Law and Philosophy Library

Volume 140

The Law and Philosophy Library, which has been in existence since 1985, aims to publish cutting edge works in the philosophy of law, and has a special history of publishing books that focus on legal reasoning and argumentation, including those that may involve somewhat formal methodologies. The series has published numerous important books on law and logic, law and artificial intelligence, law and language, and law and rhetoric. While continuing to stress these areas, the series has more recently expanded to include books on the intersection between law and the Continental philosophical tradition, consistent with the traditional openness of the series to books in the Continental jurisprudential tradition. The series is proud of the geographic diversity of its authors, and many have come from Latin America, Spain, Italy, the Netherlands, Germany, and Eastern Europe, as well, more obviously for an English-language series, from the United Kingdom, the United States, Australia and Canada.

Gonzalo Villa-Rosas • Torben Spaak
Editors

Legal Power and Legal Competence

Meaning, Normativity, Officials and Theories

Springer

Editors
Gonzalo Villa-Rosas
Centre for Research in Philosophy and Law
Externado University
Bogotá, Colombia

Department of Legal and Constitutional History, Faculty of Law
University of Vienna
Vienna, Austria

Torben Spaak
Department of Law
Stockholm University
Stockholm, Sweden

ISSN 1572-4395 ISSN 2215-0315 (electronic)
Law and Philosophy Library
ISBN 978-3-031-28554-7 ISBN 978-3-031-28555-4 (eBook)
https://doi.org/10.1007/978-3-031-28555-4

This Springer imprint is published by the registered company Springer Nature Switzerland AG
The registered company address is: Gewerbestrasse 11, 6330 Cham, Switzerland

Contents

Contributors

Brian H. Bix Law School, University of Minnesota, Minneapolis, MN, USA

Luka Burazin Faculty of Law, University of Zagreb, Zagreb, Croatia

Alejandro Daniel Calzetta Alberto Hurtado University, Santiago, Chile

Jorge Luis Fabra-Zamora University at Buffalo School of Law, State University of New York, Buffalo, NY, USA

Riccardo Guastini Tarello Institute for the Philosophy of Law, Department of Jurisprudence, University of Genoa, Genoa, Italy

Jaap Hage University of Maastricht, Maastricht, The Netherlands

Carla Huerta Law Research Institute, National Autonomous University of Mexico, Mexico City, Mexico

Visa Kurki Law Faculty, University of Helsinki, Helsinki, Finland

Josep Joan Moreso Department of Law, Pompeu Fabra University, Barcelona, Spain
BIAP, Barcelona Institute of Analytic Philosophy, Barcelona, Spain

Corrado Roversi Department of Legal Studies, University of Bologna, Bologna, Italy

Jan-Reinard Sieckmann Law Department, Faculty of Business, Economics, and Law, Friedrich-Alexander-University Erlangen-Nürnberg, Erlangen, Germany

Torben Spaak Department of Law, Stockholm University, Stockholm, Sweden

Guillaume Tusseau Sciences Po Law School, Paris, France

Gonzalo Villa-Rosas Centre for Research in Philosophy and Law, Externado University, Bogotá, Colombia
Department of Legal and Constitutional History, Faculty of Law, University of Vienna, Vienna, Austria

Monika Zalewska Department of Theory and Philosophy of Law, University of Łódź, Lodz, Poland

Introduction

Gonzalo Villa-Rosas and Torben Spaak

Abstract By the term 'legal power', we refer to a range of practices common to all modern legal systems in which persons are intentionally empowered by the legal system to bring about changes in it by affecting their own legal position or that of others. The fourteen essays included in this volume explore this fundamental concept through an approach to five major themes. The chapters of the first part deal with still open questions about the meaning of legal power and legal competence. The second part offers an analysis of the normativity of legal power. The third part is devoted specifically to exploring the relationship between legal power and constitutive norms. The fourth part is composed of chapters dealing with the analysis of legal offices and legal officers. Finally, the last part of this volume groups together chapters analysing various theories of legal power and legal competence.

By the term 'legal power', we refer to a range of practices common to all modern legal systems in which persons are intentionally empowered by the legal system to bring about changes in it by affecting their own legal position or that of others. For example, we usually refer in our daily lives to the power of judges to try cases; the power of legal officers to issue administrative directives; the power of members of parliament to enact laws; and even the powers of laypersons to enter into contracts, to appoint general or special agents, or to make wills. As Hart argued, 'the structure of a modern legal system, and indeed some most important aspects of law, cannot be

G. Villa-Rosas (✉)
Centre for Research in Philosophy and Law, Externado University, Bogotá, Colombia

Department of Legal and Constitutional History, Faculty of Law, University of Vienna, Vienna, Austria
e-mail: gonzalo.villa@uexternado.edu.co; gonzalov93@univie.ac.at

T. Spaak
Department of Law, Stockholm University, Stockholm, Sweden
e-mail: torben.spaak@juridicum.su.se

G. Villa-Rosas, T. Spaak (eds.), *Legal Power and Legal Competence*, Law and Philosophy Library 140, https://doi.org/10.1007/978-3-031-28555-4_1

understood unless the notion of legal powers and of the rules which confer them are understood'.[1]

Moreover, understanding legal power and the rules which confer it sheds light on an intuition of great importance for contemporary legal philosophy. For it seems intuitively correct to argue that legal systems do not belong to that group of naturally occurring entities but are, rather, entities produced by human beings. As Burazin observed,[2] this intuition has unsurprisingly remained unchallenged by contemporary natural law jurists and is reflected in the expression 'positive law'; namely, law established through 'intentional human acts aimed at regulating human conduct'.[3] Moving away from the deep ontological foundations to which this intuition may lead[4] and focusing instead on its more everyday consequences, not only can we recognise that law is a collective human enterprise but also that legal systems are artifacts in perpetual change. As Kelsen argued, a very significant peculiarity of these systems is that they regulate their own creation.[5] Legal systems are artifacts constantly modified by their authors, primarily[6] using the powers that the legal systems themselves provide for this purpose.

As Alexy stated,[7] although there appears to be generally uniform agreement on the phenomena that can be described as exercises of legal power, several perplexities arise when inquiring into the very concept of legal power. These are compounded by the variety of terms we use to refer to legal phenomena which are seemingly closely related to legal power.[8] As Spaak concludes, the fact that jurists, judges and lawyers, as well as legislators and framers of the constitution, use a wide variety of terms with apparently similar meanings to legal power justifies asking whether the use of this term adds something essential to the conceptual apparatus used in practice.[9] Furthermore, the variety of expressions we use to refer to legal phenomena close to legal power shows not only the differences between the various legal systems but also the

---

[1] Hart (1972), p. 800.

[2] Burazin (2018), p. 112.

[3] MacCormick (2007), p. 243.

[4] See i.a. Roversi (2018); Burazin (2016, 2018); Roversi (2015).

[5] Kelsen (2017 (1960)), § 133, p. 140.

[6] As artifacts constitute a certain kind of object intentionally produced for a certain purpose, they are causally dependent on their authors insofar as they present an intended character. This has been referred to as the problem of authorship (Hilpinen 2011; Thomasson 2007). It should be noted that, insofar as legal systems cannot be reduced to the set of rules resulting from the exercises of legal power, the concept of legal power cannot offer a comprehensive solution to the problem of the collective authorship of law qua institutional and abstract artifacts. However, assuming that it is indisputable that at least an important part of the components of a legal system finds the basis of its validity in the acts attributable to persons empowered by the rules of the system for its production, the concept of legal power does constitute a necessary but not a sufficient condition for the solution of the problem of the collective authorship of law qua institutional and abstract artifacts.

[7] Alexy (2008), p. 43.

[8] Spaak (1994), p. 12.

[9] Spaak (1994), p. 12.

differences between the various sets of norms that compose each of these systems when considered individually. Thus, the application of some of these terms may have a general scope within a legal system when referring to characteristics attributable to all the subjects that participate in its creation; for example, the term legal capacity to act (*Geschäftsfähigkeit*). Nevertheless, the application of other terms may be restricted to the participation of certain subjects in the normative creation of certain sets within a single legal system; for example, the expressions, delegation, empowerment, representation, procuration or procedural capacity (*Prozessfähigkeit*).[10] To the extent that the term 'legal power' encompasses expressions such as these and many others, it has an all-encompassing character, one which makes the term independent of the contextual characteristics of a particular legal system. Therefore, a theory that accounts for legal power can claim to have a general explanatory scope—that is, an explanatory scope with respect to every conceivable legal system.[11] This general explanatory scope corresponds to one of the tasks attributed to the development of analytical jurisprudence since Bentham.[12]

As a contribution to this task attributed to analytical jurisprudence, the fourteen essays included in this volume explore the fundamental concept of legal power through an approach to five major themes. The chapters of the first part deal with still open questions about the meaning of legal power and legal competence. The second part offers an analysis of the normativity of legal power. The third part is devoted specifically to exploring the relationship between legal power and constitutive norms. The fourth part is composed of chapters dealing with the analysis of legal offices and legal officers. Finally, the last part of this volume groups together chapters analysing various theories of legal power.

1 The Meaning of 'Legal Power' and 'Legal Competence'

The analysis of the still open questions on the definition of legal power and legal competence, to which the chapters of the first part are devoted, begins from a terminological inquiry. An extensive body of writing argues that the expressions 'legal power' and 'legal competence' refer to the same phenomena. In fact, the title of this compilation, as well as the treatment we give to the term 'legal power' in this introduction, follow this trend, according to which the justification for the use of different terms with the same meaning lies in the different linguistic tradition from

[10] On the competence concepts of positive law see Spaak (1994), pp. 11–19.

[11] On legal concepts which are common to different systems of law and different parts of individual systems as the subject of the analytical tradition of jurisprudence see e.g., Lindahl (1977), pp. 3–4.

[12] Bentham called the jurisprudence responsible for the study of concepts common to all legal systems 'universal' (Bentham 2000 (1781), p. 235).

which the sources originate. Indeed, authors such as Alexy,[13] Spaak,[14] Bulygin[15] and Lindahl,[16] have argued that whereas British and American writers prefer the use of the term 'power', writers from the Scandinavian, continental European and Latin American tradition within the philosophy of law speak rather of 'competence'. Nevertheless, various contributions have argued for distinguishing between the two terms.[17] In particular, authors such as Kurki[18] and Hage,[19] following in the wake of Ross[20] and MacCormick,[21] have recently advocated for the differentiated use of these expressions.

As part of this development, the volume begins with Jaap Hage's challenge to the view that the expressions 'legal power' and 'legal competence' are essentially synonymous. According to this challenge, although these notions are related, important differences remain. In its broad sense, unconnected to juridical acts or to the law, 'powers' refer to capabilities to do something. In this sense, powers are a social phenomenon, even though they have a basis in physical reality. By contrast, in its narrower legal meaning, 'power' represents the capability to bring about legal consequences via 'juridical acts'. Nevertheless, unlike competences, powers are not directly rule-based. For the law, one important method of limiting the number of powers is to require a legal competence for the valid performance of a juridical act. That is why legal competences, unlike powers, are typically directly granted by a legal rule, and legal competences are necessary for the existence of legal powers. To justify his position, Hage revisits well-known examples provided by the literature on legal power such as the story of Supertramp, moving from one city to another, administrative dispositions, house searches, legislation and contracting.

Moreover, an important aspect of the definition of exercises of legal power and their legal effects has revolved around the discussion of the role played by legal intention. Thus, two opposing approaches can be identified regarding the characteristics that make it possible to distinguish exercises of legal power from other phenomena. On the one hand, some authors have recognised the preponderant role played by the empowered person's legal intention in determining the legal effects of an exercise of legal power.[22] On the other hand, some positions postulate the overriding task performed by the legal system in determining exercises of legal power and their effects.[23] However, even with respect to the latter positions, it is

[13] Alexy (2008), p. 43.

[14] Spaak (1994), pp. 1–4.

[15] Bulygin (1991), pp. 201–202.

[16] Lindahl (1977), p. 194.

[17] See Hage and Kurki in this volume.

[18] Kurki (2017).

[19] Hage (2011, 2013).

[20] Ross (2009 (1968)), p. 130.

[21] MacCormick (2007), p. 156.

[22] See e.g., Lindahl and Reidhav (2017), pp. 160 and 170–171; Halpin (1996), p. 145.

[23] See e.g., Raz (2002), p. 102. On criticisms against Raz's position see Köpcke (2019a), pp. 36–38.

difficult to deny that the integration into the legal system of the normative results of the acts performed by the empowered person presupposes her knowledge and intention to carry them out when those acts are identified as exercises of legal power.[24] Indeed, they are identified in such a manner that, as an outcome of the standard approach, the empowered person's knowledge and intention are part of the minimum necessary conditions for the identification of her acts as exercises of legal power.[25] As part of this debate, the second and third chapter of this compilation explore the challenges and normative consequences of the concept of legal power and legal competence analysed via the concept of legal intention.

Thus, in Chapter 'Expanding Agency and Borders of Competence' of this volume, Visa Kurki discusses two challenges to this view. To explore these challenges, Kurki first argues for a distinction between two senses of the term 'autonomy'; namely, (i) the extra-legal sense of autonomy, which refers to a set of capacities that together provide an entity with the capacity for independent action, and (ii) autonomy as a normative status. The latter sense of the term comprises two different elements. First, to autonomy as a normative status belongs a static element, which consists of a sphere wherein one enjoys bodily integrity and may freely decide whether to engage in a wide range of conduct without interference from others. Second, autonomy as a normative status is also comprised of a dynamic element, which consists of the possibility of modifying and determining the boundaries of one's sphere of freedom. The intentional change of one's legal boundaries to which the law gives legal effect amounts to an exercise of legal competence. Thereby, competence is a central element of legal self-determination. Based on these

[24] Indeed, according to Köpcke's criticism against Raz's position, it is an empty criterion of definition to simply affirm that it is up to the legal system to define the exercises of legal power. In fact, it would suffice to inquire which criteria a legal system should consider in order to posit such a definition (Köpcke 2019a, pp. 36–38). The definition of exercises of legal power presupposes both the intention of the empowered person and the criteria for the integration of her exercise of legal power into the legal system. There are changes in legal situations that are recognised by the legal system as the result of facts. For the sake of clarity, consider the definition of the legal effects of birth (§ 1 BGB) and death (§ 1922 Par. 1 BGB) according to German civil law. The fundamental difference between such facts and exercises of legal power lies in the recognition of the latter as intentional acts by the legal system. Whereas intention is the basis of the recognition by the legal system of the exercises of legal power, as in the case of entering into contracts or the passing of laws in parliament (another aspect of the discussion is whether or not this intention is presupposed by the law through the definition of the exercises of legal power. On this point see the Chapters written by Hage and Sieckmann for this volume), integration is the legal basis of the coercive enforcement mechanisms by which the legal system characteristically backs the exercises of legal power—which have been recognised by it—for their effectiveness. Indeed, on the basis of the legal system it might also be contended that as the normative result of an exercise of legal power does not belong to the legal system, it will not be backed by the coercive enforcement mechanisms that the legal system provides (on invalidity and defeasibility of exercises of legal power see Sieckmann in this volume). We call this sanction the 'invalidity' of the exercise of legal power.

[25] Some positions have argued that these minimum necessary conditions are presupposed by the legal system based on the claim to correctness that raises the exercises of legal power. (On this point see the Chapters of Hage and Sieckmann in this volume.)

distinctions, the author questions the idea that legal intention can serve as the basis for the concept of competence. First, the paradigm change occurring in disability law has allowed us to extend competences even to persons with severe cognitive disabilities. Given that the standard method of exercising competences requires the intention to effect a change of a legal position, and that this intention implies the capacity to understand the legal reality and fundamental legal concepts, this paradigm change can be problematic for standard theories of competence. Kurki proposes that this challenge can be met by abandoning the strictly atomistic understanding of cognition and instead adopting a relational approach. Second, he uses consent-based rape laws as an example of cases that should be plausibly understood as competences yet appear excluded by the standard model of legal competence. He suggests that this challenge can be met by accepting the broader concept of soft competence that allows us to include extensional competences, such as those of persons with severe cognitive disability and even nonhuman animals, in the category of legal competences.

In Chapter 'Structures of Legal Competences', which closes the first part of this volume, by exploring the normative consequences of the definition of legal competence as the power to determine a normative situation in a legal system according to one's will, Jan-Reinard Sieckmann revisits different questions related to the identification of logical structures that make competences and competence norms an important element of legal systems. According to Sieckmann, the intention in exercising a legal competence implies the presumption of legal competence and that it was correctly exercised. Therefore, legal competence must relate to a claim to correctness. The existence of a competence requires the recognition of the power to make valid a certain norm under certain conditions, which is why legal competences include the power to establish legal reasons. Therefore, the exercise of a competence has a normative effect: it creates a legal argument on its own. If there are no counterarguments, then the competence norm in conjunction with its exercise will determine a legal situation. If there are counterarguments, a balancing will be required, and the law-applying organ must establish the definitively valid norm. Nevertheless, legal systems may attribute an exclusive competence to law-applying organs, excluding the consideration of competing arguments. If principles are understood as normative arguments and competences as reasons for the validity of norms, then competences appear connected with the notion of principles. However, competence norms always have the structure of rules, consisting of antecedent and consequence, and a competence is a position that exists on the basis of a competence rule. Finally, Sieckman holds that there is a relation between legal competence and permission as a legal competence to enact N implies that enacting N is not strongly prohibited.

2 The Normativity of Legal Power and Legal Competence

The chapters in the second part of this volume address the normativity of legal power. The normative account of legal power proposes that, through an understanding of the norms that both confer and regulate legal power, it is possible to explain the fundamental characteristics of any legal system, such as its formal structure and its changes, as a result of normative creation.[26] The notion of legal power qua power conferred by the law enables the general explanatory scope of the normative account of legal power.[27] As Köpcke established, for centuries legal thought operated without an ultimate legal basis for legal power.[28] This method of operation was reflected in theoretical strands not only from natural law but also from classical English legal positivism and the Pandectist movement.[29] Indeed, the theoretical construct of legal power qua power conferred by the law is relatively recent. Such a theoretical construct and its general explanatory character was proposed by Merkl in his *Stufenbau* theory.[30] As Paulson argued, the integration of Merkl's *Stufenbau* as an essential component of the Pure Theory of Law had vast implications that led Kelsen to reformulate his general theory of norms in terms of empowerment, beginning in the 1930s.[31] Nevertheless, the dominant streams of legal thought that have contributed to the contemporary expansive character of the normative account of legal power include not only Kelsen's Pure Theory of Law, which has exerted a great influence on continental and Latin American legal philosophical tradition, but

[26] At this point, it is worth clarifying two ideas related to the concept of normative creation. First, if the concept of normative creation is based on the concept of legal power, then it is a concept with a restricted explanatory scope. Indeed, legal power is an intrasystemic concept. In other words, legal power is a power created and regulated by norms that belong to a given legal system (this does not prevent some positions from arguing for the possibility of including within the legal system social power-conferring rules—on this point regarding the definition of legal officials see the Chapter by Fabra-Zamora in this volume). Thus, if a legal system is an artifact, changes of an ontological nature may occur—such as its own creation and disappearance as a system—that cannot be explained through the concept of legal power. Therefore, if the concept of normative creation is based on the concept of legal power, it will only refer to that normative creation which occurs on the basis of the possibilities provided by the norms that create and regulate legal power within a given legal system. Second, this intrasystemic normative creation is an essential characteristic of the legal system. Indeed, as Merkl (1931, pp. 253, 281) and Kelsen (1945, pp. 122–123) clarified, normative creation is a feature that distinguishes the legal system from other normative systems, such as morals and customs. As Paulson stated, '[a] creative dimension [in law] is undeniable, for there is an unavoidable element of discretion involved in the issuance of the lower-level norm. In other words, the determination of lower-level norm by higher-level norm is never complete.' (Paulson 2013).

[27] See Villa-Rosas in this volume.

[28] Köpcke (2019b), pp. 8, 115–145.

[29] See Villa-Rosas in this volume.

[30] See Villa-Rosas in this volume.

[31] Paulson (2019); Paulson (2000), esp. pp. 146–150; Paulson (2013).

also Von Wright's[32] and Hart's work,[33] which have had a transformative impact on the normative explanation of legal power.

As a result of these influences, we can identify three distinct trends regarding the norms of legal power. The first is composed of those theories according to which the norms of legal power must be understood either as fragments of complete legal norms *or* as norms that impose indirect obligations on the addressees of the norms issued on the basis of the norms of legal power. In the former group, we find the writings of Kelsen[34] and Spaak.[35] In the latter group are authors such as Ziembiński,[36] Nino,[37] Ross[38] and MacCormick.[39] The second trend includes those writings that defend either the permissive character of the legal power-conferring norms *or* their resemblance with permissive norms. In the former, we have the writings of Von Wright,[40] Alchourrón and Bulygin[41] and Lindahl,[42] and for the latter, those of Raz.[43] In the third trend, we group those theories that elucidate the norms of legal power as a normative social, legal conceptual, anankastic, pragmatic or institutional phenomenon. According to these theories, norms of legal power neither are nor cannot be reduced to either mandatory or permissive norms. Despite the discrepancies these theories show when compared to each other, they are all inspired by analytic philosophical insights and use the notion of constitutive rules. Examples of this stream are the theories of Hart,[44] Alchourrón and Bulygin,[45] Bulygin,[46] Atienza and Ruiz Manero,[47] Ruiter,[48] Villa-Rosas[49] and Ferrer Beltrán.[50]

[32] Von Wright (1963).

[33] Hart (2012 (1961)) and Hart (1972).

[34] Kelsen (1992 (1934)) §27–§29, pp. 55–57; Kelsen (1987), pp. 1–108; Kelsen (1960) §5(a), p. 26; §6 (d), pp. 51–52, 58; §6 (e), pp. 55–59; §28 (b), pp. 123–124; §29 (d), p. 139; §29 (f), p. 144; §30 (a), (c), pp. 150, 156; §34 (b), (c), pp. 198, 204; Kelsen (1945), pp. 60–61, 90–91, 143–144, 270–272; Kelsen (1991 (1979)), pp. 25–27, 96–105.

[35] Spaak (1994), pp. 166–181; Spaak (2003), pp. 89–104; Spaak (2005).

[36] Ziembiński (1970), pp. 24–25.

[37] Nino (1985), p. 86; Nino (1986), p. 48.

[38] Ross (1958), pp. 32–33. On Ross' theory of legal power see Alexy (2008).

[39] MacCormick (2008 (1981)), ch. 7; MacCormick (2007), ch. 9; MacCormick (1998), pp. 493–506; MacCormick and Bankowski (1986), pp. 121–134.

[40] Von Wright (1963), p. 192.

[41] Alchourrón and Bulygin (1971), p. 151.

[42] Lindahl (1977), p. 212.

[43] Raz (2002 (1975)), p. 106; Raz (1972), pp. 87–92.

[44] Hart (2012 (1961)), pp. 27–42.

[45] Alchourrón and Bulygin (1991 (1983)), p. 463.

[46] Bulygin (1991), pp. 201–216. On Bulygin's theory of power-conferring rules see Villa-Rosas (2017, 2018).

[47] Atienza and Ruiz Manero (2007 (1996)), pp. 69–114.

[48] Ruiter (1993), pp. 67–80, 91–102.

[49] Villa-Rosas (2017, 2018).

[50] Ferrer Beltrán (2000), pp. 123–166.

The second part of this volume opens with a chapter by Guillame Tusseau in which he criticises the described trends regarding norms of legal power. Tusseau maintains that, although actors—such as constituent authorities, legislators, administrators, and citizens concluding contracts or wills—tend to endow the fragments of legal discourse that mention terms such as 'competence', 'authority', 'empowerment', 'incompetence', 'jurisdiction' and so on with a distinctive and important role in legal practice, from the conceptual perspective it is unclear whether a legal theory must provide legal disciplines with a specific concept of power-conferring norm to deal with these fragments of legal discourse. In fact, many authors have rejected such a concept, either because they deny conceptual legitimacy to any other concept than that of a mandatory norm or because they prefer resorting to concepts such as permissive or constitutive norms. Based on a normativist standpoint, according to which jurists can benefit from considering a bundle of phenomena through the lens of the concept of legal norm, Tusseau proposes an original unified concept of the power-conferring norm. This concept includes the following four elements: first, the actor being empowered to produce legal norms; second, an action by means of which acts can produce norms; third, the range of application of the power-conferring norm; and fourth, the range of regulation, which refers to the kind of normative meanings that a power-conferring norm empowers to produce. This latter element refers to the types of norms that the acts can produce and their normative level in the hierarchy. To demonstrate the utility of his conception, Tusseau offers a general taxonomy of examples of power-conferring norms according to their elements. Finally, he identifies and illustrates the kinds of normative relations that exist among these norms, such as coordination—i.e. parcelling competences and competence of attribution—and the different forms of hierarchisation—such as delegation, and typical and non-typical primacy. Based on the preceding assumptions, the author defends a normativist standpoint, considering not that the legal phenomena consist of norms but, more precisely, that jurists can benefit from considering the global bundle of phenomena which are *hic et nunc* called 'legal' via the concept of a legal norm. Tusseau dispenses with any other concept (principle, institution, value, policy, etc.) as not useful for his purposes. One of the advantages of the concept of a legal norm is that it is familiar to many legal scholars. Moreover, it is not linked to any specific legal, domestic, national or statist context and can, accordingly, be used as the concept of a general legal analysis. However, concerning the puzzles resulting from power-conferring norms, Tusseau argues that the statement that legal phenomena are composed solely of norms (or that they are preferably conceived in this manner) does not tell us the whole story. In fact, we still need to explicity state whether there is a single type of legal norm so that we can establish of a single concept can be used throughout legal analysis or whether an entire taxonomy of norms should preferably be used.

In Chapter 'On the Function of Competence Norms in a Legal System', which ends the second part of this volume, Carla Huerta addresses the analysis of the function of competence norms that confer power to officials and argues that competence must be understood as a normative power given to officials to create and apply legal norms and change legal positions. Competence results from the legal norms that attribute this power and regulate its exercise. Based on Raz's critique of Hartian insights, Huerta argues that the distinction between primary and secondary norms does not posit a different category of norms. Thus, it cannot be ruled out that secondary norms have a prescriptive function. Consequently, competence norms as secondary rules may be conceived as norms that rule the conduct of public officials who aim to perform some action related to the transformation of the legal system. In this sense, competence norms for Kelsen may be expressed not only in terms of permission but also of obligation, specifically regarding norms that regulate normative actions or a judge's duty to render a decision. Huerta adopts the semantic conception of norms that allows a norm to be separated from its validity, and according to which a normative sentence is the linguistic expression of a norm and a norm is the content of a normative sentence. The semantic conception of a norm enables the reconstruction of a normative sentence whose content is a competence norm as a unit. Based on this reconstruction, and following Von Wright's contributions, Huerta finally argues that competence norms should be conceived as prescriptions, for they perform a prescriptive function which guides public officials' behavior. These norms operate in a manner that enables public officials to create, eliminate and apply norms, and thereby transform the legal system.

3 Legal Power and Constitutive Rules

As we advance in the introduction to the second part of this volume, the notion of constitutive rules has played a critical role in developing a prominent group of theories regarding the norms of legal power. As Lorini and Żełaniec have argued, the comprehensive presentation of deontic logic[51] and the distinction between constitutive rules and regulative rules prompted the two drastic turns that the theory of norms and normativity underwent in the twentieth century.[52] The inclusion of constitutive rules added an ontological role to the traditional deontic functions associated with norms. This ontological role of rules[53]—or of a certain kind of rules[54]—is premised on the recognition that with rules we can not only command, permit or prohibit but also 'do things'—inspired by the spirit of Austin's work.[55] Constitutive rules determine the conditions of possibility of new forms of behavior

[51] Ernst Mally proposed for the first time a formal system of deontic logic in his *Grundgesetze des Sollens. Elemente der Logik des Willens* in 1926. The seminal paper published by G. H. von Wright in 1951 is considered a milestone in the development of deontic logic. (On the history of deontic logic see Hilpinen and McNamara (2013); Føllesdal and Hilpinen (1981 (1971)).)

[52] Lorini and Żełaniec (2018), p. 9.

[53] On a defining pragmatic perspective of constitutive rules see Roversi in this volume.

[54] On a defining structural perspective of constitutive rules see Moreso in this volume.

[55] Austin (2009 (1962)).

that would not even be conceivable without them.[56] For the sake of clarity, let us turn to a paradigmatic case intended to reflect an 'orthodox view of constitutive norms'.[57] Consider that, if the rules of chess did not exist, then even if it occurred to me to move a black wooden piece on a board composed of black and white squares, no scheme of interpretation would be available to have full epistemic access to this movement of my hand. Without the rules that define what we mean by this game, this move of my hand would appear to you as a brute fact; that is, inexplicable. In contrast, if the rules of chess existed and you knew them, your knowledge of them would allow you to recognise the movement of my hand as a move in the game of chess you look at, and if your knowledge of the rules of chess were sufficiently deep, you could even define our possible future moves as your knowledge of the rules of chess would make every move in the chess game performed by us completely explicable as an instance of the rules of chess. Similarly, without the legal rules that define who the legally empowered person is and the acts, with respect to which she is legally empowered, she could not be a legally empowered person, and her acts and their effects could not be interpreted as part of the law.

Despite the apparent clarity of this theory, several perplexities arise upon closer examination. In fact, the boundary upon which the distinction between constitutive and regulative norms is based remains contested. Although authors such as Searle[58] and Von Wright[59] have not ruled out the regulative function of constitutive rules, others—such as Bulygin[60]—have denied that these rules play any motivational role.[61] The first two chapters of the third part of this volume argue for the latter thesis, which proposes the strict mutual exclusion between constitutive and regulative rules. This strict mutual exclusion thesis is based on a dichotomy concerning the constitutive rules. This dichotomy was elsewhere enunciated by Bulygin;[62] to wit, on the one hand, if constitutive rules define, then they can be expressed as analytic judgments. If constitutive rules can be expressed as analytic judgments, then they cannot regulate. On the other hand, if constitutive rules regulate, then they can be expressed as synthetic judgments. If constitutive rules can be expressed as synthetic judgments, then they cannot define. Therefore, if we accept the defining function of

[56] As Searle has written: '[W]e might say that regulative rules regulate antecedently or independently existing forms of behavior; for example, many rules of etiquette inter-personal relationships which exist independently of the rules. But constitutive rules do not merely regulate, they create or define new forms of behavior. The rules of football or chess, for example, do not merely regulate playing football or chess, but as it were they create the very possibility of playing such games.' (Searle 2009 (1969), p. 33.)

[57] The expression is used by Moreso in this volume. We refer here to the contribution of e.g., Rawls (1955); Anscombe (1958); Midgley (1959); Alston (1964); Ransdell (1971); Cherry (1973); Conte (1995); Lagerspetz (1995); Ruiter (1997); Searle (1964, 1965, 1995, 2006, 2009 (1969), 2010).

[58] Searle (2009 (1969)), p. 34.

[59] Von Wright (1963), p. 6.

[60] Bulygin (1991), pp. 213–214.

[61] Villa-Rosas (2017), p. 93.

[62] Bulygin (1991), pp. 213–214.

constitutive rules, we must exclude any regulative function they may possess. Hence, if we define legal power-conferring rules as constitutive rules, we must conclude they are conceptual criteria that allow us to identify the empowered persons and their legal acts.

Based on this thesis, we could even argue that the rule of recognition is a conceptual criterion for identifying a given legal system. This is the main thesis proposed by Ricardo Guastini in Chapter 'Recognition' of this volume. According to Guastini, the rule of recognition is a constitutive rule; that is, a definition. Consequently, the rule of recognition is not a duty-imposing rule. As a definition, it is neither valid nor invalid; therefore, it is not a 'basic norm' in the Kelsenian sense. Neither is the rule of recognition a rule of change in the Hartian sense as it does not belong to the legal system and it is required for recognising the constitution. For logical reasons, it cannot be a legal rule as it is required for recognising the legal system. It belongs to the meta-legal discourse of those who aim to identify the rules of a legal system. Nevertheless, identifying the rules of a legal system can mean either identifying its sources—leaving aside its interpretative practices—or identifying their normative contents—including the interpretative practices of the legal system. For this reason, two distinct rules of recognition must be identified. The rule of recognition of the legal sources identifies their original source. The rule of recognition of legal norms can refer to the identification of valid norms, existing norms or the norms in force within the legal system. Regarding the recognition of norms, the author distinguishes between two recognition statements; that is, sentences that are the conclusion of an argument whose premises include a rule of recognition. On the one hand, an internal statement of validity which presupposes the non-axiological acceptance of the rules of recognition. On the other hand, an external statement according to which a particular rule is valid if the recognition criteria of the rule of recognition are met.

In Chapter 'Institutions and Constitutive Rules', JJ Moreso defends the thesis of strict mutual exclusion between constitutive and regulative rules as part of what he calls the 'orthodox view of constitutive rules'. According to this view, whereas constitutive rules constitute the actions to which they refer, prescriptive rules regulate the behaviours that exist outside them. Constitutive rules cannot be violated but regulative rules can. Although the canonical form of constitutive rules is 'X counts as Y in context C', regulative rules are paradigmatically expressed in imperative mode, as in 'Do X'. Moreso defends this orthodox view against powerful objections, in particular the recent challenge of Timothy Williamson's so-called Rule of Knowledge ('One must: assert that P only if one knows that P'). In addition, Moreso presents a method by which constitutive rules can indirectly provide reasons for action and discusses whether the existence of these rules is given in virtue of moral facts or not. Based on these arguments, the author maintains that although constitutive rules are essential elements of our institutional systems, effectively practiced institutional systems must also include regulative rules. In this union lies the institutional nature of law, which allows it to be made into an authoritative practice and, when it meets certain requirements, provides us with reasons to act. Such institutions require, as their initial input, that we can identify the norm-creating and norm-applying bodies without recourse to evaluative considerations. Furthermore, as their final output, such institutions require final and individual decisions that irrevocably and non-controversially resolve the cases submitted to the jurisdiction.

At this point, let us return to our paradigmatic case but this time present an alternative view. Consider that you observe our chess moves and, based on your deep knowledge of the rules of chess, you conclude that our game is rather wild and that you cannot see any consistent strategy in our moves. Consequently, you advise me to make a certain strategic move to win the game against my partner. Surprised, I reply that for us, this is not a game. Neither my objective nor that of my partner is to win. We have simply been hired to mechanically follow this set of rules in each of our countless games to analyse their logical possibilities.[63] This teleological discordance between the ends of the activity you presuppose and the one we practice demonstrates that the rules and following them are insufficient to define the activity of playing chess.[64] This is precisely the main criticism that Schwyzer raises against Searle.[65] It is as impossible to play a game of chess without the rules of chess as without the concepts of playing and winning.[66] Playing chess is a competitive and playful activity, but these two concepts are not in its rules but lie beyond and before them, as Miller argued.[67]

On the basis of these pragmatic criticisms against the 'orthodox view of constitutive rules', in the closing chapter of this part, Corrado Roversi explores the relationship between constitutive rules and institutional power. According to his first thesis, being constitutive is not a structural feature of some rules but a way in which they are used. In other words, being constitutive is a pragmatic feature of those rules which not only declare what an artifactual status is via a connection between conditions for its instantiation and normative consequences but also regulate the interaction of agents with such status. According to his second thesis, there is no conceptual necessary connection between constitutive rules and power-conferring rules. On the one hand, constitutive rules may attribute power to statuses, but they can also attribute disabling modalities such as duties and prohibitions. On the other hand, power-conferring rules may not be constitutive, because they can attribute to the functional role of an institutional status that it is not essential. This idea relates to the teleological background of institutional entities, which is the subject of his third thesis. According to this, power in a given institution is not exhausted by the rules of that institution. On the contrary, the ontology of an institution is the outcome of three interlocking layers that Roversi calls meta-institutional, institutional and para-institutional. The meta-institutional layer is

---

[63] Let us introduce this example as an approximate version of Schwyzer's example of the 'Ruritanians'. (See Schwyzer 1969, pp. 456–462.)

[64] Schwyzer (1969), p. 456. Miller (1981), p. 188.

[65] Schwyzer (1969).

[66] See e.g. Roversi (2018), p. 144.

[67] Miller (1981), p. 189.

provided by the deeper social practice the institution is embedded in, which gives it its overall purpose and meaning. This layer is cross-institutional and can be accounted for both in normative and causal terms. The institutional layer includes all the rules the institution is made of, be they authoritative or customary, regulative or constitutive. The para-institutional layer includes all the features of the institution that depend not on its actual rules but on the manner in which these rules are practiced in a given social context. It is true that both meta-institutional and para-institutional powers are quite vague. Nevertheless, restricting the notion of legally relevant power to institutional power—that is, restricting this notion to a formalistic attitude in legal philosophy and social ontology which maintains that power depends only on rules based on formal procedures or a collective acceptance—would imply renouncing the possibility of fully understanding the ontology of institutions. On the contrary, it may be the case that a non-formalised kind of power provides the original power to enact formalised rules. If this were so, power would not depend on constitutive rules; rather, constitutive rules would depend on that original power.

4 Legal Officials and Legal Offices

The prominence of the State as the main concern of jurisprudential theories throughout the twentieth century[68] has meant that, alongside theories focused on the analysis and formalisation of legal relations,[69] the most influential contemporary theories of legal power have concentrated mainly on the role of legal officials in the creation of law. However, these widely accepted theories have, so far, kept open a number of fundamental questions. On the one hand, some fundamental concerns that highlight a lacuna in contemporary legal scholarship relate to the very concept of legal office, legal officials and their relationship to legal powers. The first two chapters of this part of the volume address these concerns. On the other hand, another set of persistent fundamental questions concern the relationship between the actions of legal officers and concepts such as legal validity and legal truth. The final chapter, incorporated into this part of the volume, addresses these fundamental questions.

The fourth part of this volume opens with a chapter written by Luka Burazin, in which he analyses the relationship between legal offices and legal powers. Based on the definition of legal offices as immaterial institutional artifacts, Burazin argues for

[68] On the question 'why do so many jurisprudential theories focus on the state?' see Raz (2017).

[69] Hohfeld's contribution (Hohfeld 1923) has produced a revolution in legal thought. As Sartor exposed, (Sartor 2006) among contemporary research on formal models of normative concepts, a line of logical-philosophical studies has been inspired by Hohfeld's insights. This line of research has continued the foundations laid down by the Scandinavian tradition with the works of Kanger (2001 (1972)), Kanger and Kanger (2001 (1966)) and Lindahl (1977). In this line, formal analyses have been developed by Pace and Schapachnik (2012). Sartor (2006, 2009), Makinson (1986), Guibourg (1997), Allen and Saxon (1995), Jones and Sergot (1997), Sergot (2001) and Saunders (1989), among others.

four main theses. First, a set of legal positions which constitute a legal office necessarily include at least one legal power. This is so as legal offices, by definition, put their holders in a position of legal authority, and legal authority is intrinsically connected to legal powers. Second, legal offices are always constituted by power-conferring norms, whether social (in the case of original legal offices) or legal (in the case of derived legal offices). Third, legal offices necessarily include at least a minimum liberty to exercise the powers of the office. In arguing for this, Burazin maintains that in the absence of such a liberty, a purported legal office would be constitutively incapable of performing the characteristic function of the kind of social artifacts to which it belongs. Finally, contrary to the dissociation thesis defended by J. Almäng and J. Rust, Burazin argues that a legal office, although retaining its identity if its non-essential powers are modified, nonetheless changes its identity if it is deprived of its essential legal powers; even more so, it ceases to exist if it is deprived of all its legal powers.

In Chapter 'A Hartian Account of Legal Officials', Fabra-Zamora articulates a renewed account of legal officials based on the criticisms against Hartian insights. According to the author, despite 'legal officials' being one of the central elements of HLA Hart's theory of law, this theory does not offer us a thorough account of legal officials. As critics have rightly argued, three related questions remain unanswered: 'What is an official?' (The Conceptual Problem); 'Who are the officials of a given legal system?' (The Identification Problem), and 'How are these officials empowered by the system's secondary rules?' (The Empowerment Problem). These issues have generated suggestions for eliminating legal officials from theoretical inquiries, leading to a larger question: 'What role do officials play in legal theory?' (The Explanatory Role Problem). Fabra-Zamora's renewed account of legal officials reinterprets the central insights of Hart's theory of legal systems as a general theory of practice-based normativity. With this position, the author's responses to each problem are advanced. To address the Conceptual Problem, he argues that officials are agents that make peremptory decisions (enactments and settlements) on behalf of a given community, whereas legal officials are agents that make such decisions on behalf of political communities. In response to the Identity Problem, Fabra-Zamora holds that the identification of officials demands the recognition of two kinds of agents: order-constituted officials created by the system's valid norms and identified by the rule of recognition and through a doctrinal analysis; and order-constitutive officials created by the system's secondary rules and identified through a quasi-sociological inquiry. A detailed clarification of the power-conferring character of social rules is developed in response to the Empowerment Problem. Finally, in response to the Explanatory Role Problem, Fabra-Zamora clarifies the relevance of officials, both for jurisprudence and social philosophy.

In the closing chapter of this part of the volume, Brian H. Bix explores the manner in which improper and erroneous actions by legal officials are, or should be, understood in terms of legal truth. His analysis shows not only a tension within legal systems between authority and correctness but also between legal positivism and natural law theory regarding the nature of law. According to Bix , although legal officials have the competence to create new legal norms, from the perspective of conventional doctrinal analysis, the content of new legal norms may be ultra vires or erroneous. On the one hand, this phenomenon demonstrates an instability in the concept of competence as the powers to change the law may be different from the standards prescribed and in ways that are not always predictable. This instability is exacerbated by the fact that sometimes mistakes are not corrected, and at the time the mistake is made, it is often hard to predict whether it will be corrected. On the other hand, this phenomenon evidences an instability regarding that which could be described as 'true' or 'false' for relatively narrow and specific propositions ascribing legal rights and duties to individual parties regarding a jurisdiction (legal system) at a certain date. Sometimes the simple bivalence of 'x is the law' and 'x is not the law' may not fully hold.

5 Theories of Legal Power and Legal Competence

The last part of this volume focuses on the contributions of Bentham, Merkl and Kelsen. As Hart argued, Bentham 'alone among analytical jurists has attempted a detailed analysis of [the notion of power]'.[70] Indeed, as stated by Tusseau, in comparison with Bentham's work, Austin's contributions must be considered as 'derivative and considerably less developed'.[71] Nevertheless, few of Bentham's contributions impacted the nineteenth-century origins of Anglo-American jurisprudential studies about legal power.[72] As Lindahl contended, although the origin of the study of fundamental legal concepts, and especially legal power, is usually attributed to Bentham, 'the work developed by him in Of Laws in General remained virtually unknown until the 1970s when Joseph Raz, H L A Hart, and David Lyons drew attention to it.'[73] From the interest aroused by these authors, in recent years we have witnessed a resurgence of studies of Bentham's crucial contributions to the theory of legal power, which has been reflected especially in the works of Moreso,[74] and Tusseau.[75]

In Chapter 'An Analysis of Jeremy Bentham's Quasi-Realistic Model of Legal Competence', Alejandro D. Calzetta argues that the Benthamian model of legal power can be deemed a quasi-realist model. According to Calzetta, for Bentham, only a political community that is willing to obey a sovereign can be subjected to her. The sovereign subjects her political community by means of the power of

[70] Hart (1972), p. 800.

[71] Tusseau (2007a).

[72] Dickey (1971), p. 60, note 6. Given this historical background related to the publication and reception of Bentham's work, it seems appropriate to highlight the influence of Austin and Holland on Hohfeld's work as presented by Kurki (2019, p. 59).

[73] Lindahl (1977), p. 5.

[74] Moreso (e.g., 1989, 1992, 2014).

[75] Tusseau (e.g., 2006, 2007a, b).

contrectation and the power of imperation. The former is the power that the sovereign and his delegates exercise to make effective both the threats of pain or sanctions and the promises of pleasure or rewards that come with the orders issued via the power of imperation. The latter is the sovereign's competence to issue orders backed by threats and rewards. According to Calzetta, for Bentham, the interaction between these two powers is the key for understanding the legal phenomenon. Although the power of contrectation and the power of imperation are normative powers, the sovereign is a factual power. The sovereign does not owe her position to any type of normative framework; on the contrary, she is the one who creates the normative framework. Nevertheless, according to Calzetta, Bentham recognises that the sovereign cannot do everything by herself. For this reason, the power of imperation must be divided into parcels and shared among the sovereign's delegates. The power of imperation is exercised by two manners, either as power *de classibus* or as power *de singulis*. By means of the power of imperation *de classibus*, the sovereign creates imperatives with respect to a class. These imperatives must be general as they will be applied to an indeterminate number of individuals, who share one or more properties that make them members of the class. However, these imperatives that the sovereign creates are necessarily incomplete as although they determine a class, they do not determine which individual or specific member of the class should meet the imperative. The determination of an individual requires the creation of an individual rule. The sovereign's delegate exercises the power of imperation *de singulis*, though which she determines a concrete individual who meets the criteria of membership to the class described by the general imperative created as an exercise of the power of imperation *de classibus*. What the delegate does is to impose an obligation or a prohibition to a specific individual belonging to the class described by the general imperative, with the threat of sanction or the promise of reward in the event of noncompliance. Calzetta concludes, based on his reading of Tarello's account of legal realism, by observing that the main claim behind any realist legal approach is that the law, in the sense of the content of legal norms, depends on the ultimate instance on the judges, not on the legislators. This being the core of realist theories of legal interpretation. In this manner, given that the Benthamian model describes the task and the role of judges in current legal systems fairly accurately, it can be deemed what Calzetta calls a "quasi" realist model, despite the fact that using this adjective may be considered anachronistic.

In Chapter 'Merkl's Stufenbaulehre in the History of the Theory of Legal Power', Gonzalo Villa-Rosas explores the contributions of the theory of the hierarchical structure of the legal system (*Stufenbaulehre*) advanced by Adolf Julius Merkl to the normative account of legal power—that is, the theoretical development that provides an explanation of legal power through the study of the rules that confer and regulate it. Although Merkl's contributions to the Vienna School of Legal Theory and to twentieth-century Austrian administrative and constitutional law are widely known,[76] the importance of Merkl's work for the development of the theory of legal power is mediated by the almost automatic reference to its integration into Hans Kelsen's Pure Theory of Law (*Reine Rechtslehre*).[77] Nevertheless, as Wiederin claimed, 'even authors who consider the theoretical edifice of the *Reine Rechtslehre* as a whole to be built on sand, attest that the *Stufenbaulehre* stands on solid ground and dare to predict that, on the whole, it will endure, for it is almost paradoxical that even its harshest critics, those who have not even a good word to say about the theory, confirm its dogmatic legal usefulness'.[78] The main thesis of this chapter argues that Merkl's theory of the hierarchical structure of the legal system provides a general scope to the normative account of legal power. In effect, with his *Stufenbaulehre*, Merkl rejects any formal pre-legal foundation of power by providing a legal foundation of power with respect to the ultimate basis of the legal system and its intermediate and lower structures, as well as with respect to the power to enter into voluntary legal obligations. Merkl's theory of the hierarchical structure of the legal system corresponds to an analytical achievement that formally substantiates the thesis of the separation of law and morals by reacting on the one hand against the remnants of the Pandectist movement that still resonated in its time and, on the other hand, against the statutory positivism of the nineteenth century.

As Paulson argued, the integration of Merkl's theory of the hierarchical structure of the legal system into the Pure Theory of Law had vast implications that led Kelsen to reformulate not only his general theory of norms concerning empowerment, beginning in the 1930s, but also his own concept of law.[79] In the last chapter of this volume, Monika Zalewska analyses the problem of empowerment in the context of vertical and horizontal relations in Kelsen's General Theory of Norms. In this work, Kelsen reformulates his theory. First, the vertical aspect is bound up with the hierarchical structure of law. In the Pure Theory of Law, Kelsen maintains that the lawmaker only produces legal raw material, which is subsequently cognised as legal norms. In this work, Kelsen understands the hierarchical structure of law in formal terms. Nevertheless, in his realistic phase, Kelsen perceives norms as cognition-independent entities which grant the lawmaker a more central position in his theory. By contrast, in the General Theory of Norms, Kelsen maintains that a norm is the meaning of the act of will. As this will is not an intellectual act, it can be irrational. Consequently, Kelsen denies the possibility that logic can be applied to norms. The rejection of the logic of norms affects the hierarchical structure of the law and raises questions regarding its empowerment function. The rules of inference provided the tool that guaranteed an empowered organ would issue a norm in accordance with the content of the empowering norm; as such rules are gone, such a link between the higher organ of empowerment and the empowered norm appears be

---

[76] On the life and work of Adolf Julius Merkl, see e.g., Schambeck (1993, 2018), Fuertes (1998), Walter (1990), and Grussmann (1989).

[77] Fuertes (1998), p. 419.

[78] Wiederin (2011), p. 81.

[79] Paulson (2019); Paulson (2000), esp. pp. 146–150; Paulson (2013).

absent. What remains in the law-making process is the lawmaker's act of will, which might or might not conform with the empowerment stemming from the higher norm. However, for Kelsen this leads to unwanted consequences. Namely, if the lawmaker decides whether, which and how to apply the norm, the clarity between what law is and what law is not vanishes. This would mean that Kelsen's theory is leaning towards the 'Is sphere' in a manner which could decompose Kelsen's sophisticated idea of law embedded in normativity. That begs the following question: if a norm is the meaning of an act of will, and if the will can sometimes be irrational, how can empowerment be of any relevance to norms? Kelsen partially answers this question by pointing out that although the rules of inference and the rule of contradiction do not apply to legal norms, they apply to statements about legal norms, which are the statements of legal science. However, these statements are used not during the law-making process but only *ex post* analysis of the legal application. Second, the horizontal relations result from the application of a coercive act. The coercive act is the last level of the chain of the *Stufenbau*. That is why the most important element of horizontal relations, the one setting the entire process in motion, is imputation. Imputation must be understood as the link between condition and consequence. The question this raises is how to understand the nature of imputation in the General Theory of Norms as it lost its Neokantian function of a relative a priori category. Zalewska criticises the attempt to assign a pragmatic function to imputation and proposes an alternative approach. Imputation is, in fact, a supervenience relationship that confirms the existence of the principle of equality in the positivistic paradigm.

References

Alchourrón C, Bulygin E (1971) Normative systems. Springer, New York

Alchourrón C, Bulygin E (1991 (1983)) Definiciones y normas. In: Alchourrón C, Bulygin E (eds) Análisis lógico y derecho. Centro de Estudios Políticos y Constitucionales, Madrid, pp 439–463

Alexy R (2008) Alf Ross' Begriff der Kompetenz. In: Hoyer A, Hattenhauer H, Meyer-Pritzl R, Schubert W (eds) Gedächtnisschrift für Jörn Eckert: 15. Mai 1954 bis 21. März 2006. Nomos, Baden-Baden, pp 43–64

Allen LE, Saxon CS (1995) Better language, better thought, better communication: the A-Hohfeld language for legal analysis. In: Proc. 5th Int. Conf. on AI and Law, College Park, Md., pp 219–228

Alston WP (1964) Linguistic acts. Am Philos Q 1(2):138–146

Anscombe GEM (1958) On brute facts. Analysis 18(3):69–72

Atienza M, Ruiz Manero J (2007 (1996)) Las piezas del derecho. Teoría de los enunciados jurídicos, 4th edn. Ariel Derecho, Barcelona

Austin JL (2009 (1962)) How to do things with words. Oxford University Press, Oxford

Bentham J (2000 (1781)) An introduction to the principles of morals and legislation. Batoche Books Kitchener, Ontario

Bulygin E (1991) On norms of competence. Law Philos 10:201–216

Burazin L (2016) Can there be an artifact theory of law? Ratio Juris 29(3):385–401

Burazin L (2018) Legal systems as abstract institutional artifacts. In: Burazin L, Himma KE, Roversi C (eds) Law as an artifact. OUP, Oxford, pp 112–135

Cherry C (1973) Regulative rules and constitutive rules. Philos Q 23(93):301–315

Conte AG (1995) Filosofía del Linguaggio Normativo II Studi 1982-1994. Con una lettera di Norberto Bobbio. G Ciappichelli Editore, Torino
Dickey A (1971) Hohfeld's Debt to Salmond. West Aust Law Rev 10:59–64
Ferrer Beltrán J (2000) Las normas de competencia. Un aspecto de la dinámica jurídica. Centro de estudios políticos y constitucionales, Madrid
Føllesdal D, Hilpinen R (1981 (1971)) Deontic logic: an introduction. In: Hilpinen R (ed) Deontic logic: introductory and systematic readings. D. Reidel Publishing Company, Dodrecht, pp 1–35
Fuertes M (1998) Adolf Julius Merkl: Un jurista tan citado como desconocido. Revista de Administración Pública 146:419–428
Grussmann WD (1989) Adolf J. Merkl. Leben und Werk. Schriftenreihe des Hans-Kelsen-Instituts 13. Manz Verlag, Vienna
Guibourg RA (1997) Formalization of competence. In: Valdés EG, Krawietz W, von Wright GH, Zimmerling R (eds) Normative systems in legal and moral theory. Festschrift for Carlos E. Alchourrón and Eugenio Bulygin. Duncker & Humblot, Berlin, pp 455–473
Hage J (2011) A model of juridical acts, part 1 and part 2. Artif Intell Law 19:23–73
Hage J (2013) The deontic furniture of the world. In: Stellmach J, Brozek B, Hohol M (eds) The many faces of normativity. Copernicus Center Press, Krakow, pp 73–114
Halpin A (1996) The concept of a legal power. Oxford J Leg Stud 16(1):129–152
Hart HLA (1972) Bentham on legal powers. Yale Law J 81(5):799–822
Hart HLA (2012 (1961)) The concept of law. Oxford University Press, Oxford
Hilpinen R (2011) Artifact. In: Zalta EN (ed) The Stanford encyclopedia of philosophy (Winter 2011 edition). URL: http://plato.stanford.edu/enies/artifact/
Hilpinen R, McNamara P (2013) A historical survey and introduction. In: Dov G, Horty J, Parent X, Van der Meyden R, Van der Torre L (eds) Handbook of deontic logic and normative systems. College Publications, Rickmansworth, pp 3–136
Hohfeld WN (1923) Fundamental legal conceptions as applied in judicial reasoning and other legal essays. Peters R.S. ed., New Haven
Jones AJI, Sergot MJ (1997 (1996)) A formal characterisation of institutionalised power. In: Valdés EG, Krawietz W, von Wright GH, Zimmerling R (eds) Normative systems in legal and moral theory. Festschrift for Carlos E. Alchourrón and Eugenio Bulygin. Duncker & Humblot, Berlin, pp 349–367
Kanger S (2001 (1972)) Law and logic. In: Hintikka GH, Lindström S, Sliwinski R (eds) Collected papers of Stig Kanger with essays on his life and work. Springer, Dordrecht, pp 146–169
Kanger S, Kanger H (2001 (1966)) Rights and parliamentarism. In: Hintikka GH, Lindström S, Sliwinski R (eds) Collected papers of Stig Kanger with essays on his life and work. Springer, Dordrecht, pp 120–145
Kelsen H (1945) General theory of law and state. Harvard University Press, Cambridge
Kelsen H (1960) Reine Rechtslehre. 2. Auflage. Franz Deuticke, Wien
Kelsen H (1987) Recht und Kompetenz: Kritische Bemerkungen zur Völkerrechtstheorie Georges Scelles. In: Kelsen H (ed) Auseinandersetzungen zur Reinen Rechtslehre. Springer, Wien
Kelsen H (1991 (1979)) General theory of norms. Clarendon Press, Oxford
Kelsen H (1992 (1934)) Introduction to the problems of legal theory (trans: Paulson SL, Litschewski Paulson B). Clarendon Press, Oxford
Kelsen H (2017 (1960)) Reine Rechtslehre. Mit einem Anhang: Das Problem der Gerechtigkeit. Studienausgabe der 2. Auflage 1960 unter Berücksichtigung von Kelsens Änderungen anlässlich der Übersetzung ins Italienische 1966 herausgegeben und eingeleitet von Matthias Jestaedt. Mohr Siebeck Verlag, Wien
Köpcke M (2019a) Legal validity. The fabric of justice. Hart Publishing, Oxford
Köpcke M (2019b) A short history of legal validity and invalidity. Foundations of private and public law. Intersentia Ltd, Cambridge
Kurki VAJ (2017) Legal competence and legal power. In: McBride M (ed) New essays on the nature of rights. Hart Publishing, West Sussex, pp 31–47
Kurki VAJ (2019) A theory of legal personhood. Oxford University Press, Oxford

Lagerspetz E (1995) The opposite mirrors. An essay on the conventionalist theory of institutions. Kluwer, Dordrecht
Lindahl H (1977) Position and change: a study in law and logic. Springer Science, Dordrecht
Lindahl L, Reidhav D (2017) Legal power: the basic definition. Ratio Juris 30(2):158–185
Lorini G, Żełaniec W (2018) The background of constitutive rules. Introduction. Argumenta 4(1): 9–19
MacCormick N (1998) Powers and power-conferring norms. In: Paulson SL, Litschewski-Paulson B (eds) Normativity and norms: critical perspectives on Kelsenian themes. Clarendon Press, Oxford, pp 493–506
MacCormick N (2007) Institutions of law. An essay in legal theory. Oxford University Press, Oxford
MacCormick (2008 (1981)) H L A Hart, 2nd edn. Stanford University Press, Stanford
MacCormick N, Bankowski Z (1986) Speech acts, legal institutions and real laws. In: Birks P, MacCormick N (eds) The legal mind: essays for Tony Honoré. Clarendon Press, Oxford, pp 121–134
Makinson D (1986) On the formal representation of rights relations. J Philos Log 15:403–425
Mally E (1926) Grundgesetze des Sollens. Elemente der Logik des Willens. Leuschner & Lubensky, Graz
Merkl AJ (1931) Prolegomena einer Theorie des rechtlichen Stufenbaues. In: Verdross A (ed) Gesellschaft, Staat und Recht. Untersuchungen zur Reinen Rechtslehre, Festschrift Hans Kelsen zum 50. Geburtstag gewidmet. Springer, Vienna, pp 252–294
Midgley GCJ (1959) Linguistic rules. Proc Aristot Soc 59:271–290
Miller D (1981) Constitutive rules and essential rules. Philos Stud 39(2):183–197
Moreso JJ (1989) Cinco diferencias entre Bentham y Austin. Anuario de Filosofía del derecho VI:351–375
Moreso JJ (1992) La teoría del derecho de Bentham. PPU, Barcelona
Moreso JJ (2014) Bentham's deontic logic. In: Tusseau G (ed) The legal philosophy and influence of Jeremy Bentham. Routledge, London, pp 71–80
Nino CS (1985) Las limitaciones de la teoría de Hart sobre las normas jurídicas. Anuario de Filosofía Jurídica y Social 5:75–94
Nino CS (1986) El concepto de Derecho de Hart. Revista de Ciencias Sociales 28:33–54
Pace G, Schapachnik F (2012) Types of rights in interacting two-party systems: a formal analysis. In: Schafer B (ed) Legal knowledge and information systems: JURIX 2012: the Twenty-Fifth Annual Conference, Frontiers in Artificial Intelligence and Applications, vol 250. IOS Press, Amsterdam, pp 105–114
Paulson SL (2000) The weak reading of authority in Hans Kelsen's pure theory of law. Law Philos 19:131–171
Paulson SL (2013) How Merkl's Stufenbaulehre informs Kelsen's concept of law. Revus. J Const Law Philos Law 21:29–45. https://doi.org/10.4000/revus.2727
Paulson SL (2019) Empowerment: Hans Kelsen e la teoria radicale delle norme giuridiche. Analisi e diritto 1:21–66
Ransdell J (1971) Constitutive rules and speech-act analysis. J Philos 68:385–400
Rawls J (1955) Two concepts of rules. Philos Rev 64:3–32
Raz J (1972) Voluntary obligations and normative powers. II-Joseph Raz. Proc Aristot Soc, Suppl Vol 46:79–102
Raz J (2002 (1975)) Practical reason and norms. Oxford University Press, Oxford
Raz J (2017) Why the State? In: Roughan N, Halpin A (eds) In pursuit of pluralist jurisprudence. Cambridge University Press, Cambridge, pp 136–162
Ross A (1958) On law and justice. Stevens & Sons, London
Ross A (2009 (1968)) Directives and norms. Humanities Press, New York
Roversi C (2015) Legal metaphoric artifacts. In: Brozek B, Stelmach J, Kurek L (eds) The emergence of normative orders. Copernicus Center Press, Krakaw, pp 215–280
Roversi C (2018) Constitutive rules and the internal point of view. Argumenta 4(1):139–156

Ruiter DWP (1993) Institutional legal facts. Legal powers and their effects. Kluwer Academic Publishers, Dordrecht
Ruiter DWP (1997) Basic classification of legal institutions. Ratio Juris 10(4):357–371
Sartor G (2006) Fundamental legal concepts: a formal and teleological characterisation. Artif Intell Law 14:101–142
Sartor G (2009) Legal concepts as inferential nodes and ontological categories. Artif Intell Law 17(3):217–251
Saunders KW (1989) A formal analysis of Hohfeldian relations. Akron Law Rev 23(3):465–506
Schambeck H (1993) Einführung. In: Mayer-Maly D, Schambeck H, Grussmann WD (eds) Adolf Julius Merkl. Gesammelte Schriften. Erster Band, Grundlage des Rechts. Erster Teilband, pp VII–XVIII
Schambeck H (2018) Adolf Merkl (1890–1970). In: Kilian M, Wolff HA, Häberle P (eds) Staatsrechtslehrer des 20. Jahrhunderts: Deutschland - Österreich – Schweiz. De Gruyter, Berlin, pp 431–448
Schwyzer H (1969) Rules and practices. Philos Rev 78:451–467
Searle JR (1964) How to derive 'ought' from 'is'. Philos Rev 73:43–58
Searle JR (1965) What is a speech act? In: Black M (ed) Philosophy in America. Allen and Unwin, London, pp 221–239
Searle JR (1995) The construction of social reality. Allen Lane, London
Searle JR (2006) Social ontology: some basic principle. Anthropol Theory 6(1):12–29
Searle JR (2009 (1969)) Speech acts. An essay in the philosophy of language. CUP, Cambridge
Searle JR (2010) Making the social world. The structure of human civilization. OUP, Oxford
Sergot M (2001) A computational theory of normative positions. ACM Trans Comput Log 2(4): 581–622
Spaak T (1994) The concept of legal competence. An essay in conceptual analysis. Dartmouth Publishing Company Limited, Aldershot
Spaak T (2003) Norms that confer competence. Ratio Juris 16:89–104
Spaak T (2005) The concept of legal competence. The IVR encyclopaedia of jurisprudence, legal theory, and philosophy of law. URL: http://SSRN-id923531%20(1).pdf
Thomasson AL (2007) Artifacts and human concepts. In: Margolis E, Laurence S (eds) Creations of the mind: theories of artifacts and their representation. Oxford University Press, New York, pp 52–73
Tusseau G (2006) Les normes d'habilitation. Dalloz, Paris
Tusseau G (2007a) Positivist jurisprudents confronted. Jeremy Bentham and John Austin on the concept of a legal power. Revue d'études benthamiennes [e-journal] 2. http://etudes-benthamiennes.revues.org/130
Tusseau G (2007b) Jeremy Bentham on power-conferring laws. Revue d'études benthamiennes [e-journal] 3. https://doi.org/10.4000/etudes-benthamiennes.160
Villa-Rosas G (2017) Commanding and defining. On Eugenio Bulygin's theory of legal power-conferring rules. Crítica. Revista Hispanoamericana de Filosofía 49(146):75–105
Villa-Rosas G (2018) Prescribir y definir. Cuatro tesis para una teoría de la competencia jurídica. Revus. J Const Theory Philos Law 36:111–141
Von Wright GH (1951) Deontic logic. Mind 60:1–15
Von Wright GH (1963) Norm and action. A logical enquiry. Routledge and Kegan Paul, London
Walter R (1990) Adolf J. Merkl – Persönlichkeit und wissenschaftliches Werk. In: Walter R (ed) Adolf J. Merkl. Werk und Wirksamkeit. Ergebnis eines Internationalen Symposions in Wien (22.-23. März 1990). Manzsche Verlags- und Universitätsbuchhandlung, Vienna, pp 9–36
Wiederin E (2011) Die Stufenbaulehre Adolf Julius Merkls. Rechtstheorie. Forschungen aus Staat und Recht 136:81–134
Ziembiński Z (1970) Norms of competence as norms of conduct. Archivum Iuridicum Cracoviense 3:21–31

Part I
The Meaning of 'Legal Power' and 'Legal Competence'

Capabilities, Powers and Competences

Jaap Hage

Abstract The article tries to articulate the distinction between powers and competences. Moreover, it also aims to embed these notions in social ontology and the theory of actions.

The argument of the first part is bottom-up: it starts with a discussion of actions and capabilities to act and defines powers as capabilities to act. Then follows a brief discussion of juridical acts, as the performance of juridical acts is one important way to exercise powers. The power to bring about legal consequences by means of a juridical act, the legal power, is a special case of power in the broader sense. Legal competence is a legal status which is necessary for the existence of legal powers.

The second part consists of a number of applications of the theory about competences and powers that was developed in the first part. These applications are also used for distinguishing my view from other views.

1 Introduction

In the jurisprudential literature, the notions of legal power and legal competence are usually not well distinguished, if they are distinguished at all. For instance, in his classic paper on the subject, Hohfeld (1913) only writes about (legal) powers, not about competences. Spaak (1994), following Lindahl (1977), claims that the terms 'competence' and 'power' are used for the same thing by authors on the European continent, respectively from the Anglo-/American tradition. To confirm this theory, Hart (2012), MacCormick (1981) and Raz (1972) wrote about powers. Lindahl and Reidhav (2017) remain in the Swedish tradition by claiming that powers and competences are the same. Kurki (2017), finally, considers competences to be a subset of powers.

J. Hage (✉)
University of Maastricht, Maastricht, The Netherlands
e-mail: jh-science@jaaphage.nl

G. Villa-Rosas, T. Spaak (eds.), *Legal Power and Legal Competence*, Law and Philosophy Library 140, https://doi.org/10.1007/978-3-031-28555-4_2

The present chapter tries to articulate the distinction between the two notions. Moreover, it also aims to embed them in social ontology and the theory of actions. More about that soon.

Obviously, a theory of powers and competences should use the words ‘power’ and ‘competence’ by and large in their ordinary meanings. However, these ordinary meanings are ambiguous, and arguments that develop well-defined notions must unavoidably deviate from some forms of parlance. The argument in this chapter should be read as a plea to use the words ‘power’ and ‘competence’ in a particular well-defined way, and does not aim to capture all aspects of how these notions are used in legal practice or the jurisprudential literature. I do not care much about words. The distinctions that the argument makes matter; the precise words that are used for them do not.

The distinction between powers and competences is blurred by the fact that the word ‘power’ is ambiguous. In its broader meaning, ‘power’ stands for the capability to do something. This meaning is used in, for instance the sentence ‘Making it to the finale of Wimbledon turned out to be beyond Jaap Hage’s power.’ In its narrower meaning, it stands for the capability to bring about legal consequences by means of a ‘juridical act’. This meaning is used in, for instance, the sentence ‘It lies within the power of the Constitutional Court to declare this provision null and void.’ I will call these latter powers ‘legal powers’. The notion of a legal power is related to the notion of a legal competence, although important differences remain.

This chapter consists of two main parts. The argument of the first part is bottom-up: it starts with a discussion of actions and capabilities to act, and defines powers as capabilities to act (Sects. 2–4). Then follows a brief discussion of juridical acts, because the performance of juridical acts is one important way to exercise powers. The power to bring about legal consequences by means of a juridical act, the legal power, is a special case of power in the broader sense (Sect. 5). Legal competences are necessary for the existence of legal powers. This is the argument of the first part of this chapter and at the same time the master argument of the chapter as a whole (Sect. 6). The second part consists of a number of applications of the theory about competences and powers that was developed in the first part. These applications are also used for distinguishing my view from other views (Sect. 7). The chapter is concluded in Sect. 8.

The master argument of the chapter can be formulated without connecting it to social ontology and with only a modicum of theory of action. However, that would leave the argument open to objections based on misunderstandings of what capabilities, actions and intentions are. By embedding the basic argument in a setting of social ontology and action theory, I hope to avoid at least some of these objections.

2 Actions, Capabilities and Attribution

Let me start the argument at the bottom, with events. An event is a change in the set of all facts. Examples of events are that it stopped raining, that the stock market plummeted, that Liverpool FC won the UEFA Champions League 2018/19, that a baby was born, that the victim of a car accident died in the hospital, that Maria and Mateo got married, that Luigi hit a homerun in baseball, and that Christina took a walk.

Some of these events are actions. From the examples above, the events that Luigi hit a homerun and that Christina took a walk are certainly actions. That Maria and Mateo got married is perhaps also an action, just as winning the Champions League. Being born and dying are less obvious actions, although disagreement is still possible. If it stops raining and if the stock market plummets, we consider that as events, but not as actions.

These examples are meant to illustrate that sometimes it is not obvious whether an event counts as an action. Actions are not a natural kind that we discover in a mind-independent reality. Consciously or unconsciously, we single out particular events as actions. Often, people do this in similar ways; they agree on what events count as actions. If that is the case, events that are generally recognized as actions *are*, or *count as*, actions. Actions are socially defined, and I use the phrase 'counts as' to highlight this social construction of actions.[1]

If an event is an action, there is also an agent: no action without an agent and no agent without an action. Because being an action is a matter of social reality, the same holds for being an agent. If we consider getting married as an action of the marrying persons, we attribute the status of agents to these persons. If winning the Champions League is an action, the team that performed this action counts as an agent. If we attribute the status of an action to being born, we attribute the status of an agent to the baby that was born. If we do not want to do the latter, we should refrain from the former.

Having identified actions and agents as elements of social reality, it is time to turn to capabilities. Capabilities are important for my argument, because—as I will later define—powers are nothing other than capabilities. If, as I will argue, capabilities are a matter of status attribution, powers are for the same reason a matter of status attribution.

Having a capability means being able to perform some kind of action. For instance, having the capability to walk means being able to perform actions of the type walking. The presence of such a capability can be established if an agent actually performs the kind of action in question. If somebody walks, this proves that she could (had the capability to) walk. If somebody commits arson, this shows that he is capable to do so. Actions are always actions of some particular kind.

[1] In social reality there is no difference between what something is and as what something counts. Everything in social reality is what it counts as.

Therefore, the performance of an action of some type is definitive proof that the agent had the capability to perform that kind of action.

Notice that even if a capability is established from its exercise, the presence of the exercise itself is a matter of status attribution. We ascribe to a human being the status of an agent, because we ascribe to some event the status of a particular kind of action, such as walking. Moreover, given these status attributions, we can conclude that the agent apparently had the capability to walk.

Notice also that if an agent has the capability to perform some kind of action, for instance walking, this does not imply that the agent can perform all actions of this kind. Being able to walk does not imply the capability to walk on water. However, an agent who cannot walk, cannot walk on water either.

Often, however, we ascribe capabilities to agents even though the relevant actions have not been performed yet. We know that Elisabeth can take the train to Moscow, although she never did that. Moreover, we know that our children can finish a particular kind of education, because we have seen them perform so many other actions that require the same kind of skills. Also these capabilities are a matter of attribution; they do not exist in a mind-independent reality, but we attribute them to agents because of other characteristics of these agents.

No matter whether we conclude to the presence of a capability from an action that we see as its exercise, or whether we conclude that an agent must have a certain capability because of other characteristics he has, in both cases capability is a matter of attribution. Such attribution is based on facts that are believed to be present, such as the exercise of the capability, or the possession of other capabilities, but the capabilities are not identical to these facts. They are facts that are added to, supervene on, other facts—performance of actions, or performance on other tasks—in social reality.

Just like necessity and possibility, capability is a matter of constraints.[2] These constraints may be physical, as when a person lacks the capability to stand up because he is tied to a chair. They may be psychological,[3] as when a person with an anxiety cannot bring herself to travel by airplane. They may also be geographical as when Jean, who is in France, lacks the capability to cross a bridge in Melbourne.

On purpose, the last example concerns a borderline case. Some would object that Jean is capable of crossing this bridge in Melbourne; he only has to travel to Melbourne to do so. The obvious rejoinder to this objection is that at present Jean lacks the capability, but that he may gain this capability by travelling to Melbourne. To that, it can be objected again that Jean already has the required capability, and that the trip to Melbourne is only necessary to exercise it.

---

[2] An extended argument why possibilities and necessities depend on, and are relative to, constraints can be found in Hage (2015, 2017).

[3] This not meant as the claim that the physical and the psychological are completely different domains. On the contrary: what is psychological is—at least in some sense—also physical. But that is a different topic.

The exchange of arguments can go into even more detail, but the message that should be retained is that the answers to questions about capabilities cannot to be found in nature only. Human practices are also relevant. What constraints do we take into account in determining whether somebody is capable to do something? Is geographical location one of them? And psychological limitations and, if so, what limitations? Does laziness also count as a limitation on capabilities? To find out what basic capabilities a person has, we should not only study the hard facts, but also our social practices (Hage 2017). Sometimes our practices are ambiguous, or in flux, and then there may be no one right answer to the question what a person is capable of.

People have some capabilities because, given the facts and our social practices, we attribute these capabilities to them. We will call these capabilities 'basic capabilities'. Next to basic capabilities, there are also 'derived capabilities'. These exist because the possession of a more basic capability implies[4] the possession of the derived capability. Walking is a way of moving; therefore the capability to walk implies the capability to move. Firing a gun will cause a person to be hurt; therefore, the capability to fire the gun is also the capability to hurt this person. Signing a contract counts—under suitable circumstances—as the transfer of a home; therefore, under these circumstances, the capability to sign the contract also is—counts as—the capability to transfer the home.

Derived capabilities are the result of some underlying capability, basic or itself also derived, and a 'link' that attaches the derived capability to its underlying capability. This link can be causal, but it can also be a rule.[5] If the link is causal, I will speak of causal capabilities; if the link is based on a rule, I will speak of rule-based capabilities. An example of a causal capability would be Dieter's capability to open the door. This capability is based on Dieter's capability to turn the key and the causal laws that make the door open as soon as the key is turned. An example of a rule-based capability would be that Charlène has the capability to reduce her tax obligations. This capability depends on Charlène's capability to move from Belgium to Monaco and on the tax laws of Belgium and Monaco, more in particular the differences between them.

[4]The notion of implication is on purpose left vague here. As an approximation the following 'definition' may be helpful: Capability A implies capability B, if and only if capability B is typically assumed to exist whenever capability A is assumed to exist. The double use of the word 'assumed' signals that the existence of a capability, whether basic or derived, is always a matter of attribution.

[5]In this connection, the word 'rule' is used in the broad sense of a connection between kinds of facts (including capabilities) based on a social practice which may, but need not, be the law. More on this conception of rules in Hage (2018), pp. 57–70.

3 Kinds of Rules and Kinds of Powers

We have distinguished three 'sources' of capabilities: attribution for basic capabilities, and causal links and rules for derived capabilities. All capabilities, no matter what their source is, are sometimes called 'powers'. Here I will also use the term 'power' for a capability. These are powers in the broader sense, which must be distinguished from a subcategory, legal powers. In the following, I will use the term 'power' without the addition 'legal' for powers in this broader sense, that is for capabilities. I will return to legal powers later. In this section and the following, I will focus on powers in general, and in particular on rule-based powers, because these are most easily confused with competences.

There are different kinds of rules, depending on the kinds of consequences to which they lead. These differences are reflected in different kinds of powers. All rules attach 'new' facts to 'old' ones, and they can do this in two main ways.

Some rules make that facts of one kind go together in time with facts of another kind. Elsewhere (e.g. Hage 2018, p. 93), I called these rules 'static rules'. Counts as-rules, such as the rule that—under suitable circumstances—signing a contract counts as undertaking an obligation or as the transfer of a good, are typical examples.

Some other rules attach facts to the occurrence of an event. I have called these rules 'dynamic rules', because these rules deal with the succession of facts in time (Hage 2018, pp. 94–96). The law contains many dynamic rules, such as the rule that attaches the liability to be punished to the occurrence of crimes, rules that deal with the succession of roles (e.g. the role of chairperson) or possessions in case somebody passes away, and rules that attach the existence of obligations to torts or to contracts.

Both static and dynamic rules underlie powers. If signing a contract counts as the transfer of real estate, the power to sign the contract implies the power to transfer real estate. (Legally, it is more complicated because competences play a role, but that is for later.) If there is a rule that attaches the status of commander-in-chief of the American army to the status of being the President of the USA, the power to marry the President implies the power to marry the commander-in-chief. If unlawfully causing damage to somebody else leads, according to the rules of tort law, to liability for damages, the power to unlawfully cause damage to somebody else implies the power to become liable for damages. And, finally, because of the rule that validly created statutes lead to valid legal rules, the power to create a statute implies the power to make law.

For many, only the last example will be a real example of a power. It is true that only the last example illustrates a *legal* power. A legal power is defined as the power (that is: a capability) to bring about legal consequences by means of a juridical act. I will return to the importance of juridical acts in connection to legal powers and competences, but in the next section I first will pay some more attention to the ways in which facts, including the existence of powers, depend on rules.

I cannot move to the next section, however, before having pointed out that an agent never needs the power to do something in order to do it. Two examples can illustrate this. Andrew has the power to walk and exercises this power by walking.

Andrew can do this because he has legs, sufficient muscle power and sufficient strength of will to walk, and there are no physical or mental impediments that withhold him from walking. All these combined factors, positive or negative, which make that Andrew walks, also—and for the same reason—make that Andrew can, has the capability, or has the power to, walk. The power does not add anything to what makes Andrew walk.

If we consider a juridical act, and the exercise of a legal power, the story is similar. If Parliament makes a new legal rule, there were a number of factors present that made Parliament do this. These factors include the presence of legal rules giving Parliament the competence (to be explained later) to legislate, but also the possibility for MP's to vote, perhaps to be physically present and no doubt many other factors. These factors make Parliament do something (create a new rule) and at the same time and in the same way enable Parliament to do so. Parliament has the power to create new rules, and this power has the same ground as the actual rule-making action. The power does not add anything to the causes of what Parliament does. If we say that Parliament exercises its power to create new rules, we say nothing other than that Parliament makes new rules. The power-talk is an unnecessary addition. As will see, the story is different for competences; competences do add to other factors to make particular kinds of action (juridical acts) possible.

4 Directly and Indirectly Rule-Based Facts

In Sect. 6, I will argue that a major difference between powers, including legal powers, and competences is that competences are directly rule-based, while powers are at most indirectly rule-based. To facilitate this argument, I will say a little about facts and entities that are directly or indirectly rule-based.

A fact is directly rule-based if there is a rule that attaches the existence of this fact to one or more other facts. A non-legal example is based on the semantic rule that unmarried men of marriageable age are (called) bachelors. If Harry is 35 and still (or again) unmarried, this semantic rule makes Harry into a bachelor. The fact that Harry is a bachelor has been attached by a semantic counts as-rule to the facts that Harry is 35 (and therefore of marriageable age) and unmarried. The new fact is an instantiation of the rule conclusion, and therefore this fact is based directly on the rule.

Not only does the application of this rule create a new fact, it also creates a new thing, namely a bachelor. This does not mean that this particular bachelor, Harry, did not exist before the rule was applied, but merely that Harry's status as a bachelor depends on the rule. Suppose that a particular society does not attach any significance to men of a certain age being unmarried, and therefore also has no special word for such men. Suddenly—say, because of an influential vlog—this changes. Not only has it become important whether a man of marriageable age is married, but also a special word for such men, 'bachelor', has become popular. This sudden change in social reality has created a lot of bachelors, while before there were only unmarried men. Physically, not much has changed,[6] but social reality has been enriched with a lot of new bachelors.

Law abounds with examples of facts that are directly rule-based. I will take an example from the Charter of the United Nations (Art. 2, Section 3):

> All Members shall settle their international disputes by peaceful means in such a manner that international peace and security, and justice, are not endangered.

This provision creates a rule of public international law, even though the provision calls it a 'principle'. If this rule is applied to some Member State of the UN, say France, it imposes on France the duty to settle its international disputes by peaceful means in such a manner that international peace and security, and justice, are not endangered. In other words, this rule attaches the duty to the fact that France is a Member of the UN. A new duty has entered into existence because of the rule, and at the same time a new fact, namely that France has this duty. Moreover, the duty and its existence follow directly from the rule—they are mentioned in the rule conclusion—and are therefore directly rule-based.

Let us now take a look at facts and things that are indirectly rule-based. The simplest way to do so is by means of an example. Contract bridge leagues in many countries award so-called 'masterpoints' to players who have achieved particular results. How many points a player gets for a particular achievement is determined by rules of the national league. These masterpoints are collected in a record, that keeps track of the total amount of masterpoints a player has. To my present knowledge, masterpoints do not lead to much other than the honour and status of the players who collected them. However, one can imagine that a player who has gathered sufficient points is granted the honorific title of 'bridgemaster'. The rules of the national bridge leagues determine how many points are needed for this title.

Let us fill in some details. Remember, all of this is pure fiction. In Belgium, a player needs 5000 master point in order to be a bridgemaster; in the Netherlands a player needs 'only' 4000 points. Suppose that both in Belgium and the Netherlands there are two players with 4500 masterpoints each, and one player with 5100 masterpoints. There are no other players that might qualify for the title of bridgemaster.

Although the situations in Belgium and the Netherlands are in a sense equal, the difference in rules between the two countries makes that there are three bridgemasters in the Netherlands (fact 1) and only one in Belgium (fact 2). As a result, there are more bridgemasters in the Netherlands than in Belgium (fact 3). It is obvious that the facts 1–3 all depend on the rules concerning the assignment of masterpoints and of the title of bridgemaster. Therefore, these three facts are in a sense all rule-based. However, neither the Netherlands nor Belgium has rules with as conclusion that there are so-many bridgemasters, or that one country has more

---

[6] A change in social reality is brought about by a change in minds, which is in turn brought about by a change in the physical carriers of minds, typically brains. This means that changes in social reality typically are accompanied by changes in brains. For my present purposes, this is a side-path however.

bridgemasters than another country. So, although the facts are rule-based, they are not directly based on any rule.[7] They are only indirectly rule-based.

Similar phenomena also play a role in law. The rules of a particular jurisdiction determine at what age minority ends. The fact whether a particular person is a minor is therefore directly rule-based. The rules defining minority indirectly also determine how many minors there are at a particular moment. However, this number of minors is not directly based on a legal rule, but only indirectly. The point that I want to make in the next section is that the fact that an agent has the power to do something by means of a juridical act is in a similar way indirectly rule-based.

5 Juridical Acts

There are many ways in which legal rules can provide agents with the power to bring about legal consequences. One way is if a legal rule makes that some kind of action also counts as an action of another kind. In that case, the power to perform the former kind of action also is (counts as) the power to perform the latter kind. For example, the power to create legislation is also the power to make law.

A second way is if a legal rule makes that one kind of fact goes together with another kind of fact. In that case, the power to bring about the former kind of fact goes together with the power to bring about the latter kind. In this way, the power to become the President of the USA goes together with the power to become the Commander in Chief of the US army.

A third way is if a legal rule attaches consequences to an action. In that case, the power to perform that kind of action is also the power to bring about these consequences. For example, the power to commit a tort goes together with the power to incur an obligation to repair the damage.

All three cases have in common that the rule that creates the power does not have as its consequence that this power exist. The rule leads to a legal consequence and indirectly provides an agent with the power to bring about this consequence. That is precisely the point that I want to make: powers brought about by legal rules are always the indirect consequences of these rules.

On purpose, I have chosen three examples that do not deal with the legal power that most people have in mind: the power to bring about legal consequences by means of a juridical act. I will argue that the situation with regard to juridical acts is no different from the situations dealt with in the three examples I have given. There are no rules which directly give agents the power to bring about legal consequences by means of a juridical act.

---

[7] This may be disputed, because the facts are based on rules of arithmetic. However, the point I wanted to make is that the facts in question are only indirectly based on the rules concerning masterpoints and concerning the title of bridgemaster. Analogously, it will turn out to be possible to distinguish between facts that are directly based on legal rules, and which are only indirectly based on legal rules (although perhaps directly on non-legal rules).

Juridical acts are special in the sense that they involve the capability (power), within important limits, to bring about the legal consequences that the agent intends to bring about. Actions by means of which agents use this capability are called 'juridical acts'. In Germany the notion of a juridical act, a *Rechtsgeschäft*, is limited to private law, where the performance of a juridical act tends to be an exercise of autonomy. However, these private juridical acts have close relatives in public law, for example in the form of legislation, of administrative dispositions, and of judicial verdicts. These juridical acts are essential for a proper understanding of legal powers, legal competences, and the difference between them.

The notion of a juridical act is almost as ambiguous as the notions of a competence or a power. The following definition can therefore not do full justice to the use of the notion in legal theory, doctrine or practice. Nevertheless, I find it satisfactory.

A juridical act is an action performed with the intention to bring about particular legal consequences, to which the law attaches consequences that are to a substantial extent determined by what the agent intended to bring about.[8]

Some comments can perhaps avoid misunderstandings.

1. The intention with which a juridical act is performed is not a conscious state of mind or a mental event, such as a decision (cf. Halpin 1997, pp. 60–68). It is as much the result of attribution as the action itself.[9] Members of society, including judges, attribute a particular intention to a person to whom they also attribute agency, and in doing so they can take everything into account which they deem relevant. However, if there is a recognizable conscious mental state, this will typically play an important role in the attribution of an intention.
2. Although the definition does not mention it, a typical juridical act will consist of the expression of an intention. If intention were taken to be a state of consciousness, the intention itself and the expression thereof would be different things. However, if intention is a matter of attribution, intention and the expression thereof may conceptually be closer to each other than is often assumed. This becomes clear if one considers a juridical act where the intention and its expression are almost indistinguishable, as when somebody thoughtlessly buys a leaf of bread from a vending machine. Another example, provided by Lindahl and Reidhav (2017) is that unsold goods belonging to a company are thrown into a container outside the company's premises. Here the implicit intention is to abandon the ownership on these goods. One way to express this closer relation is to say that the intention is 'read off', rather than inferred, from its expression.[10]

[8]There is some obvious affinity here with Halpin's view that if a power is exercised, the decision of the power holder influences legal positions. Cf. Halpin (1997), p. 60.

[9]Thanks to Hester van der Kaaij who insisted on this while writing her PhD-thesis (Van der Kaaij 2019). It took me some years to realise that she was right after all.

[10]Much more can be said about the close relation between an intention and the action that expresses the intention. The possibility that entities without consciousness, such as legal persons or artificially intelligent agents, express intentions would be a case in point. The present remarks are no more than

3. The intended legal consequences are the starting point for the legal consequences which the law attaches to a juridical act. However, not all intended legal consequences will necessarily become real. Moreover, there will typically be more legal consequences than only the intended ones. In the latter case, the content of the juridical act—the intended consequences—will normally determine the additional consequences to a large extent. For example, if the intended consequences make a contract into a sales contract rather than a lease contract, this determines the supplementary law that also becomes applicable.
4. In legal practice it is sometimes assumed that a juridical act has taken place, even though it has become clear that the required intention was absent.[11] The typical reason to do so is to protect justified reliance. Given the present definition of a juridical act, these situations do not involve juridical acts. This does not exclude that, for reasons of legal certainty, the legal consequences are precisely those that would have existed if the juridical act had taken place. The juridical act is not a necessary condition for these consequences.

There is a trade-off in concept-formation here. It is possible to assume that a valid juridical act exists, every time the law assigns to some event all the consequences that the juridical act would have had. For instance, in order to promote legal certainty, the law assumes a valid contract every time there was justified reliance that the relevant intention was present, even if this intention was actually lacking. It is also possible to promote conceptual consistency and deny the existence of a juridical act if the crucial intention was lacking. To protect justified reliance, the law can still assume that the consequences of a juridical act set in, even though the juridical act itself is not recognised as valid. Above, I have chosen for this second option.

Given the definition of legal powers in terms of juridical acts, and the definition of juridical acts in terms of the relation between agent's intention and legal consequences, legal powers are by definition powers to bring about the legal consequences that one intends to bring about. However, a rule that brings about the intended consequences, has as its consequence that the intended consequences become real, and nothing else. More in particular, the rule does not assign a legal power. Therefore, also in the case of juridical acts, powers are an indirect effect of legal rules, not a direct effect.

Why do some people nevertheless believe that there are rules to confer powers upon legal agents and that juridical acts are exercises of this pre-given power? The answer may be that they confuse legal powers with legal competences.

---

a suggestion that it is perhaps better not to distinguish too sharply between an intention and its expression.

[11] Another complication might be that the required competence was lacking. See the next section.

6 Competence

Not everybody can—has the power to—perform every kind of juridical act. For example, the legislator as such cannot conclude a sales contract, a private citizen cannot issue an administrative disposition, a court cannot legislate (although it may be able to create law), and an administrative organ as such cannot judge individual cases (although some administrative organs may have a subsidiary judicial function).

Moreover, even if a kind of agent has the power to perform juridical acts of a particular kind, there may be sub-kinds of agents that lack the relevant power. For example, human agents can typically enter into contracts, but very young children, or persons with a mental handicap, may lack this power.

There are even more special cases: an insolvent agent may lack the power to alienate the goods he still owns; sale between spouses may be impossible (to prevent fraudulent sales contracts); persons who lack the relevant nationality may not be appointed as judges, and so on ...

The law uses different labels to deal with these impossibilities, but a very important group of them are dealt with under the heading 'lack of competence'. Competences are particularly relevant for an agent who lacks them, because without the required competence a juridical act with a particular content will be invalid (null and void). If, in the Netherlands, a private citizen performs a marriage, the 'marriage' will be invalid. If an insolvent person tries to transfer his car to somebody else, the transfer will be invalid. If the legislator makes the last will of a private citizen, there will be no valid last will.

For every juridical act it holds that the agent performing it needs the competence to perform this kind of juridical act, with this particular content. The law uses the mechanism of withholding competence as a means to control the legal consequences that can be brought about by means of juridical acts. In public law in many countries, the principle of legality brings about that an agent lacks the competence to perform juridical acts in the sphere of public law, unless the agent was granted this competence by written law.[12]

In private law, it is typically the other way around: every legal subject has by default the competence to perform many private juridical acts with any content, unless the competence was explicitly withheld. However, sometimes an explicit attribution of competence is also required in private law. For example, one cannot transfer ownership or any other right without the competence to do so, and this competence is typically attached to having the right that is to be transferred (the *nemo plus* ...-, or the *nemo dat*...-principle). Because this attribution of the competence to transfer is usually taken for granted ('unwritten law'), the necessity to have this competence is not always obvious. However, if the competence is lacking—e.g. when a non-owner sells something—it becomes clear that it was necessary to have the competence which the law attaches to ownership.

[12]Notice that such a competence is not a permission, although a competence without matching permission makes little sense.

So, the general idea is that for every juridical act with a particular content, there is a precondition that the agent who performs the action needs a competence to perform this particular kind of juridical act, with this content. Moreover—and here comes the contrast with powers—competences are typically directly granted by a legal rule. That this is done directly means that the rule has the consequence that somebody has this competence. For instance, there is a rule that grants Parliament—perhaps in cooperation with some other State organ- the competence to create statutes. Or, there is a rule that grants owners of a good the competence to alienate this good. Or, there is a rule that grants courts the competence to issue binding decisions in cases brought before them. Where powers are not directly rule-based, competences typically are.[13]

Finally a brief reply to the possible objection that the law sometimes allows a juridical act to be valid, even if the agent performing it lacked the required competence. Just like in the case of lacking intention, we have two possibilities here. The one is to adhere to common legal usage and accept an incoherent theory of juridical acts and competences. The other one is to stick to the coherent theory and to argue that the law perhaps rightly assigns the legal consequences of a valid juridical act to a case, but that the proper way to construct this is to say that these consequences do not flow from a juridical act. For instance, if a good is transferred by a person who lacks the required competence, the beneficiary of the alleged transfer may have become the new owner. One way to construe this is to assume that in some cases, in particular when the beneficiary of the transfer acted in good faith, a transfer can also be valid without the relevant competence. The other way is to assume that the beneficiary has become the new owner, but that this ownership is not the result of a valid transfer, but—for instance- of a rule that protects contract parties who act in good faith. Here, this second option is chosen.[14]

The argument leading to a distinction between powers and competences is finished now. In summary, powers in the broad sense are capabilities to perform particular kinds of actions. Legal powers are a subcategory of powers in the broad sense. Their distinguishing characteristic is that they are exercised by means of a juridical act. Legal powers are forceful instruments and the law limits their number. One important way to do so is to require a legal competence for the valid performance of a juridical act, and to withhold this competence where the power to bring about intended legal consequences is not desirable. The existence of the relevant competence is a necessary condition for the valid performance of a particular kind of juridical act with a particular content, and in that way also for the possession of the

[13] 'Typically', because facts in social reality, including the existence of competences, can always exist because they are broadly accepted without an intervening rule. However, even then there is a contrast between powers and competences, because powers cannot exist purely because they are accepted, without any support in other facts. Elaboration of this contrast would go beyond the scope of this chapter, however.

[14] As Hegel allegedly claimed: 'Wenn die Tatsachen nicht mit der Theorie übereinstimmen – umso schlimmer für die Tatsachen.' (If the facts do not match the theory, all the more worse for the facts.) This may sound stupid, but for non-realist domains, where the facts are mind-dependent, it may be a very brief formulation of a deep insight.

legal power to bring about this content. In contrast to powers, competences are factors that contribute to the juridical acts based on them. Saying that an agent exercised a legal competence to bring about legal consequences says more than merely that the agent brought about these consequences.

7 Examples

7.1 Super-Tramp

To obtain a better understanding of the theory that was developed in the sections above, I will discuss a number of examples. MacCormick introduced the example of Super-Tramp who always committed offences in early winter in a town with a tolerably comfortable jail, in order to get convicted and imprisoned.[15] The point of this example was to refute the theory that every way of acting in knowledge of the law and with a view to making the law's provisions serve one's ends, can be viewed as an exercise of legal power.

I think it is fair to translate the phrase 'exercise a legal power' as 'perform a juridical act'. Given this translation, MacCormick was correct in claiming that Super-Tramp did not perform a juridical act. Going by Dutch law, the main legal consequence of committing an offence would be the liability to be punished. This liability does not come into existence because of the intention to bring it about. The legal consequences of Super-Tramp's behavior are not determined by the intention with which this behavior was performed. Therefore, the offences committed by Super-Tramp were no juridical acts, and Super-Tramp did not exercise a legal power. A consequence would be that he did not need any competence to perform his offences.

Notice, by the way, that the imprisonment of Super-Tramp is no legal consequence of his offences. The only legal consequence is the liability to be punished. It depends on the behaviour of the public prosecutor and the judiciary whether this liability will be actualized. In terms of the theory exposed above: it depends on whether there is a causal link between the offence and the imprisonment. If this causal link exists, Super-Tramp has the causal power to become imprisoned.

As this Super-Tramp example illustrates, the intention to bring about legal consequences by means of actions that can be subsumed under legal rules does not make these actions into juridical acts. Intentions are relevant, but the mere intention to use legal rules in order to create legal consequences does not suffice. Something more, even something completely different is needed.

[15]MacCormick (1981), p. 75.

7.2 *Moving House*

An example that is related to the Super-Tramp case, but slightly different in an illuminating manner, is the case of moving house.[16] Suppose that Charlène lives in Belgium and that she has to pay a high tax on her yearly income. If she would move house to Monaco, that would result in reduced tax obligations. This means that Charlène can intentionally modify her legal obligations.

Because Charlène can modify her legal obligations, she has by definition the power to do so. She can exercise this power intentionally, that is: she can move to Monaco with a view to reducing her tax obligations. However, just like in the Super-Tramp case, the fiscal consequences do not depend on Charlène's intentions. This means that modifying tax obligations by moving house is not a juridical act, and that no competence is required for it.

However, there is an important difference with the Super-Tramp case. In the latter case, the link between the underlying action (committing an offence) and the derived action ('earning' an imprisonment) was based on a causal link. In the case of moving house, the link is based on a rule, or—more precisely—on the difference between the tax rules of Belgium and of Monaco. This means that Charlène's power to reduce her tax obligations is rule-based, but in an indirect manner. There is no single rule with as its consequence that Charlène's tax obligations have been reduced; the reduction is based on the comparison of the legal consequences of two different rule sets. So there are two major differences between the Super-Tramp case and the case of moving house. One difference is that in the former case the power to earn imprisonment was based on a causal link, while in the latter case the power to reduce tax obligations was based on rules. The second difference is that in the former case, the power was *directly* based on a causal link—the offences caused the imprisonment—while in the latter case, the power to reduce tax obligations was *indirectly* based on the tax rules of Belgium and Monaco.

7.3 *Administrative Dispositions*

Administrative dispositions are juridical acts by means of which organs of the administration establish legal consequences for concrete cases. Their nature varies from imposing parking fines and establishing tax obligations to issuing permits and granting social security benefits. In all of these cases, the legal consequences depend on the intentions of the decision making organ. Administrative dispositions are juridical acts and can only be made by agents who have the necessary competence.

If the required competence is lacking, for instance if a tax inspector writes a parking ticket, the disposition is invalid, null and void. At least, that is what the theory requires. Legal practice is often different. Dispositions made by an organ that

[16] This example was inspired by Raz (1972) and the subsequent discussion in Kurki (2017).

lacked the competence to do so are often merely avoidable, or sometimes outright valid. The reasons why this is the case may vary, but often legal certainty has much to do with it. If somebody enjoyed a social security dole for months, it will often not be possible to decide that the payment of this dole was unjustified and that the beneficiary must repay all the money. The same holds if an industrial plant was built on the assumption that the required licenses were all granted.

If an administrative disposition remains valid, even if the agent making it lacked the required competence, the agent apparently had the power to make this disposition. Not the legal power, to be sure, because for legal powers the relevant competence is a necessary condition. However, the agent had a power in the broader sense, because she succeeded in making the disposition with its legal consequences.

This example illustrates that the law sometimes gives agents powers to do things which would normally be done by means of a juridical act, but which can in exceptional cases also be done with the (indirect) help of rules that protect justified expectations or other forms of legal certainty. In the present example, the juridical act was invalid because of a lack of competence. Other reasons why the juridical act is invalid, such as a lack of an appropriate intention, can also be overcome by such additional rules.

7.4 House Search

House search is an example that is mainly mentioned to point out a common confusion. In the investigation of a crime, the police can under suitable circumstances search a house that is somehow related to the crime, for instance the home of a suspect. The word 'can' in the previous sentence may be a source of confusion, because it wrongly suggests the presence of a capability or power.

Of course, the police can only search a house if they are capable of doing so. That is a basic physical capability, based on direct attribution. However, that is not what is typically meant by saying that the police 'can' search a house. What is meant by this 'can' in not a capability or power in the broader sense, let alone a legal power , but that the police are allowed or permitted to do so.

Permissions are sometimes confused with legal powers, and—it is true—permissions and legal powers sometimes go hand in hand.[17] A legal power typically only makes sense if the holder of this power is also permitted to exercise it. For instance, if all people would have the legal power to contract with the usual legal consequences, this would be almost useless if all people were also prohibited to contract. However, sometimes it makes sense to prohibit behavior that was legally empowered. An

[17] Perhaps the most important point that Hohfeld (1913) made in his work on basic legal concepts is that there is an important difference between the deontic concepts claim, duty and permission (I use modern terminology) and the 'anankastic'—Von Wright's (1963, p. 10) term—concepts of power and liability.

example is when a museum that owns of an important work of art is forbidden to transfer the work in order to prevent the work from leaving the public domain. Such a prohibition typically leaves the competence to transfer intact and perhaps also the power to transfer.

However, there is a complication here. A juridical act may lead to consequences that are forbidden or that conflict with the public order. Think for example for a contract with a hired killer, or a permit for a nuclear plant that creates an irresponsible safety risk for society. It is possible that the law does not allow these legal consequences to set in: the juridical acts lack their normal consequences. This can be construed in two ways. One way is to assume that a conflict with the existing legal order may be a reason to hold a juridical act to be void and without consequences. The other way to construe this is to assume that the legal consequences set in *pro tanto*, and that a normative conflict results between the pre-existing legal order and the newly created legal consequences. If this conflict is solved in favour of the pre-existing legal order, then all things considered, the new consequences do not set in. (See also the discussion of legislation, below.)

No matter how this is construed, in the end the legal consequences of the (attempted) juridical acts do not set in. The agent apparently lacked the legal power to bring these consequences about. So permission may be relevant for (legal) power. However, neither one of the constructions makes use of the notion of competence, and permission and competence remain unrelated.

As is well-known from a James Bond movie, secret agents need a license—that is a permission—to kill, but killing is not a juridical act, and the capability to kill is therefore not a *legal* power. This means that the license to kill is not and does not include a competence to kill. However, permissions typically do go together with powers. The reason is that permissions are the opposite of prohibitions and are often given to make an exception to a prohibition. This is only useful for actions that the agent can perform. For instance, it makes little sense to give an agent permission to walk on water, or to hold her breath for five minutes.

The house search example illustrates that permissions should not be confused with legal powers or their underlying competences. Moreover, it inspires the observations that permissions often—namely in the case of non-juridical acts—concern actions for which no legal power exists, but for which the agent usually has a power in the broader sense (a capability).

7.5 Legislation

Legislation is a juridical act by means of which the legislator, typically an agent consisting of more than one person, intends to make laws and where the law attaches the validity of these laws to the legislative action. As legislating is a juridical act, an agent can only have the legal power to legislate if she has the relevant competence. This should all be straightforward now.

Legislating is nevertheless an interesting example with regard to the distinction between legal powers and competences because of a limitation on the power of legislators. This limitation is that a legislators cannot make laws that conflict with fundamental rights.[18] Because of this limitation, the legislator does not have the power to make such laws. As legal powers are a special case of powers in the broader sense, this also means that the legislator lacks the legal power to make such laws.

This raises the issue of competence. The requirement of competence is a tool used by the law to limit the number of legal powers. Fundamental rights have, amongst others, the same function. Can we therefore say that human rights function as restrictions on competence and that the legislator therefore lacks the competence to make laws that conflict with fundamental rights? In that case we conclude from the absence of a legal power that the relevant competence was lacking. At the same time, we conclude from the absence of a competence that there is no legal power. If legal reasoning with regard to powers and competences works in this way, does that not show that competences are nothing other than legal powers?[19]

This objection against the distinction between legal powers and competences is even strengthened by the facts that legal competences are often assigned implicitly, and that we can only conclude that a competence must have been lacking from the fact that an attempted juridical act did not lead to the intended consequences.

The objection does not cut ice, however. Even if, very theoretically, a legal power and a legal competence always go together, this does not show that they are the same things. As a matter of fact, they could not be the same things, because legal competences are directly assigned by a legal rule, while powers—including legal powers—cannot be directly assigned by a legal rule. (See Sect. 4.) We must therefore conclude that competences and powers cannot be the same.

However, perhaps every limitation on a legal power may be caused by a lack of competence. If that were the case, there would still be a very close connection between legal competence and legal power, because there would only be two kinds of cases: those with a legal power and a legal competence, and those without a legal power and without a legal competence.

There is no univocal answer to the question whether this close connection between legal powers and competences exists. The law uses several mechanisms (personhood, capacity, competence, superior law) to limit legal powers. Perhaps the difference between these mechanisms does not make a difference and can only be explained from the historical development of the mechanisms.

From a logical perspective, it makes perhaps little sense to distinguish between these mechanisms as they have all the same effect: lack of legal power. For instance, if a legislator cannot make rules that conflict with fundamental rights, should we then say that the legislator lacked the competence to do so, or should we say that the intended rules are null and void because of a rule conflict? The theoretical difference

---

[18] It is assumed here that this is indeed impossible and that legislation in conflict with fundamental rights is null and void, rather than merely avoidable.

[19] Thanks to Visa Kurki for suggesting this objection to me.

seems to make no practical difference: legislation that conflicts with fundamental rights is—let us assume—invalid, and the precise reason does not matter. From this point of view, there is something to be said against distinguishing between different kinds of invalidity.[20] Every cause may be called a lack of competence.

However, from the point of view of a person who wants to argue that particular legislation does not lead to valid rules, it may be useful to have a repertoire of different kinds of reasons to substantiate that conclusion. Then it may also be useful to distinguish between the ground for invalidity that an agent was never assigned the competence to legislate and the ground that the result of the legislation violates fundamental rights. Having a conceptual difference between lack of competence and a rule conflict may make it easier to distinguish between different kinds of reasons. So, even if legal powers and competences would always go together, it would still make sense to distinguish them. First, because competences need to be assigned directly by the law, while powers cannot be assigned directly by the law. Second, because the distinction between legal powers and competences makes it easier to identify different kinds of reasons why juridical acts may lack the intended consequences.

7.6 Contracting

The doctrine of juridical acts was developed out of contract doctrine and for many, contracts will still be the juridical acts *pur sang*. Most human beings have the competence to contract, even without an explicit rule stating so. That may be one of the reasons why the requirement of a competence, next to the notion of a legal power, has escaped many.

In the examples above, we have already encountered two important phenomena related to the distinction between powers and competences: powers without a competence (administrative dispositions) and competences without powers (legislating). Moreover, we have seen the difference between competence and power on the one hand, and permission on the other hand (house search). All of these issues also play a role in contracting. It is not necessary to repeat the discussions, and I will confine myself by pointing out how these issues play a role in contracting.

Power without competence. The doctrine of justified reliance plays a crucial role in contract law. It is sometimes presented as if there were two grounds for the existence of a valid contract, exchange of expressions of a shared intention, or justified reliance. However, here we have chosen for a coherent doctrine of juridical acts which prefers to keep justified reliance outside the doctrine of contracting (and juridical acts in general).

[20] Even then there is a distinction between kinds of validity that still makes sense, namely the distinction between source validity and validity as existence in social reality ('binding force'). For this distinction (and even a third kind of validity), see Hage (2018).

Competence without power. Most legal subjects are competent to contract but not all intended contracts are valid. There are several reasons for this, including lack of matching intentions, undesirable content, and a prohibition to contract. In all of these cases, the power to contract was lacking, although the necessary competence was present.

Prohibited contracts. Sometimes the conclusion of particular contracts is forbidden. Sale of drugs may in many countries be a case in point. Contracts with hired killers are another example. If concluding a particular kind of contract is legally forbidden, the contract may still be valid. For example, if you buy something in a shop after mandatory closing time, the sales contract will still be valid. The sanction is punishability, or in some cases liability for damages. However, if a contract belongs to a kind that was forbidden, this may be a reason that the contract is invalid (null and void). In that case, the contracting parties lacked the power to conclude such a contract, even though they were competent to do so.

8 Conclusion

In this paper I have argued that it is possible to distinguish two notions that play a role in the debate on powers and competences. My main point is that the two notions are really different. They are not two words for the same thing, neither are competences a subset of powers, or the other way around. In the end, I do not care which words are used to denote the two notions, but—not very originally—I have adopted the words 'power' and 'competence'. I am aware that my use of these two words deviates in a number of ways from common parlance, to the extent that common parlance exists in this field.

The structure of my basic argument is as follows: I use the word 'power' in a broad sense for all capabilities to do something. In this broad sense, powers are not particularly connected to juridical acts or to law. Powers are a social phenomenon, although they have a basis in physical reality. They can be based directly on acceptance or recognition, but they can also depend on other powers, in combination with causal laws or with rules. For law, the latter—rule-based—powers are the more interesting category. Some of these rule-based powers are based on legal rules and are exercised by means of juridical acts. Juridical acts are actions to which the law attaches legal consequences that are to a large extent determined by the intention in the juridical act. Powers exercised through the performance of a juridical act are called 'legal powers'. The law limits the possibilities for agents to create legal consequences by means of juridical acts by requiring a competence to do so. Examples are the competence to issue administrative dispositions, to give judicial verdicts, to legislate, to contract, or to alienate goods. By withholding the relevant competence from a category of agents, the law can make it impossible for these agents to perform that particular kind of juridical act, and indirectly also to exercise the corresponding legal power. So, competences are necessary conditions for the existence of legal powers.

This basic argument has been embedded in a theoretical framework that deals with the existence of powers and of intentions in social reality, and with the distinction between facts and entities that are directly or indirectly rule-based. It was complemented by a discussion of a number of examples, some of which played an important role in earlier debates on the nature of powers and competences.

References

Hage J (2015) Separating rules from normativity. In: Araszkiewicz M, Banaś P, Gizbert-Studnicki-T, Pleszka K (eds) Problems of normativity, rules and rule-following. Springer, Cham, pp 13–30
Hage J (2017) The compatibilist fallacy. Revus 32:97–118. https://doi.org/10.4000/revus.3861
Hage J (2018) What is legal validity? Lessons from soft law. In: Westerman P, Hage J, Kirste S, Mackor AR (eds) Legal validity and soft law. Springer, Cham, pp 19–46
Halpin A (1997) Rights & law. Analysis & theory. Hart Publishing, Oxford
Hart HLA (2012 (1961)) The concept of law, 3rd edn. OUP, Oxford
Hohfeld WN (1913) Some fundamental legal conceptions as applied in judicial reasoning. Yale Law J 23(1):16–59
Kurki V (2017) Legal competence and legal power. In: MacBride M (ed) New essays on the nature of rights. Hart Publishing, London, pp 31–48
Lindahl L (1977) Position and change. A study in law and logic. Reidel, Dordrecht
Lindahl L, Reidhav D (2017) Legal power: the basic definition. Ratio Juris 30:158–185
MacCormick N (1981) H.L.A. Hart. Edward Arnold, London
Raz J (1972) Voluntary obligations and normative powers. II-Joseph Raz. Proc Aristot Soc, Suppl Vol 46:79–101
Spaak T (1994) The concept of legal competence. An essay in conceptual analysis. Darthmouth, Aldershot
Van der Kaaij HDS (2019) The juridical act. Springer, Cham
Von Wright GH (1963) Norm and action. A logical enquiry. Routledge and Kegan Paul, London

Expanding Agency and Borders of Competence

Visa Kurki

Abstract This chapter will offer a suggestion for a moderate rethinking of legal competence. It will first discuss the purpose of theorizing about competence. It will consider two main examples that challenge especially intention-based accounts of legal competence. First, the chapter will focus on the implications that the Convention on the Rights of Persons with Disabilities has for a theoretical understanding of competence. The Convention will pose problems for an intention-based understanding of competence. It is argued that such an account of competence can be salvaged, at least partially, by using a non-atomistic account of agency. Second, the chapter will consider consent-based rape laws, and argue that as a conceptual matter, they do not entail competences to potential victims. Such capacity to consent can be included as a competence, however, by introducing a broader notion of soft competence. The chapter will present such a notion and discuss some of its application.

1 Introduction

This chapter will offer a suggestion for a moderate rethinking of legal competence. In particular, I will consider two potential problems that challenge the extensional adequacy of the view that associates competence with the intention to change legal relations.

Let us briefly consider some of the different approaches that scholars have taken with regard to legal competence. First, a very broad account of competence equates it with any capacity to change legal relations through volitional control. Following

I would like to thank Torben Spaak and Gonzalo Villa-Rosas for their help, feedback and patience; Kelly Dhru for her highly perceptive comments; and Roosa Niklander for her help in finalizing the chapter.

V. Kurki (✉)
Law Faculty, University of Helsinki, Helsinki, Finland
e-mail: visa.kurki@helsinki.fi

G. Villa-Rosas, T. Spaak (eds.), *Legal Power and Legal Competence*, Law and Philosophy Library 140, https://doi.org/10.1007/978-3-031-28555-4_3

Wesley Newcomb Hohfeld, I have denoted such legal positions "powers".[1] Under this broad conception, even nonhuman animals have legal powers: a dog can attack Kate, and thereby through volitional action provide her with the liberty to defend herself from the attack. I will here call such normative positions "wide powers".[2] Many theorists think an account of wide powers alone does not manage to capture the distinctive nature of, say, contracting, consenting and so on. When attempting to descry the distinctive features of such acts, scholars have taken two main approaches. First, some focus on the beneficiality or desirability of being able to effect such legal consequences as a contract.[3] The other approach is to define the intention to change a legal relation as a distinct feature of competences. I have opted for the latter approach, offering the following account of competences:

Legal competence:

(1) x holds the competence C to effect the legal consequence r if and only if x can perform an act-in-the-law to bring about r.

Act-in-the-law:
Act a, performed by x, constitutes an act-in-the-law if and only if

(1) x performs a with the intention to bring about the legal consequence r, and
(2) the fact that x has performed a in order to bring about r is an element of a set of actually occurrent conditions minimally sufficient for r.[4]

One holds a legal competence to effect a legal consequence if and only if can one perform an act-in-the-law to bring it about. An act-in-the-law is an act that is performed with the intention to bring about a legal consequence, and the intention is part of the reason why the legal consequence is brought about. Accounts such as mine thus presuppose the capacity to form intentions regarding the content of the legal system: one must be able to form intentions regarding legal norms, i.e. what one is legally permitted to do and so on. I call such mental states *legal intentions*.

I will in this chapter consider two potential problems that may beset this legal-intention-based understanding of legal competence.

First, I will discuss the paradigm change that has been taking place in disability law. Recent changes in disability law purport to extend competences to the vast majority of individuals with disabilities, including those with severe cognitive disabilities. Such cases might be problematic for theories of competence because, roughly put, possessing competences presupposes the capacity to understand the legal reality and ideas such as obligation, right and so on. Only an entity with the

[1] See Kurki (2017).

[2] The term "power" in a broad sense can be confusing especially because I will below discuss power-conferring rules, which do *not* deal with powers in this broad sense but rather in a narrower sense. The phrase "wide power" is inspired by Joseph Raz' recent discussion of "wide normative powers". Raz (2019).

[3] This is Raz's and Kramer's approach. See Maccormick and Raz (1972) and Kramer (2021).

[4] Kurki (2017).

capacity to understand such notions can be endowed with competences because the standard way of exercising these competences requires the intention to effect a legal change. For instance, consider contracts. Entering a contract is a paradigm case of an exercise of a legal competence. One enters a contract by performing a specified action with the intention to be bound by the contract. Such an intention, then, is only possible if one can understand the relevant legal concepts—and some cognitive disabilities might, arguably, entail difficulties in reaching such an understanding. However, I will suggest that this problem may be averted—at least partly—if we abandon the strictly atomistic understanding of cognition, and instead adopt a relational approach.

The second challenge has to do with cases that should plausibly be understood as competences but seem to be excluded by the legal-intention-based model of competence. I will take consent-based rape laws as an example. Even though sexual consent should plausibly be understood as a competence, at least my legal-intention-based account of competences seems to exclude it. However, I will suggest that a broader account of competence—which I will label "soft competence"—will be able to account for criminal consent. Roughly put, soft competence involves law's giving legal recognition to normative (but non-legal) intentions.[5] Such an account might be able to include some further competences of persons with cognitive disabilities, even when the relational understanding of agency cannot adequately account for such competences. It might even allow for the extension of competences to nonhuman animals.

The essay is structured as follows. Section 2 will briefly adopt a meta-perspective and discuss the purpose of theorizing about competence. I will argue here that competence is a central element of legal self-determination. Section 3 will then discuss whether the legal-intention-based account of competence can account for the recent extension of self-determination to individuals with disabilities, concluding that if autonomy is understood relationally, then at least some competences can be accounted for. The section will also analyze the competences that individuals with disabilities have, based on a distinction between dependent, independent, and negative competences. In Sect. 4, I will argue that the legal-intention-based explanation of competences cannot account for consent in criminal law, unless the account is revised. The section will offer a suggestion for such a revision, and then briefly discuss whether the revised account might also apply to nonhuman animals. The essay will then conclude.

[5]Hence, as Kelly Dhru correctly pointed out, soft competences and wide powers differ in that Hohfeldian wide powers do not even require non-normative intentions. Hence, the volition required of wide powers is broader than normative non-legal intentionality.

2 Functions of Competence

Let us briefly consider a meta-level matter: what is theorizing about competence all about? Consider these two cases:

(1) The duty to help someone in mortal danger.
(2) The competence to enter a contract.

It is natural to think of these two as exemplifying different types of norms: (1) is about a duty-imposing norm, (2) about a competence-conferring norm. However, one might potentially understand both (1) and (2) as conditional obligations: "*If* you meet someone in mortal danger, then you have the duty help them", and "*If* you enter a contract, then you have the duty to fulfil your contractual obligations". Essentially, all contracts merely trigger the general norm of *pacta sunt servanda*. The issue confronting a legal theorist, then, is what kind of norms are special enough to merit their own conceptual category, rather than being merely conditional duties.

The puzzle of distinguishing between competences and conditional duty-imposing norms has recently been discussed by David Enoch in the context of reason-giving and legal normativity. Enoch notes that it is difficult to distinguish robust reason-giving—i.e. the giving of new reasons-for-action—from what he calls a "triggering case of reason-giving", i.e. the triggering of existing reasons:

> Think about my request that you read my [academic paper] draft. We are assuming that before the request you had no reason to read the draft, and after it you do. But this means that the conditional "If I ask you to read the draft, you will have a reason to read it" was true all along, or anyway shortly before – and independently of – my actually making its antecedent true (by requesting that you read the draft). But then it is very tempting to think of this case as yet another triggering case of reason-giving: For all I did here is to manipulate the non-normative circumstances so as to trigger your conditional reason to-read-the-draft-if-I-ask-you-to. Are all cases of robust reason-giving, then, cases of triggering reason-giving – perhaps appearances notwithstanding?[6]

Enoch's puzzle is, really, a generalized version of an issue relating to competence that legal theorists have been aware of for a long while. For instance, Hans Kelsen argued famously that putative competence-conferring norms are really mere norm fragments:

> Human behaviour which is qualified neither as a duty nor as a right occurs also among the conditions of a sanction. Let us consider as an example the legal norm which obligates a debtor to return a loan to his creditor. Schematically, this norm may formulated thus: If two individuals make a loan contract, if the debtor does not return the loan in due time, and if the creditor brings a suit against the debtor, then the court has to order a certain sanction against the debtor.[7]

---

[6]Enoch (2011), p. 6.

[7]Kelsen (2006), p. 90.

The competence of the creditor is thus ultimately, according to Kelsen, analyzable in terms of the conditions under which the court has an obligation to order a sanction. Matthew Kramer calls this view the "Subsumability Thesis".[8]

Enoch's solution to the reason-giving problem is that robust reason-giving is simply a special instance of triggering reason-giving—but "a very special particular instance".[9] The same is true of demarcating between duty-imposing and power-conferring norms. The distinction between these two types of norms is not "already there", ready for the theorist to discern; rather, demarcating these categories involves active categorizing by the theorist. Kelsen is, in a sense, right in that competence-conferring norms are reducible to conditional duty-imposing norms. However, the former are still in various ways special, deserving their own conceptual category. But special in what way?

For Hart, the special status of power-conferring rules had to do with their special social function:

> But there are important classes of law where this analogy with orders backed by threats altogether fails, since they perform a quite different social function. Legal rules defining the ways in which valid contracts or wills or marriages are made do not require persons to act in certain ways whether they wish to or not. Such laws do not impose duties or obligations. Instead, they provide individuals with facilities for realizing their wishes, by conferring legal powers upon them to create, by certain specified procedures and subject to certain conditions, structures of rights and duties within the coercive framework of the law.[10]

Scott Shapiro provides a similar argument in his response to Kelsen: "We might say, then, that power-conferring rules are not primarily for guiding officials on how they can help power holders; rather, they are for instructing power holders on how they can help themselves."[11]

Of central importance for this essay will be competences' role in autonomy and self-determination, which I take to be one of the central functions of competences. Competences are, of course, not *always* about providing people "with facilities for realizing their wishes". Officials, such as judges, hold various legal competences that they are legally obligated to exercise in a specific way; these competences do not exist in order for the officials to realize their wishes. However, competences do regardless have an instrumental role in the legal realization of self-determination.

2.1 *Autonomy, Self-Determination and Competence*

I use the terms "autonomy" and "self-determination" in specific senses here. I will first consider autonomy, as I take self-determination to be an aspect of autonomy.

---

[8] See Kramer (2021).

[9] Enoch (2011), p. 10.

[10] Hart (1994), pp. 27–28.

[11] Shapiro (2011), p. 68.

"Autonomy" is used by scholars to refer various things. Autonomy can, for instance, be understood as a set of capacities that together provide an entity with the capacity for independent action. Talk of autonomous weapons systems rely on this notion of autonomy. Such a notion of autonomy is extra-legal in the sense that one may possess autonomy regardless of one's status in the prevalent legal system. Relational accounts of autonomy—addressed later in this article—fall under this sense of "autonomy" as well, even if such accounts understand autonomy as partly socially constituted. On the other hand, "autonomy" can also refer to a normative status. For instance, the Åland Islands, situated between Finland and Sweden, is a part of Finland but often described as an "autonomous area". This status means that they have their own parliament, with competence to pass laws pertaining to the internal affairs of the area. It is this autonomy-*qua*-status with which I am mainly concerned here, though I will focus on the autonomy of individual human beings and animals rather than of polities.

We can distinguish different elements even in this narrower context of autonomy-*qua*-status. First, such autonomy consists of a "sphere of freedom" wherein one enjoys bodily integrity and may freely decide whether to engage in a wide range of conduct without interference from others. Being permitted to go for a walk every day without being prevented by others is an instance of this element of autonomy. Obviously, others may interfere in some ways: for instance, others are usually permitted to criticize my going for a walk. However, they may not physically restrain me from going on the walk or, say, threaten to kill me if I go for the walk. In Hohfeldian terms, this element of autonomy consists primarily of liberties and claim-rights: liberties to engage (and not to engage) in all sorts of conduct, and claim-rights protecting the liberties in various ways.[12] This element of autonomy is *static* because the boundaries of the sphere remain constant.

On the other hand, an important element of autonomy has to do with modifying and determining the boundaries of one's static sphere of freedom.[13] This is the *dynamic* element of autonomy, which I will call self-determination, following Jan Beckmann.[14] For instance, others may not normally inject vaccines into my body, but I can give a doctor the permission to do so: I can change the doctor's duty-not-to-inject-me-with-a-vaccine into a corresponding liberty. My giving the doctor this permission amounts to *consent*—a concept that has recently become very topical.

Note that the "triggering puzzle" applies here. We can perceive the situation as static if we think of the doctor's liberty-to-administer-the-vaccine as conditional: she already has the liberty-to-administer-the-vaccine-to-me-if-I-give-permission. In this sense, my giving the permission merely means triggering this existing liberty. But

---

[12] See Hohfeld (1913).

[13] However, not all aspects of the sphere of freedom are subject to being changed. First, the legal system may deny self-determination to some beings altogether; second, even for those whose self-determination is not systematically restricted, there may be limits to the sphere of freedom that they cannot change. For instance, one may be unable to consent to being tortured.

[14] See Beckmann (2017).

giving permissions, consenting, agreeing and so on are special cases because they involve the intentional changing of one's boundaries: one normally permits, consents, and agrees with the intention to change one's legal boundaries, and the law gives legal effect to this intention. Hence, we may wish to accord such acts a special status—by classifying them as legal competences.[15] Thus, classifying consenting as an exercise of a legal competence—and therefore as part of the dynamic element of autonomy, i.e. self-determination—is very natural.

3 Competence and Disability Law

Legal systems have traditionally denied competences—and thereby self-determination—to many persons with disabilities. The latter have often been relegated to a status of "objects of protection", whose interests have been protected through paternalistic legislation, rather than being treated as active decision-makers. They have been unable to decide about their affairs, consent to medical procedures or even consent to sex.[16] However, recent developments in disability law have emphasized the agency, autonomy and self-determination of persons with disabilities, with the Convention on the Rights of Persons with Disabilities spearheading a new approach. The Convention requires that states parties ensure both the static and dynamic autonomy of persons with disabilities. For instance, according to Article 14(1),

> States Parties shall ensure that persons with disabilities, on an equal basis with others:
>
> a) Enjoy the right to liberty and security of person;
> b) Are not deprived of their liberty unlawfully or arbitrarily, and that any deprivation of liberty is in conformity with the law, and that the existence of a disability shall in no case justify a deprivation of liberty.

Francesco Seatzu explains that even though this provision does not prohibit the involuntary placement of persons with disabilities into institutions, it does prohibit such placement based on discriminatory grounds: mere disability *alone* can never justify such placement.[17] The provision thus serves to protect disabled individuals' static sphere of freedom.

However, the Convention also contains provisions that are most plausibly understood as promoting the self-determination of persons with disabilities. Especially those with cognitive disabilities have traditionally often been denied the competence to decide about their own affairs. Instead, they have needed legal representatives to make decisions on their behalf. However, this state of affairs has started to change, with the Convention spearheading a new approach. Article 12 of the Convention includes the following sections:

---

[15] For an account of consenting as a normative power, see Dougherty (2015).

[16] On the last point, see Arstein-Kerslake (2015); Fridström Montoya (2015), p. 79.

[17] Seatzu (2017), p. 299.

1. States Parties reaffirm that persons with disabilities have the right to recognition everywhere as persons before the law.
2. States Parties shall recognize that persons with disabilities enjoy legal capacity on an equal basis with others in all aspects of life.
3. States Parties shall take appropriate measures to provide access by persons with disabilities to the support they may require in exercising their legal capacity.
4. States Parties shall ensure that all measures that relate to the exercise of legal capacity provide for appropriate and effective safeguards to prevent abuse in accordance with international human rights law. Such safeguards shall ensure that measures relating to the exercise of legal capacity respect the rights, will and preferences of the person, are free of conflict of interest and undue influence, are proportional and tailored to the person's circumstances, apply for the shortest time possible and are subject to regular review by a competent, independent and impartial authority or judicial body. The safeguards shall be proportional to the degree to which such measures affect the person's rights and interests.

A word about the terminology used here. In some contexts, the phrase "legal capacity" is understood as equivalent of the continental notion *Rechtsfähigkeit*, i.e. capacity to hold (private-law) rights and duties. This is an element of what I term passive legal personhood, i.e. the type of legal personhood with which even new-born children are endowed.[18] The Convention employs a different terminology. Section 1 of the article—affirming the right to recognition as a person before the law—pertains to the passive aspect of legal personhood. However, "legal capacity" in the Convention denotes instead an element of what I term *active legal personhood*, i.e. the capacity to administer one's own legal situation through legal competences.[19] Occasionally, the phrase is also used to refer to *both* passive and active legal personhood.[20] For instance, a report by the Council of Europe Commissioner for Human Rights defines the phrase as follows:

> Legal capacity can be described as a person's power or possibility to act within the framework of the legal system. In other words, it makes a human being a subject of law. It is a legal concept, a construct, assigned to most people of majority age enabling them to have rights and obligations, to make binding decisions and have them respected.[21]

Here, "legal capacity" is both described as the "power [...] to act within the framework of the legal system", that normally only adults have, but also as "being a subject of law", "enabling [one] to have rights and obligations". The definitions seem to fluctuate between active and passive legal personhood, and occasionally "legal capacity" is taken to comprise both "legal standing", meaning here the capacity to hold rights and duties, and "legal agency", meaning the capacity to exercise said rights and duties.[22] It is very unclear how this "legal standing" is then different from the right to recognition as persons before the law, affirmed in article

[18] See Kurki (2019).

[19] The other central incident of active legal personhood has to do with bearing legal duties and being held responsible in criminal and tort law.

[20] See Dhanda (2007), pp. 442–443.

[21] Nilsson (2012), pp. 9–10.

[22] Devandas Aguilar (2017), p. 4. I should note that I do not agree with this definition of "legal standing" as the capacity to hold rights and/or duties.

14(1). At any rate, in what follows, I take "legal capacity' to refer to active legal personhood, and in particular to legal competences.

According to Catalina Devandas Aguilar (acting as Special Rapporteur on the rights of persons with disabilities) this new approach, "universal legal capacity", has the following central implications:

> States must recognise universal legal capacity for all persons with disabilities, including for those requiring more intensive support. That entails adopting legislation that explicitly recognizes the capacity of persons with disabilities to create, modify or end legal relationships, as well as providing effective legal protection against any interference with such capacity. That recognition must include the exercise of the right to property, access to all forms of financial credit and the right to control one's own financial affairs.[23]

Thus, to put it in Hartian and Shapiroan terms, the Convention requires that States Parties provide disabled individuals with facilities for realizing their wishes, thus enabling them to help themselves. This has clearly to do with extending competences to such individuals and thereby expanding their self-determination.

On the other hand, the Convention requires abolishing "regimes of substituted decision-making". By such regimes, Devandas Aguilar means situations where "legal capacity is removed from a person (even if limited to a single decision) and a substitute decision maker appointed by a third party takes decisions based on what he or she considers is in the best interests of the person concerned, even if that goes against the will of the latter".[24]

Here, many theorists interested in normative powers and competences may be puzzled. Namely, the requirement of legal intention—the intention to effect a legal change—may be difficult to fulfil in the case of some individuals with cognitive disabilities. Such an intention requires some level of understanding of the legal system, norms and so on. Can all persons with cognitive disabilities, therefore, possess competences? However, the Convention relies on a new kind of understanding of agency. According to Michael Bach and Lana Kerzner, under this new model, decision-making *ability* and *capability* are distinguished. The former can be based on two criteria:

> 1) my capacity to express my will and/or intentions, at least to others who know me well, and who can then 'confer' or ascribe agency to my actions in their descriptions of me to others; and 2) being able to tell 'who' I am, my life story of values, aims, needs and challenges, or having my community of knowing and valuing others do that for me, and using that narrative coherence of my life to help direct the decisions that give effect to my intentions.[25]

This decision-making ability is, according to Bach and Kerzner, the minimum threshold for legal capacity. This ability can, then, become decision-making *capability* if the individual is provided sufficient "supports and accommodations". The notion of support means that people who know the individual well assist them in decision-making in various ways, helping them for instance in "formulating [their]

---

[23] Devandas Aguilar (2017), p. 19.

[24] Devandas Aguilar (2017), p. 7.

[25] Bach and Kerzner (2010), pp. 65–66.

purposes, to explore the range of choices and to make a decision" as well as supporting them in decision-making processes with other parties and in acting on decisions that have been made.[26] Decision-making capability is thus here understood socially: one is an agent "through" others.

What about individuals who do not meet the criteria of decision-making ability? Here, judgments seem to diverge somewhat. Devandas Aguilar argues that in situations where a person's will cannot be determined, one must instead ascertain what they would have wanted, including "consideration of the previously manifested preferences, values, attitudes, narratives and actions, inclusive of verbal or non-verbal communication, of the person concerned".[27] Substituted decision-making, based on the person's best interests, is not allowed. Many scholars accept, however, that this orthodoxy is unrealistic in some cases—as with comatose people—even if it should always be seen as a baseline.[28]

Now, can competences be extended to individuals with disabilities who require support in order to make decisions? What about individuals who are part of the facilitated decision-making scheme? And if the answer to either question is affirmative, are such competences qualitatively different from those held by individuals not under the support-model regime?

As regards the "can" question, we should first note what exactly is at stake here. The scrutiny here need not necessarily question the support model or the idea of universal legal capacity per se. Rather, the question has to do with how to analyze this model, and how to relate it to the theoretical notion of a legal competence. As noted above, the main difficulty has to do with the notion of a legal intention: can (all) persons with disabilities who rely on supported-decision making in order to exercise their legal capacity form intentions about legal consequences?

Note that the threshold for legal intentions cannot be very high, for a number of reasons. First, in most cases, one need not understand the *exact* legal consequences of an act. Individuals without disabilities seldom understand all of the legal consequences of even relatively simple contracts. Second, the conceptual threshold we are debating here does not have to do with whether one is capable of making "good" (prudent, well-reasoned) decisions. There may be reasons for restricting people's competence to make bad decisions. However, if an individual, say, enters a contract with very poor terms—but a valid contract nevertheless—the transaction is certainly an exercise of a competence. The issue is simply whether one can have legal intentions: whether one can, for instance, intend to be legally bound by a contract.

Let us first consider supported decision-making. First, many individuals with disabilities can form legal intentions. When discussing children's competences, James Dwyer notes that even relatively young children can possess a rudimentary understanding of the legal system: "If not at three then at least by five the average child could comprehend in a rough way the ideas of a legal duty and a powerful,

[26]Bach and Kerzner (2010), p. 73.

[27]Devandas Aguilar (2017), para. 31.

[28]Flynn and Arstein-Kerslake (2014), p. 98.

governing entity called a 'court' or 'judge' who can order people to do or not do certain things."[29] If the bar for legal intentions is set this low, then most individuals who rely on supported decision-making can likely have at least some legal intentions. Members of the individual's circle of support can, at least in many cases, explain the situation in terms that the individual can understand.

The idea of supported decision-making is clearly related to what philosophers and cognitive scientists call the *hypothesis of extended cognition*. According to this hypothesis, human cognition does not wholly happen inside one's head, but is rather supported by "hybrid coalitions of neural, bodily and environmental elements".[30] Traditional examples of extended cognition are notebooks and smartphones, which can serve a central role in supporting one's cognitive processing. However, an idea that is gaining traction is what Mason Cash calls "socially and culturally distributed cognition", which he labels the "third wave" of arguments for the hypothesis of extended cognition. According to this idea, "individual cognition takes place within, is supported by, and is mutually co-constructed with larger social, institutional, normative, political, technological, and cultural systems and practices".[31]

Researchers working in this field have in particular been interested in the idea of socially distributed memory. One group of researchers mentions this example of a married couple remembering their honeymoon, which had taken place 40 years earlier:

> Wife: And we went to two shows, can you remember what they were called?
>
> Husband: We did. One was a musical, or were they both? I don't... no... one...
>
> W: John Hanson was in it.
>
> H: Desert Song.
>
> W: Desert Song, that's it, I couldn't remember what it was called, but yes, I knew John Hanson was in it.
>
> H: Yes.[32]

Memory is an important part of our cognition, and *understanding* is likely socially supported in similar ways as well. When trying to understand law—for instance, to understand the legal consequences of a complicated contract—we rely on help, perhaps from lawyers and perhaps also from people who can help explain what the lawyer said. Our understanding of law is likely also supported by language and the *linguistic division of labour*: even if I might not have a full grasp of what "law" or "contract" refers to, I can still employ these terms because the meaning of terms "is determined at least in part by the linguistic usage in [one's] community, including, if necessary, expert usage".[33] The original idea of this kind of externalism about

---

[29] Dwyer (2020), p. 17.

[30] Cash (2013), p. 61.

[31] Cash (2013), p. 61.

[32] Sutton et al. (2010), p. 522.

[33] Haslanger (2013), p. 305.

meaning is that we can use terms successfully without fully understanding them. However, if one takes the idea of extended cognition seriously, one could argue that the linguistic division of labour is not only about successfully using terms that we do not understand. Rather, if understanding itself is a socially embedded process, then the linguistic division of labour supports, and perhaps even forms part of, our understanding. As Cash puts it,

> an "intelligent" agent is not one who is intelligent independently of the physical and social factors that shape, scaffold and support their cognitive abilities. An agent's intelligence is the acumen, skill, expertise, and "tools for thinking" with which they have surrounded themselves through a lifetime of development within and through ongoing engagement with this technological, linguistic, institutional, and normative environment.[34]

Thus, on this understanding, one's facility to form legal intentions is partly socially constituted and supported, also in the case of individuals with cognitive disabilities. The idea of socially distributed cognition has its share of persistent problems, however. A particularly tricky issue has to do with the question of "cognitive bloat", i.e. where to draw the line between genuine cognition and its support mechanisms, and who "owns" distributed processes. Cash suggests a normative way of drawing the line, grounded in normative practices: actions and thought processes are "mine" if I ought to take responsibility for them in light of current normative practices.[35] This answer sidesteps the question of who *should* be held responsible in light of ideal rather than current normative practices. However, the question of who owns normative processes can be anchored in the normative practice of giving and asking for reasons. If an individual can—at least with help of their support network—provide reasons for, say, consenting to a medical procedure, then it is likely meaningful to ascribe the act of consenting to the individual.

I thereby conclude that many individuals with cognitive disabilities can hold at least some legal competences if we accept the idea of extended cognition. However, this conclusion likely does not apply to all individuals with cognitive disabilities. It is certainly not obvious that individuals falling under the scheme of facilitated decision-making really are capable of making any kind of decisions about their legal situation. Imagined will and preferences are just that—imagined. We can certainly imagine, for instance, our dead loved ones' will and preferences, but that does not mean that they are in a position to exercise their will.

I will now briefly discuss the kinds of competences that individuals with cognitive disabilities are endowed with.

---

[34] Cash (2013), p. 66.

[35] Cash (2013), pp. 67–68.

Table 1 The relationship between the child's competence and his/her guardian's[a]

Child	Guardian or e.g. authority
No competence	*Independent competence*: guardian may decide over child's situation without being subject to child's veto, cancellation etc.
Negative competence: child's approval required, or child may veto decision	*Dependent competence*: guardian's competence subject to child's approval or veto
Dependent competence: child may initiate a legal change, but subject to guardian's veto, permission or cancellation.	*Negative competence*: Guardian's approval required, or they may veto or cancel the legal effect.
Independent competence: child may exercise competence without supervision.	*No competence* to decide over child's situation or to veto child's exercise of competence.

[a] The table is originally published in Kurki (2021), p. 408

3.1 *Taxonomy of Competences*

I've elsewhere analyzed the competences of children—another group whose members are not treated as fully legally competent.[36] I've put forward that children's competences can be divided into three main groups:

- *Negative competences.* The child can prevent or revert a legal change, thus protecting the status quo.
- *Dependent competences.* The child can effect a legal change, subject to the approval or a "veto" of e.g. her parent/guardian.
- *Independent competences.* The child can effect a legal change independently.

For instance, Finnish legislation on the freedom of religion distinguishes between four different categories regarding religious affiliation:

(1) Children under 12 years old, whose religious affiliation is decided by those who have custody of them.
(2) Children between 12–17 years, who must consent to a change in their religious affiliation (*negative competence*, "veto").
(3) Children between 15–17 years, who can initiate a change in their religious affiliation, though requiring the consent of their guardians (*dependent competence*).
(4) Adults, who may freely decide over their religious affiliation (*independent competence*).

The competences of a child and their guardian form an interesting relationship, which is laid out in Table 1. For instance, holding a dependent competence involves—by definition—that the desired legal consequence only comes about if some other party approves, or does not veto, the exercise of the competence. Hence, if a child can veto a change in their religious affiliation, those who have custody over

[36] Kurki (2021). The following paragraphs contain some excerpts from said article.

them hold dependent competences; whereas if the child can initiate such a change subject to the approval of their parents, the child holds a dependent competence and the parent a negative competence.

Can the legal situation of individuals with disabilities be analyzed along similar lines? First, following Eilionóir Flynn and Anna Arstein-Kerslake, we can now distinguish four different categories:

(1) Legally independent decision-making: One makes decisions independently, even if one may receive all sorts of assistance and accommodation.
(2) Supported decision-making: Assistance is provided to the individual, such as a circle of support consisting of people who are familiar with the individual. The individual may at any time reject the support.
(3) Facilitated decision-making: In this case, no-one can reasonably interpret the will and preferences of the individual. Instead, "an appointed facilitator takes decisions on behalf of the individual, but does so with the will and preferences of the individual at the centre of the decision-making process and in the manner which best augments the person's autonomy and decision-making capability".[37] The facilitator must "imagine what the person's will and preferences might be and to make the decision on this basis", and they may *not* make the decision based on an objective determination of the individual's best interests.
(4) Substituted decision-making: In this case, decisions are made "on behalf of the individual by a representative, and [. . .] can be imposed against the will of the individual".[38] Such schemes are prohibited under the Convention.

Now, one might think that "legally independent decision-making" would correspond to independent competences, and "supported decision-making" to dependent competences. However, the matter is somewhat more complicated. In fact, individuals with disabilities falling under the supported decision-making scheme are, in this classification, endowed with independent competences. This is so because under supported decision-making, the disabled individual always has the "final say", and may always reject the help and suggestions of those who support him or her. However, an interesting special case is so-called "co-decision making". Devandas Aguilar describes this regime as follows:

> an individual appoints a co-decision maker who will make decisions jointly with the appointer in order for those decisions to have legal effect. Such arrangements are usually implemented through private agreements, although some legal frameworks require court intervention. In most jurisdictions, however, the co-decision maker has the power, in certain circumstances, to veto a person's decision, thus restricting the exercise of their legal capacity.[39]

[37] Flynn and Arstein-Kerslake (2014), p. 95.
[38] Flynn and Arstein-Kerslake (2014), p. 96.
[39] Aguilar (2017), para. 45.

Such an arrangement is classifiable as dependent competences: one can initiate a legal change, but only with the approval of the co-decision maker. If the co-decision maker can also initiate legal changes that can be vetoed by the disabled individual, then both parties have dependent *and* negative competences. However, under the supported decision-making scheme, the dependency of one's competences are voluntary: one can at any time rescind the arrangement, thus reverting one's competences to independent. If the disabled individual cannot rescind the arrangement, it does not constitute a form of supported decision-making according to Devandas Aguilar.[40]

Thus, supported decision-making entails independent competences, even if the disabled individual may change the form of their competences to dependent.

To sum up, individuals with disabilities can hold competences even under the legal-intention-based account of competences, and these competences have interesting features of their own. However, this account of competences cannot account for some instance of self-determination, such as consent-based rape laws. I will address this issue next.

4 Soft Competence

Consent-based rape laws criminalize at least some sexual acts that the other party has not consented to. They therefore relate to self-determination in the sense outlined above: by consenting, one lowers one's claim-right barriers. However—perhaps surprisingly—it is not obvious that laws introducing consent-based regulation of rape entail the legal competence-to-consent for the affected parties. The reason for this surprising result is that such laws typically do not place any weight on legal intentions. Consider for instance this excerpt from Chapter 6, Section 1 of the Swedish Criminal Code:

> A person who performs sexual intercourse, or some other sexual act that in view of the seriousness of the violation is comparable to sexual intercourse, with a person who is not participating voluntarily is guilty of rape and is sentenced to imprisonment for at least two and at most six years. When assessing whether participation is voluntary or not, particular consideration is given to whether voluntariness was expressed by word or deed or in some other way.[41]

The section then goes on to enumerate situations where participation is never to be considered voluntary.

Now, as noted, the provision gives no relevance to legal intentions. The intention to *legally* allow the sexual act is never part of a set of facts minimally sufficient for a valid act of consent. Let us briefly consider the notion of minimal sufficiency that is

---

[40] Aguilar (2017), para. 45.

[41] Swedish Criminal Code, official, constantly updated translation at www.government.se (visited on April 28, 2021).

operative here. As noted above, one holds a competence to effect legal consequence *r* if and only if one can perform an act-in-the-law to effect *r*. Act *a*, performed by *x*, constitutes an act-in-the-law if and only if

(1) *x* performs *a* with the intention to bring about the legal consequence *r*, and
(2) the fact that *x* has performed *a* in order to bring about *r* is an element of a set of actually occurrent conditions minimally sufficient for *r*.

The notion of minimal sufficiency likely needs elaboration. A set is minimally sufficient for some result *r* if it is sufficient and it contains no redundant elements. Thus, one could not remove any fact from the set without also rendering it insufficient for *r*. However, consenting to sex (under Swedish legislation) cannot constitute an act-in-the-law, because in no situation is it relevant for the validity of the consent whether one is even aware of the consent-based rape legislation. Otherwise, one might imagine a case where X consents to sex with Y, but the consent is not valid because X is not aware that consent is legally required, and Y is thereby guilty of rape.[42] It is of course possible to imagine consent procedures where awareness of the legal relevance is pronounced: so-called sexual consent applications have been developed for mobile phones. The prospective sexual partners use such an application to register their consent before the sexual act. However, though one likely uses such an application only with a legal intention, said intention can regardless be redundant for the validity of the consent.

Thus, it would seem that at least some types of criminal-law rules that criminalize nonconsensual acts do not entail legal competences. Such acts of consent are certainly acts of communication, but not competences. They can, however, be classified as wide powers.

Note that the issue has merely to do with the proper theoretical classification of the legal positions flowing from consent-based rape laws such as that of Sweden. Whether such laws are justified is a different question altogether. What I am concerned with here is whether the relevant normative positions should be classified as competences, or rather merely as wide powers. As noted at the beginning of the chapter, wide powers are a very broad category. For instance, the capacity to commit a tort is a wide power, but likely does not fall under what Hart envisaged under his power-conferring rules. With this background, should the result—that consent-based rape laws do not entail competences[43]—trouble a competence theorist? Perhaps it should not. It may be a perfectly acceptable result that competences should play a

[42]Thinking of minimal sufficiency in terms of examples is somewhat difficult. Legal intention need not be (though it can be) *necessary* for some legal consequence in order for the power to effect said legal consequence to be classified as a competence. However, there must be at least one set of facts that is sufficient to effect the legal consequence, and that would be rendered insufficient for the consequence if the legal intention were not present, in order for there to be a legal competence. In the case of consent-based rape legislation, the legal intention is never necessary for the validity of the consent.

[43]They do of course entail *some* competences, such as some new competences for prosecutors and judges.

relatively minor role in the area of criminal law. However, if we take competences to be an important legal position for realizing autonomy and self-determination, the result may be more troublesome. Western criminal law is, at least partly, founded on the protection of the autonomy of persons, and paternalistic criminal law is generally frowned upon, even if Western countries have not eschewed it completely.[44] Many criminal provisions reflect implicitly or explicitly the *volenti non fit iniuria principle* ("injury is not done to one who is willing"). The fact that individuals with disabilities have not been able to consent to sex in some jurisdictions can certainly be seen as an affront to their autonomy and self-determination. Furthermore, being able to consent to sex certainly serves one central function of power-conferring rules, as identified by Hart: it provides individuals with facilities for "realizing their wishes". Hence, classifying the legal position resulting from consent-based rape laws merely as a wide normative power is an unhappy result. It distinguishes some types of consent from others in problematic manner.

A competence theorist who is troubled by the result has at least three possible alternatives. The first is to tweak the notion of competence. I will below offer a rough account of how I think it could be tweaked. Second, one can employ these examples as arguments against my account of legal competences, and in support of some other account. Though such a route is of course possible, I do not intend to pursue it here. Third, one could introduce yet another category. For instance, Kramer suggests that the normative positions resulting from Hart's power-conferring rules could be understood either as competences or as (wide) powers that are typically beneficial for their holders.[45] He suggests that these different accounts are extensionally equivalent. However, typically beneficial powers would clearly cover the case of sexual consent, whereas I have argued that competences do not, so their extensions are in fact different. The solution could then be to distinguish between competences and typically beneficial powers.

Now, the solution preferred by me—which I can only sketch here—is the following. Legal competences, and especially acts-in-the-law, are an instance of a phenomenon that can be discerned in all sorts of social practices: we can agree, consent, promise and so on even outside of law. Such speech acts are performed with normative intentions: one promises with the intention to be committed, and consents with the intention to permit something.[46] Whether the normative force of such speech acts flows only from morality, or also from e.g. mere commitment, is contested and need not be settled here.[47] At any rate, law can be seen as interacting with these practices, and occasionally giving legal effect to "acts-outside-of-the-law" or "non-legal competences".

---

[44] See e.g. Hurd (2018).

[45] Kramer (2021).

[46] For a classic treatment, see Searle and Vanderveken (1985), p. 192.

[47] For instance, Margaret Gilbert has argued that commitment has non-moral normative force. See Gilbert (2018).

The interrelations between law and relationships outside of the law have recently been explored by John Gardner, who in his last book puts forward the idea that many legal relationships are nested in non-legal relationships. For instance, romantic companionship is not a legal relationship, but it can be given legal recognition as marriage. These ideas echo those of the great German legal scholar Friedrich Carl von Savigny. In his treatment of private law, Savigny argued that private law has to do with legal relationships (*Rechtsverhältnisse*). For Savigny, a legal relationship has two elements: the relationship itself (the "material element") and the legal recognition of the relationship (the "formal element"). Savigny notes that relationships can be brought into the legal domain completely or partially, or they can be left outside of it. Property ownership is an institution completely subsumed into the law and marriage partially subsumed, whereas friendship remains an extra-legal relationship, according to Savigny.[48] I would submit that sex is also primarily an extra-legal institution, especially in modern liberal states: even if sex legally regulated, this is mainly to prevent certain transgressions of sexual autonomy and bodily integrity. However, the practice of sex is not immersed in law in the same way as e.g. contracting is.

Law can give legal recognition to primarily extra-legal practices in various ways. One such way is to recognise exercises of non-legal competences as having legal effect. In such cases, the law does not require *legal* intentions as necessary components of set of facts minimally sufficient to effect a legal change, but rather *normative* intentions. A "normative intention" is an intention to cause a normative change. Consenting is normally done with the intention to allow something, and the law can give significance to this intention in, for instance, consent-based rape laws. Such competences can for instance be labelled "soft competences".

Should we accept such a category of competences, then the extension of competences might be expanded somewhat. If competences can be understood as giving legal effect to normative non-legal intentions, the notion of extending competences to individuals with cognitive disabilities could become somewhat less problematic, as talk of their competences would not necessitate their being able to conceptualise the legal system. However, they would still need to be able to form normative non-legal intentions.

One could even argue that even some nonhuman animals could potentially be endowed with soft competences, if they can be said to be participating in practices such as consenting. Before concluding the essay, I will address this idea.

4.1 Soft Competences of Nonhuman Animals

Most of modern animal ethics has approached animals as moral patients: animals are not moral agents, but they have moral standing regardless. This is not to say that

[48] von Savigny (1840), book 2, § 52.

animals have been denied autonomy altogether—Tom Regan, for instance, has argued that animals have "preference autonomy"[49]—but the question of autonomy has not been seen as central with regard to their moral value. However, more recently, scholars have started arguing that the autonomy of animals should have a more prominent place in theorizing about their correct moral treatment. Some examples include Natalie Thomas's work, as well as *Zoopolis* by Sue Donaldson and Will Kymlicka.[50] What is noteworthy is that Donaldson and Kymlicka have employed the very idea of supported decision-making to argue for their point. Their particular focus is on the fact that animals—especially domesticated animals that have learned to communicate with human beings—can express their subjective good to us by for instance "meow[ing] in front of the fridge" and "drag[ging] a leash from the cupboard to signal walk time".[51] However, the authors note that animal communication must be fostered and supported in various ways: "First we must recognize that animals are trying to communicate, then we need to observe carefully to interpret individual repertoires, and finally we need to respond appropriately–confirming for the animal that attempts to communicate with us are not a wasted effort."[52] More recently, scholars have also started paying increasing attention to the question of animals' capacity to consent.[53]

What is the import of these ideas for legal competence? Note, first, that wide powers can certainly be held by animals. Animals can effect legal changes in all sorts of ways: a dog can, for instance, attack a human being and thereby change the latter's duty-not-to-punch-the-dog into a liberty-to-punch-the-dog-for-the-purposes-of-self-defence. However, it is doubtful that nonhuman animals could have intentions pertaining to the legal system, even with the help of support: the idea of legal contracts, for instance, likely cannot be explained to a nonhuman animal, even in a highly simplified form. But what about soft competences? Consider the relatively famous experiment where researchers performed transactions with monkeys. In one scenario, two monkeys both received cucumber in exchange for tokens; in the other, one monkey received cucumber and the other a grape—a tastier food. In the latter scenario, the monkeys who received cucumber were likely to refuse the exchange.[54] Though the experiment is usually used to show that monkeys have a sense of fairness, it also shows that the monkeys can perform transactions. Such transactions likely involve normative intentions: the monkeys understand in some sense that the token is "theirs" and if they exchange it for a grape, the fruit becomes theirs instead. They thus likely perform the exchange with a normative intention, which law could give legal effect to—for instance by recognizing that the monkeys can own property

---

[49] Regan (1983), pp. 84–86.

[50] Thomas (2016) and Donaldson and Kymlicka (2011).

[51] Donaldson and Kymlicka (2011), p. 108.

[52] Donaldson and Kymlicka (2011), p. 109.

[53] Blattner (2021) and Healey and Pepper (2021).

[54] De Waal and Brosnan (2003).

as well as perform transactions with it. Whether such a legal arrangement would be meaningful is a different question.

5 Conclusion

I have here addressed some new developments and difficult cases pertaining to legal competence. The traditional understanding of legal competence can account for the competences of individuals with cognitive disabilities, especially if agency is understood relationally. However, legal-intention-based accounts of competence are regardless too narrow for this purpose, and should be amplified by an account of how law can recognise non-legal normative intentions. I have sketched such an account here, but a full-blown definition of soft competence remains to be provided.

References

Aguilar CD (2017) Universal legal capacity to ensure the equal recognition of persons with disabilities before the law. Report of the Special Rapporteur on the rights of persons with disabilities A/HRC/37/56

Arstein-Kerslake A (2015) Understanding sex: the right to legal capacity to consent to sex. Disabil Soc 30:1459–1473. https://doi.org/10.1080/09687599.2015.1116059

Bach M, Kerzner L (2010) A new paradigm for protecting autonomy and the right to legal capacity. Law Commission of Ontario

Beckmann JP (2017) Autonomie und Selbstbestimmung auch am Lebensende. Überlegungen aus ethischer Sicht. In: Welsh C, Ostgathe C, Frewer A, Bielefeldt H (eds) Autonomie und Menschenrechte am Lebensende. Grundlagen, Erfahrungen, Reflexionen aus der Praxis. Transcript Verlag, Bielefeld, pp 27–43

Blattner CE (2021) Turning to animal agency in the Anthropocene. In: Bovenkerk B, Keulartz J (eds) Animals in our midst: the challenges of co-existing with animals in the Anthropocene. Springer International Publishing, Cham, pp 65–78

Cash M (2013) Cognition without borders: 'Third wave' socially distributed cognition and relational autonomy. Cogn Syst Res 25–26:61–71. https://doi.org/10.1016/j.cogsys.2013.03.007

De Waal F, Brosnan S (2003) Monkeys reject unequal pay. Nature 425:294–297. https://doi.org/10.1038/nature01987.1

Dhanda A (2007) Legal capacity in the disability rights convention: stranglehold of the past or lodestar for the future. Syracuse J Int Law Commerce 34:429–462

Donaldson S, Kymlicka W (2011) Zoopolis. OUP, Oxford

Dougherty T (2015) Yes means yes: consent as communication. Philos Public Aff 43:224–253. https://doi.org/10.1111/papa.12059

Dwyer JG (2020) Clarifying questions about the nature of rights. Jurisprudence 0:1–22. https://doi.org/10.1080/20403313.2020.1836905

Enoch D (2011) Reason-giving and the law. In: Green L, Leiter B (eds) Oxford studies in philosophy of law, vol 1. OUP, Oxford

Flynn E, Arstein-Kerslake A (2014) Legislating personhood: realising the right to support in exercising legal capacity. Int J Law Context 10:81–104

Fridström Montoya T (2015) Leva som andra genom ställföreträdare - en rättslig och faktisk paradox. Iustus, Uppsala

Gilbert M (2018) Rights and demands. A foundational inquiry. OUP, Oxford
Hart H (1994) The concept of law. Clarendon Press, Oxford
Haslanger S (2013) Resisting reality: social construction and social critique. OUP, Oxford
Healey R, Pepper A (2021) Interspecies justice: agency, self-determination, and assent. Philos Stud 178:1223–1243. https://doi.org/10.1007/s11098-020-01472-5
Hohfeld WN (1913) Some fundamental legal conceptions as applied in legal reasoning. Yale Law J 23:16–59
Hurd HM (2018) Paternalism and the criminal law. In: Grill K, Hanna J (eds) The Routledge handbook of the philosophy of paternalism. Routledge, Oxfordshire, pp 277–292
Kelsen H (2006) General theory of law and state. Transaction Publishers, New Brunswick, New Jersey
Kramer MH (2021) Hart on legal powers as legal competences. Can J Law Jurisprud 36:1–19
Kurki VAJ (2017) Legal power and legal competence. In: McBride M (ed) New essays on the nature of rights. Hart Publishing, Oxford, pp 31–48
Kurki VAJ (2019) A theory of legal personhood. OUP, Oxford
Kurki V (2021) Active but not independent: the legal personhood of children. Griffith Law Rev 30: 395–412. https://doi.org/10.1080/10383441.2021.1996881
Maccormick N, Raz J (1972) Voluntary obligations and normative powers. Proc Aristot Soc 46:59–102
Nilsson A (2012) Who gets to decide? Right to legal capacity for persons with intellectual and psychosocial disabilities. Council of Europe Commissioner for Human Rights
Raz J (2019) Normative powers (revised). King's College London
Regan T (1983) The case for animal rights. University of California Press, Oakland
Searle JR, Vanderveken D (1985) Foundations of illocutionary logic
Seatzu F (2017) Article 14 [Liberty and Security of Person]. In: Della Fina V, Cera R, Palmisano G (eds) The United Nations Convention on the rights of persons with disabilities: a commentary. Springer, pp 295–306
Shapiro S (2011) Legality. Harvard University Press
Sutton J, Harris CB, Keil PG, Barnier AJ (2010) The psychology of memory, extended cognition, and socially distributed remembering. Phenomenol Cogn Sci 9:521–560. https://doi.org/10.1007/s11097-010-9182-y
Thomas N (2016) Animal ethics and the autonomous animal self. Palgrave Macmillan, London
von Savigny FC (1840) System des heutigen Römischen rechts. Veit, Berlin

Structures of Legal Competences

Jan-Reinard Sieckmann

Abstract A legal or, more generally, normative competence might be understood as the power to change the normative situation according to one's will. Competence norms are norms that confer such a power to a particular agent, of course with certain conditions. Several doubts remain:

- Must there be a change, or might the use of a competence merely confirm the existing normative situation, however, creating an independent normative reason?
- Must the will to determine the normative situation be the reason for recognizing a certain norm as valid, or might it be only a circumstance that figures in the justification of this norm?
- Does the exercise of a competence create an object that otherwise would not exist, or does it define the validity of a norm?

On the other hand, it is clear that competences are not merely permissions. But what are the relations between competence and permission? Can the exercise of a competence be completely prohibited, or must it in some sense be permitted?

And how does the notion of a competence relate to the distinction of definitive norms and norms that are valid only in principle?

I would like to thank Rosaline Bates Anoma for corrections and improvement on the English language.

J.-R. Sieckmann (✉)
Law Department, Faculty of Business, Economics, and Law, Friedrich-Alexander-University Erlangen-Nürnberg, Erlangen, Germany
e-mail: jan.sieckmann@fau.de

G. Villa-Rosas, T. Spaak (eds.), *Legal Power and Legal Competence*, Law and Philosophy Library 140, https://doi.org/10.1007/978-3-031-28555-4_4

1 Introduction

Legal or, more generally, normative competences can be understood as the power to change a normative situation by a particular action intending to bring about this change.[1] Competence norms are norms that confer such a power to an agent, depending on certain conditions.

However, several doubts remain: must there be a change, or might the use of a competence merely confirm the existing normative situation? Must the intention to determine the normative situation be the reason for recognizing a certain norm as valid, or might it be only a circumstance that figures in the justification of this norm? What is the structure of legal competences as legal relations, in particular, regarding relations between legislator, law-applying organ, and legal subjects? And how does the notion of a competence relate to the distinction of definitive norms and norms that are valid only in principle? On the other hand, it is clear that competences are not mere permissions. But what is the relationship between competence and permission? Can the exercise of a competence be completely prohibited, or must it in some sense be permitted?

These are questions that I will address in my paper. I will not, however, try to reconstruct the use of the term "competence" or any other related term. Rather, my aim is to identify logical structures that make competences and competence norms an important element of legal systems. The interesting point about normative competences (or powers[2]) is that they make the validity of norms to depend on intentional acts aimed at establishing this validity.[3] In short, normative competences enable the transformation of will to "ought". I will focus on legal systems, as the notion of competence is mostly discussed with respect to law, although I think that the notion of competence and of competence norms is of interest for moral or other normative systems as well.

2 Problems of Defining Legal Competence

I will suggest that a legal competence is the power to determine the normative situation in a legal system according to one's will. The existence of a normative situation can be presented as the validity of a norm of certain content.[4] A normative competence hence is the power to determine that a particular norm is valid

[1] See Hohfeld (1919), p. 50f.; Hart (1994), p. 27; Ross (1968), p. 130; Spaak (1994), pp. 9, 75; Lindahl and Reidhav (2017), p. 158. For different notions and their inadequacies see e.g., Lindahl and Reidhav (2017), pp. 159 ff.

[2] Regarding the terminology see Lindahl and Reidhav (2017), p. 158 f.

[3] See also Lindahl and Reidhav (2017), pp. 162, 171.

[4] One might doubt whether all normative situations can be represented by statements of the validity of norms. A normative situation might be, for example, a legal status, as that of a judge. It is not

according to one's will. We can also say, it is the power to enact or bring into existence a norm of certain content.[5] This can also be referred to as achieving a legal effect.[6] Any legal effect may be expressed in the form of a statement of the validity of a legal norm. It does not matter, however, whether there is a normative change in the sense that the legal position of someone has changed.

Competence norms are norms that ascribe a certain competence to some agent, with conditions regarding the holder, the existence, and the exercise of the competence. The exercise of the competence may concern procedural aspects but also the content of the norms that might be enacted.

We might define a competence of someone (A) regarding some norm (N) accordingly as the capacity to make this norm valid (VAL) by acting in a certain way (ACT)[7] intending (INT) the validity of this norm:

$$\mathrm{COMP}(A, N) =: \mathrm{ACT}(A, \mathrm{INT}(\mathrm{VAL}(N))) -> \mathrm{VAL}(N)$$

This first approach to legal competences, however, needs clarification.[8]

---

clear that such a status can be represented completely by statements of norms. However, I will ignore such cases.

[5] See also Ruiter (1993), p. 92; MacCormick (1986), p. 65.

[6] See Lindahl and Reidhav (2017), p. 158.

[7] The predicate "ACT" might include procedural and substantive conditions regarding the successful exercise of the competence. One could explicate these conditions, but for reasons of simplicity I leave this predicate unanalysed. For a more complex definition see, for example, Spaak (2008), p. 5.

[8] In a similar vein, Lindahl and Reidhav (2017), p. 169, emphasize the element of intention in the exercise of legal competences. Their definition of immediate legal power might, however, lead to contradictions. According to this definition, in a situation S, X has the immediate power to achieve C by doing B, if B is such that in situation S:

(D I.1) X's behaviour B is a legal ground for the legal result C,
(D I.2) X's behaviour B manifests that X intends to achieve legal result C by B, and
(D I.3) X's behaviour B not manifesting that X intends to achieve legal result C by B is a legal ground for C not to follow from B.

It seems that (D I.1) can be assessed without reference to the intention of X. Then, it is possible that X's behaviour B is a legal ground for the legal result C, but that X's behaviour B is not manifesting that X intends to achieve legal result C by B. Consequently, (D I.1) makes behaviour B a legal ground for the legal result C, but (D I.3) implies that this behaviour is a legal ground for C not to follow from B. The problem occurs because behaviour B does not refer to the intention of X. It seems that (D I.1) and (D I.2) cannot be separated in the way Lindahl and Reidhav suggest. However, as Torben Spaak has suggested, one can avoid this problem by a modification D.I1-2: "X's behaviour B manifests that X intends to achieve legal result C by B, and X's behaviour B is a legal ground for the legal result C".

2.1 The Notion of Intention

A first point concerns the intention as a feature of exercising a legal competence. In some paradigm cases of legal competences, the validity of a norm does not depend on the will of the holder of the competence. For example, if at an auction someone raises her arm this counts as an offer although there was no intention to make an offer. The reason for this interpretation is that in the situation of an auction raising one's arm is usually regarded as an offer, so that other agents will understand this move in this way. The intention is ascribed according to the objective meaning of an action, not according to the real will of the agent. Still, the act is regarded as an intentional act aimed at establishing a particular normative situation. The problem is one of interpretation. The interpretation is based, however, not on a psychological fact but on the common understanding of a certain behaviour in a certain context.

One should also note that intentions must not necessarily be psychological phenomena, which only individual agents could have. Intentions might also be an ascription to collectivities or to agents participating in certain procedures for example, of legislation. Intentions can be the result of a social or normative construction.[9]

As to the content of the intention required in exercising a legal competence, it must include at least awareness of the possibility that one has the power one purports to exercise. One need not be sure that one has this competence, even less one must know exactly its legal foundation. But one cannot intend to bring about a certain state of affairs if one does not believe (at least implicitly) that it is possible to achieve the respective aim by the applied means. Therefore, the intention in exercising a legal competence implies that one at least presumes that one has the respective legal competence and, in addition, that one is exercising it in a correct manner. This point is of interest regarding the thesis that law is necessarily connected with a claim to correctness. The exercise of a legal competence must claim that the normative conditions of its exercise are fulfilled. In this sense, it must be connected with a claim to correctness.[10]

2.2 Competences and Reasons

Another point of clarification is that the capability to determine the normative situation is not enough to constitute a legal competence.[11] For example, by beating up someone else, one creates an obligation for legal organs to prosecute, and a right

[9] See also Lindahl and Reidhav (2017), p. 163 f.

[10] Law's necessary claim to moral correctness is a thesis of Robert Alexy (2002a), pp. 35 ff. It is not quite clear to what extent and in which respect this thesis is justified, in particular, whether the claim to correctness must be a moral claim. But at least there are necessary elements of law that display a certain claim to correctness.

[11] See also Spaak (2008).

of the victim to compensation for damages. However, one would not say that one has a legal competence to create these obligations or rights. One might speak of a legal ability or perhaps even of a legal power to bring about certain legal effects, but not of a legal competence. Holding a legal competence implies that the normative situation is determined according to one's will, because of this will. By contrast, the obligation to prosecute comes into existence independently of what the agent wants.

A normative competence is therefore the power to make a norm valid because of one's will to do so. We might define a normative competence accordingly as follows:

(DC1) An agent A has a normative competence to determine that a certain norm N is valid if the norm N will be valid because A has performed an act of a certain character with the intention to make N valid.

The "because" must be read as the condition that the intention of A to make N valid is the reason for the validity of N, not merely a condition of its validity.[12] As a reason, it is a sufficient argument for recognizing the validity of N, that is, N would be valid if this argument is not superseded by counterarguments. Accordingly, the exercise of a legal competence constitutes a reason for the validity of the respective norm.

However, the fact that an act is a reason for the validity of N is not sufficient to constitute a legal competence, because counterarguments might exclude recognition of such a competence. For example, the fact that a child wants to make a contract may be a reason to recognize this contract as valid, but counterarguments lead to the exclusion of such a competence. It seems that the existence of a competence requires recognition of the power to make valid a certain norm under certain conditions (that is, a hypothetically sufficient reason),[13] not only recognition that the intention to make this norm valid is a reason for its validity.[14]

2.3 Competences and Constitutional Restrictions

Competences hence constitute reasons to recognize certain norms as definitively legally valid. Correct exercise of the competence leads to the legal validity of the enacted norm. It constitutes a sufficient reason for recognizing the legal validity of the enacted norm.

---

[12] In this respect, the "because" is stronger than the legal ground-consequence relation used by Lindahl and Reidhav (2017), p. 166.

[13] See Spaak (2008): hypothetical notion of competence.

[14] See also Lindahl and Reidhav (2017), p. 166. They argue that the general idea of drawing conclusions that are not merely of a *prima facie*-character, from a set of premises, is indispensable in the law. This argument does not seem to be sufficient, however, to show that competences must have definitive character. Nevertheless, this interpretation seems most plausible regarding the typical cases of legal competences.

One might ask whether a legal competence can ever fulfill the condition that its exercise constitutes a sufficient reason for the validity of the established norm. In particular, in a constitutional system any enacted norm must conform with constitutional law. Exercise of a competence therefore is not sufficient to create a valid norm, but this norm must conform with constitutional law. One might respond to this problem in two ways.

Firstly, one might restrict the scope of the legislative competence, including only the enactment of laws that conform with constitutional law. A disadvantage of this approach is that one could not state that the Legislature has the competence to enact a certain law without constitutional review of this law. One might regard this disadvantage as a mere technical drawback, requiring a more precise statement of the scope of the Legislature's competence. However, it is also a practical problem regarding arguments of judicial deference to decisions of a democratic Legislature. If one cannot state the competence of the Legislature before constitutional review, one cannot assume that there is a constitutional reason for judicial restraint against the Legislature.

Secondly, a legislative competence might include the power to establish, not definitive validity, but a legal reason for the recognition of the definitive validity of an enacted law. It is sufficient to establish this reason, although it might not be sufficient to establish the validity of the enacted law itself. One could explain this distinction referring to the difference between rules in the sense of definitively valid norms and principles in the sense of reasons for balancing judgements.[15] The exercise of a legislative competence constitutes a norm with the character of a principle, not of a definitively valid norm.

This has consequences for the usual positivist representation of the dynamics of legal systems.[16] According to the positivist view, legal norms are created by legislative acts complying with the requirements of norms conferring legislative powers. In the model of the "Stufenbau" of the legal order, the constitution confers powers to legislative organs to enact statutes; statutes may delegate powers to executive organs to enact legal instruments; finally courts or administrative organs are empowered to take final decisions in particular cases. The legal validity of the established norms or decisions follow from the power conferred by some legally valid power-conferring norm.

In a complex legal system including substantive constitutional requirements superior to other legal norms, however, no power-conferring norm can guarantee that an act complying with this norm creates a valid legal norm. All that can be created is a legally valid argument to recognize the enacted norm as valid. This argument is directed, in particular, to the law-applying organs. These organs have to check whether there are competing legal requirements which act against recognition of the legal validity of the enacted norms. The final decision on the definitive legal validity of a norm has to be taken by the law-applying organ in charge.

---

[15] See Sieckmann (1990), pp. 54 ff., regarding Dworkin's distinction of rules and principles.

[16] Kelsen (1960) and Hart (1994).

The model of the "Stufenbau" of the legal order therefore grasps only a special case of a legal system, which is strictly hierarchically ordered and does not include substantive constitutional requirements. By contrast, modern constitutional systems require a more sophisticated model of the structure of legal systems. A crucial element of this model is understanding legal competences as power to create legal arguments, not as power to create definitively valid norms.

This implies a modification of the role of intention in the creation of norms. The intention seems to be directed towards creating the definitive validity of a norm. The legal effect is, however, the creation of a legal argument to recognize the enacted norm as legally valid. The intention might then have two objectives: creation of a legal argument, or creation of a definitively valid legal norm.

If the intention is creating a legal argument, we have no problem with the notion of intention. However, legislators usually will not understand their intention as creating a legal argument, but as creating a definitively valid legal norm.

If the intention is creating a definitively valid legal norm, we have a problem. Following the analysis above, the legislator will not be able to establish a definitively valid norm by his decision alone. However, an intention to do something does not presuppose the ability to achieve these aims. It does presuppose knowledge of the possibility to bring about the intended result. However, the possibility to bring about a definitively valid norm exists, although the final recognition of the definitive validity of a norm is not in the hands of the legislator, but in those of the law-applying organs. It is therefore also admissible to say that the legislator intends to establish the definitive validity of a norm.

2.4 Competences and Legal Change

Another problem of the suggested definition of legal competences is that a norm that someone wants to enact might be valid anyway. "Norm" is understood here as a normative meaning content, to which validity is ascribed. There may be diverse reasons for this ascription of validity. The validity of a norm may thus have several sources.

Although it is quite common to describe legal competences as the power to bring about a normative change,[17] it seems that the consequence of exercising a competence does not necessarily result in a change of the normative situation. The normative situation might remain the same. For example, the legislature might grant a right that already exists according to constitutional law. A court might grant a right according to valid law. A contract might confirm a right that already exists according to law.

One might argue in favour of the definition of legal competence as the power to bring about legal change, for it seems that there is at least the possibility that

[17] See above; see also Köpcke (2019).

exercising a legal competence leads to a change of the legal situation. It does not matter what other grounds exist for the validity of the intended norm. Exercising a legal competence is a sufficient reason for the validity of this norm. Even if the normative situation were different at the start, the result would be the same. In this sense, a legal competence implies the hypothetical possibility to bring about legal change according to one's will. However, in this sense, whether legal change occurs seems to be accidental and not an essential feature of legal competence.

Anyway, even in the cases where the legal situation is not changed the exercise of a competence has normative effect. It creates a legal argument on its own. In case the alternative foundation would cease to exist, the legal situation would continue as it is, being determined by the exercise of the competence. One can hence maintain the thesis that the exercise of a competence brings about a normative change. This change need not, however, concern the level of action-guiding norms, but might merely affect the level of the sources of law. The respective exercise of a competence hence is a sufficient argument for the existence of a certain normative situation, not a necessary condition for it. But it constitutes an independent argument for recognizing the validity of a certain norm, which would persist even if other sources for the validity of a norm would cease to exist.

2.5 *Competences as Power to Create Legal Arguments*

The suggestion to regard the creation of a legal argument as a legal change corresponds to the above thesis that legal competences include the power to establish legal reasons, although these might be valid only in principle, not as definitively valid norms. As a principle, the competence norm in conjunction with its exercise is a sufficient argument for the validity of the respective norm in case that there are no counterarguments.

We can then describe the structure of a normative competence as follows:

(DC2) A has the competence to make N valid iff it is the case that if A acts in a certain way with the intention to make valid N, then this act constitutes a reason (sufficient argument) for the validity of N.

$$\mathrm{COMP}(A, N) =: \mathrm{ACT}(A, \mathrm{INT}(\mathrm{VAL}(N))) \text{ −> } \mathrm{REASON}(\mathrm{VAL}(N))$$

The competence thus defined is a definitively valid legal position. It includes the power to create legal arguments, which are requirements to recognize the enacted norms as definitively legally valid.

The created norm will be definitively valid if there are no counterarguments. One can include the absence of counterarguments as a condition of the norm that defines legal validity based on acts of the legislator:

$$\text{ACT}(\text{A}, \text{INT}(\text{VAL}(\text{N}))) \ \& \ \text{NO} - \text{REASON}(\text{NOT} - \text{VAL}(\text{N})) \ {->} \ \text{VAL}(\text{N})$$

In this sense, the legislator has a conditional competence to create definitively valid norms. However, the competence as such includes only the power to create legal arguments.

In the case that counterarguments exist the definitively valid norm can only be established by the law-applying organ in charge. Counterarguments lead to a conflict with the legislated norm. Thus, a balancing will be required, which defines the norm that is to be regarded as definitively valid.

Regarding the enactment of definitively valid norms, one might assume that existence of a legal competence to establish a definitive reason for the validity of N corresponds to that in principle (PR) a competence exists to establish the definitive validity of the respective norm.

$$\text{COMP}_{\text{PR}}(\text{A}, \text{N}) =: \text{ACT}(\text{A}, \text{INT}(\text{VAL}(\text{N}))) \ {->} \ \text{REASON}_{\text{DEF}}(\text{VAL}(\text{N}))$$

However, this conclusion is not justified. If a competence existed in principle, there would be a requirement of recognizing this competence as far as there are no superseding counterarguments. However, if exercise of a competence is incompatible with higher law, there is no argument that one should recognize this competence as legally valid. All one could justify is a statement of a *prima facie*-competence, that is, an imprecise statement disregarding the possibility of legal restrictions of the exercise of this competence.

3 Competences as Legal Positions or Relations

Having a legal competence to bring about a certain normative situation is a legal position of the competence holder. The legal situation of the competence holder includes this normative power. Competence norms are norms that ascribe such position.

Competences are described, however, also as legal relations. In Hohfeld's scheme of legal relations, competences are the opposite of the subjection of someone to the respective competence. Accordingly, one can present the structure of legal competences as[18]

$$\text{COMP}(\text{a}, \text{b}, \text{N})$$

That is, some individual "a" has against individual "b" the competence to bring about a normative situation N. Reverse, "b" is subject to the competence of "a" regarding N:

[18] Following Alexy (2002b).

$$SUBJ(b, a, N)$$

That is, some individual "b" is subject to the power of "a" to bring about N.

The present analysis suggests that this must be refined. The normative situation "N" is presented by a norm referring to certain addressees. The addressees of the norm are not, however, the addressees of the competence. Since the legal competence is the power to create a legal argument that must be considered by the law-applying organs in charge, the addressees of the legal competence of the legislator are the law-applying organs. They are subject to this competence, and as a consequence of the legislative act, they are under an obligation to apply the legislated norm.

This application may take two forms. If there are no counterarguments against the definitive validity of the legislated norm, the legislative act creates a definitively valid norm. Judicial application consists in following a conditional rule that (as a criterion of legal validity) determines the definitive validity of norms based on legislative acts if there are no counterarguments.

If, however, counterarguments exist against the definitive validity of the legislated norm, the definitive norm must be established by the law-applying organ by means of balancing, determining a priority among the competing demands.

Regarding the legal relations involved, we have to distinguish several legal relations:

(1) The legislator has the legal competence to create an obligation for law-applying organs to consider the enacted norm N as a legal argument.
(2) The law-applying organ has the legal competence to create an obligation for the addressees of N to follow N, given the condition that the legislator has enacted N.
(3) The legislator and the law-applying organ together have the legal competence to create an obligation for the addressees of N to follow N.
(4) The legislator has the factual ability to bring about an obligation for the addressees of the enacted norm N to follow this norm, depending on the expectation that the law-applying organs will apply N.

Regarding the creation of a definitive obligation of law subjects, one might ask whether again, as in the case of the legislator, counterarguments might occur so that the judicial decision only creates a legal argument. However, legal systems may attribute an exclusive competence to law-applying organs, excluding the consideration of competing arguments. In a legal system with this structure, decisions of the law-applying organs will be definitive. Of course, the legal system may be challenged by other normative systems. However, from the point of view of a particular legal system, competences to establish definitively valid norms are possible.

The analysis of the relations between legislator, law-applying organs, and law subjects is interesting also regarding the distinction of primary and secondary norms. The common understanding is that primary norms are directed to the citizens, or legal subjects, whilst secondary norms refer to primary norms and include in particular the obligation of law-applying organs to apply legal norms.[19] By contrast, Kelsen considered the norms directed to law-applying organs as the primary norms (Kelsen 1925, p. 51; 1934, p. 30).[20] The present analysis gives some support to Kelsen's view. The norms that the legislator can create are norms directed to the law-applying organs. Norms directed to the citizens are created only at second place by law-applying organs.

4 Definitive Norms and Validity in Principle

The relation of competences and competence norms to the distinction of rules and principles needs clarification. The model of principles of law, which is presupposed also in this analysis, assumes that legal systems include as well rules in the sense of definitively valid norms as principles in the sense of legal arguments requiring recognition of certain as definitively valid. One might ask how competences fit in this model.

In particular, one might doubt that competence norms can have the character of principles. Competences are normative relations, which, depending on certain conditions, exist or do not exist, principles include an ideal "ought", which exists only as an ideal, not as a real relation.[21] On the other hand, if principles are understood as normative arguments and competences as reasons for the validity of norms, competences seem to be connected with the notion of principles.

Principles should be understood as normative arguments, which, just in the situation of conflict with competing arguments, require that a certain result of a balancing be accepted. This makes them (reiterated) requirements of validity regarding a norm whose definitive validity is in question and might be the result of a balancing.[22] As requirements of validity, however, normative arguments have categorical structure. That is, they include an unconditional "ought". Although this "ought" is to be applied in a certain situation of conflict (a certain justificatory context), this situation does not constitute an antecedent of the normative argument that is to be applied. The validity of the normative argument is constituted by the possibility to justify its reiteration. It does not depend on the situation in which the argument is applied. Therefore, the normative argument holds categorically, not only conditionally. In addition, the situation of conflict actually exists, hence the normative argument actually applies in this situation.

By contrast, competence norms have conditional structure. They make the validity of a particular norm depend on the exercise of the competence, which might be subject to further conditions. It seems that competence norms always have the

[19] See also Hart's distinction of primary and secondary rules, Hart (1994), pp. 79 ff.

[20] But see also Kelsen (1979), pp. 115 f., retracting from his former view.

[21] Sieckmann (1990), p. 75; id. (2018), p. 102 f.

[22] Sieckmann (2012), p. 46; id. (2018), p. 113.

structure of rules, consisting of antecedent and consequence, and a competence is a position that exists on the basis of a competence rule. Accordingly, the demand that a certain competence should exist or ought to be recognized, is not the statement of a competence, and a corresponding norm demands in principle recognition of a certain competence, but does not confer this competence to a competence holder.

Demands or requirements referring to the existence of competences might be regarded as competence norms in a wider sense. In the case of principles, they may be called "formal principles". In this sense, formal principles are normative arguments for ascribing certain competences to certain subjects.[23] Still, norms regarding competences in the narrow sense have a structure different from that of principles.

The distinction of principles and competence norms presupposes that one must distinguish two normative structures:

It ought to be valid that if A enacts[24] N then N is valid.
If A enacts N then N ought to be valid.

Formally:

$$O\,(ENACT(A, N) \rightarrow VAL(N))$$

$$ENACT(A, N) \rightarrow O\,VAL(N)$$

Both forms are not equivalent. The basic structures are:

$$O\,(p \rightarrow q)$$

$$p \rightarrow Oq$$

Besides these logical issues, there is a practical difference between the competence to enact a norm that is valid in principle, and a principle that one has the competence to enact a definitively valid norm. If this principle is superseded by a competing principle, there is no competence at all, and not a competence to enact a norm that is valid in principle. Hence, we must distinguish both structures.

One might doubt this opposition of competence norms and principles, for competences make certain acts a reason for the validity of an enacted norm. As a reason, they might be connected with principles.

It is true that reasons need not have the structure of principles, but might be deductive arguments. A competence norm and the act of exercising the respective competence together constitute a reason for the validity of the enacted norm. This is a deductive argument.

However, one might ask what its foundation is. Thus, we have a problem of justification. In the first place, the reason for recognizing the validity of a certain

[23] Sieckmann (2018), p. 196.

[24] I will understand enactment of a norm N by an agent A as an intentional act of making this norm valid: ENACT(A,N) =: ACT(A,INT(VAL(N))).

norm is the competence norm. But the next question is what justifies the competence norm. There might be higher competence norms and corresponding acts, but this line of justification will come to an end. If there should be a successful justification, it must refer to some norm that is not a competence norm but justifies the validity of the competence norm of the highest order. For example, one might accept the competence of a certain legislative authority because it will secure peace and order, or justice, or human rights. The justification of a legal competence will hence depend on material, substantive principles. The dependence of substantive principles does not exclude recognition of legal competences. However, in a rational legal system it will have two effects.

First, there will be substantive restrictions of the scope of the competence, which aim at guaranteeing deference to the relevant substantive principles.

Second, the exercise of a legal competence must be orientated towards fulfilment of the relevant substantive principles.

As a consequence, in a legal system there will be no unlimited or unbound legal competences. In this sense, legal competences have a necessary connection with principles, although competence norms in a narrow sense cannot have the structure of principles.

5 Competence and Permission

Legal competences have sometimes been interpreted as permissions,[25] or as related to permissions.[26] The definition as permissions is certainly not adequate, as permissions do not include conditions for the validity of norms.[27] It is also claimed that competences may but need not be conjoined with liberties.[28] On the other hand, the interpretation of competences as the power to bring about legal effects is regarded as inadequate, for this cannot be regarded as a right.[29] Therefore, the issue remains whether a relation exists between competence and permission. In particular, a legal competence might imply that the exercise of the competence is permitted, or at least not completely forbidden.

Alas, there cannot be a strict implication that a legal competence implies permission of an act that exercises this competence. For example, an administrative act might be legally valid although it is illegal. A statute might be valid although it violates constitutional law. Not permitted exercises of a competence may constitute valid legal norms.

---

[25] von Wright (1963), p. 192.

[26] Alchourrón and Bulygin (1971), p. 151 f.

[27] See also Spaak (1994), p. 80; Lindahl and Reidhav (2017), p. 160.

[28] For example, Kramer (1998), p. 106.

[29] Weissenbauer (2019), p. 170.

On the other hand, if someone (A) has the competence to enact a norm N, then it cannot as such be prohibited for A to enact N. There may be modes of exercising this competence that are illegal. But exercising a legal competence cannot as such be prohibited. A legal system would be inconsistent if it granted a legal competence and declared forbidden (F) any use of it.

However, it is not clear whether this inconsistency amounts to a logical contradiction. At first sight, the prohibition to bring about validity of N and a competence to bring about validity of N are not contradictory. Leaving aside differences between definitive validity and validity as an argument, a competence of A to make N valid might be notated as

$$\mathrm{ENACT}(A, N) \mathrel{-}> \mathrm{VAL}(N).$$

The prohibition of bringing about validity of N would be:

$$O\neg \mathrm{ENACT}(A, N)$$

Exercise of the competence would violate the prohibition, but this is not logical contradiction. However, we must consider that in a normative system prohibitions and norms of competence need justification. Therefore, if there is a prohibition to bring about validity of N, there must be a requirement that there ought to be a prohibition to bring about N:

$$O\ \mathrm{VAL}O\neg \mathrm{ENACT}(A, N).$$

This presupposes that there is a reason that N ought not be enacted by A, for if there were no reason against enactment of N by A, there would be no justification for a complete prohibition of A enacting N. Hence

$$O\neg \mathrm{ENACT}(A, N).$$

The reason for a complete prohibition of A enacting N must, however, be that N ought not to be made valid by A. For, if there were no such reason but only reasons regarding other aspects of A or enactment of N by A, there would be no justification for a complete prohibition of A enacting N. Therefore, there must be a requirement that N is not made valid by enactment of A:

$$O\neg(\mathrm{ENACT}(A, N) \mathrel{-}> \mathrm{VAL}(N)).$$

On the other hand, if there is a competence of A to bring about N there must be a requirement that there ought to be a competence of A to bring about N:

$$O\ (\mathrm{ENACT}(A, N) \mathrel{-}> \mathrm{VAL}\ N).$$

Thus, we have a contrariety of the structure $Op \wedge O\neg p$. This still is not a logical contradiction. However, regarding definitively valid norms, contrariety implies a contradiction, for $O\neg p -> \neg Op$, and hence we get $Op \wedge \neg Op$.

We can conclude then that in a normative system, in which all norms are rationally justified, the existence of a competence to enact N and a prohibition of exercising this competence are contradictory as far as definitively valid norms are concerned. On the other hand, regarding norms that are valid merely in principle, the conflict of competence and prohibition of its exercise merely amounts to contrariety.

That is, it cannot be true that:

$$\mathrm{COMP(A, N)} \wedge \mathrm{F\ ENACT(A, N)}$$

or more precisely, stating definitive validity,

$$\mathrm{VAL_{DEF}\ COMP(A, N)} \wedge \mathrm{VAL_{DEF}\ F\ ENACT(A, N)}$$

Therefore, not every exercise of a competence (EXE-COMP) can be forbidden (x is a variable for actions). By contrast, necessarily (**N**) some exercise of a legal competence must be legally permitted (P):

$$\mathbf{N}\neg(x)(\mathrm{EXE-\ COMPx} -> \mathrm{F\ DOx})$$

$$\mathbf{N}(\exists x)(\mathrm{EXE-\ COMPx} \wedge \mathrm{P\ DOx})$$

On the other hand, it is not necessarily true (N) that each exercise of a competence is permitted (P):

$$\neg\mathbf{N}(x)(\mathrm{EXE-\ COMPx} -> \mathrm{P\ DOx})$$

These relations require distinguishing strong and weak forms of deontic modalities. A strong form means that all instances of a certain type of action are permitted/forbidden/required. A weak form means that there are instances of a certain type of action that are permitted/forbidden/required. Accordingly, we have to distinguish the following alternatives:

Strong permission: $(x)(Ax -> Px)$

No strong permission: $\neg(x)(Ax -> Px)$

Strong prohibition: $(x)(Ax -> \neg Px)$

Weak permission: $\neg(x)(Ax -> \neg Px)$

Strong prohibition: $(x)(Ax -> Fx)$

No strong prohibition: $\neg(x)(Ax -> Fx)$

Strong permission: $(x)(Ax -> \neg Fx)$

Weak prohibition: $\neg(x)(Ax \rightarrow \neg Fx)$

Accordingly, one cannot define permission as no-prohibition, and vice versa. The equation of prohibition and non-permission ($Fp \leftrightarrow \neg Pp$) is at least misleading. It can correctly be stated that strong prohibition excludes strong permission, and vice versa. Weak permission is equivalent to the negation of strong prohibition. Negation of strong permission is equivalent to weak prohibition.

We have to conclude then that a relation between legal competence and permission exists: A legal competence to enact N implies that enacting N is not strongly prohibited. Therefore, it implies a weak permission regarding the exercise of the competence.

6 Conclusion

I would like to summarize three main theses:

(1) The structure of a normative competence is:

(DC2) A has the competence to make N valid if it holds that if A acts intending to make valid N, then this act constitutes a reason (sufficient argument) for the validity of N.

$$\mathrm{ACT}(A, \mathrm{INT}(\mathrm{VAL}(N))) \rightarrow \mathrm{REASON}(\mathrm{VAL}(N))$$

(2) Competence norms in a narrow sense cannot have the structure of principles. However, the need to justify competence norms implies that in a legal system there will not be unlimited or unbound legal competences. In this sense, legal competences have a necessary connection with principles.

(3) A relation between legal competence and permission exists: A legal competence to enact N can only be valid if enacting N is not strongly prohibited. Therefore, it implies a weak permission regarding the exercise of the competence.

References

Alchourrón CE, Bulygin E (1971) Normative systems. Springer, Wien/New York

Alexy R (2002a) The argument from injustice. Oxford University Press, Oxford

Alexy R (2002b) A theory of constitutional rights. Oxford University Press, Oxford

Hart HLA (1994) The concept of law, 2nd edn. Clarendon Press, Oxford

Hohfeld WN (1919) Fundamental legal conceptions as applied in judicial reasoning and other legal essays. Yale University Press, New Haven

Kelsen H (1925) Allgemeine Staatslehre. Springer, Berlin

Kelsen H (1934) Reine Rechtslehre, 1st edn. Deuticke, Leipzig/Wien
Kelsen H (1960) Reine Rechtslehre, 2nd edn. Böhlau, Wien
Kelsen H (1979) Allgemeine Theorie der Normen. Manz, Wien
Köpcke M (2019) Legal validity. Hart Publishing, Oxford/Portland (Oregon)
Kramer M (1998) Rights without trimmings. In: id., Simmonds, Steiner (eds) A debate over rights. Oxford University Press, Oxford, pp 7–111
Lindahl L, Reidhav D (2017) Legal power: the basic definition. Ratio Juris 30:158–185
MacCormick DN (1986) Law as institutional fact. In: MacCormick DN, Weinberger O (eds) An institutional theory of law. Springer, Dordrecht, pp 49–76
Ross A (1968) Directives and norms. Humanities Press, New York
Ruiter DW (1993) Institutional legal facts. Springer, Dordrecht
Sieckmann J (1990) Regelmodelle und Prinzipienmodelle des Rechtssystems. Nomos, Baden-Baden
Sieckmann J (2012) The logic of autonomy. Hart Publishing, Oxford/Portland (Oregon)
Sieckmann J (2018) Rechtsphilosophie. Mohr, Tübingen
Spaak T (1994) The concept of legal competence. Dartmouth, Aldershot
Spaak T (2008) Explicating the concept of legal competence. In: Hage JC, von der Pfordten D (eds) Concepts in law. Springer, Dordrecht, pp 67–80
von Wright GH (1963) Norm and action. Routledge & Paul Kegan, London
Weissenbauer J (2019) Content and competence. Mohr, Tübingen

Part II
The Normativity of Legal Power and Legal Competence

Testing the Utility of a Concept of Power-Conferring Norm: A Proposal

Guillaume Tusseau

Abstract According to a conventionalist perspective, legal discourses admit several possible reconstructions. Their respective values depend on a form of epistemological utilitarianism. Legal practice tends to endow fragments of legal discourse that mention terms such as "competence", "authority", or "jurisdiction" with a distinct role. One wonders whether legal theory should provide legal disciplines with a specific concept of power-conferring norm to deal with these sentences. I propose such a concept, whose canonical formulation reads: "If an actor *a* accomplishes the action – i.e., follows the procedure – *p* having the subjective meaning of a norm *n* relative to a range of application *ra* and included in the range of regulation *rr*, then its objective meaning ought to be." Such a norm makes the behaviour *p* of a given actor *a* the condition of production of a norm *n* bearing on the domain (e.g. activity, territory, class of persons, etc.) *ra* and having the normative meaning *rr* (e.g. mandatory, permissive, power-conferring, etc.). A first taxonomy exemplifies classes of power-conferring norms, and proves the wide applicability of the proposed concept across domestic, international, public, and private laws. A second one deals with the kinds of relations that exist between power-conferring norms: coordination and hierarchisation.

1 Ordinary Legal Language and Conceptual Discomfort

In ordinary legal language, many expressions relate to the idea of a capacity to produce new legal entities. For example, pursuant to Article I of the Constitution of the United States, "The Congress shall have Power To lay and collect Taxes, Duties, Imposts and Excises, to pay the Debts and provide for the common Defence and general Welfare of the United States." Section 192(1) of the Nigerian Merchant Shipping Act, 2007 (No. 27 of 2007) similarly reads "The Minister may make regulations for the prevention of accidents, the protection of health in employment

G. Tusseau (✉)
Sciences Po Law School, Paris, France
e-mail: guillaume.tusseau@sciencespo.fr

G. Villa Rosas, T. Spaak (eds.), *Legal Power and Legal Competence*, Law and Philosophy Library 140, https://doi.org/10.1007/978-3-031-28555-4_5

and may by regulations specify measures for the prevention of accidents which are peculiar to maritime employment." Article 95 of the Constitution of South Korea provides that "The Prime Minister or the head of each Executive Ministry may, under the powers delegated by Act or Presidential Decree, or ex officio, issue ordinances of the Prime Minister or the Executive Ministry concerning matters that are within their jurisdiction." Pursuant to Article 17(6) of the Treaty on European Union, "The President of the Commission shall: (a) lay down guidelines within which the Commission is to work; (b) decide on the internal organisation of the Commission, ensuring that it acts consistently, efficiently and as a collegiate body; (c) appoint Vice-Presidents, other than the High Representative of the Union for Foreign Affairs and Security Policy, from among the members of the Commission."

These fragments of legal discourse, which belong to the object-language of positive law, can be styled "power-conferring sentences". At the metalinguistic level, jurists deal with them by using expressions such as "règle de competence", "norme attributive de pouvoir", "norma che conferisce potere", "Ermächtigungsnorm", "authorizing norm", "norm of competence", "kompetansenormer", "komptencji normodawczej". The use of such a specific terminology is very widespread among lawyers, whatever the specific field of positive law they study. Though the use of a given word by no means warrants that a specific thing exists,[1] it is possible to surmise that if a given linguistic community, such as jurists, uses a word, this is because this word has a specific function among this community. Using such a term is meant to meet specific needs and solve specific problems that the jurists face.

Nevertheless, this common legal parlance is obviously at odds with the dominant representation of what defines a legal norm. The latter is traditionally understood, with more or less important qualifications, as determining what ought to be and stipulating a coercive sanction in case the norm addressee does not comply. In spite of the many differences between their respective theories, John Austin[2] and Hans Kelsen[3] for example share the idea that basic legal entities—be they called laws or norms—impose obligations and rely on coercion. The apparent conflict between the felt need to single out the doctrinal apprehension of power-conferring sentences, on the one hand, and the dominant implicit representation of legal norms, on the other, leads to an important conceptual question regarding the existence of "power-conferring norms" properly so called.

---

[1]Bentham (1997), p. 87.

[2]Austin (1913), pp. 11–12.

[3]Kelsen (1934), pp. 32–33; Kelsen (1997), pp. 69–80; Kelsen (1962a, b), pp. 33–55.

2 Conceptual Conventionalism

Trusting what the contemporary theory of knowledge has adopted as its main principle, I rely on the presupposition and adopt the framework of 'conceptual conventionalism'.[4] This perspective rejects the conception according to which scientific theories start with neutral observation of brute facts, faithfully identify the entities and processes that truly exist, display the reality in itself, infer laws through induction, and thus offer indications on the objective nature of the world.[5] The basic tenet of conventionalism is ontology's relativity.[6] According to it, the world we inhabit has no natural, necessary, objective, a priori structure. It is shaped by the ways we conceive of it, i.e. the ways we cut in the magma of sensitive perceptions, impressions, feelings, and experiences, several units that prove meaningful and useful from a specific viewpoint. Karl R. Popper suggestively recounts the following experience:

> Twenty-five years ago I tried to bring home the same point to a group of physics students in Vienna by beginning a lecture with the following instructions: 'Take pencil and paper; carefully observe, and write down what you have observed!' They asked, of course, what I wanted them to observe. Clearly the instruction, 'Observe!' is absurd. (It is not even idiomatic, unless the object of the transitive verb can be taken as understood.) Observation is always selective. It needs a chosen object, a definite task, an interest, a point of view, a problem. And its description presupposes a descriptive language, with property words; it presupposes similarity and classification, which in its turn presupposes interests, points of view, and problems.[7]

The myth of the given, i.e. of a neutral, universal and anhistorical observation thus needs to be abandoned.[8] The concepts one resorts to do not result from the nature of things, but from choices. Consequently, they depend on a project and a commitment, which are themwelves determined by contextual—historical, cultural, linguistic, economic, etc.—factors. As John Dewey puts it, more than "*data*" or "*givens*", the objects that science cuts, isolates, selects, abstracts, reconstructs, etc. are to be regarded as "*takens*".[9]

Therefore, in the legal context, there are several 'ways of legal worldmaking',[10] i.e. several ways to conceive of the basic legal formants of any legal phenomenon. This is the reason why some authors adopt a twofold vision of the basic elements of a

[4] Barberousse et al. (2000) and Laugier and Wagner (2004a, b).

[5] Giere (2006), pp. 1, 4.

[6] Quine (1969).

[7] Popper (1962), p. 46.

[8] See Hanson (1958); Kuhn (2008), pp. 157–188; Sellars (1997); Sellars (1981); Putnam (1981), pp. 49–74; Forrai (2001); Stengers and Schlanger (1991); Fuller (1988), pp. 233–249; Tusseau (2021a).

[9] Dewey (1929), pp. 170–194, esp. p. 178. See also Bedoya Giraldo (2017), esp. pp. 45–103, 129.

[10] Goodman (1978).

legal phenomenon: Dworkin[11] thus opposes rules and principles. Manuel Atienza and Juan Ruiz Manero[12] distinguish between principles, rules, and values. Others conceive of the legal phenomenon as composed of norms or rules. Nevertheless, several options must be distinguished. Some consider that two types of rules must be distinguished: primary and secondary rules, as in Hart's terminology.[13] Others refuse to admit to their conceptual apparatus more than one type of legal norm. Such was Kelsen's option until 1962.[14] Others consider that legal phenomena should be analysed thanks to the identification of eight 'fundamental legal conceptions' corresponding to the situations of the legal subjects.[15] Depending on the chosen conceptual apparatus, one can give several accounts of one and the same bundle of phenomena. In this respect, Willard van Orman Quine notices that "If you take the total scattered portion of the spatiotemporal world that is made up of rabbits, and that which is made up of undetached rabbit parts, and that which is made up of rabbit stages, you come out with the same scattered portion of the world each of the three times. The only difference is in how you slice it."[16] One and the same phenomenon can thus be conceived of in three different ways. Three distinct and nevertheless equally complete descriptions can be offered depending on the fact that in order to analyse it, science has resorted to the concept of rabbit, of undetached rabbit parts, or of rabbit stages.

Such an approach does not imply adopting a relativistic position. Not all the possible ontologies are equal. The choice among them is guided by the search for "real explanatory power,"[17] thanks to which "we reduce the complexity of our stream of experience to a manage able conceptual simplicity."[18] It depends therefore on its utility in carrying out a certain task. For the traditional empirical sciences, this involves in particular developing a division of the world that allows the prediction of future events. From a pragmatist perspective, the essence of intellectual operations thus consists in developing a conceptual order that, by its discrete divisions, disciplines a continuous perceptual flow according to certain goals. Scientific investigation, made of successive conceptual bets that are in turn tested from the point of view of their practical consequences for the one who employs them, is connected to the local interests of the one who leads it. William James, for example, notes in this sense that "We say this theory solves it on the whole more satisfactorily than that theory; but that means more satisfactorily to ourselves, and individuals will

[11] Dworkin (1978).

[12] Atienza and Ruiz Manero (1996).

[13] Hart (1961).

[14] Compare Kelsen (1962a), on the one hand, with Kelsen (1962b, 1979), on the other hand. See also Tusseau (2007).

[15] Hohfeld (1978).

[16] Quine (1968), p. 189.

[17] Quine (1948), p. 30.

[18] Quine (1948), p. 36.

emphasize their points of satisfaction differently."[19] Any concept therefore depends on cognitive interest. It follows, according to Jean-Pierre Cléro, that "If one needs these commensurabilities [between objects of study], one must be able to give them to oneself and, rather than encounter ontology as an obstacle, admit the primacy of deontology and practice in order to give oneself the ontological operations, that is to say the commensurabilities, that one needs."[20]

Based on the preceding assumptions, I will adopt a normativist standpoint, considering not that the legal phenomena consist of norms but, more exactly, that jurists can benefit from considering the global bundle of phenomena which are hic et nunc called 'legal', through the lens of the concept of a legal norm. I will dispense with any other concept (principle, institution, value, policy, etc.) as not useful for my purposes. One of the advantages of the concept of a legal norm is that this concept is familiar to many legal scholars. Moreover, it is not linked to any specific legal context, domestic, national, statist, etc. and can, accordingly, be used as the concept of a general legal analysis. However, with respect to the puzzles that result from power-conferring sentences, considering that legal phenomena are only composed of norms (or are preferably conceived of this way) is not the whole story. One must still make explicit whether there is only one sort of legal norm, so that a single concept would be used in the whole legal analysis, or whether a whole taxonomy of norms should preferably be used.

3 A Theory of Power-Conferring Norms

In the field of legal theory or jurisprudence, the literature on the concept of a legal power and on power-conferring norms has recently been burgeoning. Several learned and doctrinal proposals have been made by scholars, including Rupert Stettner,[21] Hajime Yoshino,[22] Ota Weinberger,[23] Rafael Hernández Marín,[24] Torben Spaak,[25] Jordi Ferrer Beltrán,[26] Andrew Halpin,[27] Manuel Atienza, Juan Ruiz Manero,[28] and Hubert Schnüriger.[29] All of them intend to devise the conceptual tools which are best suited for the legal analysis of legal expressions which are prima facie related to the idea of a power to create norms, and for legal reasonings which

[19] James (1907), Lecture II.

[20] Cléro (2014), p. 234.

[21] Stettner (1983)

[22] Yoshino (1995a, 1995b)

[23] Weinberger (1995).

[24] Hernández Marín (1998).

[25] Spaak (1994, 2009).

[26] Ferrer Beltrán (2000).

[27] Halpin (1996).

[28] Atienza and Ruiz Manero (1996).

[29] Schnüriger (2013).

imply assessing the legal faculties of a legal actor (e.g. considering one's own range of possible actions, considering the possibility of appealing for the judicial review of the validity of legal norms, etc.).

In another context,[30] I have reviewed several individuations of the basic elements of legal phenomena, in order to assess their respective merits and demerits. I rejected as inappropriate to the activities of most legal scholars and legal practitioners several theories that I considered reductionist. These theories refuse to use a concept of power-conferring norm, and prefer to embark on legal tasks by resorting only to the concept of prescriptive norm, i.e. the concept of a norm imposing a sanction in case a given behaviour is not adopted. According to such theories, all the raw legal material is to be reconstructed so as to fit into this conceptual pattern. Power-conferring sentences are consequently understood either as fragment of complete legal norms[31] or as indirectly enunciated mandatory norms.[32] I also rejected non-reductionist theories, which, contrary to the preceding ones, consider it more convenient to add other concepts of norms to that of prescriptive norm. According to my own position, for reasons that would be too long to give here, neither the addition of the concepts of permissive norm[33] and constitutive norm[34] can be regarded as sufficient.

I have relied on a functional and on a structural analysis in order to advocate (once again: not the necessity but) the opportunity of using a concept of power-conferring norm in legal analysis. Studying a legal order's functions as a dynamic normative system in Merkl[35] and Kelsen's sense, and from the point of view of Hart's 'descriptive sociology'[36] invites one to devise a specific concept in order to account for the importance of power-conferring sentences in ordinary legal reasoning. Such is also the case when one focuses on the analysis of subjective legal positions and legal actors' practical reasonings when they are confronted with a power-conferring sentence. After examining thesis which, such as Ruiter's,[37] Weinberger's,[38] or Guastini's,[39] recommended individuating several types of norms on the production of norms, I sided with MacCormick[40] in proposing a unique and richer concept of power-conferring norm.

[30] Tusseau (2006).

[31] Kelsen (1997), pp. 197–198; Kelsen (1962a, b), p. 74.

[32] Ziembiński (1970), pp. 24–25; Ziembiński (1988), pp. 174–177; Ross (1958), pp. 32–33; Kelsen (1996), pp. 348–349.

[33] Von Wright (1963), p. 192; Von Wright (1982); Alchourrón and Bulygin (1971), pp. 73–74, 151; Alchourrón and Bulygin (1979), p. 41; Lindahl (1977), p. 212. See also ibid., pp. 219, 229; Lindahl (1994), pp. 898–899.

[34] Hernández Marín (1984), pp. 40, 151–152, 162–163; Hernández Marín (1989), p. 395; Hernández Marín (1998), pp. 188–189, 233, 316; Carcaterra (1974), p. 86; Roversi (2012); Ramírez Ludeña and Vilajosana Rubio (2022).

[35] Merkl (1931), p. 252.

[36] Hart (1961).

[37] Ruiter (1993, 1998).

[38] Weinberger (1991), p. 22; Weinberger (1973), pp. 124–125; Weinberger (1981), p. 62.

[39] Guastini (1994). For a discussion, see Tusseau (2019).

[40] MacCormick (1998).

This concept is adopted only as a matter of choice, of theoretical decision, which is revisable and must be tested against its utility for legal scholars' and legal practitioners' tasks. The proposed concept includes four elements. The first is that of an actor being empowered to produce legal norms. The second is that of an action by means of which that actor can produce norms. The other two elements determine the norms that this actor is allowed to produce, provided it follows the procedure. The third element, called the 'range of application' of the power-conferring norm, refers to the area of reality, which is determined by territorial, temporal, material, and/or personal criteria, that an actor is empowered to govern. The fourth and final element is called the 'range of regulation'. It refers to the kinds of normative meanings that a power-conferring norm empowers to produce, i.e. both to the types of norms (according to the taxonomy I choose to adopt: prescriptive, permissive, derogating, and power-conferring) the legal actor can produce, and their level in the normative hierarchy. Therefore, I propose the following concept of a power-conferring norm:

> if an actor *a* accomplishes the action—i.e. follows the procedure—*p* having the subjective meaning of a norm *n* relative to a range of application *ra* and included in the range of regulation *rr*, then its objective meaning ought to be.

Such a norm makes the behaviour of a given actor *a* the condition of production of a norm *n* bearing on the domain *ra* and having the normative meaning *rr*. Apart from a power-conferring norm, no one can produce any norm. No norm can result from a logical deduction. This power-conferring norm is the only condition to produce norms. My concept thus states the necessary and sufficient conditions for an actor to produce a legal norm.

In order to substantiate these abstract reflections and make use of this theoretical suggestion, I will proceed in two steps.[41] Drawing on various areas of positive law, I will first offer a general taxonomy of examples of power-conferring norms. I will then identify and illustrate the kinds of normative relations that can exist among them.

4 Types of Power-Conferring Norms

4.1 A Twofold Theoretical Construction

Following Charles Eisenmann,[42] I suggest that in order to design a useful conceptual tool, it is necessary at first to stay at a strictly theoretical level, and to map out abstractly all the theoretical possibilities. Classes of possibilities are identified, divided, and subdivided in an ordered way, so as to offer a complete map of what

---

[41] See also Tusseau (2014).

[42] Eisenmann (1948, 1966).

may (but need not) appear in practice. Classes must be elaborated so as to be both jointly exhaustive with regard to the field studied, and mutually exclusive of one another. Once these logical prerequisites for a sound intellectual framework are satisfied, an infinity of classifications is possible according to the criteria which are considered interesting.[43] In the present case, my purpose is to design, by way of example and by no means with a view to exhaust the conceivable possibilities, a series of typologies of the classes of power-conferring norms that may appear concretely in the legal practice. Only after completing this first operation will it be appropriate to identify actual cases that fit in one of the theoretical hypotheses previously identified. This legal casuistry is the second step. It allows the ordering of the several power-conferring norms which can be identified in the object-language, according to the four components of the concept of a power-conferring norm that I have suggested.

4.2 *Outline of a Typology of Power-Conferring Norms*

4.2.1 The Actor

First, with respect to the composition of the actor, one can oppose power-conferring norms the addressee of which is a single individual and those the addressee of which is an actor consisting of several individuals. As an example of the former situation, according to Article 109 of Constitution of Azerbaijan,

> The President of the Republic of Azerbaijan shall have the following powers: [...] (5) to appoint and dismiss members of the Cabinet of Ministers of the Republic of Azerbaijan; [...] (8) to repeal resolutions and orders for the Cabinet of Ministers of the Republic of Azerbaijan and the Cabinet of Ministers of the AUtonomous Republic of Nakhchivan, and acts of central and local executive bodies; [...] (12) to appoint and dismiss the Supreme Command of the Armed Forces of the Republic of Azerbaijan; [...] (25) to declare general and partial mobilization, and demobilization; [...] (27) to appoint the Security Council of the Republic of Azerbaijan; [...] (29) to declare a state of emergency and martial law;

In the latter case, where a plurality of individuals is empowered, one can moreover distinguish between power-conferring norms the addressee of which is a single collective institution—for example the Spanish Congress of Deputies, the European Court of Justice, the Italian Constitutional Court, etc.—and those the addressees of which are several institutions. In this last situation, the empowered actor is in fact a set of co-authors, whose converging consent is necessary for the production of a norm. Among many examples where several institutions have to cooperate, each having a veto power—be it in the form of an initiative, a proposal, or the consent to a proposed norm—in order for a norm to be adopted, Article 168 of the Spanish Constitution reads:

[43] Tusseau (2009), pp. 41–42.

1. If a total revision of the Constitution is proposed, or a partial revision thereof, affecting the Introductory Part, Chapter II, Division 1 of Part I, or Part II, the principle of the proposed reform shall be approved by a two-thirds majority of the members of each House, and the Cortes Generales shall immediately be dissolved.
2. The Houses elected thereupon must ratify the decision and proceed to examine the new constitutional text, which must be passed by a two-thirds majority of the members of each House.
3. Once the amendment has been passed by the Cortes Generales, it shall be submitted to ratification by referendum.

In this case, the complex empowered actor consists of (1) the current Congress of Deputies, (2) the current Senate, (3) the newly elected Congress of Deputies, (4) the newly elected Senate, and (5) the people.

Another possibility is to distinguish between particular and general power-conferring norms according to the description of the empowered actor. A particular norm's addressee can either be an individual identified by his full name or a class of individuals of which only one individual can be a member at the same time. An example of the former case is offered by Article 39 of the French Constitution of Year VIII, which expressly empowered citizen Bonaparte as the "Premier consul". The previous example from Azerbaijan corresponds to the second type of particular power-conferring norm. On the contrary, a general power-conferring equally gives powers to a class of actors that are similarly and simultaneously allowed to act. Such is the case of Section 133(2) of the Companies Act, 2017 of Pakistan. By stating that "The board may at any time call an extraordinary general meeting of the company to consider any matter which requires the approval of the company in a general meeting," it empowers any board of any firm.

4.2.2 The Action or Procedure

Secondly, with respect to the action or procedure, one can first oppose power-conferring norms depending on the material nature of this action. Some norms can only be produced as the result of an explicit action. Such is for example the case of getting married, issuing a judicial ruling or enacting a statute, which require an express manifestation and the explicit following of all the required procedural steps. On the contrary, some norms can be produced in a tacit way. For example, pursuant to Section 83 of the Colombian Code of administrative procedure, "After three months from the presentation of a petition without notification of a decision to resolve it, it will be understood that it is negative."

A second criterion distinguishes power-conferring norms that allow for several actions to result in the production of a new norm and those that impose resorting to one specific action. For example, generally under French contract law, no specific procedure needs to be followed. Pursuant to Article 1128 of the civil code, "The following are necessary for the validity of a contract: 1° The consent of the parties; 2° Their capacity to contract; 3° A lawful and certain content." Nothing is required regarding the procedure. Article 1109 confirms that "The contract is solemn when it is formed by the sole exchange of consents regardless of the mode of expression. The contract is solemn when its validity is subject to forms determined by law. The contract is real when its formation is subordinated to the delivery of a thing." Similarly, by providing that "[t]he [Economic and Social Committee] may be consulted by [the European Parliament, the Council or the Commission] in all cases in which they consider it appropriate," Article 304 of the Treaty on the Functioning of the European Union introduces some kind of indifference as to the legal procedure which is to be used in order to establish a norm. It appears that, for every power-conferring norm in the Treaties, the empowered actors have a choice between following a procedure where they do not consult the Economic and Social Committee, and one where they proprio motu decide to ask for its advice. On the contrary, many provisions of the Treaty prove more constraining. Consultations as such do not amount to a sharing of the normative power. As a consequence, they do not affect the identity of the empowered legal actor, but only the way it makes its decisions and produces norms. Such is, for example, the case of Article 43(2) of the Treaty on the Functioning of the European Union, which reads: "[t]he European Parliament and the Council, acting in accordance with the ordinary legislative procedure and after consulting the Economic and Social Committee, shall establish the common organisation of agricultural markets provided for in Article 40(1) and the other provisions necessary for the pursuit of the objectives of the common agricultural policy and the common fisheries policy."

4.2.3 The Range of Application

Thirdly, with respect to the range of application, one can oppose power-conferring norms according to the criterion or the combination of criteria that are used to define the subject matter the regulation of which is entrusted to the empowered legal actor. For example, Article 94 of the Japanese Constitution uses a material criterion to define the local authorities' competence, as it stipulates that "Local public entities shall have the right to manage their property, affairs and administration and to enact their own regulations within law." On the contrary, Article 43(4) of the Greek Constitution defines the range of application of the power-conferring norm using material and temporal criteria when it states that "By virtue of statutes passed by the Plenum of the Parliament, delegation may be given [to the President of the Republic] for the issuance of general regulatory decrees for the regulation of matters specified by such statutes in a broad framework. These statutes shall set out the general principles and directives of the regulation to be followed and shall set time-limits within which the delegation must be used." Finally, using a personal criterion, Article 34 of the Canadian Constitution Act 1867 states that "The Governor General may from Time to Time, by Instrument under the Great Seal of Canada, appoint a Senator to be Speaker of the Senate, and may remove him and appoint another in his Stead."

Another classification can oppose power-conferring norms that are dedicated to only one object to those which enjoy a wider scope. For example, Article 137 of the

Austrian Constitution is only dedicated to one strictly defined object. According to this provision, "The Constitutional Court pronounces on pecuniary claims against the Federation, the Laender, the municipalities and municipal associations which cannot be settled by ordinary legal process nor be liquidated by the ruling of an administrative authority." Similarly, a principle of specialty traditionally applies to the competences of international organisations. This is why the International Court of Justice denied the World Health Organisation any competence to deal with nuclear weapons. In the opinion of the Court, "to ascribe to the WHO the competence to address the legality of the use of nuclear weapons - even in view of their health and environmental effects - would be tantamount to disregarding the principle of speciality; for such competence could not be deemed a necessary implication of the Constitution of the Organization in the light of the purposes assigned to it by its member States."[44] Thus this power-conferring norm can be deemed "special". On the contrary, Article 248 of the Indian Constitution regarding the residuary powers of legislation broadly states that "1. Subject to article 246A, Parliament has exclusive power to make any law with respect to any matter not enumerated in the Concurrent List or State List. 2. Such power shall include the power of making any law imposing a tax not mentioned in either of those Lists." Thus, this is a "generic" power-conferring norm.

4.2.4 The Range of Regulation

Fourthly, with respect to the range or regulation, one may oppose power-conferring norms that confer a broad discretion to the empowered actor as to the types of norms it may produce, and power-conferring norms that only confer the power, if one chooses to exercise it, to produce a single, totally predetermined norm.

For example, although sometimes material limits are imposed on it,[45] the constituent power is generally very free to produce any norms it wants, and is therefore presented as sovereign. Similarly, in France, pursuant to article L. 223-18 of the commerce code, "In relations with third parties, the manager [of a limited liability company] is invested with the broadest powers to act in all circumstances on behalf of the company, subject to the powers that the law expressly grants to the partners."

On the contrary, other provisions tend to predetermine the kinds of norms that can be produced by the empowered authority. Pursuant to Article 37(2)(a) of the Constitution, when it decides to extend a state of emergency, the South African Parliament can only do it "for no more than three months at a time." Pursuant to Article R. 2162-7 of the French code of public procurement, when a framework-agreement has been passed between a contracting public authority and another party, the power-conferring norm both enjoy is strictly limited: "The subsequent contracts

[44] Legality of the Use by a State of Nuclear Weapons in Armed Conflict, Advisory Opinion, I. C. J. Reports 1996, p. 66, p. 79.

[45] Rigaux (1985); Ragone (2011); Gözler (2008); Tusseau (2021b), pp. 749–754, 790–798.

specify the characteristics and the methods of execution of the services requested which were not fixed in the framework agreement. They cannot lead to substantial modifications of the terms of the framework agreement." Even more strictly, Article 115l(2) of the German Basic Law only allows the adoption of one (derogation) norm: "The Bundestag, with the consent of the Bundesrat, may at any time, by a decision to be promulgated by the Federal President, declare a state of defence terminated. The Bundesrat may demand that the Bundestag reach a decision on this question. A state of defence shall be declared terminated without delay if the conditions for determining it no longer exist."

Therefore, it remains useful to distinguish as suggested, so as to obtain the general mapping outlined in Table 1.

Thus far, power-conferring norms have been considered in isolation. However, when one ponders over such a topic, one also has in mind the way several power-conferring norms, which empower various authorities, interlock with one another, how an empowerment in one site impacts upon the legal situation in another site, and how the ensuing normative productions themselves interact.

5 Types of Relationships Between Power-Conferring Norms

5.1 Coordination and Hierarchisation of Power-Conferring Norms

One of the advantages of a theoretical approach is, at least provisionally, to ignore the traditional terms which are used by scholars and practitioners. This allows for the avoiding of the emotive—positive or negative—connotations these terms may convey. By focusing on the power-conferring norms and their relationships, it also allows one to escape from the ambiguities of terminologies which, though traditional, are more or less metaphorical and are not always understood in the same ways by several authors, such as 'concurrent', 'parallel', 'shared', 'complementary', 'coordinate', 'joint', etc. powers.

Two major modes of relationship between norms are usually distinguished in the Italian theory of legal sources.[46] The 'principle of hierarchy' imposes upon some actors the need to respect and to conform to the normative production of other actors. When norms conflict, the superior one prevails and the other is invalid. The power of the actor whose norms are called 'inferior' is limited to the production of norms that respect the norms produced by the actor whose norms are called 'superior'. On the contrary, the 'principle of competence' does not operate on a vertical scale, but on a horizontal one. Its function is to specialize sources of law. Any source can only

[46] Ruggeri (1977) and Guastini (1998).

Table 1 Types of power-conferring norms

Actor						Procedure					Range of application						Range of regulation	
Composition			Description			Nature of the action		Regulation of the action			Criteria for defintion				Scope		Degree of flexibility	
Monopersonal	Collective body or bodies		Particular		General	Implicit	Explicit	Free	Formalist		Territorial	Temporal	Material	Personal	Special	Generic	Discretion	Predetermination
	Single collective institution	Co-authors	Intuitu personae	Class of one member					Variety of admissible procedures	One exclusive procedure								

produce norms that bear on a specific subject matter. No other source can operate in this field. The relationship is not of superiority and inferiority, but of exclusion.

I propose to restate these two principles of normative ordering within the theory of power-conferring norms. The principle of hierarchy operates between the normative qualifications that can be produced thanks to several power-conferring norms. The relationship between power-conferring norms is thus situated at the level of their respective ranges of regulation. There is a hierarchy between two power-conferring norms when the normative productions that the range of regulation of the inferior one authorizes cannot violate the normative productions that the range or regulation of the superior one authorizes. The principle of competence, which I rename 'coordination of power-conferring norms', distinguishes power-conferring norms not according to the normative meanings they authorize, but according to the matters, objects, persons, territories, etc. about which they authorize the production of norms. In other words, the relation of power-conferring norms is thus situated at the level of their respective ranges of application.

Starting with this basic bifurcation, one can offer a more detailed analysis of several types of coordination and hierarchisation.

5.2 *Outline of a Typology of Relationships Between Power-Conferring Norms*

5.2.1 Forms of Coordination

Several techniques can result in the establishment of a relationship of coordination between two power-conferring norms. A first one can be identified, which I call 'parcelling competences'. An activity, a territory, a time span, or a group of human beings is divided into fragments. Thus, the coordinated power-conferring norms are 'special', for they only authorize the production of norms about that range of application. The various actors between whom the range is divided have an identical power-conferring norm. Such is for example the case of all the provincial governments in Ecuador, which, pursuant to Article 263 of the Constitution,

> shall have the following exclusive jurisdictions, without detriment to others as established by law:
>
> 1. To plan provincial development and draw up the respective land use development and management plans in coordination with national, regional, canton and parish planning.
> 2. To plan, build and maintain the road network within the scope of the province, not including urban zones.
> 3. In coordination with the regional government, to execute works in watersheds and micro watersheds.
> 4. Provincial environmental management.
> 5. To plan, build, operate and maintain irrigation systems.
> 6. To foster the farm and livestock activities.
> 7. To foster provincial production activities.
> 8. To secure international cooperation for the fulfillment of their competences.

Within the scope of their jurisdictions and territory, and in the exercise of their powers, they shall issue provincial ordinances.

This competence is equally divided from a material point of view, according to the territorial jurisdiction of each.

A second way to create a coordination of power-conferring norms is to distinguish between what French doctrine calls “compétence de principe” and “compétence d’attribution”. A global range of application is divided into two parts, only one of which is precisely defined. The other one is defined as “all that remains”. Thus the coordination is between a “special” and a “generic” power-conferring norm. For example, this operation of coordination is present in Article 73 of the Constitution of the Russian Federation, according to which “Outside the limits of authority of the Russian Federation and the powers of the Russian Federation on issues under the joint jurisdiction of the Russian Federation and constituent entities of the Russian Federation, the constituent entities of the Russian Federation shall enjoy full State power.” Article 3 of the Constitution of Switzerland similarly reads: "The Cantons are sovereign except to the extent that their sovereignty is limited by the Federal Constitution. They exercise all rights that are not vested in the Confederation.”

5.2.2 Forms of Hierarchisation

Relations of hierarchisation can take two broad forms. In a relation of “delegation”, a superior power-conferring norm limits itself to empowering an actor to produce norms that deal with the totality or part of its own range of application. Such is, for example, what is envisioned in Article 124 of the Constitution of Costa Rica, which stipulates: “The Legislative Assembly may delegate, in permanent commissions, the cognizance and the approval of bills of law. However, the Assembly may retract to itself, at any moment, the debate or the vote of the bills that have been [the] object of delegation. The delegation does not proceed if it concerns the bills of law relative to electoral matters, to the creation of national taxes or to the modification of the existing [ones], to the exercise of the faculties specified in paragraphs 4), 11), 14), 15) and 17) of Article 121 of the Political Constitution, to the convocation to a Constituent Assembly, to any effect, and to the partial reform of the Political Constitution.” This power-conferring norm, the range of regulation of which is limited by the specifications of the article itself, empowers an actor to empower another actor to produce norms. Similarly, Article 76 of the Italian Constitution reads: “The exercise of the legislative function may not be delegated to the Government unless principles and criteria have been established and then only for a limited time and for specified purposes.”

As distinguished from the relation of delegation, the relation of ‘primacy’ limits the normative productions that are possible thanks to an inferior power-conferring norm. The study of relations of primacy among power-conferring norms must be twofold. 'Typical' (i.e. relatively intuitively perceived and known) relations of primacy are of two types, between which the difference is more of degree than of nature.[47] The first is the relation of 'conformity', i.e. a strict correspondence between the normative productions that the inferior power-conferring norm authorizes and those that the superior power-conferring norm authorizes. The second typical relation of primacy is that of 'compatibility'. It is looser than the previous one. A simple absence of conflict between normative productions is sufficient for the inferior norm's validity. Both are related to the way a superior norm is applied or executed by an inferior norm.

Article 108 of the Belgian Constitution seems, on the face of it, to characterize a relation of conformity, as it empowers the Head of State to execute in a strict manner the will of the legislator: "The King makes decrees and regulations required for the execution of laws, without ever having the power either to suspend the laws themselves or to grant dispensation from their execution." Because of its range or regulation, the inferior power-conferring norm can only authorize the production of norms that strictly respect what has been decided when the superior power-conferring norm was employed.

Article 116 of the Constitution of Ukraine seems closer to a relation of compatibility, as it appears to leave more space for the Cabinet of Ministers' autonomous decision: It "ensures the state sovereignty and economic independence of Ukraine, the implementation of domestic and foreign policy of the State, the execution of the Constitution and the laws of Ukraine, and the acts of the President of Ukraine."

In contrast to typical ones, two types of 'non-typical' relations of primacy can be identified. In the first case, the range of regulation of the superior norm is itself limited. Therefore, the empowered actor is not left free to produce any norm it wants, and to limit accordingly the ambit of the inferior power-conferring norm, which empowers other actors (or the same actor) to execute the first norms. While it uses its own, superior, power-conferring norm, the actor must leave enough leeway for the inferior power-conferring norms. Such is the situation, which seems to be implied by the principle of subsidiarity that must be observed in the allocation and performance of state tasks pursuant to Article 5a of the Constitution of Switzerland. Article 43a (1) reads: "The Confederation only undertakes tasks that the Cantons are unable to perform or which require uniform regulation by the Confederation." Pursuant to Article 149(1) of the Spanish Constitution,

> 1. The State shall have exclusive competence over the following matters: [...]
>
> 11th. Monetary system: foreign currency, exchange and convertibility; bases for the regulations concerning credit, banking and insurance. [...]
>
> 13th. Basic rules and coordination of general economic planning.

With respect to the relations between the statutes that determine the "basic principles" and the "acts of development" that may be adopted by the Autonomous Communities, the Constitutional Tribunal made it clear that enough room should be

[47] Eisenmann (1957).

left for the action of the inferior power-conferring norm: "The establishment by the State of the bases of the regulation cannot reach such a degree of development that it leaves the correlative competence of the Community empty of content."[48]

As a consequence, the whole regulation of the range of application in discussion cannot be dealt with in totality by the State's authorities. Whatever the norms they are empowered to produce, they must be limited, so as to guarantee some autonomous legal action at the community level.

The second type of non-typical relations of primacy, I propose to call 'relations of intensification'. In this case, the inferior normative productions do not strictly implement—within the framework of strict conformity or looser compatibility—the superior ones. They can only increase the effect of the superior norms. Such is the case, for example, in Article 193 of the Treatise on the functioning of the European Union, which reads: "[t]he protective measures adopted pursuant to Article 192 shall not prevent any Member State from maintaining or introducing more stringent protective measures. Such measures must be compatible with the Treaties. They shall be notified to the Commission." Both the States and the European institutions are empowered to produce norms regarding the range of application of the protection of environment (Article 191 TFEU). However, the inferior normative productions, which in this case are the national ones, must not only respect what the superior normative productions have established. They can only pursue the continuation of the normative dynamics in one sense.

Similarly, Article L. 2251-1 of the French Labour code recites: "A convention or agreement may contain stipulations more favourable to employees than the legal provisions in force. They cannot derogate from the provisions which are of a public order nature." Article L. 2254-1 of the same code recites: "When an employer is bound by the clauses of a convention or an agreement, these clauses apply to the employment contracts concluded with him, unless more favourable stipulations exist." In both cases, the hierarchisation of power-conferring norms relies on a relation of betterment that illustrates the "principe de faveur" that dominates the hierarchy of norms in labour law.

The general mapping that results from this examination is shown in Table 2.

6 Conclusion

Power-conferring norms are not something that is already given to the jurist. She faces an amount of raw legal phenomena, and it belongs to her to deal with them in a what appears to her a fruitful way. Deciding to adopt a concept of a power-conferring norm and retaining a specific conception of it certainly violate the principle of Ockham's razor. However, creating entities without necessity does not mean creating entities without utility for legal science. Conceptual creativity is admitted as a

[48] STC 1/1982.

Table 2 Types of relationships between power-conferring norms

Coordination		Hierarchisation				
Parcelling competence	Special v. generic power-conferring norm	Delegation	Primacy			
			Typical		Non-typical	
			Compatibility	Conformity	Limitation of the inferior range or regulation	Intensification

crucial factor in order to propose new theories, to give a unified view of problems that traditionally remain separated, to distinguish more precisely what is often confused, or to renew the explanation of legal processes. The ensuing attempt, as the one proposed in this chapter, naturally remains open to criticism and improvement, in a reflexive progress through which legal science, like any other scientific enquiry, tries to correct itself.[49]

References

Alchourrón CE, Bulygin E (1971) Normative systems. Springer, Wien, New York

Alchourrón CE, Bulygin E (1979) Sobre la existencia de las normas jurídicas. Universidad de Carabobo, Oficina latinoamericana de investigaciones jurídicas y sociales, Valencia

Atienza M, Ruiz Manero J (1996) Las piezas del derecho. Teoría de los enunciados jurídicos. Ariel, Barcelona

Austin J (1913) Lectures on jurisprudence or the philosophy of positive laws. John Murray, London

Barberousse A, Kistler M, Ludwig P (2000) La philosophie des sciences au XXe siècle. Flammarion, Paris

Bedoya Giraldo H (2017) La construcción epistémica del derecho. Universidad Externado de Colombia, Bogotá

Bentham J (1997) De l'ontologie et autres textes sur les fictions. Seuil, Paris

Carcaterra G (1974) Le norme costitutive. Edizione provvisoria. Giuffrè, Milano

Cléro J-P (2014) Essai sur les fictions. Hermann, Paris

Dewey J (1929) The quest for certainty: a study of the relation of knowledge and action. Gifford Lectures 1929. Minton, Balch & Company, New York

Dworkin RM (1978) Taking rights seriously, 2nd edn. Harvard University Press, Cambridge

Eisenmann C (1948) Centralisation et décentralisation. Esquisse d'une théorie générale. LGDJ, Paris

Eisenmann C (1957) Le droit administratif et le principe de légalité. In: Etudes et documents du Conseil d'Etat. Imprimerie national, Paris, pp 25–40

Eisenmann C (1966) Quelques problèmes de méthodologie des définitions et des classifications en science juridique. Archives de philosophie du droit 11:25–43

Ferrer Beltrán J (2000) Las normas de competencia. Un aspecto de la dinámica jurídica. Centro de estudios políticos y constitucionales—Boletín oficial del Estado, Madrid

Forrai G (2001) Reference, truth and conceptual schemes. A defense of internal realism. Kluwer, Dordrecht

Fuller S (1988) Social epistemology. Indiana University Press, Bloomington

Giere RN (2006) Scientific perspectivism. University of Chicago Press, Chicago

Goodman N (1978) Ways of worldmaking. Harvester Press, Hassocks

Gözler K (2008) Judicial review of constitutional amendments. A comparative study. Ekin Press, Bursa

Guastini R (1994) Invalidity. Ratio Juris 7:212–226

Guastini R (1998) Teoria e dogmatica delle fonti. Giuffrè, Milano

Halpin A (1996) The concept of a legal power. Oxford J Leg Stud 16:129–152

Hanson NR (1958) Patterns of discovery. An inquiry into the conceptual foundations of science. Cambridge University Press, Cambridge

Hart HLA (1961) The concept of law. Clarendon Press, Oxford

[49] On this conception of science, see especially Zolo (1989) and Sellars (1997).

Hernández Marín R (1984) El Derecho como dogma. Tecnos, Madrid
Hernández Marín R (1989) Teoría general del derecho y de la ciencia jurídica. PPU, Barcelona
Hernández Marín R (1998) Introducción a la teoría de la norma jurídica. Marcial Pons, Madrid, Barcelona
Hohfeld WN (1978) Fundamental legal conceptions as applied in judicial reasoning. Greenwood Press, Westport
James W (1907) Pragmatism. A new name for some old ways of thinking. Popular lectures on philosophy. Longmans, Green, and Co., London, New York
Kelsen H (1934) Reine Rechtslehre. Einleitung in die Rechtswissenschaftliche Problematik. Franz Deuticke, Leipzig
Kelsen H (1962a [1960]) Théorie pure du droit. Dalloz, Paris
Kelsen H (1962b) Derogation. In: Newman RA (ed) Essays in jurisprudence in honor of Roscoe Pound. The Bobb Merrill & Co., Indianapolis, New York
Kelsen H (1979) Allgemeine Theorie der Normen. Manz, Vienna
Kelsen H (1996 [1979]) Théorie générale des normes. PUF, Paris
Kelsen H (1997 [1945]) Théorie générale du droit et de l'Etat suivi de La doctrine du droit naturel et le positivisme juridique. LGDJ, Bruylant, Paris, Bruxelles
Kuhn TS (2008 [1962]) La structure des révolutions scientifiques. Flammarion, Paris
Laugier S, Wagner P (dir) (2004a) Philosophie des sciences I. Théories, expériences et méthodes. Vrin, Paris
Laugier S, Wagner P (dir) (2004b) Philosophie des sciences II. Naturalismes et réalismes. Vrin, Paris
Lindahl L (1977) Position and change. A study in law and logic. D. Reidel Publishing Company, Dordrecht, Boston
Lindahl L (1994) Stig Kanger's theory of rights. In: Prawitz D, Skyrms B, Westerstahl D (eds) Logic, methodology and philosophy of science IX, Studies in logic and the foundations of mathematics, vol 134, pp 889–911
MacCormick N (1998) Powers and power-conferring norms. In: Paulson SL, Litschewski Paulson B (eds) Normativity and norms. Critical perspectives on Kelsenian themes. Clarendon Press, Oxford, pp 493–506
Merkl AJ (1931) Prolegomena einer Theorie des rechtlichen Stufenbaues. In: Verdross A (ed) Gesellschaft, Staat und Recht. Untersuchungen zur reinen Rechtslehre. Festschrift Hans Kelsen zum 50. Geburtstag gewidmet. Springer, Vienna, pp 252–294
Popper KR (1962) Conjectures and refutations. The growth of scientific knowledge. Basic Books, New York
Putnam H (1981) Reason, truth and history. Cambridge University Press, Cambridge
Quine WVO (1948) On what there is. Rev Metaphys 2:21–38
Quine WVO (1968) Ontological relativity. J Philos 65:185–212
Quine WVO (1969) Ontological relativity, and other essays. Columbia University Press, New York
Ragone S (2011) I controlli giurisdizionali sulle revisioni costituzionali. Profili teorici e comparativi. Bononia University Press, Bologna
Ramírez Ludeña L, Vilajosana Rubio JM (2022) Reglas Constitutivas y Derecho. Marcial Pons, Madrid
Rigaux M-F (1985) La théorie des limites matérielles à l'exercice de la fonction constituante. Larcier, Bruxelles
Ross A (1958) On law and justice. Stevens & Sons, London
Roversi C (2012) Costituire. Giappichelli, Torino
Ruggeri A (1977) Gerarchia, competenza e qualità nel sistema costituzionale delle fonti normative. Giuffrè, Milano
Ruiter DWP (1993) Institutional legal facts. Legal powers and their effects. Kluwer Academic Publishers, Boston and London: Dordrecht
Ruiter DWP (1998) Legal powers. In: Paulson SL, Litschewski Paulson B (eds) Normativity and norms. Critical perspectives on Kelsenian themes. Clarendon Press, Oxford, pp 471–491

Schnüriger H (2013) Der Begriff der Kompetenz. Archiv für Rechts- und Sozialphilosophie 99:77–94
Sellars W (1981) Foundations for a metaphysics of pure process: the Carus lectures. Monist 64:3–90
Sellars W (1997) Empiricism and the philosophy of mind. Harvard University Press, Cambridge
Spaak T (1994) The concept of legal competence. An essay in conceptual analysis. Dartmouth, Aldershot
Spaak T (2009) Explicating the concept of legal competence. In: Hage JC, von der Pfordten D (eds) Concepts in law. Springer, Dordrecht, Heidelberg, London and New York, pp 67–80
Stengers I, Schlanger J (1991) Les concepts scientifiques. Invention et pouvoir. Gallimard, Paris
Stettner R (1983) Grundfragen einer Kompetenzlehre. Duncker & Humblot, Berlin
Tusseau G (2006) Les normes d'habilitation. Dalloz, Paris
Tusseau G (2007) De quelques énigmes du kelsénisme. Int J Semiot Law 20:367–393
Tusseau G (2009) Classificazioni. In: Pegoraro L (ed) Glossario di Diritto pubblico comparator. Carocci, Roma, pp 41–42
Tusseau G (2014) Theoretical deflation: the EU order of competences and power-conferring norms theory. In: Azoulai L (ed) The question of competence in the European Union. Oxford University Press, Oxford, pp 39–62
Tusseau G (2019) Riccardo Guastini et la théorie des métanormes sur la production du droit. In: Chiassoni P, Comanducci P, Ratti GB (eds) L'arte della distinzione. Scritti per Riccardo Guastini, vol II. Marcial Pons, Madrid, Barcelona, Buenos Aires, São Paulo, pp 561–577
Tusseau G (2021a) Droit comparé et théorie générale du droit. Notes sur quelques allers- retours aporétiques. Les presses de l'Université Laval, Sainte-Foy
Tusseau G (2021b) Contentieux constitutionnel comparé. Une introduction critique au droit processuel constitutionnel. Lextenso, Paris-La Défense
Von Wright GH (1963) Norm and action. A logical enquiry. Routledge and Kegan Paul, London
Von Wright GH (1982) Norms, truth and logic. In: Martino AA (ed) Deontic logic, computational linguistics and legal information systems 2. North-Holland Publishing Company, Amsterdam, New York, pp 3–20
Weinberger O (1973) Der Erlaubnisbegriff und der Aufbau der Normenlogik. Etudes de logique juridique 5:113–142
Weinberger O (1981) Normentheorie als Grundlage der Jurisprudenz und Ethik. Eine Auseinandersetzung mit Hans Kelsens Theorie der normen. Duncker & Humblot, Berlin
Weinberger O (1991) The theory of legal dynamics reconsidered. Ratio Juris 4:18–35
Weinberger O (1995) Normological inferences and the generation of legal norms. Ratio Juris 8: 261–270
Yoshino H (1995a) The systematization of legal meta-inference. In: Proceedings of the 5th International Conference on Artificial Intelligence and Law, May 21–24. University of Maryland College Park, MD USA. ACM Press, New York, pp 266–275
Yoshino H (1995b) The logical structure of legal meta-inference. Eur J Law Philos Comput Sci 1–2: 425–434
Ziembiński Z (1970) Norms of competence as norms of conduct. Archivum Iuridicum Cracoviense 3:21–31
Ziembiński Z (1988) Le contenu et la structure des normes concédant les compétences. In: Di Bernardo G (ed) Normative structures of the social world, Poznań studies in the philosophy of science and the humanities, vol 11, pp 159–182
Zolo D (1989) Reflexive epistemology. The philosophical legacy of Otto Neurath. Kluwer Academic Publishers, Boston: Dordrecht

On the Function of Competence Norms in a Legal System

Carla Huerta

Abstract Norms are in general considered a basic element of law and competence norms, definitely, lie at the core of a dynamic legal system and its validity. This may be due to their function. Yet, what is the function of competence norms? The analysis of the function of competence norms, distinguishing private from public competence, addresses the conceptual question. Competence is here understood as the faculty to create, modify, or extinguish legal norms, and is only analyzed as a power given by the legal system to an agent acting as an authority.

Though scholars widely accept that legal norms are given to direct human behaviour in society, to create legal relations or establish some obligations, prohibitions, or permissions, not all legal norms have been deemed to be properly characterized by resorting to these modalities. For some authors, the explanation of legal competence specifically is not satisfactory in such terms. So, for the purpose of the determination of the function of competence norms, Hart's explanation of secondary rules will be revisited and Kelsen's theses on the function of norms will be discussed.

1 Introduction

Competence norms are a central feature of a legal system, but even if it is generally accepted that competence norms play an important role in legal systems, their nature and function is still being debated. The working hypothesis is that competence norms, understood as public power conferring norms, can be considered as prescriptions and, to that end, their function is analyzed. The approach is analytical and, thus, different concepts such as function, norm and competence will be briefly reflected upon simply to establish the conceptual background of the analysis.

In legal theory, it is common to distinguish private powers (capacity) from public powers (competence), despite the fact, that they both serve to empower actors. The

C. Huerta (✉)
Law Research Institute, National Autonomous University of Mexico, Mexico City, Mexico
e-mail: chuerta@unam.mx

G. Villa Rosas, T. Spaak (eds.), *Legal Power and Legal Competence*, Law and Philosophy Library 140, https://doi.org/10.1007/978-3-031-28555-4_6

term competence is used hereinafter in relation to public powers exclusively. I will therefore focus only on the attribution of powers to public officials, since in my opinion the fact that the normative subject has a position of authority is relevant to the effect of the characterization of the function of the competence norm.

Contemporary legal theorists maintain that law can only be understood if a distinction between rules that confer powers and those that impose duties is made. Following that argument, the general notion of empowerment is commented on to delimit the concept of competence norms, and the description of these norms as secondary rules in the sense of Hart's classification will also be reviewed to examine the effect of this distinction on the explanation of the function and nature of competence norms in a legal system.

It is commonly considered that legal norms are issued to direct human behaviour in society in terms of obligation, prohibition, or permission, to create legal relations or positions.[1] It is not clear though how some of the functions of legal norms are to be deontically expressed, and legal competence specifically might not be adequately characterized in terms of mere permission.

The object of this paper is therefore to analyze the norms that attribute power to officials, that is, norms of public law, in order to explore what their function is. In that regard, I will focus here mainly on Kelsen's position on this subject in *General Theory of Norms* in the light of the analysis of competence norms according to their ideal and logical structure as normative sentences.

2 Some Conceptual Considerations

2.1 On the Notion of Function

In philosophy, as well as in other sciences, the notion of function has been used in diverse senses meaning operation or set of operations that determine what a reality is or that allow us to understand that reality, as activity, or as purpose or end, for example.[2] The polysemic term of function has been used in law and legal doctrine to address different issues regarding mainly the purpose or operation of something. For that reason, it is convenient to start by clarifying what is here meant by function and competence, before addressing the question of the specific function of competence norms. Still, a definition of the term function will not be proposed.

In general, in the social sciences the notion of function refers, in a broad sense, to the ends, objectives and effects of the law within a social system. Regarding law, we can speak of the function of the law itself or of the function of the norms, or even speak of legislative, administrative, or judicial functions, for example. It seems

---

[1]A legal position is understood as Lindahl does, as a kind of relation that does not necessarily involve exactly two parties. See Lindahl (1977), p. 85.

[2]Ferrater Mora (1994), pp. 1408, 1409.

though, that in these cases the term function is used with different meanings, that is, as purpose, operation, and empowered action, respectively.

Raz mentions that it is surprising that legal theorists have not paid more attention to the elucidation of the notion of the function of law,[3] a subject relevant for the present investigation, because of its connection to the answer to the question about the function of competence norms. Even if he does not explain the concept of function, he holds that, among the direct functions of law, the primary one is to guide behaviour and it affects the general population, while the secondary one, has more to do with the operation of the legal system, with the procedures to change the law and the functioning of the organs that apply it. In his words, it deals with the maintenance of the legal system.[4] Raz distinguishes more functions than Hart. Yet, Raz considers that it is not possible to ascribe to every law or legal norm a distinct "social function", because these correspond rather to legal institutions.[5] Nevertheless, he mentions that, in some cases, it can be useful to investigate the function of particular legal norms.[6]

Despite the similarities and the fact that Raz's analysis on the social functions of law is based on Hart's ideas, in his opinion Hart's classification does not distinguish clearly "between normative types and social functions". So, he obscures the different functions of norms.[7] This is perhaps also due to the rigorous distinction between primary and secondary rules that has led scholars to believe that secondary rules can only perform one function, while legal norms often perform more than one as Raz mentions as well. He also maintains that duty-imposing norms play an important role in performing secondary functions.[8]

Law is a functional institution, that is, it is instrumental. That means that it serves some purpose. It is created to serve as a tool to regulate changing social relations. That is why it is designed as a dynamic order that can be transformed by including new norms or eliminating existing rules. So, considering its form and structure, the function of law concerns its operation, how the system works, and how its norms produce legal effects. But, when speaking of the function of law, reference is often made to what the legislators intend with a law, or what administrative agencies expect to achieve with a regulation.

If law is to serve as an instrument for the conformation of changing social relations, it should then be conceived as a dynamic order that is continuously modified to adapt to new circumstances. Consequently, the function of law is to enable human conduct, for change happens because of human action. The transformation of the legal system, therefore, occurs by means of the actions taken according

[3]Raz (2009), p. 169.

[4]Raz (2009), p. 168.

[5]The institutional character of law is for Raz the way of identifying a legal system, especially through the rules of competence. Raz (2009), pp. 88, 105 ff.

[6]Raz (2009), p. 167.

[7]Raz (2009), p. 179.

[8]Raz (2009), p. 179.

to the regulated competence norms. The meaning of the term function in relation to the norms will be discussed in Sect. 3.

2.2 *The Concept of Competence*

Despite the different terms used in relation with a variety of legal powers, the terminological aspects regarding competence norms will not be discussed. Kelsen explains four terms used in German law,[9] but for him the difference between these different cases of the empowering function of norms is not substantial, since they all correspond to a normative function that attributes an agent the possibility to create or apply norms.[10] So, even if various terms have been used in legal theory to describe this legal phenomenon, I will mainly use here the term "competence," unless otherwise required to preserve a specific author's narrative. The concept of competence will be understood, in a broad sense, as the capacity to create, modify or extinguish legal norms, and will be, hereinafter, used only in relation to a power given by a posited legal norm to an agent acting as a public authority.

Here the discussion on competence revolves around legal power, and legal power "is normative power, power confined to the realm of the 'ought'."[11] Competence norms are, then, an expression of a form of ought or duty -*sensu lato*-, of a *Sollen*; and so, empowerment may be considered in terms of Kelsen as a normative necessity, a "*Sollfunktion*",[12] and as such a normative function. Thus, the notion that underlies the concept of competence norm is that of power, and it regards an acquired power, vested in a person by law.

Neil MacCormick points out that "power in its widest sense is the ability to cause or to prevent change in some prevailing state of affairs."[13] Legal power can be therefore understood as the ability to produce changes according to law. Competence specifically is, then, as Ross wrote, "a special case of power" and the purpose of a competence norm is to regulate the ability and the conditions for its exercise. For him competence is "the legally established ability to create legal norms (or legal effects.)"[14] In this same sense Spaak mentions that "competence is regularly conferred on the agent by norms" and "the exercise of competence regularly affects norms."[15] Competence can consequently be considered as a normative power that brings about changes in legal relations and, also, legal effects.

[9] Kelsen (2000), pp. 150 ff.

[10] Kelsen (1991), pp. 102 ff.

[11] MacCormick (1997), p. 222.

[12] For Kelsen a norm decrees an 'ought', and 'ought'—that is '*Sollen*'—is for Kelsen a basic category, that expresses a normative necessity. Kelsen (1991), pp. 2, 9.

[13] MacCormick (1998), p. 494.

[14] Ross (1968), p. 130.

[15] Spaak (1994), pp. 2–11.

So, competence in a general sense can be understood as a normative power given to officials to create and apply legal norms and change legal positions. It results from the legal norms that attribute this power and regulate its exercise. Within the realm of law competence and its exercise depend, therefore, on norms. But, what kind of norms? To attempt an answer for the purpose of this inquiry the concept of norm will be next delimited.

2.3 The Semantic Conception of Norms

The delimitation of the notion of 'norm', as it will be here understood, is relevant because as von Wright acknowledges in the first chapter of *Norm and Action*: "The word 'norm' in English and the corresponding word in other languages is used in many senses and often with an unclear meaning."[16] And as Mazzarese has mentioned, this is also a source of problems for the possibility of resorting to deontic logic to explain legal norms.[17] In addition to the ambiguity of the term, it is known that disputes regarding competence norms specifically, are often due to the fact, that experts hold different conceptions regarding the ontological status of norms.

As Kelsen wrote, "the word 'norm' comes from the Latin *norma* and has been adopted in German to refer primarily, though not exclusively, to a command, a prescription, an order."[18] Accordingly, the term norm is generally used in reference to provisions as to how individuals should behave. Von Wright dedicates the first chapter of *Norm and Action* to the concept of norm and distinguishes three major types of norms. Prescriptions, or regulations, are one of them. In his opinion, they are, commands, permissions or prohibitions, which are given or issued to agents by a norm-authority.[19] A prescription is then a norm given by the legal authority to the effect that something can or must be done or not done.

'Norm' is a central concept of jurisprudence, and following Kelsen's opinion, the distinction between 'is' and 'ought' is at the basis of the concept of the norm,[20] and, also, of the analysis of the function of competence norms. For those reasons, the semantic conception of the norm is here adopted, not only because I consider it to be best suited for the analysis of competence norms from the deontic point of view, but also because it allows legal philosophers to separate the norm from its validity.[21] Hence, norms are here conceived as prescriptions, as von Wright does, resorting to the contrast 'descriptive and prescriptive' to distinguish norms from other things

---

[16] von Wright (1963), chap. I, section 1.

[17] Mazzarese (1991), p. 376.

[18] Kelsen (1991), pp. 1, 21, 106.

[19] von Wright (1963), chap. I, section 10.

[20] Kelsen (1941), pp. 54, 55.

[21] Validity questions regarding competence norms will not be here addressed.

with similar nature.[22] For the semantic conception, the normative sentence is the linguistic expression of a norm, and this is its content.[23]

These notions seem to point towards the hyletic conception of norms, which as explained by Alchourrón and Bulygin, conceives "norms are proposition-like entities, that is, the meanings of certain expressions called normative sentences."[24] A normative sentence is, accordingly, the linguistic expression of a norm, and a norm is considered its deontic meaning. In other words, normative sentences have prescriptive meaning, and are thus prescriptive in nature. Normative propositions, on the other hand, are descriptive propositions about a set or system of norms. We find indications of this line of thought in the *General Theory of Norms*, when Kelsen writes that a norm can be understood "as a meaning (or meaning-content)" that "is said to be that something 'ought' to be or 'ought' to happen -especially that a person ought to behave in a certain way."[25] And Ross in *Directives and Norms* holds that the norm as a linguistic phenomenon is a meaning content.[26]

In legal discourse different levels of analysis have been suggested from the semantic point of view, I here propose to distinguish three:

1. the norms, understood as the prescriptive meaning of a normative sentence,
2. the normative sentence, issued by the authority with competence to do so, which has a prescriptive function, and
3. the norm proposition that describes a legal sentence or a norm.

Many legal theorists have made a similar distinction, though maybe not expressly distinguishing three different levels of analysis as suggested before. This proposal is useful because it offers the possibility of considering for the analysis two prescriptive levels and a descriptive one, so that the structure and elements of normative sentences and norms as normative entities can be differentiated and better explained. Since normative sentences may need to be reconstructed from different legal sentences to their ideal form (see below Sect. 5), the term legal sentence is here used as a neutral term that refers to posited sentences, and it is not equivalent to normative sentence nor to norm.

Kelsen considered only two semantic levels. For him norms are "prescriptions concerning people's behaviour towards each other," and its "linguistic expression is

[22] See chap. 1, section 1. This contrast allows von Wright to distinguish between norm and norm-formulation, for him the norm-formulation are the words used in enunciating the norm. von Wright (1963), chap. VI, section 1.

[23] The terminology used in legal theory is not uniform, many terms have been used to distinguish at least two different types of entities from the linguistic perspective, and the theoretical foundation and meaning of the terms used often differ. On this issue see Alexy, who uses the terms '*Norm*' and '*Normsatz*' for example, Alexy (1996), pp. 42 ff.

[24] Alchourrón and Bulygin (2015), pp. 147, 148.

[25] Kelsen (1979–1991), p. 97.

[26] Ross speaks of directives, and a directive is an action-idea conceived as a pattern of behaviour Ross (1968), pp. 34, 80, 81.

an imperative or a *Sollen*-sentence."[27] Here the semantic conception of the norm can be perceived, though the first two levels mentioned before that have a prescriptive function, are considered as one by him—as in general most legal philosophers do.

From the linguistic perspective, normative sentences and norm propositions have a different function.[28] It is often said that legal discourse is prescriptive in opposition to descriptive discourse, and the prescriptive character is the key to a general characterization of norms. Norms and normative sentences have a prescriptive function, but norms, understood as the deontic contents of normative sentences, can only be known by interpreting the legal sentence.[29] Norm propositions on the other hand, are statements issued by legal scholars or persons interested in knowing their meaning and are therefore mere descriptions of the law. That is why they have no directive force. The term 'norm' will be hereinafter used to refer to the deontic meaning of legal sentences in positive law, and law is understood as a system of general and individual norms.

The nature of normative sentences that regulate competence is disputed not only due to the variety of legal sentences that can be identified as such, but also because they seem to be of a different kind since they do not usually express a command or permission, but rather establish some conditions (personal, procedural, and substantial conditions of the competence.) In Ross's opinion, for example, "a norm of competence prescribes the conditions for the creation of a norm,"[30] and in so doing competence norms could be conceived as the content of legal sentences that establish the conditions of the exercise of the power given to the specific officials to create and apply norms. Consequently, competence norms could be considered as prescriptions because those conditions must be satisfied to create or apply norms, and as von Wright wrote: "human acts through which norms come into existence may themselves be obligatory or permitted or forbidden."[31] It could then be said that competence norms—as genus—are the meaning of legal sentences that establish the conditions of the exercise of that power, and therefore, norms in the strict sense.[32]

---

[27] Kelsen (1991), pp. 1, 2.

[28] Here function means what can be done with words, language has three major functions: informative, expressive and directive, and two less common types of use: ceremonial and performative. *Cfr.*. Copi et al. (2014), pp. 68, 69.

[29] For Ilkka Niiniluoto to say that a norm is the content or meaning of a normative sentence is an interpretative statement. Niiniluoto (1991), p. 367.

[30] Ross (1968), p. 130.

[31] von Wright (1963), chap. X, section 1.

[32] This does not mean though that there is only one type of competence to be exercised, but rather that the competence norm regulates human action and that often it is posited in different normative sentences.

3 On the Function of Hart's Secondary Rules

Nowadays legal systems are usually considered as consisting of two kinds of norms: duty-imposing norms and norms conferring powers to issue other norms. This statement reflects one of the most important theses of contemporary legal philosophy.[33] Hart's distinction between 'primary' and 'secondary rules', as he calls them, explains the complexity of law as a dynamic system.[34] But despite its importance, in my opinion, this distinction does not generate a different category of norms that would imply that secondary rules are not prescriptions in the strict sense.

To speak of competence norms implies a dynamic conception of law. The legal system is thus created and modified in accordance with procedures that it establishes. It follows then, as MacCormick wrote, that "when we represent a normative order in a dynamic way, we represent it in terms of the norms that regulate change, individuated as norms of competence, power-conferring rules, institutive rules of legal institutions,"[35] and so competence norms are placed in a prominent position in the legal system. Of this same view is Kelsen for whom it is undeniable, that, "[s]ince the law regulates its own creation and application, the normative function of empowering plays a particularly important role in law."[36]

Hart's model of law as the union of primary and secondary rules is the result of the analysis and criticisms he makes of the theories that conceive law as a set of coercive orders. For him, it is not only "the key to the science of jurisprudence,"[37] but it is "at the centre of a legal system."[38] The identification of the rules of behaviour as primary is indicative of his conception of law.[39] That is why he considers power-conferring rules as accessory to the other rules.[40] Nevertheless, he does not deny that empowering norms are important and needed to remedy the static character of primary rules.[41]

The criterion used by Hart for the distinction is the purpose for which norms are given, they are either to direct human conduct or to regulate the legal system. So, primary rules are rules of obligation, while secondary rules like the rules of

[33] Not only Hart and Raz considered that distinction, for Ross for example, legal norms are divided in two groups according to their content: norms of conduct and norms of competence or procedure, Ross (1974), p. 32.

[34] Hart (1979), pp. 98, 99.

[35] MacCormick (1997), p. 233.

[36] Kelsen (1991), p. 102.

[37] Hart (1979), p. 81.

[38] Hart (1979), p. 99.

[39] Ross emphasizes instead the relevance of the competence norms. For him, "legal rules govern the structure and functioning of the legal machinery", the whole set of institutions and agencies, Ross (1968), p. 91.

[40] He considers them 'parasitic' upon or secondary to primary rules. Hart (1979), p. 81.

[41] Hart (1979), p. 94.

recognition, of change and adjudication regulate the legal system.[42] For Hart, to the basic type of legal norms belong those that require human beings "to do or abstain from certain actions," that is, duties. The secondary type of rules, confer powers to introduce, modify or extinguish rules. For him, secondary rules are concerned with primary rules because they "specify the ways in which the primary rules may be conclusively ascertained, introduced, eliminated, varied, and the fact of their violation conclusively determined."[43] He so attributes a different function to each type of rules that results in the distinction of two seemingly distinct groups of legal norms.[44] This has led scholars to various interpretations of the nature of the secondary rules.

So, secondary rules can be identified by their function regarding other norms in the legal system. Following Hart's classification we can speak of three functions regarding what the norms perform: the identification of the norms that are part of the legal system, the transformation of those norms, and the application of norms to concrete cases, which correspond to the rules of recognition, of change and of adjudication, respectively. The rule of recognition, that according to Hart serves as a criterion for the identification of the rules of the legal system,[45] will not be discussed here as a competence norm, because such an enterprise would require a special investigation.

But what is the function of competence norms for Hart? The answer to this question requires that we explore the category of secondary rules to which they may belong. For Hart, the function of rules of change is to confer powers, 'define' legal concepts, identify the competent officials, and 'define' the procedure to be followed.[46] Rules of change establish the competent organs or individuals to give or eliminate norms, as well as the procedures and conditions to be followed, so we can safely say, that competence norms are rules of change. Adjudication rules warrant in each case the specific prescriptive content of the other norms of the legal system. There are different kinds of norms in this group depending on their content, because they enable someone with authority, establish and organize the courts and regulate the procedures to follow. So, among adjudication rules at least those that enable judges can be considered as norms of competence *stricto sensu*.

The main object of these two types of secondary rules is to empower and establish procedures. Adjudication rules and rules of change are concerned with organs and institutions. Even if their content may vary, an important group of norms that belong to this type of secondary norms are norms of competence. That is, norms that

---

[42] So defined, secondary rules can be conceived as metarules. For Hart the structure that results from the combination of primary and secondary rules is not only at the heart of the legal system, but also "a powerful tool of analysis". Hart (1979), p. 98.

[43] Hart (1979), p. 94.

[44] Hart speaks of "the different social functions which different types of legal rule perform", Hart (1979), p. 38.

[45] Hart (1979), p. 95.

[46] Hart (1979), p. 97. It is important to point out, as Bulygin does, that "Hart does not actually say that power-conferring rules are definitions, but it is remarkable that he uses repeatedly the verb "define" in connection with such rules". Bulygin (2015), p. 277.

empower some agents or institutions to create and apply the law. These norms are usually expressed in a regulative or behavioural manner, as permissions or obligations. Some of them, nevertheless, seem to be written out as definitions.

In Hart's opinion, primary and secondary rules are of a different kind because the latter do not impose duties, they confer legal powers and cannot "be construed as orders backed by threats."[47] However, we could rethink this idea. As Kelsen wrote in the second edition of the *Reine Rechtslehre*, the empowering function of the legal order refers only to human behaviour.[48] So, the purpose of issuing competence norms would be to direct the conduct of officials, the persons qualified by the legal system, to act in accordance with the powers given. It seems that Hart would agree, at least regarding private powers, when he says that the purpose of power-conferring rules is to "confer on individuals power to vary their initial positions under the primary rules."[49] It must be noted, though, that since Hart does not distinguish functionally public from private powers,[50] private power-conferring rules can be considered as secondary rules. He maintains though that the "kinship of these rules with the rules of change involved in the notion of legislation is clear,"[51] because part of their function is to create norms. Competence norms can so be conceived as norms that direct human conduct, that of public officials, to perform some action related to the transformation of the legal system.

According to Hart, legal rules that confer powers on private individuals may relate to capacity or minimum personal qualifications required for the exercise of the power, or the conditions of such exercise.[52] Similarly, public power-conferring rules enable officials to create or apply norms. In his opinion, public legal powers seldom seem to be orders given to officials (legislative, administrative, or judicial,) because rules of adjudication, for example, "do not impose duties but confer judicial powers and a special status on declarations about the breach of obligations."[53] For him, rules imposing legal duties related to the exercise of public power are additional to competence norms.[54] And that is why he maintains that secondary rules are on a "different level" from primary rules, "though they may be reinforced by further rules imposing duties on judges to adjudicate."[55]

In my view, Hart's distinction does not imply that one group of norms excludes the other completely, since legal sentences may contain a duty and a rule of

---

[47] Hart (1979), p. 79.

[48] "*Die als Ermächtigung bezeichnete Funktion der Rechtsordnung bezieht sich nur auf menschliches Verhalten.*" Kelsen (2000), p. 150.

[49] Hart (1979), p. 96.

[50] Hart (1979), p. 81.

[51] Hart (1979), p. 96.

[52] Hart (1979), p. 28.

[53] Hart (1979), p. 97.

[54] By calling them 'additional' rules he seems to intend to exclude them as secondary rules, and specifically as competence norms. Hart (1979), p. 29.

[55] Hart (1979), p. 97.

procedure, as is the case of competence norms, for example. Hart's distinction serves the purpose to explain that a legal system is dynamic and, therefore, more complex than a mere set of norms because it regulates its transformation. Yet, this classification is not intended to clarify the nature of legal norms but instead that of the legal system. It sets a methodological assumption for its explanation: that of considering that norms have diverse functions, still this does not necessarily result in different normative types.

To sum up: we can say that for Hart, the primary function of law is to guide human behaviour. Norms directed to officials, should, therefore, also be considered as primarily guiding their behaviour. Nevertheless, for him, the function of secondary norms is to enable for the application and transformation of the law, which includes making laws and the power to carry out sanctions. Yet, to ensure this end, shouldn't competence norms guide the officials' behaviour? In my opinion, to reduce competence norms to the functions related to the transformation of the legal system does not exclude the possibility that competence norms direct the acts or actions of officials to whom they are given.

4 Kelsen's View on the Function of Competence Norms

As was mentioned before, the term function is polysemic,[56] and so, when we speak of the legal system, for example, it seems that it is mainly used as equivalent to the purpose of law, of giving norms. In relation to a norm, on the other hand, it can refer to what can be done or achieved with it, or how it operates from the deontic point of view. It can also mean that a norm can execute or perform something as we will see from Kelsen's theses on the function of norms as suggested in his *General Theory of Norms*.

Let us start by reflecting with Kelsen upon the function of norms. For him, if the function of a norm is conceived in relation to the production of some legal effect, or the transformation of the legal system or the position of the norm subject, we can speak of a normative function.[57] In that sense, we should recall that before addressing the diverse functions of the norms, Kelsen commences by stating that every norm establishes an ought, a '*Sollen*'. He does however clarify that the term 'ought' is used in a more general sense than that in ordinary speech when holding

---

[56] Among the multiple meanings we can find in the dictionary, for the explanation of the function of the norms, I have decided to focus on: perform, execute, purpose, act, operate, work as, action, activity and performance. Webster's (1951), p. 1019.

[57] The function is called normative in relation to the prescriptive nature of law, for as Kelsen wrote: "*Das Recht gebietet, erlaubt, ermächtigt, es 'lehrt' nicht*". Kelsen (2000), p. 73.

that every norm decrees an ought, because in so doing it includes all possible normative functions such as command, empower,[58] permit or derogate.[59]

But what does Kelsen mean by the function of a norm? The first clue is that for him law is an order of human conduct,[60] another is that he considers that "the specific function of a norm is to *command* a certain behaviour,"[61] and he understands 'to command' as "synonymous with 'to prescribe', as opposed to 'to describe'."[62] Hence, the purpose of every norm is to regulate behaviour, but they can be differentiated according to their function. As to the prescriptive character of competence, Kelsen expressly maintained that "an empowering norm decrees an 'ought' and that an 'ought' obtains even in the case of a permission- since empowering and permitting are essentially related to an Ought- then the word 'ought' expresses the three *normative functions* (commanding, empowering, and permitting.)"[63] Consequently, all legal norms, no matter their function, have a prescriptive character, even competence norms, because they establish an ought.[64] One could thus conclude, that for Kelsen all norms are therefore equal in nature, but they can have a different function, and they are different because of what they give effect to in normative terms. The notion of function in Kelsen cannot therefore be understood as purpose, because the end of every norm is to regulate behaviour.

It seems, then, that the only thing the normative functions have in common is that they express a form of ought, because Kelsen considers the normative function of *empowering* to be different from that of commanding or permitting.[65] Unfortunately, he does not elaborate on this matter. Nevertheless, he points out that the normative function of empowering norms is to confer on an individual, or body of individuals, the power to posit and apply norms. Accordingly, a competence norm "empowers certain individuals to create legal norms or to apply legal norms."[66] And so, the

[58] Even if Kelsen explained the use of different terms and distinguished between private and public power, when he speaks about 'empowering' he does not use the use term competence, but his examples allow to differentiate the cases when he speaks of public power. For those cases I use here the term competence.

[59] It should be noted that derogation is explicitly added to the functions of the norms in 1979, Kelsen (1991), p. 1. In 1960, Kelsen only considers that norms command, permit and empower especially someone to issue norms ("*selbst Normen zu setzen*"). Kelsen (2000), p. 4.

[60] "*Die Normen einer Rechtsordnung regeln menschliches Verhalten*", Kelsen (2000), p. 32.

[61] Kelsen maintains that if the object of a norm is characterized as a behaviour, then there is no need to distinguish between commanding and prohibiting, these are different forms of duty. Kelsen (1991), p. 96.

[62] Kelsen (1991), p. 96.

[63] Kelsen (1991), p. 97.

[64] Von Wright is of the same view, for him: "Norms prescribe something and do not describe anything", von Wright (1998), p. 379.

[65] Kelsen (1991), p. 103.

[66] Kelsen (1991), p. 102.

content of competence norms includes the two types of action within the law that Kelsen speaks of: creation and application of legal norms.[67]

According to Kelsen, the functions of norms are to command, empower, permit and derogate, and competence norms can be conceived as duties regarding the power of positing norms, even if not always expressed as such, because as he mentions, usually the legislative organ, the courts and other officials are commanded to act, and only in those cases its omission is illegal.[68] Further support for this claim is that in his opinion: "Certain organs are empowered to create and apply law; they are not permitted to do so; and empowering is a different normative function".[69]

Kelsen also maintains that a norm can "empower someone to behave in a certain way,"[70] and in so doing it seems as if a specific way of action is determined by the norm. Since for him the purpose of norms is to command a behaviour, one could conclude that it is possible to command the exercise of the power given. Especially because as it was already mentioned, the act empowered can be commanded.[71] So, regarding the deontic status of competence norms, this could mean that they can be expressed not only in terms of permission but also of obligation, specifically regarding norms that regulate normative actions or a judge's duty to render a decision.[72]

As to what regards the difference between the function of commanding and that of empowering, Kelsen considers that it can be "expressed in the difference between *observing* (or *violating*) a norm and *applying* a norm."[73] In his opinion, "only a norm which commands (or prohibits) a certain behaviour can be observed or violated."[74] Although I can relate to the idea that the concept of obedience may not be the best suited regarding competence norms, it does not seem to me a sufficient argument to differentiate the empowering function, nor to deprive competence norms of their directive character. To speak about observing or complying with the competence norm could be acceptable rather regarding the satisfaction or fulfillment of the material fact of the normative sentence as von Wright does.[75] In relation to competence norms, it is perhaps a better idea to use the term satisfiability, particularly

---

[67] Even if for Kelsen it is incorrect to distinguish between these acts because creation is always application except in the borderline cases. Kelsen (2000), pp. 240 ff.

[68] Kelsen (1991), p. 103.

[69] Here he distinguishes though empowering from "permitting in a *positive* sense", which for him is an indirect function of the norm that repeals or restricts the validity of another norm. Kelsen (1991), pp. 98, 99, 101.

[70] Kelsen (1991), p. 97.

[71] Kelsen (1991), p. 103.

[72] Further support for this claim comes from the following passage for example: "Judges are empowered by statutes to apply general legal norms to concrete cases. As a rule they are also commanded to do so" Kelsen (1991), p. 103.

[73] Kelsen (1991), p. 104.

[74] Kelsen (1991), p. 105.

[75] "Given a norm, one may consider what has to or may be done in order to satisfy it", von Wright (1998), p. 379.

because the material fact (*Tatbestand*) of the norm can be fulfilled. In the case of a deviation from the prescribed content of the competence norm different legal consequences may arise such as liability for acting without competence or ultra-vires, and these could result in the application of sanctions.[76]

5 Competence Norms *qua* Prescriptions

In legal theory competence norms have been conceived as autonomous or in connection to other norms, such as rules of conduct.[77] In the first case, competence norms are understood as rules that while conferring powers establish either a permission or an obligation. In the second one, the competence norm is explained in relation to the results that the exercise of the power produces in terms of the creation or application of a norm.

The question to be answered here is whether legal sentences that regulate competence are prescriptions in the strict sense, that is, whether they guide some conduct. So, in accordance with the previously established theoretical and conceptual background, competence norms are analyzed to assess their nature as prescriptions. In my opinion, to achieve this, it is convenient to study the form and content of competence norms to identify their logical structure and the elements of the norms following von Wright's proposal.[78] The theory of norm-kernels has been chosen for its explanatory properties, not to analyze the logical relations of these norms,[79] even if it only takes into account the character, the content and the condition of application of the norms, omitting from the consideration the authority and subject which are defining elements of competence norms.[80] This procedure requires to differentiate the logical structure of the norm-kernel from the ideal structure of the normative sentence.[81]

[76] Other consequences are possible regarding the validity of the act, but that discussion exceeds the purpose of the present paper.

[77] As Ross does in *On Law and Justice* by stating that competence norms are indirectly expressed norms of conduct directed to the courts, Ross (1974), p. 33; or Kelsen by establishing the connection between the competence norm and a norm that establishes a sanction. Kelsen (2000), p. 150.

[78] von Wright (1963), chap. V. Paulson resorts to this theory in 1988 to analyze the ideal form of the norm in Kelsen's writings.

[79] Because as von Wright mentioned the formal apparatus for dealing with norm-kernels he developed seems to be inadequate for the analysis of competence norms, as norms of higher order. von Wright (1963), chap. X, section 1.

[80] I have previously attempted to demonstrate the prescriptive nature of transitory rules—paradigmatic legal sentences that are often regarded as something else but norms-, by identifying their norm-kernel. Huerta (2009), pp. 181–192.

[81] This process requires of course the interpretation of the legal sentences.

For von Wright, a prescription is a norm, and in his opinion: "Generally speaking prescriptions are commands or permissions given by someone in a position of authority to someone in a position of subject."[82] Since prescriptions are given to direct human behaviour, distinctive features are to be identified such as a 'norm-authority' that issues them and the 'norm-subject(s)' they are addressed to. And legal norms, as prescriptions, have six 'components': the character, the content, the condition of application, the authority, the subject(s) and the occasion. He maintains that there are two more things which belong to every prescription without however being 'components' of prescriptions in the same sense as the above six. These are the promulgation and the sanction,[83] because they are promulgated to be known, and a sanction is attached for its effectiveness. The character, the content and the condition of application form the norm-kernel that for von Wright constitutes the logical structure that prescriptions have in common with other types of norms.[84] The authority, the subject(s), and the occasion on the other hand, are specific characteristics of prescriptions that do not belong to other types of norms.[85]

Since the object of the analysis are competence norms it is important to mention that for the logical analysis of norms von Wright distinguishes two different kinds of norms in a legal system using the criterion of 'normative action', which is the human action of issuing (or cancelling) of norms (prescriptions). He calls norms of the first order those whose contents are not normative acts, that is commands and prohibitions.[86] Norms whose contents are normative acts are for him norms of higher order, and for the analysis he considers only positive prescriptions in this category.[87] Competence norms are hence norms of higher order. In addition, they are often considered by scholars as metarules, because they regulate the application of other rules.

As we will see, in the case of competence norms three elements of the norms are interrelated: the authority, the subject, and the content of the norm. The authority is the agent who gives a prescription, "who orders, permits or prohibits certain subjects to do certain things on certain occasions."[88] In the case of competence norms, it is some higher order official enabled to create norms that empower other agents, and the subject is always some public institution or person holding public office. The subject of a norm is the agent to whom it is directed, in the case of competence norms

---

[82] von Wright (1963), chap. I, section 5.

[83] von Wright (1963), chap. V, section 1.

[84] von Wright (1963), chap. V, section 1.

[85] Hart also considers some of these elements as it can be noticed for example when he says that laws are general in content and regarding the addressee, and they are also general in relation to the occasion, because they are standing orders to be followed time after time by classes of persons. Hart (1979), p. 23.

[86] Von Wright does nevertheless mention that "commands and prohibitions hold the most prominent position, though maybe not the only one", and in so doing seems to suggest that there are other possibilities, such as permissions for example. von Wright (1963), chap. X, section 4.

[87] von Wright (1963), chap. X, section 1.

[88] von Wright (1963), chap. V, section 7.

it is correlated to the content of the norm, normative action, thus the subjects of higher order norms are the agents to whom those norms are addressed to and are thus normative authorities of lower order.

Regarding the subject, for Kelsen to speak of the norm-addressee refers to the fact that "a norm is 'directed' to a person" and this means "that it is the behaviour of a person, human behaviour, which is obligatory."[89] The norm-subject of competence norms is not the legal system but a person that should act according to the norm to produce some intended legal effect.[90] For Kelsen the norm subject of competence norms are the empowered organs. So, following this argument competence norms regulate behaviour, not other norms, not the legal system, and could therefore be characterized as prescriptions.

The term 'content' refers to the regulated behaviour, what ought to be done, that is certain generic acts or forbearances. The content of competence norms, or in terms of von Wright, of a higher order norm, is a normative act "of issuing or cancelling certain norms (prescriptions) of the first order."[91] The 'character' indicates whether something ought to be done be it an obligation, prohibition, or permission, and it can, but need not be, expressed by a deontic verb.[92] The character is indicative of an ought, and the prescriptive nature of the norm.[93]

The occasion refers to the opportunity to fulfill the content of the norm, to the specific corresponding circumstances of time and place, or in other words, to the where and when to act, which is very important in the case of competence norms, especially because in my opinion, whenever the occasion is satisfied, the competence has to be exercised.[94]

Von Wright calls a condition of application "the condition which must be satisfied if there is to be an opportunity for doing the thing which is the content of a given norm."[95] It must be noted that the fact that prescriptions have a condition of application does not entail that all normative sentences are formulated in a conditional form. That conditions are a relevant element of the norm can also be perceived in Kelsen when he writes that all general norms can prescribe a behaviour but only under specific conditions.[96] Nevertheless, following the criteria of the expression of the conditions of applications von Wright distinguishes two types of prescriptions,

---

[89] Kelsen (1979–1991), p. 8.

[90] Hart holds that power conferring norms cannot be considered as directed only to officials, because there are norms that regulate private powers, but here competence norms have been defined as norms that attribute public powers, so the norm-addressee is an official. Hart (1979), p. 80.

[91] von Wright (1963), chap. X, section 3.

[92] For him, "Norms of the 'ought'—character can also be called obligation-norms and norms of the 'may'—character permissive norms". von Wright (1963), chap. V, section 2.

[93] In this sense, Ross stated that "the operator distinguishes a directive from a proposition, it indicates that the topic (being an action-idea) is presented as a pattern of behaviour". Ross (1968), p. 116.

[94] von Wright (1963), chap. V, section 10.

[95] von Wright (1963), chap. V, section 5.

[96] Kelsen (1991), p. 20.

categorical and hypothetical.[97] So, competence norms could be expressed categorically or hypothetically but there will always be some conditions for the exercise of the competence.

For Kelsen, a general norm is expressed in a sentence,[98] and in his opinion "general norms are hypothetical", that is abstract formulations that "attach a generally specified consequence decreed to be obligatory to a generally specified condition."[99] In the *General Theory of Norms* he holds that "the relation of condition and consequence contained in a norm" is a logical relation.[100] So, the norms that establish a relation between a condition and a consequence have the logical structure of a conditional, and the hypothetical structure could be considered as the logical form of the normative sentence. This does not mean though that every legal sentence is expressed in a conditional form, only that it can be reformulated into it. When analyzing the relation between a general and an individual norm, Kelsen states that the "higher norm contains three concepts: that of a competent organ, that of a conditioning state of affairs, and that of a legal consequence."[101] In von Wright's terms, we might say: the norm-subject, the condition of application, and the sanction.

When Hart comments on the idea that norms are conditional in their form, he mentions that if so, then sometimes recasting would be needed, to specify the conditions under which a legal duty arises.[102] The legal 'if-clause' has thus as antecedent the conditions for the legal consequence. And legal norms, including power-conferring norms can be restated in the conditional form. But since from the semantic perspective, norms are the meaning of normative sentences, then it is the posited sentences which must be reformulated into the conditional form, as their logical structure.

It is generally accepted among legal theorists, that the ideal or logical structure of the norm—rather of the normative sentence—consists of the material fact or hypothesis, a copula or normative link (a linking verb) and a sanction or legal consequence. The logical form of this structure would be the implication.[103] But legal sentences do not always express these elements or do not do so in that order. According to Schreiber it is a question of logical analysis to make explicit these elements.[104] Nevertheless, one could say that the elements of the ideal structure of a normative sentence are the hypothesis (the condition), the normative link (usually the verb 'to

97 The difference is that the condition of application of categorical prescriptions is given with its content, while those of hypothetical prescriptions require further conditions. von Wright (1963), chap. IX, section 1.

98 "A norm is general if it decrees some generally specified behaviour to be obligatory". Kelsen (1991), p. 7.

99 He holds also though, that some individual norms can also be hypothetical. Kelsen (1991), p. 266.

100 Kelsen (1991), p. 266.

101 Kelsen (1991), p. 262.

102 Hart (1979), p. 37.

103 In this sense see, e.g., Kelsen (1994), p. 22, Schreiber (1966), pp. 9 ff, or Larenz (1994), pp. 243, 244.

104 Schreiber (1966), pp. 24, 25.

be' that is deontically translated as a duty or permission) and a sanction (understood as legal consequence, that is, rights or duties).

That is why the notion of sanction is also considered in the analysis of legal sentences. For that purpose, the concept of sanction is here understood as legal consequences rather than as punishment because, in my opinion, legal sentences should be given so that legal effects can be produced, a legal position be modified, or the legal system be transformed. The fact that human conduct made obligatory by norms requires to be backed by some consequence is the possibility to a wider interpretation of the concept of sanction as legal consequence. Engish shares this understanding. In his opinion the legal consequence includes rights and duties, and even authorizations, and in his view not every legal consequence implies carrying out a coercive act.[105]

The main idea for this conceptualization of the sanction is that law is not merely a repressive system, rights, liberties, permissions need to be warranted. And the concept of norm is best construed around the notion of consequence. Just like any human action produces an effect, actions regulated by norms will produce some kind of legal consequence, but it does not need to be a negative consequence. To speak of a sanction in relation to competence norms means that not acting in conformity with the norm will result in liability, not only in some degree of invalidity of the norm created.

To sum up, the normative sentence has a conditional form. But as it was already mentioned, legal sentences are not always phrased in such a manner. That is why the elements of this ideal structure must be identified in the legal system and brought together. This procedure requires a systematic interpretation of the law to reconstruct the normative sentence and reformulate it to the ideal form: "If A then B." To that end the conception of the law as a system of norms that form a unity is best suited because it allows to connect the normative sentences. A similar proposal was made by Kelsen with the thesis of the non-independent norm for a different purpose, to link the normative sentences with a coercive sanction, and so connect different legal sentences to present a complete normative sentence in the ideal form.[106]

Regarding competence norms, the powers, the subject, the procedure, and the obligation to act accordingly that are regulated in different legal sentences could be reformulated as a unit. Considered separately, they do not seem to be prescriptions strictly speaking, but due to the unity of the legal system these sentences can be reconstructed as a normative sentence whose content is a competence norm that might establish an obligation for a norm subject, a public official.

In brief, a competence norm is issued by a norm-giving authority and is directed to a subject that due to the content of the norm will also be considered a norm giving authority. The character is a form of ought, there is a condition of application, and the occasion can be general or particular. Yet, given the occasion, the competence

[105] Engisch (2011), pp. 13–17.

[106] Kelsen (2000), pp. 55–59.

must be exercised.[107] Since all these elements can be identified in competence norms, be it in one or more legal sentences, it can be said that they can be called prescriptions in their own right.

If competence norms are prescriptions, then their function is to direct the conduct of officials to do or refrain from doing something—positing or applying norms—in a certain way on given occasions. So, one could say that the primary function of competence norms is to prescribe a certain form of normative action to be performed according to the established conditions on every occasion as regulated.

6 Concluding Remarks

Hart's distinction between primary and secondary norms is not about differentiating types of norms or assigning a different nature or structure to the norms. It is rather about explaining the legal system in terms of the different function of some norms, specifically competence norms. Yet, it does not entail that competence norms do not have more than one function. Legal norms can indeed be distinguished from each other by their normative function but not their structure.

Based on the analysis made following von Wright, we can say that competence norms can be conceived as prescriptions. And even when expressed in terms of possibility, it can be said that, given their nature, they express a form of 'ought' that requires that the competence be exercised when the occasion prescribed in the norm is satisfied. To identify its character, the competence norm may need to be reconstructed to the ideal form of the normative sentence from different legal sentences, including those that expressly impose a duty to exercise the power. Competence is a power vested on the authority and responsibility is therefore always attached to its exercise. The result of the normative action may be invalidated though when competence norms are not properly satisfied, but that is another question.

As it can be perceived, I consider competence norms, that is, public power conferring norms, as norms of conduct, deontic sentences that prescribe some action as obligatory or possible, or maybe both, even if the legal sentences are not formulated in such a manner. The normative function of a competence norm, a prescription, is directive, to guide a public official's behaviour, and it operates in a way that it enables a subject to create, eliminate, or apply norms and, in so doing, to transform the legal system, it can thus be said that competence norms have multiple functions.

[107] Paulson mentions that for Kelsen in 1979 the components that serve to identify competence norms are the hypothetical form, an 'empowering' modality and the legal official as addressee. Paulson (1998), p. 63.

References

Alchourrón C, Bulygin E (2015 (1981)) The expressive conception of norms. In: Bernal C, Huerta C, Mazzarese T, Moreso JJ, Navarro PE, Paulson SL (eds) Essays in legal philosophy. Eugenio Bulygin. OUP, Oxford, pp 146–170

Alexy R (1996) Theorie der Grundrechte. Suhrkamp, Frankfurt am Main

Bulygin E (2015 (1992)) On norms of competence. In: Bernal C, Huerta C, Mazzarese T, Moreso JJ, Navarro PE, Paulson SL (eds) Essays in legal philosophy. Eugenio Bulygin. OUP, Oxford, pp 272–283

Copi IM, Cohen C, McMahon K (2014) Introduction to logic. Pearson New International Edition, New York

Engisch K (2011) Introducción al pensamiento jurídico. Editorial Comares, Granada

Ferrater Mora J (1994) Diccionario de Filosofía, vol II, E-J. Ariel, Barcelona

Hart HLA (1979) The concept of law, 2nd edn. OUP, Oxford

Huerta C (2009) Artículos transitorios y derogación. In: Huerta C Teoría del Derecho. Cuestiones Relevantes. UNAM, México, pp 175–202

Kelsen H (1941) The pure theory of law and analytical jurisprudence. Harv Law Rev 55(1):44–70

Kelsen H (1991) General theory of norms. Clarendon Press, Oxford

Kelsen H (1994) Reine Rechtslehre. Einleitung in die Rechtswissenschaftliche Problematik. 1. Auflage. Scientia Verlag, Aalen, Darmstadt

Kelsen H (2000) Reine Rechtslehre. 2. Auflage 1960. Verlag Österreich, Wien

Larenz K (1994) Metodología de la ciencia del derecho. Editorial Ariel, Barcelona

Lindahl L (1977) Position and change. A study in law and logic. D. Reidel Publishing Co., Dordrecht

MacCormick N (1997) Law as institutional normative order. Rechtstheorie 28:219–234

MacCormick N (1998) Powers and power-conferring norms. In: Paulson SL, Litschewski Paulson B (eds) Normativity and norms. Critical perspectives on Kelsenian themes. Clarendon Press, Oxford, pp 492–506

Mazzarese T (1991) Deontic logic as logic of legal norms. Two main sources of problems. Ratio Juris 4(3):374–392

Niiniluoto I (1991) Norm propositions defended. Ratio Juris 4(3):367–373

Paulson SL (1998) An empowerment theory of legal norms. Ratio Juris 1(1):58–72

Raz J (2009) The authority of law. Essays on law and morality. OUP, Oxford

Ross A (1968) Directives and norms. Routledge and Kegan Paul, London

Ross A (1974) On law and justice. University of California Press, Oakland

Schreiber R (1966) Die Geltung von Rechtsnormen. Springer Verlag, Berlin-Heidelberg-New York

Spaak T (1994) The concept of competence. An essay on conceptual analysis. Dartmouth, England

von Wright GH (1963) Norm and action. A logical enquiry. Routledge and Kegan Paul, London. https://www.giffordlectures.org/lectures/norm-and-action

von Wright GH (1998) Is and ought. In: Paulson SL, Litschewski Paulson B (eds) Normativity and norms. Critical perspectives on Kelsenian themes. Clarendon Press, Oxford, pp 364–382

Webster's New International Dictionary (1951). Second edition. Merriam, Springfield

Part III
Legal Power and Constitutive Rules

Recognition

Riccardo Guastini

Abstract (1) The rule of recognition (RR) is a conceptual criterion for identifying the rules of a definite legal system. It is not a duty-imposing rule. It is neither the constitution of the legal system at hand nor the set of its rules of change. Most of all, it is not a legal rule belonging to the system—rather it belongs to the meta-legal language of those who aim to identify a legal system. (2) The RR of legal sources (statutes, the constitution, and so forth) is to be distinguished from the RR of legal norms, understood as the meaning contents of legal sources, that has to take into account the interpretive practices of judges and legal scholars. As to the RR of norms, a further distinction is in order: the RR of valid norms, the RR of existing norms, and the RR of the norms in force. Each of such rules incorporates different criteria. (3) Two "statements of recognition" can be distinguished: (i) "The norm N is valid (existing, in force)", (ii) "If these, as defined by the RR, are the criteria of recognition, then the norm N is valid (existing, in force)". The sentence (i) uses the RR and, in this sense, is "internal", but does not entail any kind of axiological acceptance, the RR being a definition, not a norm of behaviour. The sentence (ii), in turn, does not use, but only mentions the RR. In both cases, there is no connection between the recognition statements and the moral or political acceptance (the binding force) of the legal system.

R. Guastini (✉)
Istituto Tarello per la Filosofia del diritto, Dipartimento di Giurisprudenza, Università di Genova, Genoa, Italy
e-mail: guastini@unige.it

G. Villa-Rosas, T. Spaak (eds.), *Legal Power and Legal Competence*, Law and Philosophy Library 140, https://doi.org/10.1007/978-3-031-28555-4_7

1 What It Is

In view of identifying the rules of a definite legal system (the Italian, the French, the international. . .), and therefore the system itself, a criterion of identification is necessary (Bulygin 1976). In the legal-philosophical jargon introduced by Hart, such a criterion is usually called "rule of recognition" (RR).[1]

The RR, as its name aims to suggest, is a conceptual criterion for recognizing—that is, identifying extensionally—a definite legal system. A criterion of identification is but a definition: namely, an informative definition that reconstructs the (conceptual) identification practices of jurists and judges of the legal system at hand.

It can be maintained that, in a sense (namely, in Searle's sense[2]), the RR is a constitutive rule.[3] Constitutive rules, however, are neither descriptive nor prescriptive sentences—they are but definitions (although in a peculiar formulation).

According to Hart, the RR is an object of "acceptance" by legal officials and scholars. Nonetheless, it is worth stressing: first, that accepting and using a definition is quite different from accepting and using a norm (a rule of behaviour); second, that accepting the criterion of identification of a legal system is quite different from (and does not entail in any way) the axiological acceptance of the identified system and/or of the "binding force" of its rules.

2 What It Is Not

(i) The RR is not a norm of behaviour—a duty-imposing rule—commanding judges to apply valid law.[4] If a legal system does include a rule like that, such a rule has to be identified, and the RR is the criterion of identification.

Take, for example, the case of the Italian legal system. Art. 101.2 of the Constitution establishes: "Judges are subject only to the law". Such a provision has a manifold normative content, most of all because of the implications of the adverb "only" (Guastini 1994, p. 140 ff.). But, no doubt, one of the rules it expresses is that judges are under the obligation to apply the law. In other words, in the Italian legal

---

[1] Hart (1961). See Bobbio (1970, 1975); Raz (1971); Bulygin (1976, 1991a, b); Hacker (1977); MacCormick (1978); Ruiz Manero (1990, 1991); Caracciolo (1991); Muffato (2010); Ratti (2012a, b); Burazin and Ratti (2020).

[2] Searle (1969). A different concept of "constitutive rule" (*norma costitutiva*) can be found in Italian legal theoretical literature: Carcaterra (1974, 1979). See Guastini (2008).

[3] Bulygin (1976) and Vilajosana (2019).

[4] This is the prevailing view in current literature. Such a view can be traced back to Raz (1971), p. 93. According to Lamond (2013), p. 115, "the rule of recognition is a duty-imposing rule: it not only provides the criteria for the identification of the rules of the system but imposes a duty on officials to use those criteria in identifying the laws of the system". In Italian literature, the same view was held by Scarpelli (1965); see Guastini (1988).

system the judicial obligation to apply the law stems from an expressed positive constitutional norm.

Nobody would say that art. 101.2 of the Constitution is the ultimate RR of the Italian legal order. Moreover, any Italian jurist would take as quite bizarre the idea that the judicial obligation to apply the law arises not from this constitutional provision, but from a further (meta-constitutional) rule, the RR: this odd idea would be perceived as a "needless reduplication" (how Hart would say).[5]

(ii) The RR is not a "basic norm". In the sense that, unlike Kelsen's *Grundnorm*, its validity is not presupposed—the RR is neither valid nor invalid. Most of all, the RR does not provide any dynamic foundation to the validity (and binding force) of the whole legal system.[6] Founding is different from recognizing.

Any legal rule R finds its own dynamic ground of validity in a superior power-conferring rule which authorizes a definite state organ to issue R. For example, the validity ground of parliamentary acts lies in those constitutional rules which vest the Parliament with legislative power. The ground of validity of a legal system as a whole, in the final analysis, is but its (first) constitution.[7]

(iii) The RR is not the ("first") constitution of a legal system, although Hart repeatedly tends to confuse the two things.[8] This is so for at least two reasons.

In the first place, the RR, unlike the constitution, does not belong to the legal system—as we shall see in a moment, the RR is not a legal rule, but a meta-legal criterion of identification of the law.

In the second place, the constitution too has to be "recognized". Hence, the constitution is not the RR itself, but one of its objects—one of the things to be recognized.[9]

---

[5] Hart (1961), p. 293, referring to Kelsen's basic norm. Moreover, one can maintain that, in modern legal thought, judicial obligation to apply the law is implicit in the very concept of "judge": by definition, judges are under such an obligation.

[6] Notwithstanding Kelsen's view, the basic norm, too, should be deemed neither valid nor invalid. If it were valid, there would be no need to *presuppose* its validity. If it were invalid, one could not presuppose it *valid*.

[7] And, if one does not confuse between validity and binding force, no further foundation is required. The problem that Kelsen tries to solve introducing the basic norm is a false problem. See Guastini (2013), p. 63 ff.

[8] Hart (1961), p. 293. "Enactment by the Queen in Parliament", he says, is the validity criterion, that is, the RR of the United Kingdom. However, "Enactment by the Queen in Parliament" is a rule of change, a power-conferring rule, and is the very core of the constitution of the U.K. A constitution, in the "material" (Kelsenian) sense, is precisely a set of rules of change, rules about the sources of law. Hence, identifying the RR with the rules of change amounts to confusing the RR with the constitution. The same confusion can be read also in Hart (1954), p. xii: "to say that a legal system exists entails that [...] there is a general acceptance of a constitutional rule, simple or complex, defining the manner in which ordinary rules of the system are to be identified".

[9] In Kelsen there is no possible confusion between the basic norm and the constitution: the *Grundnorm* is a meta-constitutional norm, whose validity is presupposed in view of ascribing validity (legal existence and binding force) to the constitution and, from the constitution, to the legal system as a whole.

(iv) Therefore, the RR is neither the set of "rules of change" (in Hart's parlance) of the legal system, that is the rules regulating the issuance of (further) rules—the constitution in the "material sense", as Kelsen would say. Rather, it is the criterion for identifying them.[10]

At the same time, as we shall see in a moment, the RR, after identifying the original, independent (that is, constitutional), rules of change, makes reference to them in view of identifying the derived, dependent, rules (for example, statutory).

(v) The RR is not a legal rule. If its object is identifying the law, then the RR, for reasons logical in nature, is a meta-legal rule—its logical place is at a second-order language regarding the law, the law being its object-language (Caracciolo 1991, p. 298).

In other words, the RR does not belong to the legal system it refers to. Rather, it belongs to the meta-legal discourse of those who aim to identify the legal system at stake.

To be sure, the RR is neither valid nor invalid—it is a matter of course. But the reason why is not because the RR—like Kelsen's basic norm—sets the criteria of validity of the rules of the system: such criteria lie in the rules or meta-rules of the system itself, not in the RR that identifies them. The RR is neither valid nor invalid for the simple reason that it is not a legal rule at all. It can only be a sort of definition "in force", analogous to the lexical definitions that one reads in the dictionaries of a language—reconstructions of the language in use.

3 Variety of RR

The phrase "identification of the rules of a legal system" can point to two different things, depending on what one means by "legal system" (Guastini 2014, p. 219 ff.).

In a first (naïve) sense, a legal system (leaving aside customary rules) is, trivially, a set of normative texts, that is a set of sentences provided with normative meaning.[11]

In a second (a little more sophisticated) sense a legal system is a set of rules, understood as the normative meanings ascribed to such texts by jurists and officials via interpretation.

Well, one thing is identifying the sources of a legal system—the constitution, statutes, by-laws, and so forth—leaving aside interpretive practices; another quite different thing is identifying their normative contents, which, on the contrary, presupposes the knowledge of the interpretive practices of jurists and officials (Ratti

[10] In Hart, the relationship between RR and rules of change is quite unclear. The same is true also for Bobbio: see Bobbio (1970, 1975) and Ruiz Manero (2010).

[11] This folk-concept of legal system is current in common language, but can be met even in jurists' language, especially whenever they do not distinguish between legal provisions (sentences) and rules (the meaning-contents of such sentences).

2012a, b). Therefore, two distinct RRs are necessary: the RR of legal sources and the RR of legal rules.

(1) The RR of legal sources is simple enough. Roughly speaking, any legal system includes (a) its first historical constitution as well as (b) the normative texts issued by a normative authority created by the constitution (Bulygin 1991a, p. 257 ff.).

The RR of legal sources, on the one hand, identifies the original, supreme, source (the constitution in the material sense) and, on the other hand, makes reference to the original rules of change in view of identifying the dynamically derived sources (statutes and the like).[12]

(2) The RR of legal rules is more complicated, since, in this connection, a further distinction is in order: the RR of valid rules, the RR of existing rules, and the RR of the rules "in force" (in the sense stipulated by Ross 1958). Each of such RRs incorporates different criteria, but in the three cases, since the object of identification are rules (not texts), that is, meanings, the RR cannot but take into account the interpretive practices of officials and legal scholars within the system at hand.

The distinction between validity and existence (or membership), although usually neglected in current legal-theoretical literature,[13] is made necessary by the fact that any legal system includes as existing rules not only valid rules, but also: (a) rules that are neither valid nor invalid, that is the original and supreme rules (the first constitution); (b) invalid rules, whose invalidity, however, was not yet declared by the competent organ (for example, the constitutional court).

By the way, not all the valid and/or existing rules are "in force", that is subject to predictable application by judges and other officials[14]—some are in force, some are not.

Therefore, three different RRs can be envisaged.[15]

(i) The RR of valid rules incorporates the validity criteria of the legal system concerned. Roughly speaking, a rule is valid if and only if (a) it was produced in accordance with the rules of change (formal validity) and (b) it is not incompatible with "superior" rules in the "hierarchy" of legal sources (material validity).[16] For example, a statute is valid if and only if it was passed by the competent organ in accordance with the proceedings required by the constitution and (provided that the

[12] The distinction between original or independent ("sovereign") and dependent or derived norms can be traced back to von Wright (1963), ch. X, and Caracciolo (1988). As to the distinction between static and dynamic derivation see also Guastini (2014), pp. 262 ff.

[13] A remarkable exception is Ferrajoli (1989, 2007).

[14] A more refined concept of being in force can be met in Bulygin (1965).

[15] In a different sense stipulate a variety of RR Scarpelli (1971) and Jori (1976). According to them, the RR (the necessary presupposition of any "internal" description of the law) is no matter of empirical knowledge—it is a matter of political decision, aimed not at the neutral ascertainment of the existing law, but at a legal policy.

[16] That is the rules which determine the subjects and the proceedings of the creation of further rules. As to the distinction between formal and material validity (and the connected distinction among different kinds of normative "hierarchies") see Guastini (2010), ch. XXIII and XXIV.

constitution is rigid) does not contradict the substantive norms of the constitution itself.

Thus, the RR of valid rules makes a mobile reference, on the one hand, to the rules of change (original and derived) and, on the other hand, to the hierarchy of legal sources (hence to the rules from which such a hierarchy derives: for example, those rules that make rigid a constitution).

(ii) The RR of existing rules incorporates the membership criteria of the legal system concerned. Roughly speaking, a rule is held to be existent within the system if it was issued either by the constituent power, or by a constituted power *prima facie* competent to issue such a rule through proceedings *prima facie* correct.

Thus, the RR of existing rules, too, makes reference to the rules of change of the legal system at hand. Most of all, it incorporates (a) the principle of effectiveness and (b) the legal presumption of validity of dynamically derived rules.

The principle of effectiveness, which is the existence criterion of the first constitution, is a positive (customary) rule of international law.

The legal presumption (*juris tantum*) of validity of dynamically derived rules, issued by a *prima facie* competent authority, is an accepted, although implicit, principle of most legal systems, namely of all those systems where the (usually: judicial) review of the validity of rules is implemented *a posteriori*, in such a way that it is perfectly possible that an invalid rule enters the system and is even for a long time applied, until its invalidity is declared by the competent organ.[17]

(iii) Finally, the RR of the rules in force incorporates the criterion of the prevailing interpretation (Ross 1958, ch. IV).

Indeed, the rules predictably applied by the courts are those rules which, in a given moment, are the result of a by and large accepted interpretation within the existing legal culture.[18] No need to say that a special importance is due to the interpretive trends of those organs that are competent to decide ultimately and "authentically"[19] the meaning of normative texts (most of all supreme and constitutional courts).[20]

4 Recognition Statements

By "recognition statement" I mean a sentence that is the conclusion of an argument whose premises include the RR (one of the RRs mentioned in the preceding section). Leaving aside the recognition of legal sources and circumscribing the analysis to the identification of rules, one can distinguish at least two recognition statements:

[17] To be sure, only *ex post* one will be able to say, from the "external" point of view, that until then an invalid rule existed within the legal system. Troper (2014), pp. 149 ff.

[18] The "living law" (*diritto vivente*) in Italian legal parlance. See Pugiotto (1994).

[19] In Kelsen's sense, of course.

[20] Troper (2001), ch. V.

(i) "The rule R is valid (existing, in force)";
(ii) "If these (as defined by the RR) are the criteria of validity (existence, being in force), then the rule R is valid (existent, in force)".

Now, sentence (i) uses the RR and, in this sense, is an "internal" statement, which presupposes the "acceptance" of the RR. Nonetheless, since the RR is a definition (not a norm of behaviour), such an acceptance has no axiological (moral or political) flavour: it is purely theoretical, epistemic.[21] Moreover, validity—as was made clear long ago by Ross (Ross 1961)—is not, and does not entail, the binding force of the valid rules, binding force depending on the contrary on some kind of axiological acceptance (Ross 1968, p. 61).

Sentence (ii), in turn, is an "external" statement, that does not use, but only mentions the RR, and this does not presuppose any kind of "acceptance" at all, since a conditional does not affirm either the antecedent or the consequent, but only the link of entailment between them.[22]

The RR, unlike Kelsen's basic norm, does not ascribe binding force either to the legal system or its norms. There is no relationship between the meta-legal statements of recognition and the axiological acceptance of the legal system concerned—no relationship with the "internal point of view" as conceived by Hart (the standpoint of those who make claims, approve or criticize other people's behaviour, and so on). Recognition statements are normative propositions.[23]

References

Bobbio N (1970) Norme primarie e norme secondarie. In: Bobbio N (ed) Studi per una teoria generale del diritto. Giappichelli, Torino, pp 175–197

Bobbio N (1975) Per un lessico di teoria generale del diritto. In: Studi in memoria di Enrico Guicciardi. Padova, Cedam Padova, pp 135–146

Bulygin E (2015 (1965)) The concept of efficacy. In: Paulson SL et al (eds) E. Bulygin, Essays in legal philosophy. OUP, Oxford, pp 37–51

Bulygin E (1976) Sobre la regla de reconocimiento. In: Derecho, Filosofía y Lenguaje. Homenaje a Ambrosio L. Gioja. Astrea, Buenos Aires

Bulygin E (2015 (1982)) Norms, normative propositions and legal statements. In: Paulson SL et al (eds) E. Bulygin, Essays in legal philosophy. OUP, Oxford, pp 188–206

Bulygin E (1991a) Algunas consideraciones sobre los sistemas jurídicos. Doxa 9:257–279

Bulygin E (1991b) Regla de reconocimiento: ¿norma de obligación o criterio conceptual? Doxa 9: 311–318

Burazin L, Ratti GB (2020) Rule(s) of recognition and canons of interpretation. In: Chiassoni P, Spaić B (eds) Judges and adjudication in constitutional democracies: a view from legal realism. Springer, Cham, pp 123–138

[21] This is why the word "acceptance", after all, does not sound proper.

[22] A suggestion in this sense in Conte (1966), p. 67 f.

[23] See von Wright (1963), p. 106; Bulygin (1982); Ross (1962).

Caracciolo R (1988) El sistema jurídico. Problemas actuales. Centro de Estudios Constitucionales, Madrid
Caracciolo R (1991) Sistema jurídico y regla de reconocimiento. Doxa 9:295–309
Carcaterra G (2014 (1974)) Le norme costitutive. Giappichelli, Torino
Carcaterra G (1979) La forza costitutiva delle norme. Bulzoni, Roma
Conte AG (1967 (1966)) Intervento. In: Tavola rotonda sul positivismo giuridico, Quaderni della rivista Il político. Giuffré, Milano, pp 67–68
Ferrajoli L (1989) Diritto e ragione. Teoria del garantismo penale. Laterza, Bari-Roma
Ferrajoli L (2007) Principia Juris. Teoria del diritto e della democracia. Vol. I. Teoria del diritto. Laterza, Roma-Bari
Guastini R (1988) Conoscenza senza accettazione. In: Gianformaggio L, Jori M (eds) Scritti per Uberto Scarpelli. Giuffré, Milano
Guastini R (1994) Art. 101. In: Branca G, Pizzorusso A (eds) Commentario della Costituzione, Artt. 99-103 (Gli organi ausiliari. La magistratura, I). Zanichelli-Il Foro Italiano, Bologna-Roma
Guastini R (2008) Normativismo mágico. Analisi e diritto 2008:251–262
Guastini R (2010) Le fonti del diritto. Fondamenti teorici. Giuffré, Milano
Guastini R (2013) The basic norm revisited. In: Duarte d'Almeida L, Gardner J, Green L (eds) Kelsen revisited. New essays on the pure theory of law. Hart Publishing, Oxford, pp 63–74
Guastini R (2014) La sintassi del diritto, 2nd edn. Giappichelli, Torino
Hacker PMS (1977) Hart's philosophy of law. In: Hacker PMS, Raz J (eds) Law, morality and society. Essays in honour of H.L.A. Hart. Clarendon, Oxford, pp 1–25
Hart HLA (1954) Introduction. In: Hart HLA (ed) The province of jurisprudence determined. Weidenfeld & Nicolson, London, pp vii–xxi
Hart HLA (1961) The concept of law. Clarendon, Oxford
Jori M (1976) Il metodo giuridico tra scienza e política. Giuffré, Milano
Lamond G (2013) The rule of recognition and the foundations of a legal system. In: Duarte D'Almeida L, Edwards J, Dolcetti A (eds) Reading H.L.A Hart's "The Concept of Law". Hart Publishing, Oxford, pp 97–122
MacCormick N (1978) H.L.A. Hart. Edward Arnold, London
Muffato N (2010) Norme e discorsi su norme. Aracne, Roma
Pugiotto A (1994) Sindacato di costituzionalità e "diritto vivente". Giuffré, Milano
Ratti GB (2012a) Regola di riconoscimento e realismo giuridico. In: Ratti GB (ed) Diritto, indeterminatezza, indecidibilità. Marcial Pons, Madrid
Ratti GB (2012b) Reglas de reconocimiento, cánones interpretativos y realismo jurídico. In: Luque Sánchez P, Ratti GB (eds) Acordes y desacuerdos. Marcial Pons, Madrid, pp 315–328
Raz J (1979 (1971)) The identity of legal systems. In: Raz J (ed) The authority of law. Clarendon, Oxford, pp 78–102
Ross A (1958) On law and justice. Stevens & Sons, London
Ross A (1988 (1961)) Validity and the conflict between legal positivism and natural law. In: Paulson SL, Litschewski Paulson B (eds) Normativity and norms. Critical perspectives on Kelsenian themes. Clarendon Press, Oxford, pp 146–163
Ross A (1962) "Review" of H.L.A. Hart's, the concept of law. Yale Law J LXXI:1185–1190; Italian translation: Ross A (1990 (1962)) Il concetto di diritto secondo Hart. In: Castignone S, Guastini R (eds) Realismo giuridico e analisi del linguaggio. Testi di Karl Olivecrona e Alf Ross, 2nd edn. ECIG, Genova, 1990, pp 195–203
Ross A (1968) Directives and norms. Routledge & Kegan Paul, London
Ruiz Manero J (1990) Jurisdicción y normas. Dos estudios sobre función jurisdiccional y teoría del derecho. Centro de estudios constitucionales, Madrid
Ruiz Manero J (1991) Normas independientes, criterios conceptuales y trucos verbales. Respuesta a Eugenio Bulygin. Doxa 9:281–293
Ruiz Manero J (2010) Bobbio y los conceptos de norma juridícamente última. Analisi e diritto 2010:95–106
Scarpelli U (1965) Cos'è il positivismo giuridico. Comunità, Milano

Scarpelli U (1982 (1971)) Il metodo giuridico. In: Scarpelli U (ed) L'etica senza verità. il Mulino, Bologna, pp 179–203
Searle JR (1969) Speech acts. An essay in the philosophy of language. CUP, Cambridge
Troper M (2001) Une théorie réaliste de l'interprétation. In: Troper M (ed) La théorie du droit, le droit, l'État. PUF, Paris, pp 69–84
Troper M (2014) Une théorie réaliste de la validité. Analisi e diritto 2014:149–164
Vilajosana JM (2019) Guastini y el realismo de la regla de reconocimiento. In: Chiassoni P, Comanducci P, Battista G (eds) L'arte della distinzione Scritti per Riccardo Guastine, 1st edn. Marcial Pons, Ediciones Jurídicas y Sociales, Madrid, pp 489–506
von Wright GH (1963) Norm and action. A logical enquiry. Routledge & Kegan Paul, London

Institutions and Constitutive Rules

Josep Joan Moreso

Abstract In this paper, the orthodox view of constitutional rules is defended. For this view, the division between prescriptive rules and constitutive rules is mutually exclusive: while constitutive rules constitute the actions to which they refer, prescriptive rules regulate behaviours that exist apart from them; constitutive rules cannot be violated, whereas regulative rules can; and the canonical form of constitutive rules is "*X counts as Y* in context *C*", while regulative rules are paradigmatically expressed in the imperative mood—as in "Do *X*". This view is defended from powerful objections, particularly the recent objection of the so-called *Knowledge-Rule* by Timothy Williamson ("One must: assert that *P* only if one knows that *P*"). Furthermore, it is presented a way in which constitutive rules can indirectly provide reasons for action and it is analysed whether the existence of these rules is given *in virtue of* moral facts or not.

> También el jugador es prisionero (la sentencia es de Omar) de otro tablero de negras noches y de blancos días.
>
> Dios mueve al jugador, y éste, la pieza. ¿Qué dios detrás de Dios la trama empieza de polvo y tiempo y sueño y agonías?
>
> "Ajedrez", Jorge Luis Borges (1960)[1]

[1] The player is also a prisoner/ (the sentence is Omar's) of another/ board of black nights and white days./ God moves the player, and he, the piece./ What god behind God begins the web/ of dust and time and dreams and agonies?

J. J. Moreso (✉)
Department of Law, Pompeu Fabra University, Barcelona, Spain

BIAP, Barcelona Institute of Analytic Philosophy, Barcelona, Spain
e-mail: josejuan.moreso@upf.edu

G. Villa Rosas, T. Spaak (eds.), *Legal Power and Legal Competence*, Law and Philosophy Library 140, https://doi.org/10.1007/978-3-031-28555-4_8

1 Introduction: Ydobon in the Noîsulli Islands

Alf Ross (1957), in a well-known article, tells us the fictious story of the customs of a tribe, the Noît-cif, who inhabit the Noîsulli Islands in the South Pacific, as described by the Illyrian anthropologist Ydobon.[2] According to this narrative, on that island, when one of the Noît-cif encounters their mother-in-law, kills a totem animal, or eats food prepared for the tribe's chief, that person acquires the property of being *tû-tû*, and so must undergo a special ceremony of purification. This practice of which Ross tells us can be represented by two rules:

R1: If someone encounters their mother-in-law, or if a totem animal is killed, or if someone has eaten of the food prepared for the chief, there arises what is called *tû-tû*.

R2: If someone has become *tû-tû*, they must be subjected to a special ceremony of purification.

The main purpose of Ross's article is to show that presumed expressions for properties like *tû-tû* do not refer to anything and are empty of meaning. This is a surprising conclusion if we consider that this kind of term can be eliminated in much the same way that theoretical terms for unobservable entities in scientific theories can be eliminated—by means of Ramsey sentences, for instance.[3] In any case, this was perhaps Ross's intention, for finally he also shows us in his article how to dispense with an expression like "*tû-tû*" by the simple means of substituting it with other predicates like "encounter one's mother-in-law", "kill a totem animal", and "eat food prepared for the chief", which are satisfied by certain members of the tribe in suitable circumstances.

However, it is only indirectly that I want to address this view of Ross. The simple normative system presented by him has the virtue of capturing, with only two rules, a crucial part of our institutional systems. Here I refer to the fact that while rule R2 prescribes a behaviour and, therefore, can be violated, rule R1 cannot be violated, but simply establishes that if someone is in one of the described circumstances, they acquire the property *tû-tû*.

In the literature, rules like R1 are called *constitutive* rules, and rules like R2 are called *prescriptive* or *regulative* rules. In Sect. 2 of this paper, what can be called the *orthodox* conception of constitutive rules will be presented. In Sect. 3, some objections and difficulties faced by this conception will be analysed. In Sect. 4, the question of how these rules provide reasons for action will be addressed. In Sect. 5, some clarifications will be made about the difficulties of identifying this kind of rule,

---

[2] Although Ross, jokingly, even cites the supposed work of the anthropologist Ydobon, the fictitious nature of this narrative, perhaps told with a touch of Danish humour, is obvious. (Aside from the anthropologist's dubious provenance, one only has to read his name—as well as that of the islands, and of the tribe—in reverse.)

[3] See Ramsey (1978). A clear presentation is provided by Andreas (2017).

and whether this depends in some sense on moral reasons in the case of law. Finally, Sect. 6 concludes the paper.

2 The Orthodox Conception[4]

Although there are precedents from the start of the previous century,[5] the works that have placed this notion under contemporary discussion are, in my opinion, those of John Rawls (1955), Georg Henrik von Wright (1963), and John Searle (1964, 1969, 1995, 2018).[6]

Here I will use Searle's terminology, which has gained a certain currency, and which distinguishes between *constitutive* and *regulative* rules.[7] The differences between these two kinds of rules can be identified as the following three (see Marsili 2019, pp. 3–4).

(a) While constitutive rules constitute the actions to which they refer, which are incomprehensible without them, regulative rules regulate behaviours that exist and can be understood apart from them. In written work, independently from that of Searle, the legal philosopher Ross, distinguishing between the natural activity of parking one's car and the institutional activity of playing chess, puts it thus:

> Parking a car is a 'natural' activity; by this I mean an activity whose performance is logically independent of any rules governing it. Cars were parked before parking regulations existed, and it would be an obvious absurdity if I said that I could not park my car because of the absence of parking regulations in this town. Playing chess, on the other hand, is not a 'natural' activity. To play chess is to undertake certain actions according to the rules of chess. The actions of the game consist in 'moves' which have no meaning or purpose except that they are rules of chess. A move is made by moving a piece of wood on a squared plane. That the piece of wood is a pawn and its displacement a 'move' can be understood only if the action is interpreted in terms of the rules of chess. (Ross 1968, p. 53)

(b) In this way, constitutive rules cannot be violated, whereas regulative rules can. Again in the words of Ross:

---

[4] I take this expression from Marsili (2019), who gives a perspicuous presentation of this conception, which I will draw from here.

[5] For instance, in the work of the prematurely deceased phenomenologist—and disciple of Husserl—Adolf Reinach (1913; translated into English in 1983). Conte (1985) also informs us of the distinction between constitutive rules and prescriptive rules (called *constructive* and *coercive*) found in the work of the Polish lawyer Znamierowski (1921).

[6] Around the same time, there were other analytic authors who also pointed to some ideas in the vicinity, e.g., Black (1958) and Midgley (1959).

[7] Von Wright (1963, ch. 1) calls them, respectively, *determinative norms* (or *rules*) and *prescriptive norms* (or *prescriptions*). Among philosophers of law the expression "constitutive rule" (or "constitutive norm") has become common currency, although "prescriptive rules" (or "prescriptive norms") seems to be preferred for the second kind. In the next section I will refer to Rawls's (1955) distinction between the concept of a rule as a *summary* and as a *practice*.

> The rules of chess, since they define the game, cannot, strictly speaking, be violated. A player may of course cheat by making an irregular move. But in that case what is going on is not, strictly speaking, chess. Cheating in chess requires passing off, undetected, an action as chess that is not really so. (Ross 1968, p. 54)

(c) According to Searle (1969, p. 33), the canonical form of constitutive rules is something like "*X counts as Y* in context *C*", while regulative rules are paradigmatically expressed in the imperative mood—as in "Do *X*", or "Do not park here"—or through the use of deontic expressions—as in "You should do *X*", or "Parking here is forbidden".

This second conception draws a mutually exclusive distinction between these two kinds of rules: while regulative rules can be violated, constitutive rules cannot. This does not entail that they are mutually exhaustive, however. Indeed, later on we will see that there is also another kind of rule: *technical* rules.

This is the conception that, with some nuances, has been assumed in contemporary philosophy of law. To Ross's proposal (1968) has been added H. L. A. Hart's influential book (1961, pp. 33–35), which distinguishes, as is well known, between *duty-imposing* and *power-conferring* rules. While the violation of the former may *contingently* entail a sanction, failing to meet the requirements established by a constitutive rule—e.g., moving the bishop vertically—*necessarily* entails its nullity. To move the bishop vertically is not a correct movement of that piece; properly speaking, it is not to *move* the bishop. Which amounts to saying that power-conferring rules cannot be violated, for conceptual reasons.

These ideas gave rise to an ample literature in the philosophy of law during the final decades of the twentieth century and into the start of the present one.[8]

3 Objections and Clarifications

The orthodox conception has always raised some doubts. For instance, when we teach a child to play chess, it is natural to instruct them not to move the bishop vertically. Thus the idea that constitutive rules cannot be violated has often been challenged.

The biggest challenge to this idea in contemporary philosophy comes, however, from philosophy of language. In an influential article, Timothy Williamson (1996,

[8]In English, see e.g., Raz (1975), MacCormick and Weinberger (1986), Ruiter (1993), and Marmor (2009). In Italian, see especially Carcaterra (1974, 1979) and Conte (1989, 1995, 2001), but also Guastini (1985), Mazzarese (1985), Azzoni (1988), di Lucia (2003), and Roversi (2007). And from the Hispanic world, see Alchourrón and Bulygin (1983), Hernández Marín (1984), Robles (1984), Barrère (1990), Alarcón Cabrera (1991), Bulygin (1992), González Lagier (1995), Atienza and Ruiz Manero (1996), Moreso (1998), Ferrer Beltrán (2000), Moreso and Vilajosana (2004), and Arriagada (2017).

and in the revised version of 2000) contends that assertion is governed by a rule, which he calls the *Knowledge Rule* (KR), according to which:

(KR) One must: assert that *P* only if one knows that *P*.

According to Williamson, (KR) is a constitutive rule, conceived as analogous to the rules of games (1996, pp. 489–490). However, this rule can obviously be violated, as Williamson himself recognizes, since someone could very well assert that *P* in order to induce false beliefs in their audience; and in any case one could assert that *P* when *P* is false. Still, Williamson argues that this rule is constitutive of the act of asserting, even though it can be violated.

Williamson's claim can be questioned in various ways. On the one hand, one might hold that it is not this rule that governs assertion, but rather some variant of it (see e.g. García-Carpintero 2004). Alternatively, one might oppose Williamson's claim by arguing that the norm that governs assertion cannot both regulate it and constitute it (see, with varying emphases, Hindriks 2007; Maitra 2011; Marsili 2019). However, there are also those who insist on attributing these properties to constitutive rules and reject the traditional conception (perspicuously, García-Carpintero 2021).[9]

This debate over the nature of assertion apparently remains open. Still, we would do well to notice that the traditional conception is in need of some refinements and clarifications.

The first, and perhaps the most obvious of these comes from von Wright, who distinguishes between two senses in which a rule can prescribe a behaviour. Von Wright takes logical and mathematical laws as his paradigms of constitutive rules, and explicitly compares and likens them to the rules of games. He adds:

> The *a priori* nature of the laws of logic seems easier to reconcile with a view of them as prescriptive laws. Shall we then say that the laws of logic prescribe how we *ought to* think and how we *may* and *must not* think? Perhaps we can say this, but it is also obvious on reflection that the *sense* in which the laws of logic 'prescribe' (order, permit, prohibit) is a different sense from that in which the laws of the state prescribe.

Here the idea suggests itself that the laws of logic and mathematics prescribe how one ought to think and calculate in order to think and calculate correctly. The laws of logic do not aim at making people think correctly, as the laws of the state can be said to aim at making people behave in a certain way. The laws of logic provide a standard whereby to judge *whether* people think correctly or not. This seems to be a good way of characterizing the difference between the two types of law and the different senses in which they 'prescribe'. (von Wright 1963, p. 4)

Perhaps an idea like this could also work for assertion: the rule of assertion establishes a standard for determining whether a particular assertion is correct or not, given the link—on Williamson's conception—between assertion and truth. Moreover, this could perhaps also help us to understand the two different ways in which the Rossian rules of the inhabitants of the Noîsulli Islands prescribe: while rule R1

[9] An excellent presentation of this debate is provided by Pagin (2016).

establishes a standard of correctness—one should not be *tû-tû* (it appears that on these islands, acquiring this property is bad in some sense)—rule R2 establishes a duty applicable to those who fall into that situation, without assuming any standard of correctness.[10]

The second clarification comes from Rawls's (1955) presentation in his influential article. As is well known, Rawls here tries to defend so-called *rule utilitarianism* against *act utilitarianism*. To this end he uses the examples of the justification of promises and the justification of punishment. He argues that it is important to distinguish between the justification of these institutions—which may be utilitarian, since having them yields better consequences than lacking them—and the justification of a specific rule in practice. To consider here the consequences of applying rules to specific cases would involve assuming a conception of rules as maxims of experience, which we may drop when they do not work for us (the *summary conception*). But Rawls (1955, p. 28) thinks that we should instead conceive the rules in this case as *practices*, that is, as rules without exceptions (the *practice conception*): "a particular case cannot be an exception to a rule of a practice. An exception is rather a qualification or a further specification of the rule."

However, this is a distinction between two conceptions of prescriptive rules. For instance, the rule of punishment to the effect that the innocent should not be punished is a prescriptive rule, which can be conceived as a maxim of experience that allows for exceptions in the extreme cases imagined by some act utilitarian authors,[11] or can instead be conceived as a rule without exceptions: the institution never authorizes punishing someone who is innocent.

Yet Rawls (1955, p. 25) adds another characterization of rules as practices, saying that "the rules of practices are logically prior to particular cases", and that "[w]e may think of the rules of a practice as defining offices, moves, and offenses." And he also gives the example of games. It is clear that, in chess, there is no castling outside the rules of the game. So here Rawls is not thinking of *regulative*, but rather of *constitutive* rules.[12]

I think this ambiguity in Rawls's characterization permeates the whole debate. Some regulative rules of some institutions are considered *essential* to a given institution. This is how we conceive of the rule that the innocent should not be

---

[10] Perhaps this could help to explain why some authors impugn the distinction: all constitutive rules are also regulative; see Duarte (2018).

[11] Such as the case of the desert island promise, which Smart (1973, p. 62) describes as follows: "Thus if the deontologist says that promises always should be kept (or even if, like Ross, he says that there is a *prima facie* duty to keep them) we may confront him with a situation like the following, the well-known 'desert island promise': I have promised a dying man on a desert island, from which subsequently I alone am rescued, to give his hoard of gold to the South Australian Jockey Club. On my return I give it to the Royal Adelaide Hospital, which, we may suppose, badly needs it for a new X-ray machine. Could anybody deny that I had done rightly without being open to the charge of heartlessness?"

[12] It is clear that Rawls's argument, designed to defend rule utilitarianism against act utilitarianism, still retains much of its value. But it does not adequately distinguish between regulative rules and constitutive rules. On this point, see Diver (2004).

punished: it is a prescription and can be violated, but it is *essential* to the institution of punishment, which would not be what it is in the absence of this rule.

Furthermore, this reveals another ambiguity in the properties that constitutive rules establish. An ambiguity that was already present in Searle's (1964) pioneering work on promises. How should we characterize the nature of promises? There are two initial candidates:

(Promise 1) To say "I promise" (or a similar expression) under certain felicity or sincerity conditions is to promise.

(Promise 2) To promise is to undertake an obligation to perform an action in someone's favour in the future.

This further ambiguity brings us to a third clarification. Since both of these candidates have been conceived as constitutive rules, and given that one can only promise if the institution of promising exists, both (Promise 1) and (Promise 2) can be presented in the canonical form of constitutive rules: "To say 'I promise' (in certain conditions) counts as promising", and: "Promising counts as obliging oneself to perform an action in the future"—something like alienating an episode from our future.[13]

Something similar happens with our predicate "*tû-tû*", which may equate to encountering one's mother-in-law, or killing a totem animal, or eating food prepared for the chief, but may also equate to being obliged to undergo a purification ceremony.

The same is maintained by Alchourrón and Bulygin (1983) in a seminal work in legal theory on this issue, when they affirm, for instance, that the predicate "murder" could be rendered equivalent to either "that person who killed another person" or "that person who should be condemned to a certain penalty *P*".

Moreover, what these two examples show us is that we only obtain the second sense if there is a regulative rule in this regard. A rule that, for instance, respectively establishes that one should not cross paths with one's mother-in-law, or kill a totem animal, or eat what is prepared for the chief, or that one should not commit murder. As the example of promises makes manifest, these also require a constitutive rule and a regulative rule. The first says:

(CR-Promise) To say "I promise" under certain felicity or sincerity conditions counts as promising.

And the second says:

(RR-Promise) Promises must be kept.

[13]Hugo Grocio (1625 II. XI.4) puts it in this perspicuous way: "Alienatio particulae ciuiusdam nostrae libertatis." Moreover, as is well known, since Searle (1964) takes (Promise 1) to imply (Promise 2), he takes it to be possible to move unfallaciously from "is" to "ought".

Now we can understand the sense of (Promise 2): it says that to promise is to be subject to the regulative rule (RR-Promise). Like all institutions, the institution of promising requires both kinds of rules.

Something like this distinction is proposed by Neri Marsili (2019, pp. 7–9) as an alternative reading of the rule of assertion (KR) ("One must: assert that *P* only if one knows that *P*"):

(KR′) One asserts that *P* if and only if saying *P* is subject to the duty of knowing that *P*.

But as Marsili takes care to point out, this reading is equivalent to:

(KR″) One asserts that *P* if and only if saying *P* is subject to the rule (KR).

(KR″) can be read as a constitutive rule, in the sense that asserting something counts as falling under the obligation to know it. However, as Marsili (2019, p. 7) says, this is so because (KR″) is a rule about another rule (KR)—that is, it is a meta-rule. I will come back to this point later.[14]

Conte (1985) accurately anticipates this criticism of Searle, and adds that expressions like (Promise 2)—or, for that matter, (KR′)—are constitutive not "because they constitute the institution that they are concerned with, but rather because they reflect the intrinsic constitution of that institution" (Conte 1985, p. 32).

Fourth, and partly as a consequence of the various senses of "constitutive rule", it should be pointed out that any set of rules of an institution (the rules of chess, the rules of baseball, the rules of football, the rules of the Noît-cif, the rules of promising, the rules of assertion, or the rules of law) can be presented in various ways. If the normative dimension of the institution is privileged, then all the constitutive rules are encapsulated in regulative rules. If the institutional dimension is privileged, then the regulative rules are formulated as if they were constitutive, although as we have seen, in the case of promises, the rule that says "Promising counts as placing oneself under the obligation to fulfil what was promised" presupposes the regulative rule "Promises must be kept".

In this sense, we can reconstruct the rules of chess as a set of regulative rules. For instance "The bishop can only be moved diagonally", plus a constitutive rule such as "These are all the correct moves of chess". Or, alternatively, the rules of chess can be reconstructed as a set of constitutive rules. For instance "Moving the bishop diagonally counts as a correct move of chess", plus a regulative rule such as "[In certain circumstances] one must play chess", or better, as Joseph Raz elaborates, a rule of *continuity* that says something like:

> [T]he opening player (determined in a certain way) and subsequently any player, within a reasonable (or a specified period of) time from the beginning of the game or from the time the other player made his last move, respectively, ought to use one of his powers as specified by rules of the first type. (Raz 1975, pp. 115–116)

[14] Marsili (2019), rightly in my opinion, concludes from this that Williamson cannot collapse these two rules into one.

Without this rule, chess would not be a real *game*, but only a theoretical model or something of the sort.

It is no wonder, then, that the chess rules of FIDE, the International Chess Federation,[15] use (in two parts, the first dedicated to the basic rules of the game and the second dedicated to the rules of the competition) both kinds of canonical formulations interchangeably—the constitutive rule, for instance the definition of castling in Article 3.8.2.:

> This is a move of the king and either rook of the same colour along the player's first rank, counting as a single move of the king and executed as follows: the king is transferred from its original square two squares towards the rook on its original square, then that rook is transferred to the square the king has just crossed.

and the regulative rule, with its use of deontic expressions, for instance in Article 3.2: "The bishop may move to any square along a diagonal on which it stands."

And it is no wonder for a reason that is well captured by David Lewis, with reference to the game of baseball:[16]

> The rules of baseball could in principle be formulated as straightforward directives concerning behavior, without the aid of definable terms for score and its components. Or they could be formulated as explicit definitions of the score function, the components of score, and correct play, followed by directives in which the newly defined terms appear. It is easy to see why neither of these methods of formulation has found favor. The first method would pack the entire rulebook into each directive; the second would pack the entire rulebook into a single preliminary explicit definition. Understandably averse to very long sentences, we do better to proceed in our more devious way. (Lewis 1979, p. 344)

That is, any institutional system contains, at once, both constitutive rules and regulative rules, but the system can be presented in various equivalent ways.

The fifth clarification relates to a point raised by Rawls (and suitably underscored by García-Carpintero MS). In his words:

> Blue-prints for a practice do not make a practice. That there is a practice entails that there are instances of people having been engaged and now being engaged in it (with suitable qualifications). (Rawls 1955, pp. 25–26, n. 23)[17]

This observation from Rawls is fitting for at least two reasons. The first is that Ross's practice of *tû-tû*, for instance, is only a blueprint for a practice. Since it is fictitious it has never been implemented; it has never been in force.[18] We do not know, for instance, if those rules have implicit exceptions. For instance, does it count as

[15] Approved in the 88th FIDE Congress in Antalya (Turkey), and coming into force on 1 January 2018. https://feda.org/feda2k16/wp-content/uploads/LEYES-2018-bilingues.pdf.

[16] A similar idea is found in Carcaterra (1985), where some rules for what he calls the *Pickwick Club* are imagined (clearly with reference to Charles Dickens's first novel), which can also be presented either by highlighting their normative dimension, privileging the regulative rules, or else by relying on their institutional dimension, privileging the constitutive rules.

[17] A nearby idea is this: there are no rules, neither regulative nor constitutive, besides an institutional practice. See Vega (2007).

[18] The same goes for the practice of Carcaterra's Pickwick Club, as cited in footnote 17.

encountering one's mother-in-law if one crosses paths with her, but she is in disguise and cannot be recognized?

The second reason, which follows from the first, is that the institutional systems in force tend to include exceptions and mechanisms to deal with such vicissitudes. In chess, for instance, the rules allow the validation of some incorrect movements. Thus Article 7.2.2 establishes that if, in the course of a game, it is discovered that the board was misaligned at the start (a black square was placed to the right of each player), then the game will continue but the position must be transferred to a correctly aligned board. And, of course, here again it is important to decide if we are going to treat this mechanism as a way of adding clauses to a constitutive rule, or a way of establishing exceptions to a regulative rule.

In law, this is a very commonplace situation. Is killing someone in legitimate self-defence an exception to the rule that constitutes murder, and therefore not a murder?[19] Or is it instead a murder, albeit exceptionally one that should not be punished?

Something similar happens in private law. Thus Article 688 of the Spanish Civil Code establishes the following:

> A holographic last will and testament may only be made by persons who are of legal age. In order to be valid, this last will and testament must be written out in full and signed by the testator, specifying the year, month and day on which it is made. Should it contain words that have been crossed out, amended or written between the lines, the testator shall validate these with their signature. Foreigners may make a holographic last will and testament in their own language.

Now then, what happens if a last will and testament meets these requirements, but was made under a violent threat? Is this a situation that renders the will invalid, or does it just oblige the notary not to notarize it? In the doctrine on these aspects, lawyers distinguish between *inexistence*, *absolute nullity*, and *relative nullity* or *voidability*. It is the last of these that allows for validation and, I believe, in my example it would be said that a will made in this way is *voidable*. Perhaps it would be *null and void* if it did not contain the signature of the originator, and *inexistent* if it contained just one clause leaving the planet Mars to the inheritor. However, the distinction between inexistence and absolute nullity is not sharp, because it cannot be. It depends on the context whether a certain act that appears to be legal will immediately be taken as a joke, or whether it will instead be the subject of a legal process aimed at declaring it null and void. Let us imagine the following case of procedural law: in a process of eviction for non-payment of rent, a somewhat cretinous judge issues a warrant for the arrest of the defaulting tenant. What would the tenant's lawyer do then, supposing her to be diligent? Well, I believe that in some contexts she would go to the senior judge so that this silly decision would not be followed through. But in other, more erratic contexts, she might file an appeal to

[19] In fact German criminal law doctrine has elaborated a conception called the *theory of negative elements of the type* (*die Lehre von den negativen Tatbestandsmerkmalen*), precisely designed to establish that the causes of justification, such as legitimate self-defence, make up the criminal type (e.g. murder), establishing negative conditions, precisely. See, for instance, Mir Puig (2015, lecture 6).

annul the order. The boundaries between inexistence and nullity are no longer clear.[20]

In reality, law is at once a set of substantive rules that regulate human behaviour and a set of procedural rules that establish the authorities, procedures and consequences of following or violating the substantive rules. These two kinds of rules are in tension with each other (see Ruiz Manero 2015, pp. 82–84). That is, as has been indicated, it is possible for an authority to establish that a certain substantive rule has been infringed when it has not, and vice versa.

Sixth, and finally—and developing the last point—institutional systems of norms are not fixed in time, but subject to change. Even the rules of chess are often modified by FIDE, its international federation. Hence such systems must include rules that confer powers. This idea, although present in legal theory long before, owes its present currency to Hart (1961). For Hart, as is well known, legal norms are a subclass of social rules that are distinguished from mere habits (regularities of behaviour), because (a) they arouse criticism when the participants deviate from the practice (such as, among ourselves for instance, the improper use of cutlery for eating), (b) appealing to the rule is considered a sufficient basis for criticism, and (c) in that context the use of normative language is appropriate (to continue with the example: "You *should* hold the knife with your right hand"). The fact that someone has the duty to perform a certain action, then, means that within a social practice there is a rule that prescribes performing that action. Legal norms are the subclass of social rules identified by what Hart calls the *rule of recognition*: a criterion that underlies the practice of legal operators when they identify the guidelines that are in force in their ambit. So not all rules are rules of conduct: norms that oblige, prohibit or permit, which Hart calls *primary rules*. There are also rules that deal with other rules or, in a slightly different version, *power-conferring rules*, which Hart calls *secondary rules*: first, the rule of recognition, which endows the legal system with stability by allowing us to check whether a given guideline is part of the system or not; second, the *rules of change*, which establish in what conditions, and by whom, norms can be introduced to or eliminated from the system to prevent it from ossifying; and third, the *rules of adjudication*, which establish the procedures and authorities that decide when the primary rules were infringed and, in this way, resolve conflicts. For Hart, legal systems are hence a combination of primary and secondary rules: this is the key to jurisprudence that the concept of law reveals to us.

In institutional systems, then, there is another kind of constitutive rule: those that allow us to identify new norms as norms of the system. These are rules that deal with other rules.

[20] A classical contribution in Carnelutti (1955). Another difficulty of this feature can be verified in Article 6.3 of the Spanish Civil Code: "Acts contrary to mandatory and prohibitive norms are null and void, unless these norms provide for a different effect in case of infraction." Acts contrary to these norms are illicit, but not void: it is not void to stop paying the price of what one buys, nor to steal someone's umbrella in a restaurant. But it seems to me that the legislator did not employ the concept of a constitutive rule, which was needed here.

From these six clarifications, we may conclude that, despite the various senses of the expression "constitutive rule", any institution is made up of a set including at least one regulative rule and one constitutive rule. Constitutive rules are intrinsically related to the institutional nature of our practices.

4 Are Constitutive Rules Reasons for Action?

Thanks to Raz's work, the idea that legal norms are reasons for action has become crucial to our conception of rules. According to Raz's (1975) conception, legal norms are *protected* reasons, that is, first-order reasons that prescribe behaving as the norm establishes and, at the same time, second-order reasons of an exclusive character that displace any other kind of first-order reason. This conception goes hand in hand with his conception of authority as *service* (Raz 1994: ch. 10), according to which the norms of legitimate authorities serve as mediators between our underlying reasons to act (our moral reasons) and what we should do. On this conception, the fact that legitimate legal authorities have promulgated certain norms changes our reasons to act. That is, legal norms have practical relevance to the extent that they are endowed with authority.

That is to say, legal authorities are practical authorities, and the claim to authority is essential to the nature of law. Admittedly, not all legal authorities are legitimate. However, all authorities *de facto* claim to have legitimate authority. And according to Raz, the theses that characterize legitimate authority are the following three:

> *The Dependence Thesis*: All authoritative directives should be based, among other factors, on reasons which apply to the subjects of those directives and which bear on the circumstances covered by the directives. Such reasons I shall call dependent reasons.
>
> *The Normal Justification Thesis:* The normal and primary way to establish that a person should be acknowledged to have authority over another person involves showing that the alleged subject is likely better to comply with reasons which apply to him (other than the alleged authoritative reasons) if he accepts the directives of the alleged authority as authoritatively binding, and tries to follow them, than if he tries to follow the reasons which apply to him directly.
>
> *The Pre-emption Thesis*: The fact than an authority requires performance of an action is a reason for its performance which is not to be added to all other relevant reasons when assessing what to do, but should replace some of them. (Raz 1994, p. 198)

So, on the one hand, the obligatory force of law—when the legal authorities are legitimate—derives from these robust normative facts of a moral nature, which legitimize these authorities. On the other hand, for law, in accordance with its nature, to fulfil its function, it must be identified without appealing to moral considerations; because when they are resorted to, we find ourselves compelled to analyse and weigh all the reasons, and the law thus loses its character of pre-emption. Then the directives are no longer protected: they are no longer *exclusive* reasons.

Apparently Raz is considering regulative rules under his conception here. If, as under the orthodox conception, constitutive rules cannot be violated, then they cannot be protected reasons in his sense. However, on at least one occasion, Raz has considered if, and in what sense, constitutive rules can provide reasons for action, and has said the following (Raz 2001, pp. 4–5):

> The rules of chess, i.e. those which determine which moves are allowed rather than how to win at chess, are said to be constitutive of the game. It is often said that constitutive rules are not reasons either. I think that they are, but they are (that is their existence constitutes) conditional reasons. They are reasons to behave in this way or that, reasons why you must behave this way and that, if you are to play chess and therefore, if you have reason to play chess.
>
> Many constitutive rules are themselves man-made, but not all. Many of them are conditional reasons, whose condition can be avoided. One can avoid playing chess and at least in principle one can avoid a country, or a profession. Some constitutive rules are different. The rules of mathematics and logic are—in the old terminology—rules or laws of thought, constitutive of thinking (or of central kinds of thinking). We do not make them, and we cannot avoid them, at least we cannot avoid observing some of them, so long as we continue to think. But they too may be regarded as setting conditional reasons, even though the reason cannot be avoided by anything less than opting out of all rational thought.

This idea of Raz, I believe, can be understood with the help of what von Wright (1963: ch. 1) calls *directives* or *technical norms*, such as instructions, for example. Von Wright states the idea as follows:

> I shall regard as the standard formulation of technical norms conditional sentences, in whose antecedent there is mention of some wanted thing, and in whose consequent there is mention of something that must (has to, ought to) or must not be done. An example would be 'If you want to make the hut habitable you ought to heat it'. (von Wright 1963, p. 10)

According to von Wright, this technical rule presupposes the truth of what he calls an *anankastic* proposition: "If you do not heat the hut, it will not be habitable", at least in cold places such as the author's native Finland. Or we may change the example to one closer to home, e.g. the culinary necessary truth: "If you do not cook the rice by spreading a single layer over the base of the pan, the paella will not be tasty"; a truth presupposed by the technical rule: "If you want to eat a tasty paella, then you should spread the rice into a single layer in the pan."

So, while constitutive rules are not technical rules, they may be viewed as the presuppositions of certain technical rules, which are, as Raz wants, *conditional* reasons. Returning to the previous example of the constitutive rule that defines what a holographic will is, we may extract the technical rule: "If you want to make a holographic will, you should sign it." Likewise: "If you want to play chess, you should move the bishop diagonally", and also: "If you do not want to be *tû-tû*, you should avoid your mother-in-law." So constitutive rules are the respective *presuppositions* of a class of conditional reasons.

Furthermore, von Wright adds:

> A man argues with himself: 'I want to make the hut habitable. Unless it is heated, it will not become habitable. Therefore I ought to heat it.' I shall call this type of argument a *practical inference*. (von Wright 1963, p. 11)

In this reasoning, it appears that the *operative* reason is constituted by the premise expressed by the speaker's desire, and the anankastic proposition constitutes an auxiliary reason. Perhaps, then, we could say that constitutive rules are not *operative* reasons within our practical reasoning, but instead *auxiliary* reasons.[21]

5 The Identification of Constitutive Rules and Moral Reasons

As is well known, Raz's conception of rules as reasons for action—the exclusive conception of legal norms as reasons for action—is what makes him the leading defender of the *thesis of social sources* in its strictest version, i.e. that of so-called *exclusive legal positivism*:

> A jurisprudential theory is acceptable only if its tests for identifying the content of the law and determining its existence depend exclusively on facts of human behaviour capable of being described in value-neutral terms, and applied without resort to moral argument. (Raz 1979, pp. 39–40)

This conception is confronted by so-called *inclusive legal positivism*, which favours a laxer version of the thesis of social sources, according to which identifying the content of law may depend on moral reasons, when the social sources of law (e.g., the Constitution, legislation, legal precedents) *incorporate* moral considerations.[22]

This is an ongoing debate in contemporary legal philosophy that also has to deal with those defences of anti-positivism that reject the thesis of social sources in all its forms,[23] and which involves intricate questions of metaphysics, epistemology and metaethics (see e.g., Plunkett 2019).

However, this is not what I wish to address here. I only want to analyse a recent suggestion for understanding the distinction between these various conceptions. Brian Epstein (2015, pp. 98–99), in a chapter in which he reconstructs Hart's (1961) ideas—including his distinction between primary and secondary rules—suggests the following way. According to exclusive legal positivism, neither the criteria of validity of primary rules, nor the sources of those criteria—which are *anchored* in social facts of the acceptance of secondary rules—leave any room for morality. In contrast, for anti-positivism, according to Epstein, both kinds of rules may depend on moral considerations for their identification. And this is the

[21] Although Raz (1975, pp. 108–111) criticizes Searle in order to show that, in his sense, all rules are both regulative and constitutive—arguing in a way that resembles the idea that the constitutive rule of promising can be represented both as (Promise 1) and as (Promise 2)—on at least one occasion he endorses the same idea as von Wright regarding practical inference (Raz 1975, p. 34): "Consider the inference: I want to help him. Lending him £400 will help him. Therefore, I have reason to lend him £400. The first premise states an operative reason, the second states an identifying reason. It transmits, as it were, the force of the operative reason to the particular act of lending him £400."

[22] A view defended by Waluchow (1994), Coleman (2001), and to which Hart (1994) himself seems to subscribe. For presentations of this view, see Himma (2002) and Moreso (2001, 2012).

[23] See e.g. Dworkin (2006, ch. 8), where he criticises both kinds of positivism, or more recently, Greenberg (2014).

suggestion that I will discuss now: for inclusive legal positivism, while the identification of primary rules may depend on moral considerations, the basis of secondary rules never depends on moral considerations.

Let us first see the appeal of this suggestion. If we accept the suggestion that power-conferring norms, i.e. secondary norms, are constitutive rules, then we obtain a conceptual picture like the following. Law as an institutional system is composed of constitutive rules and regulative rules. The first never depend on moral reasons for their identification. The second, however, may depend on such considerations when the social sources of law incorporate them. This picture, moreover, would be in a position to explain the *institutional* dimension of law, which is intimately linked to the presence of constitutive rules. And the institutional dimension of law is what distinguishes it from morality, even for those conceptions that treat law as part of morality, because it is *institutionalized* public morality (see e.g., Dworkin 2011: ch. 19). If the rules that confer on law its institutional dimension could also depend on morality, then this would throw us into a vicious circle of some sort. Moreover, it seems more than reasonable to accept that we need a evaluation-free mechanism for identifying the Parliament who can issue laws, or the Supreme Court, or the legal adults, or those who are *tû-tû*.

Although I believe that there is a grain of truth in this view, and despite the beautiful symmetry that it secures for institutional systems of rules, I think we should reject it. The rules that confer powers, for instance, on Parliament to legislate—at least in institutional systems—confer on it powers to promulgate laws that are not contrary to the Constitution; and this entails that in order to determine the scope of that power it is necessary to assign meaning to the articles of the Constitution. And this often involves moral deliberation: think for instance of the prohibition of inhumane and degrading treatment established by Article 15 of the Spanish Constitution. Even more directly, the norm that confers the power to enter into contracts does not grant the power to enter into contracts whose content is immoral: such contracts are null and void according to Article 1.255 of the Spanish Civil Code.

On the other hand, the institutional system requires the final decisions taken by the law enforcement bodies—which are often regulative rules ("I hereby condemn *X* to pay 2,500 euros to *Y*", "I hereby condemn *Z* to a penalty of *N* years in prison", etc.)—to be identified through mechanisms that do not make any reference to morality. Otherwise these cases would always remain open; and putting an end to disputes is a central feature of legal systems. What is more, this aspect of legal systems is crucial, and the presence of enforcement bodies is what defines this kind of system. Raz (1975, pp. 132–137), who has characterized institutional systems in this way, calls them *primary* organs.

So, accounting for the institutional nature of law requires accounting for this kind of rule whose identification does not depend on moral considerations. In reality, law is at once a set of substantive rules that regulate human behaviour and a set of procedural rules that establish the authorities, the procedures and the consequences of following or violating the substantive rules. These two kinds of rules are in tension with each other. For, as I have already said, it is possible for an authority to establish that a certain substantive rule has been infringed when it has not, and vice versa. For this reason, I think that law has a few *untouchable* parts; by which I mean, some rules whose identification cannot make reference to moral argumentation.[24] These, in my opinion, are the following (Moreso 2010, 2016, 2019):

(a) The rules, *regulative* or *constitutive*, included in those individual legal and administrative decisions that are final.
(b) The procedural rules, of a *constitutive* character, which define legal institutions such as Parliament, the Supreme Court, and the Constitutional Court.
(c) The procedural rules, also of a *constitutive* character, which establish which legal decisions are final and definitive, i.e., what is *res judicata*.

Some comments about these untouchable parts are in order. First, the particular decisions that put an end to legal disputes must be able to be identified clearly and precisely. Unlike the general norms of the penal code, a judgment must establish that *A* is to be punished with the penalty of, for instance, six years in prison; *not* that *A* is to be punished with that penalty unless *A*'s conduct was legally justified. That would simply reopen the controversy. Individual decisions must be identifiable in a way that is completely opaque with respect to their justification. Proceduralists distinguish between three kinds of legal judgments: judgments of conviction, declarative judgments and constitutive judgments. A legal judgment can also have a constitutive rule as its content, such as: "*X* is the adoptive child of *Y*."

Second, the rules that confer competences on Parliament, or on the Constitutional Court, are often sources of controversy about the content or limits of its competence, as we well know. It suffices that the untouchable part of these rules allows these institutions to be uncontroversially identified. The organ and the procedure must be settled uncontroversially. The extent of its content, however, may be subject to debate.

Finally, Dworkin seems to take into account this feature when he refers to principles of procedural structure and adds:

> [O]nce we reject the two-systems model, and count law a distinct part of political morality, we must treat the special structuring principles that separate law from the rest of political morality as themselves political principles that need a moral reading. (Dworkin 2011, p. 413)

This assertion can be interpreted in two ways. If it is interpreted as saying that the justification of the function of these principles needs a moral reading, then I agree. But if it is interpreted as saying that the identification of its content depends on the moral reading, then I do not agree. When the U.S. Supreme Court, in *Bush v. Gore*,[25] decided that the method established by the Supreme Court of Florida for recounting ballot papers entailed a violation of constitutional rights, this decision was highly controversial, and many thought it to be mistaken from the viewpoint of constitutional law.[26]

---

[24] And, for these rules and only for them, the strong thesis of social sources associated with exclusive legal positivism is true as intended.

[25] 531 US 98 (2000).

[26] See e.g., Dworkin (2002).

However, as far as I know, no one thought that the Court's judgment should not be obeyed, and that President Bush was therefore an *illegal* President, even if the legal decision that authorized his proclamation was *constitutionally* invalid. Sometimes, however paradoxical it may seem, legal procedures require *invalid* rules to be applied. This is also Raz's view:

> The fact that a court can make a binding decision does not mean that it cannot err. It means that its decision is binding even if it is mistake [. . .] This seemingly paradoxical formulation illuminates the nature and function of primary norm-applying organs. (Raz 1975, p. 135)

6 Conclusion

Let me briefly conclude by stressing that constitutive rules are essential elements of our institutional systems. However, effectively practised institutional systems must also include regulative rules. They can perform their function only if they are conceived as a set of interrelated constitutive and regulative rules. And many regulative rules can only be identified by means of other rules of a constitutive nature.

In this union lies the institutional nature of law, which allows it to be made into an authoritative practice, and when it meets certain requirements, provides us with reasons to act. Such institutions require, as their initial input, that we can identify the norm-creating and norm-applying bodies without recourse to evaluative considerations. And as their final output, they require final and individual decisions that irrevocably and uncontroversially resolve the cases submitted to the jurisdiction.

References

Alarcón Cabrera C (1991) Sobre el concepto y tipología de las reglas constitutivas. Anuario de Filosofía del Derecho 8:273–295

Alchourrón C, Bulygin E (1983) Definiciones y normas. In: Bulygin E et al (eds) El lenguaje del Derecho. Homenaje a G.R. Carrió. Abeledo-Perrot, Buenos Aires, pp 11–42

Andreas H (2017) Theoretical terms in science. In: Zalta EN (ed) Stanford encyclopedia of philosophy (Fall 2017 Edition), URL = <https://plato.stanford.edu/archives/fall2017/entries/theoretical-terms-science/>

Arriagada MB (2017) Normas de competencia y normas acerca de la competencia. Eludiendo las reglas constitutivas. Doxa 40:93–121

Atienza M, Ruiz Manero J (1996) Las piezas del derecho. Ariel, Barcelona

Azzoni G (1988) Il concetto di condizione nella tipologia delle regole. Cedam, Padova

Barrère M (1990) La Escuela de Bobbio. Reglas y normas en la filosofía jurídica italiana de inspiración analítica. Tecnos, Madrid

Black M (1958) Necessary statements and rules. Philos Rev 67:313–341

Borges JL (1960) El hacedor. Emecé, Buenos Aires

Bulygin E (1992) On norms of competence. Law Philos 11:201–216

Carcaterra G (1974) Le norme costitutive. Giuffrè, Milano

Carcaterra G (1979) La forza costitutiva delle norme. Bulzoni, Roma

Carcaterra G (1985) Le regole del Circolo Pickwick. Un modelo per la teoria del diritto. Nuova civiltà delle machine 3(3–4):16–25
Carnelutti F (1955) Inesistenza dell'atto guiridico? Rivista di diritto processuale 10:208–235
Coleman J (2001) The practice of principle: in defense of a pragmatist approach to legal theory. Oxford University Press, Oxford
Conte AG (1985) Regole eidetico-costitutive. Nuova civiltà delle machine 3(3–4):26–33
Conte AG (1989) Filosofia del linguaggio normativo. I. Studi 1965-1981. Giappichelli, Turin
Conte AG (1995) Filosofia del linguaggio normativo. II. Studi 1982-1994. Giappichelli, Turin
Conte AG (2001) Filosofia del linguaggio normativo. III. Studi 1995-2001. Giappichelli, Turin
Di Lucia P (ed) (2003) Ontologia sociale. Potere deontico e regole costitutive. Quodlibet, Macerata
Diver N (2004) Institutions and social justice. PhD dissertation, University of Pennsylvania. https://books.google.es/books?id=HjZ9zsUAWz4C
Duarte D (2018) Norms on language and the regulativeness of constitutive norms. Diritto & Questioni Pubbliche 18:135–156
Dworkin R (ed) (2002) A badly flawed election: Debating Bush v. Gore, the Supreme Court, and American Democracy. The New Press, New York
Dworkin R (2006) Justice in robes. Harvard University Press, Cambridge
Dworkin R (2011) Justice for hedgehogs. Harvard University Press, Cambridge
Epstein B (2015) The ant trap: rebuilding the foundations of the social sciences. Oxford University Press, Oxford
Ferrer Beltrán J (2000) Las normas de competencia. Un aspecto de la dinámica jurídica. Centro de Estudios Constitucionales, Madrid
García-Carpintero M (2004) Assertion and the semantics of force-markers. In: Bianchi C (ed) The semantics/pragmatics distinction. The University of Chicago Press, Stanford, pp 133–166
García-Carpintero M (2021) How to understand rule-constituted kinds. Rev Philos Psychol 13(1): 7–27
González Lagier D (1995) Acción y norma en G. H. von Wright. Centro de Estudios Constitucionales, Madrid
Greenberg M (2014) The moral impact theory of law. Yale Law J 123:1288–1314
Grocio H (1625) De Jure Belli ac Pacis, libri tres. In quibus is naturae & Gentium: ítem iruis publici preciptae expilicantur, Pariisis: Apud Nicolam Buon, MDCXXV, cum privliegio regis Via Gallica (the French National Library). https://gallica.bnf.fr/ark:/12148/bpt6k97657872/f7.item
Guastini R (1985) Teorie delle regole costitutive. Rivista internazionale di filosofia del diritto 60: 548–564
Hart HLA (1961) The concept of law. Oxford University Press, Oxford
Hart HLA (1994) Postscript. In: Bulloch P, Raz J (eds) H L A Hart. The concept of law, 2nd edn. Oxford University Press, Oxford
Hernández Marín R (1984) El derecho como dogma. Tecnos, Madrid
Himma KE (2002) Inclusive legal positivism. In: Coleman JL, Shapiro SJ (eds) The Oxford handbook of jurisprudence and philosophy of law. Oxford University Press, Oxford, pp 125–165
Hindriks F (2007) The status of the knowledge account of assertion. Linguist Philos 30(3):393–406
Lewis D (1979) Scorekeeping in a language game. J Philos Log 8:339–359
MacCormick N, Weinberger O (1986) An institutional theory of law. Kluwer, Dordrecht
Maitra I (2011) Assertion, norms, and games. In: Brown J, Cappelen H (eds) Assertion: new philosophical essays. Oxford University Press, Oxford, pp 277–295
Marmor A (2009) Social conventions: from language to law. Princeton University Press, Princeton
Marsili N (2019) The norm of assertion: a 'constitutive' rule? Inquiry: Interdiscip J Philos:1–22. https://doi.org/10.1080/0020174X.2019.1667868
Mazzarese T (1985) Metaregole. Nuova civiltà delle macchine 3(3–4):65–73
Midgley GCJ (1959) Linguistic rules. Proc Aristot Soc 59:271–290
Mir Puig S (2015) Derecho penal. Parte general. Reppertor, Madrid
Moreso JJ (1998) Legal indeterminacy and constitutional interpretation. Kluwer, Dordrecht

Moreso JJ (2001) In defense of inclusive legal positivism. In: Chiassoni P (ed) The legal ought. Giappichelli, Turin, pp 37–64
Moreso JJ (2010) La doctrina Julia Roberts y los desacuerdos irrecusables. In: Moreso JJ, Prieto Sanchís L, Ferrer Beltran J (eds) Los desacuerdos en el Derecho. Fundación Coloquio Jurídico Europeo, Madrid, pp 49–86
Moreso JJ (2012) Legal defeasibility and the connection between law and morality. In: Ferrer Beltran J, Ratti GB (eds) The logic of legal requirements: essays on defeasibility. Oxford University Press, Oxford, pp 225–237
Moreso JJ (2016) The untouchables of law. Crit Rev Int Soc Polit Philos 19:496–504
Moreso JJ (2019) Diez tesis sobre el neoconstitucionalismo (y dos razones a favor del positivismo jurídico). Revista i-latina 1:1–42
Moreso JJ, Vilajosana JM (2004) Introducción a la teoría del derecho. Marcial Pons, Madrid
Pagin P (2016) Assertion. In: Zalta EN (ed) Stanford encyclopedia of philosophy (Winter 2016 Edition). URL = <https://plato.stanford.edu/archives/win2016/entries/assertion/>
Plunkett D (2019) Robust normativity, morality, and legal positivism. In: Plunkett D, Shapiro SJ, Toh K (eds) Dimensions of normativity. Oxford University Press, Oxford, pp 105–136
Ramsey FP (1978) Theories (1929). In: Ramsey FP (ed) Foundations: essays philosophy, logic, mathematics and economics. Routledge & Kegan Paul, London, pp 101–125
Rawls J (1955) Two concepts of rules. Philos Rev 64:3–32
Raz J (1975) Practical reason and norms. Hutchinson, London
Raz J (1979) The authority of law. Oxford University Press, Oxford
Raz J (1994) Ethics in the public domain. Oxford University Press, Oxford
Raz J (2001) Reasoning with rules. Curr Leg Probl 54:1–18
Reinach A (1913) Die apriorischen Grundlagen des bürgerlichen Rechtes. Jahrbuch für Philosophie und phänomenologische Forschung 1:685–847
Reinach A (1983) The Apriori Foundations of the civil law. Translated into English by J. F. Crosby. Aletheia: Int J Philos 3:1–142
Robles G (1984) Las reglas del derecho y las reglas de los juegos. UIB, Palma de Mallorca
Ross A (1957) Tû-Tû. Harv Law Rev 70:812–825
Ross A (1968) Directives and norms. Routledge & Kegan Paul, London
Roversi C (2007) Pragmatica delle regole costitutive. GEDIT, Bologna
Ruiter DWP (1993) Institutional legal facts. Kluwer, Dordrecht
Ruiz Manero J (2015) Algunas pretensiones en conflicto en el Derecho. Analisi e Diritto 2015:71–86
Searle J (1964) How to derive 'ought' from 'is'. Philos Rev 73:43–58
Searle J (1969) Speech acts: a theory in the philosophy of language. Cambridge University Press, Cambridge
Searle J (1995) The construction of social reality. The Free Press, New York
Searle J (2018) Constitutive rules. Argumenta 4(1):51–54
Smart JJC (1973) An outline of a system of utilitarian ethics. In: Smart JJC, Williams B (eds) Utilitarianism: for and against. Cambridge University Press, Cambridge
Vega J (2007) Normas constitutivas: ¿una categoría autónoma? Sobre la problemática de la constitutividad normativa. In: Moreso JJ (ed) Legal Theory: Teoría del derecho. Legal Positivism and Conceptual Analysis/Positivismo jurídico y Análisis conceptual. Proceedings of the 22nd IVR World Congress. Granada 2005. Volume I. ARSP-Beiheft 106. Franz Steiner, Stuttgart, pp 246–258
von Wright GH (1963) Norm and action: a logical enquiry. Routledge & Kegan Paul, London
Waluchow WJ (1994) Inclusive legal positivism. Oxford University Press, Oxford
Williamson T (1996) Knowing and asserting. Philos Rev 105(4):489–523
Williamson T (2000) Assertion. In: Williamson T (ed) Knowledge and its limits. Oxford University Press, Oxford, pp 238–270
Znamierowski C (1921) Podstawowe Pojęcia Teorii Prawa, cz. I. Układ Prawny i Norma Prawna. Fiszer i Majewski, Poznań

Constituting Power

Corrado Roversi

Abstract Constitutive rules have been an important concept in philosophy over the last century. However, this concept tends to divide scholars between those who consider it to be an important explanatory tool and those who, instead, believe it to be void. In previous writings, I have tried to defend the heuristic relevance of this concept and to qualify it against several objections. In this paper, I discuss the relation between constitutive and power-conferring rules and, more in general, the relation between constitutive rules and institutional power. I argue that the set of constitutive rules and power-conferring rules overlap but do not coincide: Some, but not all constitutive rules have a power-conferring nature and, conversely, some, but not all power-conferring rules have a constitutive role. Then, I consider a broader question, namely, the relation between constitutive rules and institutional power, and I show that not all institutional power is coincident with power constituted or conferred by rules.

1 Introduction: In Defence of Constitutive Rules

Constitutive rules have been an important concept in philosophy over the last century. After the introduction of this concept by the the Polish legal philosopher Czeslaw Znamieroswki and later independently by John Rawls, the notion has played a role in debates about normativity, the nature of speech acts, the Is/Ought question, the metaphysics of the social world, to name only a few. However, this concept tends to divide scholars between those who consider it to be an important explanatory tool and those who, instead, believe it to be void. I am in the first camp, and admittedly this is not a comfortable position: Several authoritative authors have levelled important criticisms to the concept of constitutive rules, even recently.

C. Roversi (✉)
University of Bologna, Department of Legal Studies, Bologna, Italy
e-mail: corrado.roversi@unibo.it

G. Villa-Rosas, T. Spaak (eds.), *Legal Power and Legal Competence*, Law and Philosophy Library 140, https://doi.org/10.1007/978-3-031-28555-4_9

In previous writings, I have tried to defend the explanatory relevance of this concept and to qualify it against several objections.[1] Some argue, for example, that all kinds of rules can be constitutive, and that there is no structural opposition between constitutive and regulative rules. This is true, but it does not entail that constitutive rules do not exist: If we replace a strong structural distinction between constitutive "count-as" rules and regulative rules with a pragmatic distinction between constitutive vs regulative *uses* of a rule, and consider this last distinction as a continuum between two extremes rather than a dichotomy, the objection can be countered. Others argue that constitutive rules can be reduced to more ordinary regulative rules, and in particular to a regulative connection between conditions and normative consequences.[2] I have argued that this reduction does not work, because the *ratio* of the connection is not captured by it and needs instead the concept of a constituted status. Recent developments in social metaphysics replace constitutive rules with the notion of "grounding",[3] but this, I have tried to show, can cause a collapse of the strong, practical normativity of statuses on the weak, epistemic normativity of explanations. Several scholars think that constitutive rules entail a weird, platonic metaphysics of ideal entities,[4] but in fact a metaphysics of immaterial artifacts is sufficient to explain them while being consistent with an empiricist attitude. This also shows, in my view, why constitutive rules are not simply stipulative definitions:[5] because their point is not that of defining a meaning but rather that of creating an artifact's interaction plan. The consequence of this is that constitutive rules, conceived as speech acts, have a double illocutionary point: declarative *and* prescriptive. Constitutive rules are not aimed at teaching agents how to speak but rather how to behave when interacting with an institutional element. Of course, these objections do not exhaust the range of criticisms that can be raised against constitutive rules, but at least they show the reasons why the notion is still worth considering and fruitful. There is a very simple intuition according to which rules make possible new activities, new ways of talking, even new objects: This is indeed a constitutive role and I think that any empiricist caution one may have should not entail ignoring its relevance.

As I said, in defending constitutive rules I have also tried to qualify the notion. First, as already mentioned, I defend a pragmatic notion of constitutive rules and not a logical one. Hence, I do not think that constitutive rules must have a peculiar structure, for example a "count-as" structure ("X counts as Y in context C"). This is the formula that J. R. Searle has often cited as being characteristic of constitutive rules and that, according to a shared misunderstanding of his view, should be found in all constitutive rules. In reality Searle himself states clearly, already in *Speech*

[1] Roversi (2007, 2018, 2019, 2021a).

[2] Hindriks and Guala (2015), building an argument very similar to Ross (1957).

[3] Epstein (2015).

[4] Guastini (1983).

[5] Contra Guastini: see ibid.

Acts,[6] that only some constitutive rules have this form, whereas some have a more regulative structure, and that in most cases only the system of constitutive rules has this form. Searle is not alone in this regard. Amedeo Conte,[7] for instance, shows with a simple example borrowed from chess—"Bishops must move diagonally"—that the process of conceptual constitution of institutional elements involves rules that are clearly regulative in structure (he calls these rules "deontic eidetic-constitutive rules"). And, conversely, constitutive rules in the "count-as" form can have a distinctively regulative purpose. Neil MacCormick's[8] example "Broken bottles count as weapons in pub brawls" shows in a wonderfully simple and explanatory way that very often count-as statements are used only to include entities within an already rule-regulated domain. More in general, depending on context, the same statement can fulfill a constitutive or regulative function: "Well-educated people do not step onto flowerbeds" can mean that people should not step onto flowerbeds, if the statement is written on a sign in a park, thus expressing a regulative rule, but it can also be genuinely constitutive of the idea of education if included in a handbook of etiquette. The distinction between constitutive and regulative rules is not a structural distinction between kinds of rules, but rather a pragmatic distinction between different ways of using rules. This leads to a pragmatic conception of constitutive rules: being constitutive is not simply a question of semantic content but of illocutionary force.

Second, just like all speech acts, constitutive rules must fulfil some requirements. Some are formal: Constitutive rules must define the conditions for an institutional element to be instantiated in the actual practice, but they must also define what is the normative import of the element (namely, what consequences for the practice an instantiation of that element has) and what kind of regulations are involved in interacting with it. For example, chess pieces must be put on the chessboard in specific positions, but it is also crucial for players to know that all chess pieces can take other pieces and checkmate the king, and also to know how those pieces must be moved. Similarly, legal transactions are concluded if specific acts under specific circumstances are performed, but legal transactions are performed because they have consequences in terms of the obligations and rights of individuals. To use Searle's formula in the way in which it was meant since the beginning, namely, as a "useful mnemonic",[9] it can be important to remember that constitutive rules must state which X counts as Y, but also which Z is implied by Y: this is Frank Hindriks "XYZ Formula",[10] by which we can also capture Neil MacCormick's point about the need for "consequential rules" as a complement to "institutive rules".[11] Further, as it is clear in Conte's already-mentioned example "Bishops must move diagonally in

[6] Searle (1969), p. 36.

[7] Conte (1995), pp. 279–280.

[8] MacCormick (1998), p. 334 n. 25.

[9] Searle and Smith (2003), p. 301.

[10] Hindriks (2005), pp. 123 ff.

[11] MacCormick (1986), pp. 52 ff.

chess," the element Z stating the normative consequences of being a Y includes also prescriptions about how the constituted entity must behave and, conversely, about how agents must behave when interacting with that entity.

Third—and this again is no surprise given their pragmatic nature—constitutive rules are context-dependent. Apart from formal requirements, they must also fulfil substantive requirements, depending again on the context in which they are used. Rules constitutive of a game element must define conditions that players can perform and consequences that are (directly or indirectly) relevant for victory, whereas rules constitutive of a legal institutional entity will at least define the relevant conditions of existence of that entity within the legal system and the consequences of that existence in terms of rights, powers, and duties of legal subjects. As Hubert Schwyzer[12] has shown, the overall meaning of a system of constitutive rules depends on the broader social practice in which that system is embedded, and that practice sets the conceptual boundaries that the constitution of institutional elements must respect: to use an expression by Andrei Marmor,[13] the "deep" conventions in the background of which surface conventions are framed.[14]

This concludes my preliminary discussion. To capture it with a formula, being constitutive is not a structural feature of a rule but a way in which rules are used. Constitutive rules create the concept of an artifactual status by way of a connection between conditions for its instantiation and normative consequences, *plus* a point, a *ratio* given by the deeper social practice in which that status is embedded. Hence, constitutive rules both declare what the artifactual status is and regulate the interaction of agents with it: They "constitute (and also regulate)", as Searle originally said. This discussion provides the general framework within which I will address the specific topic of this paper, namely, the relation between constitutive and power-conferring rules and, more in general, the relation between constitutive rules and institutional power.

I will try to argue for two distinct theses. First, though power-conferring rules are often constitutive and constitutive rules are often power-conferring, these are two distinct sets: they overlap but do not coincide. In arguing for this conclusion, I will try to show why these two sets are related but not reducible. Second, though much of institutionally-relevant power—the kind of social power that depends on an institution—is attributed by power-conferring, possibly constitutive rules, power-conferring constitutive rules and power-conferring rules in general do not exhaust it. There is a whole domain of institutionally-relevant power that is not conferred nor constituted by an institution's rules.

[12] Schwyzer (1969).

[13] Marmor (2009), ch. 3.

[14] See also Lorini (2000), pp. 263ff.; Roversi (2010) on this.

2 Constitutive Rules and Power-Conferring Rules

2.1 Four Possible Relations

There are five possible relations between the set of constitutive rules (or better, as said: of rules used in a constitutive way) and the set of power-conferring rules: either (1) the two sets overlap, or (2) they coincide, or (3) they are entirely distinct, or (4) the first is included in the second, or (5) the former is included in the latter. However, I will rule out since the beginning alternative (3)—that the two sets are distinct—leaving only four available. Constitutive rules create statuses, and these statuses are at least sometimes connected with powers as one of their normative consequences: hence, it is apparent that constitutive rules can have a power-conferring nature and that the two sets cannot be entirely distinct. The problem is not whether constitutive rules can be put in connection with power-conferring rules, but rather what is the connection between them. Given the other four options, it seems fruitful to proceed by addressing alternatives (4) and (5)—identifying a relation of inclusion of one set into the other. If it will turn out that at least one of these alternatives is false, then (2) is false: if not all constitutive rules are power-conferring, or if there are power-conferring rules that are not constitutive, then the two sets cannot coincide either. Moreover, if it will turn out that both (4) and (5) are false, given that (3) is false, the conclusion will be (1)—the two sets overlap but do not coincide, and one is not included in the other—, which is the only other available alternative. This will indeed be my conclusion and, in order to argue for it, I will proceed as follows: I will first consider, in Sect. 2.2, whether all constitutive rules have a power-conferring nature, and I will conclude that they do not; then I will enquire, in Sect. 2.3, whether all power-conferring rules are constitutive, and again I will answer negatively. Finally, I will identify the features of the overlap between these two sets. Then, in Sect. 3, I will consider a broader question, namely, the relation between constitutive rules and institutional power—a notion that, as I will argue, is not entirely coincident with that of power constituted or conferred by rules.

2.2 Are Constitutive Rules Power-Conferring?

Several authors have underscored the fact that constitutive rules have an essentially enabling role. In a paper titled *The Nature of Institutional Obligation*, dated 1972, J. R. Cameron suggests that this enabling role is connected to the very idea of constituting new practices:

> The constitutive convention which forms the basis of such a practice, whether it be promising or playing Pontoon, is not a convention which restricts people's action or limits their freedom. Rather it plays an enabling role, making it possible for them to do things that

> they want to do, creating the possibility of a new kind of institutional status, such as that of husband or wife, which, once it exists, is a status people desire enter into.[15]

In this general sense, constitutive rules can be seen as power-conferring—they give people the power to perform a new activity—or more broadly as enabling, because by creating new activities they open spaces of possibility. If we limit our analysis in this way, constitutive rules can indeed be seen as a kind of power-conferring rules. Such an approach, however, would be quite superficial. It is helpful here to use a distinction between two senses of constitutive rule that Jaap Hage has used in his works: that between practice-defining rules and fact-to-fact rules.[16] Systems of rules can generically be qualified as constitutive because they define a practice. But, among rules constitutive in this sense, there are some rules that are constitutive in a more specific sense because they attach normative consequences and conditions of instantiation to statuses. What we are looking for is not the generic enabling nature of constitutive rules in the first sense, but rather an equivalence between power-conferring rules and constitutive rules in the second, more specific sense. Cameron's broad idea of the enabling character of constitutive rules therefore does not bring us much closer to our objective.

Let's focus then on constitutive rules that create a status. To exemplify, let's consider not the system of rules of chess as constitutive of the game of chess, but rather the specific rules that constitute chess pieces by connecting their conditions of instantiation, normative consequences, and inherent regulation within a general teleological framework. An example can be the following:

> The pieces placed on c1 and f1 count as the white bishops in chess. Bishops must move diagonally. Bishops can take other pieces and check the king. Bishops can be taken by other pieces through a valid move.

Is such a rule inherently power-conferring? Of course, this depends in large part on the notion of power-conferring rule that we assume. In his work on legal competence, Torben Spaak frames the notion of competence, similarly to Hohfeld, as the capacity to change the legal position of someone (another subject, or the acting subject) by way of an act performed with the specific intention of obtaining that change.[17] In this conception, norms of competence conditionally connect changes in legal positions with the performance of acts plus a specific intention. This general idea is shared by other legal theorists. Lars Lindahl and David Reidhav, for example, conceive competence norms as rules framing ground relations between manifestations of intentions and legal effects,[18] and Jaap Hage, too, connects competence directly to rules establishing a relation between a certain kind of legal powers and a certain kinds of intentional acts, though he argues for a distinction between legal powers and competence (the former being based on any kind of rules framing a

[15] Cameron (1972), p. 325.

[16] Hage (2018a).

[17] Spaak (2009), p. 78.

[18] Lindahl and Reidhav (2017), pp. 169–171.

relation between legal facts, while the latter being a specific legal status with the power to create particular legal consequences by means of juridical acts).[19] The trait which is common to all these analyses, therefore, is the idea that power-conferring rules, in the sense of competence norms, create the possibility to obtain some legal effects if some acts with the intention to obtain those effects are performed. So, are all constitutive rules power-conferring in this sense? The answer is no. Constitutive rules can constitute statuses that are not connected with powers, in the sense of the capacity to intentionally get effects if some acts are performed. A famous example by John Searle can help me show this point:

> Consider for example a primitive tribe that initially builds a wall around its territory. The wall is an instance of a function imposed in virtue of sheer physics: the wall, we will suppose, is big enough to keep intruders out and the members of the tribe in. But suppose the wall gradually evolves from being a physical barrier to being a symbolic barrier. Imagine that the wall gradually decays so that the only thing left is a line of stones. But imagine that the inhabitants and their neighbors continue to recognize the line of stones as marking the boundary of the territory in such a way that it affects their behavior.[20]

The border, in Searle's example, can be connected with powers (for the example, the power of chiefs to rule within the border) but it is mainly connected with an obligation, namely, the duty not to trespass: It can simply have a purely disabling role. Similarly, as Searle makes clear, status functions can be connected with "rights, responsibilities, obligations, duties, privileges, entitlements, penalties, authorizations, permissions", not simply with powers, and this is why Searle qualifies the "deontic powers" connected with status functions as being either "positive" or "negative".

> On our earlier suggestion, that in general the Y terms confers (or denies) power, the obvious hypothesis would be that there are two broad categories of such status-functions. The first is where the agent is endowed with some new power, certification, authorization, entitlement, right, permission, or qualification granting the ability to do something he or she could not otherwise have done; and the second is where the agent is required, obligated, in duty bound, penalized, enjoined, or otherwise compelled to something he or she would not otherwise have had to do. [. . .] Roughly speaking, the two major categories are those of positive and negative power.[21]

Some statuses, moreover, are inherently honorific and do not entail any kind of power or duty:

> the point of honors (and dishonors) is to have statuses valued (or disvalued) for their own sake, rather than just for their further consequences. Examples are victory and defeat in games, and institutionally sanctioned forms of public honor and disgrace.[22]

As Searle shows clearly, statuses can be connected with powers but need not, which means that constitutive rules can be power-conferring but they need not.

---

[19] Hage (forthcoming).

[20] Searle (1995), p. 39.

[21] Searle (1995), p. 100.

[22] Searle (1995), p. 101.

There remains, however, a perceived connection between constitutive rules and power-conferring rules. Searle himself, when discussing the significance of institutional facts for social life, gives priority to the enabling aspect. He writes in this regard: "The existence of institutions, as I have emphasized over and over, is enormously enabling in human life, and gives us all kinds of possibilities that we could not otherwise conceive of",[23] thus suggesting that, though the connection between constitutive and power-conferring rules is not necessary, it is quite typical. An interesting statement of this connection can also be found in Joseph Raz. When discussing constitutive rules in his *Practical Reason and Norms*, Raz writes:

> Searle has an additional test for identifying constitutive rules. They can be and often are cast in the form 'X counts as Y in the context C'. [. . .] It may be that in proposing this second test Searle is groping towards the distinction between power-conferring and mandatory norms.[24]

A few pages after this passage, Raz indeed provides a reformulation of the constitutive rules of chess pieces in terms of power-conferring rules.

> 'A player who is to make the first move or whose opponent has made the last move, has power, unless he makes another move, to move his rook to any square lying horizontally or vertically on a straight line from its present position, provided that no other piece lies between its present position and that square and that the square to which it moves is not occupied by one of his own pieces.' [. . .] Similar power-conferring rules apply to all the other pieces in the game.[25]

In Raz's view, therefore, even "deontic" constitutive rules regulating how a piece *should* behave—the kind of rules that Conte would have called "deontic eidetic-constitutive"—must be seen as modalities of exercise of a power. Searle's example of the border, however, shows that such an analysis cannot be extended to all kinds of rule-constituted institutional statuses. If constitutive rules create normative statuses, there is no conceptual reason to assume that these statuses cannot entail obligations only. To state my conclusion again: Constitutive rules can be power-conferring, perhaps they most often are, but they are not so necessarily.

Moreover, this conclusion and its underlying argument—the idea that there can be disabling, rule-constituted statuses—make it possible to counter Raz's general criticism against constitutive rules. Raz argues that, if we assume Searle's criterion for distinguishing constitutive from regulative rules, then all rules are both regulative and constitutive and the distinction loses its relevance. The criterion criticized by Raz is stated by Searle in *Speech Acts* and is formulated in terms of action-descriptions:

> There is a trivial sense in which the creation of any rule creates the possibility of new forms of behaviour, namely, behaviour done in accordance with the rule. That is not the sense in which my remark is intended. What I mean can perhaps be best put in the formal mode. Where the rule is purely regulative, behaviour which is in accordance with the rule could be given the same description or specification (the same answer to the question "What did

[23] Searle (2010), p. 124.

[24] Raz (1975), pp. 110–111.

[25] Raz (1975), p. 115.

> he do?") whether or not the rule existed, provided the description or specification makes no explicit reference to the rule. But where the rule (the system of rules) is constitutive, behaviour which is in accordance with the rule can receive specifications and descriptions which it could not receive if the rule or rules did not exist.[26]

In reality, Raz writes, a rule-dependent description of rule-following behaviour is possible for all kinds of rules. He provides two examples, each divided into a pair of act-descriptions, one that is rule-dependent and one that is not rule-dependent:

1 (a) 'Giving £50 to Mr. Jones' (b) 'Paying income Tax'

2 (a) 'Saying "I promise"' (b) 'Promising'.[27]

Given these two pairs of act-descriptions, "both the law imposing income tax and the rule about promising are each of them both a regulative and a constitutive rule".[28] Raz therefore concludes as follows:

> There is nothing in Searle's explanation to suggest that his classification is exclusive, that the same rule cannot be both regulative and constitutive. Searle assumes that the same act can be given different descriptions and that a rule is regulative if a description of a certain kind is available for acts in accordance with it, and that a rule is constitutive if a different description, which is of a kind logically independent from the first, is available to describe the same act. But it follows from this account that *all* rules are both regulative and constitutive.[29]

Raz is here arguing that, just like in the case of "citizens must pay income tax every year", *all* rules—even those that are most clearly regulative—entail a non-trivial, rule-dependent action description like 'paying income tax' as opposed to 'Giving £50 to Mr. Jones'. If this is the correct interpretation of his text, then Raz is assuming that "citizens must pay income tax every year" is clearly an instance of a regulative, non-constitutive rule. It seems to me, however, that this assumption in its own turn presupposes Raz's reading of all constitutive rules as inherently enabling—a reading that, as we have seen, is false. The rule "Citizens must pay income tax every year" is a constitutive rule of the institutional status "income tax", a status that, just like that of a border, is connected with a disabling, not enabling, institutional entity. This institution is linked with a specific field of application and exemption, a specific mode of calculation, and one main normative consequence: Citizens must normally pay the amount in money every year. Compare it with the rule "Do not park in the city centre on Thursday evenings": *that* is a regulative rule. People already park in the city centre, even without the rule, but they would not pay an income tax without its specific regulation.

Raz could reply here that the way I have framed the comparison between parking and paying income tax is biased by my own view. The problem is not whether people pay income tax without the rules, but rather whether people have an income without

[26] Searle (1969), p. 35.

[27] Raz (1975), p. 108.

[28] Raz (1975), pp. 108–109.

[29] Raz (1975), p. 109.

the rule: and they have one. The conclusion, Raz could argue, is that the rule about paying an income tax is regulative, not constitutive, because it regulates an already-existing activity, namely, that of earning an income. Even if framed in this way, Raz's position would still be wrong, but it would be so in an illuminating way. It would show a difference between two ways in which rules can be constitutive in the legal domain: They can be constitutive because they make possible an activity for ordinary citizens *and* officials, or they can be constitutive because they make possible a practice only for officials or legal experts. I still think that "paying income tax" is an institutional, rule-constituted activity both for citizens and officials, but I concede that the concept of "income tax", its regulation, all the practices that revolve around it are more a matter for accountants and tax lawyers than for non-experts. Hence, one can say that what is really constituted by the rules is not the general form of life of earning an income and giving a tribute to the State, but the highly professionalized activity of "paying income tax" as the outcome of a complex calculus, a careful consideration of strategies for tax efficiency, a deep knowledge of tax exemption zones. This is an important distinction, that can be found more clearly in other areas of the law. Consider Art. 575 of the Italian Criminal Code:

> Murder. Whoever causes the death of a human being is punishable by no less than 21 years in prison.

Despite its regulative appearance, this rule is also constitutive, and in particular it is constitutive of the concept of "murder" in criminal law. This does not mean of course that murdering people is not possible in absence of criminal law: What is not possible, however, is the highly institutionalized activity of prosecuting murder as performed by officials and lawyers. Art. 575 is constitutive not of the activity of killing people, but of the way the law responds to that activity. Identifying this ambiguity of the expression "constituting a legal practice"—an officials' practice, or a citizens' practice, or both—is an important point that must be kept in mind when dealing with constitutive rules in legal institutions, as opposed to other kinds of social institutions.

With this I conclude my treatment of the question "Are all constitutive rules power-conferring in nature?". My answer, to state it again, is: No. Constitutive rules, at least if not interpreted in a generic sense of practice-defining rules but rather as rules that constitute institutional statuses, can be power-conferring but can also create disabling statuses. There is no conceptual connection between constitutive rules and power-attribution.

2.3 *Are Power-Conferring Rules Constitutive?*

Let me now consider the second, inverse question: "Are all power-conferring rules constitutive?". This question can be reframed as follows: Do all the rules that confer power to a status constitute the concept of that status and make it possible? The answer is negative. Professors have the power to give a score to students after the exam, but they also have the power to include some research assistants in their research group when applying for research funds. If we took away from professors the power to share funds with their research assistants, for example by giving research assistant their own funds, the status of being a professor and the ensuing institutional practices would still be there in their most important elements; if we took away the power of evaluating students' knowledge, however, perhaps professorship would not exist anymore or at least it would be essentially changed. Hence it seems that, just as not all constitutive rules are power-conferring, not all power-conferring rules are constitutive: some are, some are not.

The problem here is to understand which power-conferring rules are constitutive, and which are not. I will use here Lynne Baker's concept of "primary kind property", which she developed in working to solve the problem of material constitution and understand which change an object can undergo without losing its identity. In Baker's view, objects have primary-kind properties—i.e., properties they cannot lose without ceasing to exist as such—, and artifacts are objects whose primary-kind property is a function.[30] As said, constitutive rules define the interaction plan of immaterial artifacts, hence Baker's line of argument can be extended to institutional statuses. In order to understand which power-conferring rules are constitutive of a given status, it is necessary to understand whether the conferred powers are part of the "primary function" of that status in Baker's sense, and in order to do this we must imagine counterfactually what would happen if the relevant power-conferring rule were repealed: Would that status remain the same status? Would it retain its identity, that is, its functional role in the system? These questions can be answered only by considering again the teleological background of institutional entities, a background that I have already shown to be one of the necessary elements of constitutive rules.

Of course, trying to find the functional role of an institutional status is in large part a matter of interpretation. In some cases, however, the function of a status is stated by the rules themselves, and in that case the kind of counter-factual reasoning I am proposing is easier. Consider the example of the President of the Republic in the Italian Constitution:

> Art. 87 of the Italian Constitution. The President of the Republic is the Head of the State and represents national unity.

Now, let us examine the following two power-conferring rules about the President:

> (1) Art. 74 of the Italian Constitution. The President of the Republic may send Parliament a reasoned opinion to request that a law scheduled for promulgation be considered anew. If such law is passed again, it shall be promulgated.
>
> (2) Art. 59 of the Italian Constitution: The President of the Republic may appoint five citizens who have honoured the Nation through their outstanding achievements in the social, scientific, artistic and literary fields as life Senators.

According to the kind of counterfactual reasoning I am conjecturing, Rule (1) is a constitutive power-conferring rule, whereas Rule (2) is not. Given that the President

[30] Baker (2004).

of the Republic represents National unity, it has among its primary functions that of guaranteeing the legal system's constitutional coherence: Hence, if Art 74 were repealed by a Constitutional reform, the status would lose a power which is essential to fulfill its role, because the President could not be anymore a constitutional control over the Chambers' legislative activity. On the other hand, it seems that Art 59 is not constitutive, though it is clearly power-conferring: The President can represent the Nation's unity even without being able to appoint life Senators. Of course, the system envisages other kinds of constitutional control, the Constitutional Court being the most important one. What is important for our purposes, however, is not the system as a whole but the essential function that a given status must perform within the system. If the rule-conferred power is necessary to perform that function, then it is "primary" in Baker's sense and it is an integral part of the status' identity conditions. In that case, the power-conferring rule is constitutive. On the other hand, the capacity to appoint important personalities, who played an important role in Italy's culture and progress, with the status of life Senators is *not* a primary function: It certainly represents the Nation's acknowledgment, but the President can fulfill its symbolic role even in absence of that power. Hence the power-conferring rule is not constitutive.

The whole argument rests on the assumption that trying to find the essential function of institutional entities is a meaningful endeavour, an idea some are skeptical about. In general, this is an assumption of my conception of constitutive rules and of institutions, and particularly of the idea of an essential teleological role that institutional statuses must play within an institution embedded in a deeper social practice. I cannot argue for this assumption here. As a partial support to it, one could perhaps appeal to Jaap Hage's observation, that he brings to counter Alf Ross's reductionism, according to which institutional statuses are translatable and comparable across different legal systems even if the relevant rules that constitute them are in some way different.[31] If statuses are completely expressed by the connection between its conditions and normative consequences, how can it be that different regulations concerning, say, marriage can nevertheless be compared? The answer could be, in this light: because an analogy is found not strictly between the rules, but between the teleological role these statuses play within the respective institutions, hence by finding a common "primary function" working in the background of slightly different regulations.

I have thus argued that constitutive rules and power-conferring rules can be related but that there is no conceptual connection between them: There can be constitutive rules that are not power-conferring and there can be power-conferring rules that are not constitutive. Power-conferring constitutive rules are those rules that constitute institutional statuses by attaching enabling normative consequences to them; constitutive power-conferring rules are those rules that attribute a power that is a primary-kind property, or better a primary function, of the constituted institutional status.

---

[31] Hage (2018b), ch. 2, sec. 3.4. My view on this topic can be found in Roversi (2021a).

3 Constitutive Rules and Institutional Power

I have thus far argued that the set of constitutive rules and that of power-conferring rules overlap but do not coincide, nor is one included in the other. I turn now to the more general question of the relation between constitutive rules and institutional power. What I will try to argue is that, even in those cases where power is attributed only by way of rules constitutive of statuses—where all power-conferring rules are constitutive—there are kinds of power relevant for an institution that are not constituted by rules. To put it in a formula: not all institutionally-relevant power is rule-dependent.

3.1 Three Layers of an Institution

I have argued in previous writings that the ontology of an institution can be fruitfully analyzed as an interlocking of three, metaphysically connected layers: an institutional, meta-institutional, and para-institutional layer.[32] The institutional layer includes all the rules the institution is made of, be they authoritative or customary, regulative or constitutive; the meta-institutional layer provides the teleological background of constitutive rules, that is, the broader and deeper social practice in which the institution is embedded and which gives it its overall purpose and meaning; the para-institutional layer includes all the features of the institution that depend not on its actual rules but on the way these rules are practiced in a given social context.

This distinction may seem very abstract and obscure, so an example is in order to clarify it. Let's consider a game. One could say that the game is made up of—and conceptually constituted by—rules. So, in the case of chess, there are constitutive rules that dictate how pieces are placed on a chessboard, how they must be moved, and what is their role in the game; in the case of football, rules define the number of players, how players must behave, the way a goal is scored, etc. Similarly, legal institutions are defined by rules. Rules define, for example, how a specific tax is to be calculated, when it must be paid and who should pay it, and in so doing they constitute a specific institutional concept—like the concept of income tax, used by Raz, or *IRPEF* in Italian, *imposta sul reddito delle persone fisiche*.

Even though the rules play an essential role in defining these institutions, however, they are not sufficient: It would be pointless to abide by the rules of chess or football without knowing what competitive game-playing is, and impossible to understand *IRPEF* if we did not know what a tax is for, what is the role of taxation in our political community. The overall institution constituted by rules presupposes a deeper background, that clarifies its teleology and its basic values. Some of this background can be made explicit (the duty to pay taxes in proportion to

[32] Roversi (2018, 2021b).

income is codified in Art. 53 of the Italian Constitution), some is simply given for granted (the very notion of a tax is presupposed by Art. 53, just as no rulebook explains what it means to play a game when giving you the basic rules of the game). Accordingly, some concepts that are very relevant for the institution are not constituted by the rules but rather presupposed: the rules of chess define how you can checkmate but do not explain what it means to win in a competitive game, just as Art. 2 of DPR 22/12/(1986) n. 917 defines those who are subject to *IRPEF* but do not define the notion of passive subjectivity in law. These concepts, these general principles and values—the overall conceptual background the institution presupposes to have a meaning—make up the meta-institutional layer: They are "meta" because, in a sense, they define the basic grammar of our social context and legal practice.

Distinct from the institutional is also the para-institutional layer, which includes phenomena that are made possible by the way the institution is practiced rather than by its structural features. The fact that in chess there is a slight first-move advantage, or that the Queen's Gambit is divided into two major categories based on the opponent's response, or that football teams in a 5-3-2 formation typically rely on a counterattack strategy to win, are facts that of course require the games' rules to be in place but are not constituted by them like, for example, the fact that in chess bishops can move only diagonally or that in football a goal is scored when the ball passes completely over a goal line. They are para-institutional facts as opposed to institutional, using the prefix *para-* in the same sense as it is used in terms such as paramedic, paralegal, or paralanguage, namely, as qualifying objects which in some sense attach to more fundamental entities and which are relevant for the concrete practice revolving around those entities. Phenomena of this kind are relevant for law as well, and particularly for legal sociology. The fact (1) that there are parliamentary strategies like filibustering, that (2) there were governmental practices like reiteration of decrees, that (3) a perfect two-chambers system can lead to legislative gridlocks, that (4) tax efficiency is easier when a business is based on intangible assets, or finally that (5) a receipt lottery mechanism reduces tax evasion: These are all facts made possible but not strictly constituted by the rules, hence in my terminology "para"-institutional rather than pure institutional facts.

To summarize, the ontology of an institution is the outcome of three, interlocking layers: meta-institutional, institutional, and para-institutional. An institution is explained not simply by its rules but also by its axiological and teleological background and by the emerging features of the institutional practice. What I am going to argue now is that three kinds of power relevant for an institution—and here we come back to the main topic—can be distinguished accordingly.

3.2 Three Kinds of Power Relevant for an Institution

Power can be exercised at each of the three levels of institutional ontology. Institutional power is typically rule-constituted. Enacting statutes, applying and enforcing legal norms, sending laws back to the Parliament: All these are instances of institutional power, which along with institutional duties and other rights come with the specific roles and statuses an institution creates.

Meta-institutional power depends instead not on the institution's rules, but rather on the axiological and teleological background, the broader practice in which that particular institution is embedded. When games are played in non-formalized contexts, a player or a team has the power to quit whenever he or she wants: This is an activity people perform for fun, basically. Another example of meta-institutional power is the power that a player has to propose a change or adaptation or simplification of the rules, or even propose "house rules" given certain conditions (limits given by time and context, for example): If players agree, this house rule can become part of the game in that context. Unlike institutional power, meta-institutional power can be applied to different institutions, provided that they all belong to the same meta-institutional background: In non-formalized contexts, I can quit a match of chess or football, or baseball, or tic tac toe, or of any other game.

Para-institutional power is a causal capacity to influence other people's behaviour in virtue of having an institutional status and being able to obtain concrete effects from it. To take again the example of games, as a good player of chess I can influence worse players with my moves and ideas about the game, or I can make people try to avoid me in tournaments. This does not depend on the formal powers I have as a player—all chess players have the same powers in the game—but on the way I play, hence on the way I typically make use of those powers in the actual practice. Like in the case of meta-institutional power, para-institutional power can be cross-institutional, and indeed the example just made can be applied to all kinds of competitive games, not only chess. But it can also be typical of a given institution: If, as it seems to be the case, it is a typical para-institutional fact about chess that the white player, who moves first, has a slight advantage, then as a white player I can capitalize on this slight advantage by making my opponent play in a way different from that he or she would have liked.

It is apparent that there is a strong difference between institutional, meta-institutional, and para-institutional power: The first is normative, the second can be normative or causal depending on the conception one assumes, the third is definitely causal. Normative power has to do with the normative consequences of a given status, which can be expressed by way of sentences having deontic operators. Causal power is instead a capacity, hence a disposition to obtain effects that can be expressed by way of descriptive sentences. Though several authors have argued that there is an analogy between these two senses of power,[33] and the analogy indeed lies in the fact that they both trace back to the general idea of a capacity to get effects from reality, there is a categorial distinction between the two kinds of realities these effects take place in: To use Hans Kelsen's words, power in the first sense belongs to the domain of the Ought (*Sollen*), whereas power in the second sense belongs to the domain of the Is (*Sein*).

---

[33] See for example Spaak (2009), p. 75; Hage (forthcoming).

Meta-institutional power can be interpreted as being either normative, though less formalized and transparent than institutional power, or causal, depending on the conception. An example drawn from legal theory can be used to exemplify these two possible interpretations. Let us consider norm-enacting processes in law. As Kelsen among others has shown, it is possible to conceive legal systems as hierarchical chains of validity, in which norms are valid if enacted through acts of normative power qualified by other legal norms (or fragments of norms) of the system. Hence, in my terminology, a legal system can be interpreted as a system of statuses having the institutional power to enact other norms. The problem of this approach is that it leads to a regress: if a norm is valid because enacted through institutional power, and institutional power is rule-constituted, either you have an invalid norm at the root of the system or you have a power that is not institutional. Kelsen famously solved this problem with his idea of a transcendental *Grundnorm*, that is presupposed as valid and qualifies the power of the Constitutional Assembly. Hart, on the other hand, solved this problem by stating that his basic norm, the Rule of Recognition, is not part of the formal game of validity because it is a social rule. An alternative to these normativistic solutions were those of John Austin, on the English tradition, and Carl Schmitt, on the continental: Both traced the ultimate foundation of law to a factual, causal power to become a source of directives for social behaviour in a community. I propose to interpret ontologically this long-standing and venerable problem of legal philosophy—the problem of the foundation of legal validity and authority—as a question of legal meta-institutional powers. Whether the Constituent Assembly originally had the constituent power to create the legal system is a question of meta-institutional rather than institutional power: it depends not on the power created by that legal system but on the more general concept of law. It is a feature of our concept of law (at least as it evolved in the Western legal and political tradition) that a factual capacity to enforce in a way which is superior to all other claims is necessary to create legal rules, and also that the law should be enacted primarily in the form of rules (and not paradigms, for example). The distinction between normativists like Kelsen and reductionists like Austin and Schmitt—with Hart's insistence on the rule of recognition being a fact lying in between—is a distinction among which of the two features of legal meta-institutional power should prevail. Hence my conjecture is that Kelsen and Hart conceived meta-institutional power in law as primarily normative—though both provided an account of the role of effectiveness—whereas Austin and Schmitt conceived it as exclusively causal. Of course, this interpretation would require much more discussion than the one I can give in this work, but this conjecture should give an idea of the way in which I think the concept of meta-institutional power to be relevant for legal theory.

Para-institutional power is always causal. As a player, I have the capacity to do something in the game in the normative sense, whereas as a good player I have the factual capacity to influence other players' behaviour. Para-institutional power in law can have several different forms. Professors have several para-institutional powers connected with their institutional status, for example (1) the power to have students collaborate with them in the activities they propose in class (particularly before the exam), or (2) the power to influence their students' beliefs in virtue of their role. Other examples of para-institutional power in the legal domain are the following: (3) policemen in a city square influence the behaviour of people by their mere presence; (4) new regulations on tax deductions for house renovations can make people improve the anti-sismic resilience of their home; (5) receipt lotteries can reduce tax evasion; and (6) regulations prescribing that zebra crossings be drawn three-dimensionally can foster the prudence of car drivers. All these are instances of causal capacities to influence human behaviour in virtue of institutional legal roles, though it is clear that they are quite disparate in kind. A first, necessary clarification regards the causal mechanism that underlies the capacity. In some cases, para-institutional power is based on reasoning, and in particular prudential reasoning, like in the case of (1), (3), (4), and (5): Here, people are assumed to take into consideration the institutional powers connected with a given status and behave accordingly to maximize their benefits and minimize their costs. In other cases, the mechanism is less reflective and more automatic, as in the case of (2) or (6), where behavioural dispositions are elicited by way of a sort of cognitive or perceptive suggestion. Let's introduce then a distinction between transparent vs. opaque para-institutional power, but it is worth mentioning since now that this is more a matter of degree than a dichotomy: Is fear of sanction, as in (3), a prudential calculus or a behavioural unreflective attitude, or is hope for reward in a lottery, as in (5), rational or merely reactive, a kind of compulsion? Rather than presupposing a clearcut distinction between transparent and opaque para-institutional powers, we should talk of them as being *more or less* transparent or opaque.

Another distinction that is worth mentioning is that between direct and indirect para-institutional power. In (1), (2), or (3), causal influence on people's behaviour is exercised directly, simply in virtue of someone having a given status endowed with normative powers and the factual capacity of putting these powers into effect. On the other hand, (4), (5), and (6) all involve an influence by way of law-making power: A Legislator can influence people behaviour not directly, by virtue of its being the Legislator, but indirectly, by way of its enacted laws. All these para-institutional facts depend on what the Italian legal philosopher Amedeo G. Conte called "nomotropic behaviour", namely, behaviour that is not an instance of rule-following but is performed in light of the rule or the context created by the rule.[34] An example of nomotropism in this sense is that of the thief described by Weber who, though he does not abide by the law of property, acts in light of the law of property when concealing the stolen goods. To capture the difference between direct and indirect para-institutional power in terms of the idea of nomotropism, it is important to appreciate that nomotropic behaviour can be twofold: either in light of a status' constitutive rules or in light of the regulative rules enacted by people having that status. When, for example, students show a collaborative attitude in class activities, they act in light of the rules constituting the status of professors and giving them the power to give grades at exams: Hence this is a case of direct para-institutional power. When, instead, students attend classes regularly, they possibly act in light of a rule

[34] Conte (2011), pp. 47 ff.

set up by the professor about extended reading lists for non-attending students: This is indirect para-institutional power.

If we cross the distinctions between transparent vs. opaque, direct vs. indirect para-institutional power, we can introduce a taxonomy to put some order among the examples provided above. (1) is an instance of direct and transparent para-institutional power: Students are collaborative and kind with the professor because they act prudentially in light of the professor's institutional power to give grades (of course this is a rather gloomy view about students, and I trust it is inaccurate!). (2) is instead an instance of direct and opaque para-institutional power, because in this case students do not formulate a rational calculus but are rather impressed by the professor's aura of authority. (3) can be interpreted as a direct para-institutional power that is somewhat middleway between transparent and opaque: people regulate nomotropically their behaviour out of the policemen' capacity to react and inflict sanction, and this can be seen both as a rational calculus or simply as a gut reaction out of fear. (4), (5), and (6) are instead all instances of indirect para-institutional power, because here people act nomotropically not in light of the institutionally-empowered status but of the rules enacted by that status. (4) is transparent, because people make a cost-efficiency calculus about tax deductions, whereas (6) is opaque, because car drivers react behaviourally to three-dimensional zebra crossings differently than in the case of ordinary, flat road markings. (5) is, as in the case of (3), in the middle between transparent ad opaque para-institutional powers, because as said it is not clear whether the hope for a lottery win is a rational calculus or simply an automatic, unreflective attitude. An interesting question—though one I cannot deal with here—would be where to locate "nudge-like" regulations in this framework.

3.3 Andersson and Searle on Non-Rule-Constituted Power

The phenomena I am trying to capture with the concepts of para-institutional and meta-istitutional power have been discussed in social ontology by Åsa Andersson, in her book *Power and Social Ontology*, and to some extent more recently by Searle himself in *Making the Social World* with his concept of "Background power".[35] Andersson formulates a "taxonomy of social power" distinguishing between normative and causal social power.[36] Under the normative kind of social power, she introduces a further distinction between "deontic" and "telic" powers. Deontic powers are created by an institution's constitutive rules, or more in general by status functions attributions in Searle's sense: Hence, they fall under what I call "institutional" power. Telic powers, on the other hand, are connected not with the codified powers of a given status but with the ideal normativity that depends on that status's purpose.

---

[35] See respectively Andersson (2007); Searle (2010), ch. 7.

[36] Andersson (2007), pp. 149 ff.

> Many functions are defined in terms of goals or purposes, rather than in terms of rights and obligations. We impose a purpose or telos on knives, which makes it meaningful to speak of good or bad knives. [. . .] This point holds for Searle's status functions too. A professor has certain rights and obligations in virtue of this status, but this status function can display a different kind of function, since the role is also characterized in terms of certain ideals the professors and others expect her to live up to.[37]

Andersson's concept of "telic power" seems to be broader than the concept of meta-institutional power I am presenting here. While meta-institutional power is explicitly focused on the kind of power that result from an institution's broader purpose or axiology, telic power can exist even without institutions.

> Telic power, in contrast to deontic power, is not necessarily dependent on institutions to exist, since there can be non-institutional social statuses displaying telic normativity. Some functions of being a woman is defined in terms of a purpose or goal, rather than in terms of rights and obligations, which means that there is an ideal measuring how well we live up to this purpose.[38]

On the other hand, Andersson's examples of telic power are instances of a disabling rather than enabling kind of normativity. If we consider some of the examples she provides—good professors are expected to publish high quality work beyond what is merely required, women ought to stay at home with the kids, boys ought to play soccer—telic normativity and telic power have to do with standards dictating what someone should, rather than can, do. In this sense, Andersson adopts Searle's broad notion of "power", which we have already touched upon in Sect. 2.2 above. My notion of meta-institutional power, instead, is meant to capture the enabling normative elements that can be connected with an institutional status in virtue of its conceptual background.

Andersson's other notion of power distinct from deontic powers—causal power—finds a parallel in my notion of para-institutional power. Above, I introduced para-institutional power as a kind of para-institutional fact, and defined para-institutional facts as phenomena that depend not on the institution's rules but on the way those rules are practiced. In other writings,[39] I explicitly linked para-institutional facts with what Searle calls "systematic fallouts", namely, "intentionality-independent facts about intentionality-relative phenomena".[40] Searle's idea is that some facts emerge from the way institutions are framed but are not institutional and do not carry a deontology with them:

> To take a trivial example, it has been discovered in baseball that, statistically, left-handed batters do better against right-handed pitchers, and right-handed batters do better against left-handed pitchers. This is not required by the rules of baseball; it is just something that happens. I propose to call these "third-personal fallout facts from institutional facts," or more briefly, "fallouts" from institutional facts. They are "third-personal," because they need not be known by participants in the institution. They can be stated from a third-person,

[37] Andersson (2007), p. 97.

[38] Andersson (2007), p. 151.

[39] See Roversi (2018), pp. 150 ff.

[40] Searle (2010), p. 117; see also Thomasson (2003), pp. 275–276.

> anthropological, point of view. They carry no additional deontology, and so no new power relations are created by fallouts.[41]

Searle states here that "no new power relations are created by fallouts", meaning "power" in his sense of "deontic power", namely, institutional, normative power. Andersson notes, however, that fallouts create power relations in the causal sense: not a normative qualification, but an influence on people's behaviour that emerge as a more or less indirect side-effect of the rules. First, she broadens the focus from systematic fallouts to what she calls "social macro-phenomena", and she considers the former included in the latter:

> Social macro-phenomena include social structures such as class or gender structures, economic phenomena like inflation and recession, and urbanization and migration. Some macro-phenomena are unintended consequences of other arrangements, e.g. traffic jams and migration, while others are systematic fallouts (a species of unintended consequences), e.g., that entrepreneurs sell where marginal cost equals marginal revenue, or that people who are not able to sell their labor in a market economy will be poor.[42]

Then, she focuses on social structures as a kind of macro-phenomena that can be at the root of causal power. Social structures restrict the opportunities of some and enhance the opportunity of others, whence the idea of causal power made possible by these structures.[43] They can be opaque and even unintentional and they are connected with membership in social groups, possible examples being gender inequalities, race discrimination, labour relations. Causal power can be "visible", when both the power-holder and the passive subject are aware of it, or "invisible" when either the power-holder, or the passive subject, or both are not aware of it. An example of visible causal power is the head of the central bank increasing the profit of his friend's company by simply mentioning that company as an interesting start-up.[44] The most invisible kinds of causal powers are instead dependent on existing social structures that can be in place even though the agents are unaware of them. As a result, just like in the case of telic powers compared with meta-institutional powers, Andersson's perspective on causal powers seems again broader than mine on para-institutional powers and also in some respects different. Though I explicitly made a distinction between "transparent" and "opaque" para-institutional power depending on the mechanism of motivation, para-institutional power is rooted in direct or indirect nomotropism with regard to an institutional status, hence it is in general visible in Andersson's sense. Hence, para-institutional power is only an instance and does not coincide with what Andersson qualifies as causal power. It is that kind of visible causal power that is connected with an institutional status.

Another discussion aimed at showing that the ontology of power cannot be reduced to institutional, rule-constituted power is Searle's treatment of "Background power" in Chapter 7 of his *Making the Social World*. In this chapter, Searle aims at

---

[41] Searle (2010), p. 117.

[42] Andersson (2007), p. 114.

[43] Andersson (2007), pp. 121 ff.

[44] Andersson (2007), pp. 151–152.

broadening his notion of institutional, rule-dependent deontic power to capture a broader notion of social power, and in particular the diffused, acephalous processes of social normalization that Michel Foucault labels as "bio-power". Searle defines a core notion of power as follows:

> A has power over S with respect to action B if and only if A can intentionally get S to do what A wants regarding B, whether S wants to do it or not. Special cases of this are cases in which A gets S to want to do B when he would otherwise not have wanted to do it and where S wants to do B because he has been prevented by A from seeing all the available options.[45]

Clearly, this notion of power is causal: it is described through a non-normative but modal meaning of "can". Searle, however, thinks that normative, deontic power can be included in this core causal notion by way of the notion of reason for action.

> In simple paradigmatic cases of getting someone to do something, the power wielder does not necessarily have to use force. Indeed, this is a characteristic feature of deontic powers. They involve getting people to do things without using force. [. . .] So, if I make a promise to you, then you do indeed have a deontic power over me, because I have created a binding reason on myself for doing what I promised to do. I think this is a case of a power relation, but deontic powers are typically cases in which the power consists of reasons for action. [. . .] So deontic power is legitimately described as power even though typically it is not a case of the use or threat of force.[46]

According to Searle, then, in the case of deontic powers causal influence on people's behaviour is obtained through their sensitivity to reasons for action. Here Searle is implicitly performing a semantic shift in his notion of "deontic power", because even though the kind of reason-motivated power Searle is describing certainly depends on people's acceptance of the institution's purpose and rules as standards, obviously it is not something that can be conferred through a rule, and hence it is not institutional and deontic. This is an important ambiguity to explain how Searle, with his notion of "Background power", uses a normative notion to explain causal, social processes of normalization.

> The Background and Network, as I have defined them, contain among other things, a set of norms of behaviour. If someone violates the norms of the community, various sorts of sanctions can be imposed on the violator. [. . .P]rovided that there is indeed a set of shared Background norms, *anybody* can exercise power over *anybody* else.[47]

Background power is a kind of (causal) power that society exerts on individuals, pressuring them to conformity, because in case of violation any members of society have the (normative) power to sanction through criticism or disapproval or even violence. The power conferred to individuals is normative according to Searle because he traces it to Background norms. On the other hand, the pressure society exerts in virtue of Background norms is causal according to Searle because it is expressed in terms of possible influence:

---

[45] Searle (2010), p. 151.

[46] Searle (2010), pp. 147–148.

[47] Searle (2010), p. 157.

> My knowledge that sanctions can be imposed upon me and that I would find those sanctions unacceptable places me in a power relation with those who have the perceived option of imposing the sanction. That is, they are able [a causal sense of "can"] intentionally to get me to do something, whether I want to do it or not, and that satisfies our initial core definition of power.[48]

Here the crucial expression is "perceived option": the normative power conferred by Background norms becomes a perceived option to sanction and hence a capability to causally influence others' behaviour because they act nomotropically in light of those Background norms.

This clarification about the ambiguous nature of Searle's notion of "Background power" enables me to explain the relation between that notion, on the one hand, and meta-institutional and para-institutional power on the other. Given that Searle has always used the concept of Background (and also of Network) to capture the web of concepts, capabilities and practices presupposed by institutions, my idea of meta-institutional facts as facts about the general social practices in which institutions are embedded can be seen as a specification of the Background: Hence, meta-institutional powers are a subset of Background powers. More specifically, meta-institutional powers are those Background powers that depend not simply on social norms in general, but on the specific sections of the local Background that are connected with institutions. As we have seen, however, it depends on the conception of meta-institutional powers we assume whether they are connected with Background powers in the normative or causal sense. Para-institutional powers, on the other hand, are not typically connected with the concept of Background powers, because they depend on nomotropic behaviour in light of an institutional status or of the rules enacted by that status, not in light of Background norms.

4 Conclusion: Three Theses About Rules and Power in Institutional Ontology

Given the foregoing discussion, we can now come back to our original question: Is all power relevant for an institution exhausted by the institution's constitutive or power-conferring rules? The answer is no. In giving an account of institutional ontology, institutional power is only one among three kinds that must be taken into account. Meta-institutional power does not depend on the institution's rules but rather on its conceptual, teleological and axiological background. It is cross-institutional and can be accounted for both in normative and causal terms. On the other hand, para-institutional power is a kind of causal influence on social behaviour that depends, either directly or indirectly, on institutional power and that can be more or less transparent. In some cases, it is cross-institutional, in other cases it is not. Both meta-institutional and para-institutional powers are part of the life of an

[48] Searle (2010), p. 157. Italics mine; comment in square brackets is mine.

institution, the first because it follows from that institution's conceptual background, the second because it follows from its actual social effects. Restricting the notion of legally-relevant power to institutional power create a mono-dimensional perspective, whereas a three-dimensional conception of power is required to account for a full ontology of institutions.

The outcome of this analysis is that the relation between constitutive rules and power in institutional ontology is more subtle than it may seem. One can draw from a formalistic attitude in legal philosophy and from social ontology the idea that power depends on rules based on formal procedures or collective acceptance. On the contrary, it can happen that a non-formalized kind of power is implied not strictly by the rules but rather by their teleological structure and background, the social purpose that institution is meant to play in the community. It could even be that this meta-institutional, background layer provides the original power to enact formalized rules: if this were the case, power would not depend on constitutive rules but, on the contrary, constitutive rules would depend on that original power. Moreover, rules do not even exhaust the *object* of institutional power: The set of behaviours an authority could obtain by exercising institutional power is not exhausted by rule-following behaviour. There is a whole domain of nomotropic behaviour an authority can aim at that is an indirect effect of rules enacted in virtue of normative power.

I take this to be a conclusion about the ontology of institutional power, and I think it is relevant not only for constitutive, power-conferring rules, but also for power-conferring rules in general. The examples I have used when discussing meta-institutional power, even when interpreted to be instances of normative power, clearly do not depend on the explicit rules of an institution but rather on background presuppositions. The general conventions about game-playing or the very concept of legal authority and of law in a given community are basic elements of social practices, a social grammar that the different institutions specify in various ways, depending on context: They are presupposed by the rules of these institutions, hence they are not conferred by those rules (though of course those rules elaborate on them). This means that even those power-conferring rules that, though institutional, are not constitutive cannot capture the idea of meta-institutional powers: just like constitutive, power-conferring rules do not exhaust the domain of institutionally-relevant power, neither do power-conferring rules more generally. The same holds for para-institutional powers. The examples of para-institutional power I have discussed, though clearly connected with institutional, normative powers, are instances of causal power that depend on the prudential reasoning or behavioural reactions of agents. Students who become more collaborative in the presence of professors act in light of those professors' capacity to exercise normative institutional power or simply in light of their institutional, rule-constituted status. But the institutional, rule-conferred power of professors is the normative capacity to change the student's normative situation by giving them a score at the final exam, not the causal capacity to influence them. This causal capacity of course depends on the rules but is not conferred by those rules. Just like constitutive, power-conferring rules, non-constitutive power-conferring rules cannot give professors the causal capacity that corresponds to para-institutional power. What I have argued with regard to constitutive, power-conferring rules holds as well for power-conferring rules in general.

One could object at this point that, by including into the picture both normative and causal kinds of power, I am in fact discussing two different kinds of phenomena under a single label. Under such an objection, it would be quite trivial to conclude that institutional ontology does not include instances of causal power like those I describe under the label 'para-institutional', because institutions are normative, rule-constituted entities, and then the kind of power they create cannot but be inherently normative. I think this objection can be countered by way of two distinct arguments. First, not all the examples of institutionally-relevant, not-rule-conferred power I have discussed are causal. As we have seen, under some interpretations meta-institutional power can be considered to be normative: only, it is not conferred by the rules of the institution but rather by the tacit, teleological and axiological presuppositions that form the institution's conceptual background. Second, the phenomena I have discussed are extremely relevant for institutional ontology: They are part of what an institution is. Even if all these instances of power are interpreted to be causal, they are connected with an institution's normative framework: Though they are not constituted by the institution's rules, they provide those rules' background (in the case of meta-institutional power) and they are indirect effects of those rules (in the case of para-institutional power). Their presence in the life of institutions is unavoidable: Constitutive and power-conferring institutional rules necessarily require a teleological and axiological background and necessarily will give place to peculiar kinds of nomotropic behaviour. This is the reason why I conceive the intertwining of institutional, meta-institutional, and para-institutional layers to be a metaphysical feature of institutions, and from this my thesis follows that a complete metaphysical explanation of institutional power is not restricted to rule-constituted, normative power but rather calls for a complex intertwining of normative and causal powers.

Admittedly, however, the idea of focusing only on rule-constituted, normative power has an advantage over this more complex, more shaded view of institutional ontology, and this is that rule-constituted normative power is clearly defined, whereas both meta-institutional and para-institutional powers are quite vague. Meta-institutional power is vague because the norms or causal powers that lie behind a social practice are always fuzzy, tacit, and require a great deal of interpretation to make them explicit. Para-institutional power, on the other hand, is vague because the consequences of an institutional status or of regulations on social behaviour can be very indirect, to the point of being nothing else than unintended side-effects. Hence, while in the case of meta-institutional power the content is vague, in the case of para-institutional power it is the power-holder and its intentionality that is indeterminate. We face therefore a theoretical choice between a conception that provides a seriously partial and limited view of institutional power and one that, though more complete and encompassing, concedes that some facets of power can be fuzzy and indeterminate. My conclusion goes in support of this second alternative. Despite this vagueness and the complexities involved in identifying meta-institutional and para-institutional power, these kinds of power exist and are relevant for institutional

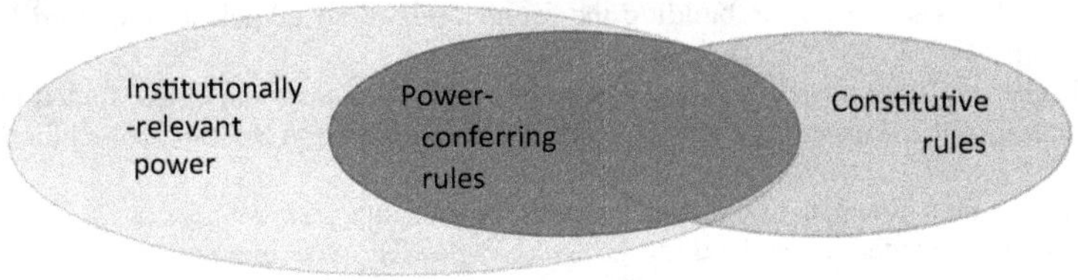

Fig. 1 Relation between rules and power in institutional ontology

ontology. Hence, constitutive and power-conferring rules do not exhaust the domain of power relevant for an institution.

In conclusion, it is possible to summarize the overall discussion by advancing three theses about the relation between constitutive rules and power in institutional ontology.

First thesis. Constitutive rules do not necessarily attribute power to statuses: They can attribute only disabling modalities, like duties or prohibitions. Being a constitutive rule does not conceptually entail being power-conferring.

Second thesis. Not all normative power in a given institution is attributed through constitutive rules. Some powers are essential to the institution, some are not. Being a power-conferring rule does not conceptually entail being constitutive.

Third thesis. Power in a given institution is not exhausted by the rules of that institution. Some powers may depend on the deeper social practice the institution is embedded in and may therefore be meta-institutional. Some powers, that I have called para-institutional, may depend on the way people act in light of the rules, either for strategic reasons or behavioural dispositions.

One could draw these relations by imagining three sets: constitutive rules, power-conferring rules, and institutionally-relevant power. As said, the relation between the first two sets is one of intersection: They have some rules in common but not everything in the two sets is shared, nor is one set included in the other. On the other hand, institutionally-relevant power includes all power-conferring rules and the intersection with constitutive rules but is not exhausted by these two sets: Some powers connected with institutional statuses do not depend on rules. Figure 1 represents the relation I have tried to reconstruct.

References

Andersson A (2007) Power and social ontology. Bokbox Publications, Malmö
Baker LR (2004) The ontology of artefacts. Philos Explor 7:99–111
Cameron JR (1972) The nature of institutional obligation. Philos Q 22:318–332
Conte AG (1995 (1981)) Regola costitutiva in Wittgenstein. In: Filosofia del linguaggio normativo. I. Studi 1965-1981. Giappichelli, Turin, pp 235–254
Conte AG (2011) Sociologia filosofica del diritto. Giappichelli, Turin

Epstein B (2015) The ant trap: rebuilding the foundations of social sciences. Oxford University Press, Oxford
Guastini R (1983) Cognitivismo ludico e regole constitutive. In: Scarpelli U (ed) La teoria generale del diritto. Problemi e tendenze attuali. Studi dedicati a Norberto Bobbio. Comunità, Milan, pp 153–176
Hage J (2018a) Two concepts of constitutive rules. Argumenta 4:21–39
Hage J (2018b) Foundations and building blocks of law. Eleven International Publishing, The Hague
Hage J (forthcoming) Capabilities, powers and competences. In: This Volume. Springer, Cham
Hindriks F (2005) Rules and institutions. Essays on meaning, speech acts and social ontology. Haveka BV, Ablasserdam
Hindriks F, Guala F (2015) Institutions, rules, and equilibria: a unified theory. J Inst Econ 11:459–480
Lindahl L, Reidhav D (2017) Legal power: the basic definition. Ratio Juris 30:158–185
Lorini G (2000) Dimensioni giuridiche dell'istituzionale. CEDAM, Padova
MacCormick N (1986) Law as institutional fact. In: MacCormick N, Weinberger O (eds) An institutional theory of law. Kluwer, Dordrecht, pp 49–76
MacCormick N (1998) Norms, institutions, and institutional facts. Law Philos 17:310–345
Marmor A (2009) Social conventions: from language to law. Princeton University Press, Princeton
Raz J (1975) Practical reason and norms. Oxford University Press, Oxford
Ross A (1957) Tû-Tû. Harv Law Rev 70:812–825
Roversi C (2007) Pragmatica delle regole constitutive. GEDIT, Bologna
Roversi C (2010) Constitutive rules in context. Archiv für Rechts- und Sozialphilosophie 96:223–238
Roversi C (2018) Constitutive rules and the internal point of view. Argumenta: J Anal Philos 4:139–156
Roversi C (2019) Six heresies on constitutive rules. Diritto e Questioni Pubbliche 2:1–25
Roversi C (2021a) In defense of constitutive rules. Synthese 119:14349–14370
Roversi C (2021b) A three-dimensional ontology of customs. In: Frezet E, Goetzmann M, Mason L (eds) Spaces of law and custom. Routledge, London, pp 27–45
Schwyzer H (1969) Rules and practices. Philos Rev 78:451–467
Searle JR (1969) Speech acts. An essay in the philosophy of language. Cambridge University Press, Cambridge
Searle JR (1995) The construction of social reality. The Free Press, New York
Searle JR (2010) Making the social world: the structure of human civilization. Oxford University Press, Oxford
Searle JR, Smith B (2003) The construction of social reality: an exchange. Am J Econ Sociol 62: 285–309
Spaak T (2009) Explicating the concept of legal competence. In: Haage J, von der Pfordten D (eds) Concepts in law. Springer, Berlin, pp 67–80
Thomasson A (2003) Foundations for a social ontology. Protosociology 18–19:269–290

Part IV
Legal Officials and Legal Offices

Legal Offices and Legal Powers

Luka Burazin

Abstract In his chapter, the author analyses the relationship between legal offices and legal powers. Based on the definition of legal offices as immaterial institutional artifacts, the author argues for four main theses. According to the first one, a set of legal positions which constitutes a legal office necessarily includes at least one legal power. This is so since legal offices, by definition, put their holders in a position of legal authority, and legal authority is intrinsically connected to legal powers. According to the second one, legal offices are always constituted by power-conferring norms, whether social (in the case of original legal offices) or legal (in the case of derived legal offices). According to the third one, legal offices necessarily include at least a minimum liberty to exercise the powers of the office. In arguing for this, the author maintains that in the absence of such a liberty a purported legal office would be constitutively incapable of performing the characteristic function of the kind of social artifacts to which it belongs. Finally, contrary to the dissociation thesis defended by J. Almäng and J. Rust, the author argues that a legal office, while retaining its identity if its non-essential powers are modified, changes its identity if it is deprived of its essential legal powers, and, even more so, ceases to exist if it is deprived of all its legal powers.

1 Introduction

One can read in the media sentences such as the following: "It then crashed as markets reacted to the coronavirus pandemic, wiping out all the gains made since President Trump took office",[1] "Louisiana's freshman class of new lawmakers, who took office in January, got little of the glad-handing, party-hopping slow start that

[1] US 2020 election: The economy under Trump in six charts, *BBC News*, https://www.bbc.com/news/world-45827430, accessed 16 December 2020.

L. Burazin (✉)
Faculty of Law, University of Zagreb, Zagreb, Croatia
e-mail: lburazin@pravo.hr

G. Villa-Rosas, T. Spaak (eds.), *Legal Power and Legal Competence*, Law and Philosophy Library 140, https://doi.org/10.1007/978-3-031-28555-4_10

traditionally kicks off a regular legislative session",[2] "Both backed the current cabinet, which took office in January",[3] "Netanyahu's new government took office last month, ending more than a year of political stalemate",[4] "The 116th U.-S. Congress took office in January, with Democrats taking control of the House while Republicans maintain an edge in the Senate".[5]

The offices mentioned or referred to in the above quotations are all examples of, *inter alia*, legal offices. In an earlier paper[6] I expounded the view that legal offices (e.g., the office of the president of the republic, member of parliament, judge, government, minister, attorney general) can ontologically best be understood as immaterial institutional artifacts. I argued that they are artifacts since they have human authors (i.e., members of a relevant community), who create them for some purpose (i.e., to enable individuals to create, apply, and enforce the law). I argued that they are institutional since they are rule-based (i.e., constituted by a social norm of recognition, in the case of original legal offices, or a positive constitutive legal norm, in the case of derived legal offices) and require for their existence collective recognition (by members of a relevant community). Finally, I argued that they are immaterial since they are nothing but status functions consisting in a set of normative (legal) positions (powers, duties, liberties, etc.) attached directly or indirectly to certain people (officeholders or officials).

In this paper I will analyse the relationship between legal offices and legal powers. I will claim that a set of legal positions which constitutes a legal office necessarily includes at least one legal power (Sect. 2). I will argue that legal offices are always constituted by power-conferring norms, be they legal or social power-conferring norms (Sect. 3). Furthermore, I will argue that legal offices necessarily include at least a minimum liberty to exercise the powers of the office (Sect. 4). Finally, I will defend a view that legal offices can never be dissociated from the powers they consist in, rejecting the so-called dissociation thesis developed in social ontology literature (Sect. 5).

---

[2] Analysis: Jarring introduction for Louisiana's new lawmakers, *The Washington Times*, https://www.washingtontimes.com/news/2020/jul/12/analysis-jarring-introduction-for-louisianas-new-l/, accessed 16 December 2020.

[3] Lebanon's top Christian clerics blast politicians as hunger, hardship bite, *Reuters*, https://www.reuters.com/article/us-lebanon-crisis-cleric-idUSKBN2460NK, accessed 16 December 2020.

[4] Hundreds of Israelis protest in Jerusalem against Netanyahu, *The Washington Times*, https://www.washingtontimes.com/news/2020/jun/27/hundreds-of-israelis-protest-in-jerusalem-against-/, accessed 16 December 2020.

[5] The changing face of Congress in 6 charts, *Pew Research Center*, https://www.pewresearch.org/fact-tank/2019/02/15/the-changing-face-of-congress/, accessed 16 December 2020.

[6] Burazin (2021).

2 Legal Offices Necessarily Include Legal Powers

In a comment on D. Renan's paper *The President's Two Bodies*,[7] P. Horwitz posed the following question: "What is an office, precisely? Is its defining feature one of powers—or of duties?".[8] I will not try to answer this question in an either/or form. Instead, I will argue that powers are necessarily a part of any office, and thus its defining feature (but, of course, not the only one). I will leave the place of duties in the concept of office for another paper.

There are different types of offices, e.g., legal, political and professional (such as academic or military) offices. What they all have in common is that they are conceived as, among other things, something that puts its holders in a position of authority.[9] And as such, i.e., as authority-providing, offices necessarily contain powers.[10]

Depending on the type of office, these powers can be factual or normative powers. MacCormick defines factual power (power-in-fact) as the ability "actually to change the factual situation so that another's interests are affected and thereby his or her reasons for action or inaction altered", and normative power as "the ability to take decisions that change what a person ought or ought not to do, or may or may not do, or what a person is able or unable to do, in the framework of some normative order, with or without the other person's consent to this change".[11] Legal offices differ from other types of offices in that they necessarily contain a special type of normative power, i.e., a legal power,[12] while other offices contain normative and/or factual social, political or professional powers.

Offices can overlap. For example, a government (a cabinet), a legislature, a member of parliament, a minister and a president of a republic are at the same time both political and legal offices. This, however, does not mean that one cannot

---

[7] Renan (2020).

[8] Horwitz (2020). Horwitz, in a different context, defends the primacy of duties in defining offices. See Horwitz (2019).

[9] See, for example, the definitions of office in *Merriam-Webster.com Dictionary*, https://www.merriam-webster.com/dictionary/office, accessed 21 August 2020, *Cambridge Dictionary*, https://dictionary.cambridge.org/dictionary/english/office, accessed 21 August 2020, *Collins Dictionary*, https://www.collinsdictionary.com/dictionary/english/office, accessed 21 August 2020, and *Black's Law Dictionary*, 8th ed., p. 1115.

[10] J. Raz, for instance, suggested that "[a] person has authority to the extent that he has power to affect norms", that is, that one has authority to the exent that he has a special type of power, i.e., a normative power. See Raz (1999), p. 467. This is true of legal offices, but I am not sure whether one should exclude MacCormick's powers-in-fact as powers which can make someone an authority (e.g., when political authorities and their respective offices are concerned).

[11] MacCormick (1999), p. 495.

[12] Another prominent (non-legal) type of normative power is moral power (e.g., power to promise and power to consent). See, for example, Koch (2018).

differentiate between the powers which define them as legal and those which define them as political offices.[13]

For the purpose of this paper, I use the notion of legal powers in Raz's sense, as an ability to effect a legal change, where legal change is defined as "a change in the existence, content, or application of a law or a legally recognized norm".[14] I also adopt Raz's distinction between norm-creating powers, i.e., "powers determining the content and existence of laws and of legally recognized norms", and regulative powers, i.e., powers which "govern the application of such norms".[15] Although all the instances of legal powers pertaining to legal offices could as well be referred to by Hart's notion of legal power which covers situations "where persons are enabled by the law either to do actions physically affecting other persons or things, or to bring about changes in the legal positions of others or of themselves, or of both themselves and others"[16] or Bentham's notions of "power of contrectation" and "power of imperation".[17]

As has been said in the Introduction, legal offices are social constructions, created by humans for some purpose. When it comes to their directly legal purposes,[18] i.e., purposes concerned with handling laws and legally recognized norms, these are reflected in legal powers they contain. As I have argued elsewhere,[19] the main legal purposes for which humans create legal offices is to enable individuals that are directly or indirectly called to the office to authoritatively, enduringly, and representatively,[20] create, change, abrogate, apply, and enforce law, which they could not do only in virtue of their physical structure. And it would intuitively be hard to square the idea of legal office as a means of enabling the individuals to carry out these tasks without these individuals being granted the requisite legal powers.[21]

Among the paradigmatic instances of these powers are: the power to issue laws (as a part of the office of the legislature); the power to vote upon legislation (a part of the office of a member of parliament); the power to issue regulations and decrees (a part of the office of government); the power to judge a lawsuit (a part of the office of a judge or judicial office); powers to issue presidential decrees, promulgation, veto, command the army in wartime (often parts of the office of the president of the

[13]On the distinction between legal and political powers see MacCormick (1999), pp. 496–497.

[14]Raz (1999), pp. 453–454.

[15]Raz (1999), p. 454.

[16]Hart (1972), p. 799.

[17]Bentham (1970), ch. IX, para. 9, pp. 81ff.

[18]Of course, legal offices are created to serve other, not technically "legal" purposes as well, e.g., keeping the peace, enhancing the economy, solving moral issues, and "legal" purposes can be understood as only the means to achieving these more substantive purposes. In fact, as will be seen in Sect. 5, legal powers of the offices are only the means to realizing the legal offices' institutional functions.

[19]Burazin (2021), p. 151.

[20]On the representative feature of offices (in the sense that office-holders act as, for, or on behalf of another) see Penner (2020).

[21]See Essert (2013), p. 431.

republic or the office of the presidency); powers to arrest, detain, search, issue orders (a part of the office of policing), and the power to execute judgement orders (a part of the office of the bailiff). In addition to the powers listed, which define the functions exercised by the holders of different offices, offices usually include powers which establish the relationships of dependency among the holders of different offices. The latter are, for example, the powers to nominate, appoint and elect officeholders (e.g., a parliament can be granted the power to elect the government and to recall a minister, a president of the republic can be granted the power to appoint judges of the Supreme Court or to nominate the prime minister, etc.). All of these powers are either norm-creating (e.g., the power to issue laws, regulations, decrees) or regulative powers (e.g., the powers to appoint, elect, execute judgement orders, arrest).

Given that legal offices are social constructions, in different legal orders they have different contents and so contain different legal powers (for example, there are important differences with respect to powers which in different legal orders pertain to the office of the presidency). Nevertheless, some legal offices often contain certain legal powers regardless of the legal order to which they belong to, and some are of such a nature that we understand them as defining the office in question, which makes it, by definition, impossible for that office not to contain them (e.g., when it comes to the power to issue laws and the office of the legislature or the power to issue adjudicative decisions and the office of a judge). These can be said to be powers which make particular legal offices (e.g., the office of a judge in Croatia, the office of a judge in Germany, the office of a judge in the USA) instantiations of their type (i.e., the office of a judge) since they are regarded as particular solutions regarding the means to realizing the institutional function of their office-types.[22]

Be that as it may, since legal offices are, by definition, (legal) authority-providing, that is, they put their holders in a position of legal authority, legal offices necessarily contain at least one legal power. How different legal powers affect the identity of legal offices will be discussed in Sect. 5.

3 Legal Offices Are Always Constituted by Power-Conferring Norms

According to J. Raz, not all legal powers are conferred by legal norms and, indeed, not all legal powers are conferred by norms at all: "legal powers may exist even if not conferred by any norm, whether legal or non-legal".[23] In arguing for this claim, Raz puts forward two examples: Austin's sovereign and 'The People's Council' which made the Israeli declaration of independence. Since both examples refer to what I call an original legal office, Raz's claim can be extended to offices as well. Thus,

[22] On the relationship between institution-types and institution-tokens (i.e., the particular instantiations of institution-types), see Guala (2016), p. 196.

[23] Raz (1999), p. 455.

Raz's view implies that there may exist legal offices that are not constituted by any norm whatsoever.

Let us take the example of 'The People's Council'. Raz says the following:

> The People's Council on the other hand was never granted powers by any law. Nevertheless it had and did exercise legislative powers by enacting the first law. (...) It is arguable whether or not there was in Palestine at the time a social norm which conferred powers on the People's Council. I doubt whether there was such a norm. The point is that the existence of such a norm does not affect the issue. It is possible for a legal power to be recognized in some such circumstances even if it is not conferred by a pre-existing social norm.[24]

My reply to Raz's argument would be this. If there was no (social) power-conferring norm, then what 'The People's Council' did was not the exercise of, strictly speaking, legislative power. These could then have only been purported legislative powers, which came to be legislative powers only after the members of the relevant community started collectively recognizing them as their officials. By doing that, they have come to regard the purported exercise of legislative power as the genuine exercise of legislative power.

This reply rests on the distinction between original and derived legal offices that I have made in an earlier paper,[25] and my artifact theory of law. Derived legal office is a legal office that is brought into existence by an existing (positive) legal norm, i.e., a norm belonging to a certain legal order. It is derived since its belonging to a legal order depends on pre-existing positive legal norms. For example, the offices of a legislature, a presidency and a judiciary are brought into existence by existing legal norms, in principle, the norms of a constitution. However, every legal order seems to have an office (like The People's Council above) which, while it does not depend on the existence of a pre-existing positive legal norm, is still regarded as a legal office. That office is the office of the constitution-maker. The constitution-maker, as understood here, is by definition the office that consists in the power to issue a norm on the production of other norms of a legal order and, in this sense, the first positive norm of a legal order. It can thus be said that the constitution-maker, at least from the point of view of a legal order, is an original or sovereign office. That is, an office which enables its holders to constitute other legal offices by issuing constitutive legal norms (i.e., derived legal offices, such as the legislature, judiciary and presidency). However, as we shall see shortly, that does not mean that the office of the first constitution-maker is itself not constituted by any norm.

The question that now arises is, what then makes the original office *legal*? What makes it possible to identify holders of the original office as legally relevant agents that exercise their powers of law-creation? What makes their powers legally significant? According to the artifact theory of law (which is expounded elsewhere),[26] the office of the constitution-maker is constituted by the norm of recognition, which itself is constituted by the practice of citizens (in the sense of members of the relevant

[24] Raz (1999), p. 456.

[25] Burazin (2021), p. 147ff.

[26] Burazin (2015, 2016, 2018).

community). Citizens (including legal officials) are those who, by their collective recognition of a constitutive norm, impose the institutional status of first or original legal office on certain people and in doing so confer on them the powers to issue the norm or norms which regulate the creation of general legal norms (i.e., norms on legislation).

Although certain people can define themselves as "first constitution-makers" by agreeing on some criteria for having this status, they do not have the said institutional status unless collectively recognized as such by a relevant community (a community in respect of which they carry out the powers which follow from their status of the first constitution-makers).[27] The "first constitution-makers" are a group, social and public phenomenon. They can exist only in a group and for a group. There can be no private constitution-makers. Constitution-makers can be said to exist as constitution-makers only if collectively recognized as such by members of a relevant community. By collectively recognizing certain people as their first constitution-makers, members of a relevant community do not identify the already existing institutional status of the first constitution-makers, but instead create this status and attach to it the corresponding power to issue the first constitution.

Since collective recognition of the original officials by members of a relevant community consists in the social practice of regarding certain people as the original officials and as having the power to issue the first constitution, and since it is performed (at least in part) for social reasons,[28] it constitutes a social (power-conferring) norm of recognition.[29] Furthermore, it is a double constitutive norm as it constitutes the institutional status of the original legal office, accompanied with the power to issue the first constitution, and makes the conceptual framework for an instantiation of their legal system, which, on the basis of the division of labour, is implemented by both the original and the derived legal officials (holders of original and derived legal offices, respectively), setting the criteria of identification of the sources of law in a relevant community. Thus, according to my artifact theory of law, the office of the constitution-maker is a legal office not because it is created by law or recognized as such through the practice of only legal officials, but because it is *collectively regarded as a legal* office by the relevant community (citizens and officials included) and thus constituted by the social norm of recognition.

To conclude: legal offices are always constituted by a norm, whether social (in the case of original legal offices)[30] or legal (in the case of derived legal offices). The (social or legal) norm (or norms) which constitutes a legal office, as implied by the previous Section, necessarily attaches certain legal powers to a certain individual

[27] Cf. Lagerspetz (1995), p. 15.

[28] Participants' social reasons to collectively recognize their original officials consists in the fact that other participants recognize it too and are expected to do so. On social reasons see Tuomela (2002), p. 79.

[29] More precisely, the norm in question is an uncodified or implicit individual constitutive norm. See Burazin (2018), p. 123.

[30] For a different argument, but the same conclusion to the effect that even the so-called constituent power is ultimately constituted by social or customary norms, see Redondo (2016).

or group of individuals. Thus, offices are constituted by power-conferring (or competence) norms. By attaching legal powers to the designated individuals or groups of individuals,[31] power-conferring norms necessarily partake in defining legal offices.[32]

4 Legal Offices Necessarily Include at Least a Minimum Liberty to Exercise the Powers of the Office

Power-conferring norms (legally) enable (make it legally possible for) the office-holders to produce institutional results or normative changes.[33] They do that by granting the officeholders the requisite legal powers. However, power-conferring norms are not deontic norms, i.e., they do not deontically regulate the exercise of the behaviour they make legally possible. In addition to power-conferring norms, there are thus usually other norms that regulate the actions of the officeholders. These norms are regulative or deontic norms (or norms of conduct). They regulate how the officeholders should exercise the powers of the office, whether their exercise is obligatory, forbidden, permitted, or facultative.

Given these regulative rules, legal offices, in addition to legal powers, usually include many different legal positions, such as duties, liberties, liabilities and immunities. For instance, judges usually have a duty to exercise their power to adjudicate cases, and a legislature is usually at liberty to exercise its power to issue laws, although in some cases it also has a duty not to exercise the said power or not to exercise it in a particular way (e.g., a ban on retroactive criminal laws, a ban on unreasonable restrictions of human rights, etc.).

However, what I want to argue for is that if something is to be a legal office, it necessarily has to include at least a minimum liberty to exercise the powers of the office. This, I argue, follows from the very concept of legal office as a social artifact.

If one accepts that legal offices are social artifacts, then they are created for some purpose. If one accepts that legal offices are constituted by a set of legal powers, then these powers are created for some purpose. As I have argued above, the (at least strictly legal) purpose for which these powers are created is to enable a certain individual or group of individuals to create, apply, and enforce laws and legally recognized norms. In order to achieve this purpose, the officeholders have to be permitted to exercise the powers they are given.[34] This, of course, does not mean that

[31] On two ways of designating the office-holders, see Burazin (2021), p. 147.

[32] On this feature of power-conferring (or competence) norms, see Bulygin (2015), p. 283.

[33] See Manero (2009), p. 277 and Spaak (2003), pp. 94–95 and 99 (for the capacitative dimension of competence or power-conferring norms).

[34] They can be permitted to exercise their powers in various ways, e.g., by permissive norms, commands (since a command to φ logically implies a permission to φ), or by some such general rule (either a positive law rule or a rule derived from the concept of the legal system) to the effect that

these powers cannot be restricted by commands and prohibitions, which they usually are (at least in modern legal systems). However, if the given powers were accompanied by a total prohibition of their exercise, one would have to say that the purported legal office fails to count as a member of an artifact kind K since it is constitutively incapable of performing the characteristic function of members of that kind,[35] i.e., the function of creating, applying, and enforcing laws. It would be a legal failure.[36] In the same vein, Atienza and Manero conclude that "it does not seem to make much sense to uphold someone as the holder of a normative power while, at the same time, totally prohibiting its exercise to that same person".[37]

5 The Puzzle of So-called Dissociation of Legal Offices and Legal Powers

According to the account given above, a legal office is a status function consisting in a set of normative (legal) positions which, as has been argued, necessarily include a legal power (or powers) and a minimum liberty to exercise it. This means that if someone (an individual or a group of individuals) has been called to the office and has thus acquired the status function of the office, she, by the fact of holding the office, also necessarily has all the normative (legal) positions, and so also all the legal powers, contained in the office. For instance, if a person has been called to the office of a judge, she, by the fact of being a judge (a holder of the office of the judge) also necessarily has the power to adjudicate cases. Or, if a group of people has been called to the office of government, the group in question, by the fact of being a government (a holder of the office of government) also necessarily has the power to issue decrees and regulations. Of course, in both examples I am assuming that the legal orders to which these legal offices belong to include the norms which confer the said powers.

However, J. Almäng argues that the relationship between status functions (in our case, legal offices) and normative positions ('powers', 'deontic powers' or 'normative powers', in the social ontology discourse used in this Section, which include not only powers in the strict sense, but also other normative positions)[38] is not that

---

what is not prohibited is permitted (of course, in the case of legal officials, this rule applies only to the powers conferred).

[35] See Crowe (2014), p. 749.

[36] See Crowe (2014), p. 750ff.

[37] Atienza and Manero (1998), p. 107, n. 8.

[38] In the social ontology discourse, normative positions associated with a status function are usually called 'deontic powers' or 'normative powers'. These include not only powers in the strict sense (in the sense in which 'powers' are used in this paper), but also rights, duties, obligations, entitlements, immunities, etc. See Searle (1995), pp. 100–101 and Searle (2010), p. 9. See also Hindriks (2020), p. 495, who thinks that Searle's term 'deontic powers' unjustifiably "excludes second-order deontic powers such as Hohfeldian powers and immunities" and thus he broadens the scope of the term to include these second-order normative positions. Although, given the examples

"intimate", since "a status function and the power it normally carries, can, as it were, become disassociated from each other".[39] Something can meet all the conditions for being assigned a status function and thus have a status function, but "lack the deontic powers normally associated with these status functions",[40] and, vice versa, something can have such powers although it does not meet the conditions for being assigned a status function and thus does not have the relevant status function. [41] This would imply that someone could acquire the status function of a particular legal office, but lack the powers belonging to that office, and that someone could have the powers belonging to a particular office even if she does not have the status function of that office. If the dissociation thesis is correct, then the definition of statuses (in our case, legal offices) as sets of normative positions fails.

However, cases which Almäng analyses in order to show how the dissociation between statuses and powers can happen[42] do not prove the dissociation thesis, understood in terms of dissociation between status functions and the normative positions these status functions carry. Some cases show that an entity has the relevant status function, and has the normative positions included in the status, but it, in fact, cannot exercise these normative positions (e.g., a real US dollar which is slightly damaged and thus not recognized in Albania as a real dollar, but as a forgery). In these cases, what becomes dissociated is not the status and the normative positions it includes, but the status (or the set of normative positions) and the possibility of exercising these normative positions.[43] Other cases show that an entity does not have the relevant status and does not have the normative positions included in the status, but it, in fact, nevertheless acts *as if* it has the status and the relevant normative positions, i.e., it actually does what would otherwise be considered the legitimate exercise of the normative positions that belong to the relevant status (e.g., a forged US dollar erroneously accepted in Albania as a real dollar). In these cases, as Hindriks argues, it only appears that an entity has the relevant normative positions, while, in fact, it neither has nor exercises them, but only mimics these

---

Searle uses (e.g., police powers or the president's power of veto), I am not entirely convinced that this interpretation of Searle's use of the term 'deontic power' is correct.

[39] Almäng (2016), p. 6.

[40] Almäng (2016), p. 5. See also Hindriks (2020), p. 483.

[41] Almäng (2016), p. 6. See also Hindriks (2020), p. 483.

[42] Well, this is at least what Almäng claims to be doing. However, although he is sometimes imprecise and inconsistent in wording, it might be that Almäng, eventually, did not want to show how statuses can be dissociated from the deontic powers they carry, but how statuses can be dissociated from their institutional functions. For Almäng, deontic powers are the means to realizing institutional functions, and in this sense statuses are deontically related to their institutional functions. So, if the status-holder cannot exercise the powers of the status, she lacks the institutional function, and if someone who does not have the status exercises the powers normally associated with that status, she has an institutional function.

[43] For a similar line of argument, which uses the distinction between 'having a power' and 'exercising a power', helped by the distinction between type and token acceptance, see Hindriks (2020), p. 489.

positions.[44] Thus, here too no dissociation between statuses and their normative positions happens.

J. Rust takes a slightly different route arguing for the possibility of dissociation, basing his account on the distinction between rules determining the conditions for acquiring a status (constitutive rules) and rules determining normative positions included in a status (i.e., rules determining the content of a status or status rules). At the same time, he follows Almäng's distinction between statuses, normative positions and institutional functions, but, more fruitfully, points also to cases where a status is deprived of the key normative positions for realizing its defining institutional function.

Rust claims that dissociation is always possible for "a class of statuses that are defined by a combination of normative powers and constitutive rules . . . such that someone (or something) could satisfy the constitutive rules associated with the status, but no longer carry normative powers associated with the status, and vice versa".[45] He adduces two examples to show how the dissociation is possible. First, he has us imagine a situation where the US presidency is, by way of a constitutional amendment, deprived of "key normative powers previously associated with the status", but constitutive rules were not changed.[46] In this case, one purportedly has a status, but has no normative powers. Second, he has us imagine a person who, by way of a *coup d'état*, comes to occupy "an office with the same normative powers as that of the presidency"[47] or the German chancellor, and who comes to be accepted as an instance of the kind in question.[48] In this case, one purportedly does not have a status, but has normative powers.

Let us first tackle the latter example. Rust infers that someone who did not acquire the status in virtue of a constitutive rule in place, and who thus does not have a status, can, nevertheless, have normative powers associated with that status. However, such examples do not tell us anything about the status itself, and whether a status can be dissociated from its powers. They only show which of the two rules is defining in considering someone a holder of a particular status. They answer the question of whether someone has a particular status because it was assigned to her in the appropriate way (in virtue of a constitutive rule in place), or because she actually has normative powers which are an appropriate means of carrying out the essential, defining institutional function of the status in question. Hence, they can only reveal whether holding a particular status is determined by the way in which someone has acquired the status or by normative positions which she has despite the fact that she acquired those positions in a way different from that determined by the constitutive rule in place.

---

[44] Hindriks (2020), p. 489.

[45] Rust (2017), p. 715.

[46] Rust (2017), p. 715.

[47] Rust (2017), p. 715.

[48] Rust (2017), p. 712.

Moreover, Rust erroneously thinks that such examples involve the issue of whether the *statuses* are defined "in terms of their constitutive rules or normative powers".[49] Instead, the main issue revealed by such examples is in virtue of what someone becomes a *status-holder*. Rust attempts to explain Almäng's puzzle by distinguishing two kinds of social kinds, a real social kind, and a conventional social kind. According to Rust,

> if a *coup d'état* results in someone's occupying an office with the same normative powers as had by previous German chancellors, and if this person comes to be accepted as an instance of the kind, German chancellor, then this kind is revealed to be a real social kind. If this person is not accepted as a German chancellor, due to the fact that they were not elected by the Bundestag, then this kind is revealed to be a conventional social kind or Searlean status.[50]

However, if the members of a relevant community accepted (recognized) as a German chancellor a person who, by way of a *coup d'état* 'took the office of German chancellor' with all the normative positions included in the office of German chancellorship by the valid norms of the German legal order, then the previous office of a German chancellorship (a status) was not replaced by the new one. It is the same office. What changed was only the fact that the members of a relevant community made an exception in a concrete case, setting aside the application of the valid positive legal rule determining the way one is called to the office of the German chancellor, replacing it with their own temporary (i.e., for this case only) constitutive social norm of recognition. Since the members of the relevant community recognized a person as a new German chancellor, and thus assigned to her the relevant status, and since she has all the normative positions included in the office of the German chancellor, no dissociation happened. Things would be different if the members of the relevant community recognized that person as the first constitution-maker. This would result in the creation of a new legal order (of course, under the assumption that it became efficacious) and, despite the fact that this person would be called 'the German chancellor', this would be a new office with a new set of normative positions (more precisely, with the power to issue the first constitution), i.e., the office of the first constitution-maker, different from the office of German chancellor established by the previous German legal order. Be that as it may, in this case too there is no dissociation between a status and its accompanying normative positions.

I now turn to Rust's first example, that is, the US presidency deprived of key normative powers previously associated with the status. Rust, just like Almäng, distinguishes between statuses, (institutional) functions of statuses, and normative powers necessary to realize the functions associated with statuses. However, unlike Almäng, who focuses on the effects of the non-exercise of normative powers conducive to the realization of the status's institutional function, Rust focuses on the effects of the status being deprived of key (essential) normative powers

[49] Rust (2017), p. 709.

[50] Rust (2017), p. 712.

conducive to the realization of the status's institutional function. Thus, according to Rust, the dissociation happens when a status is deprived of its key normative powers, i.e., there is a status, but no (key) normative powers.

Although this is closer to showing the possible dissociation between statuses and the normative powers they consist in, I argue that the given example still fails to uphold the dissociation thesis. However, it sheds light on an important issue of the identity of legal offices as statuses. We can distinguish at least three situations. First, if a legal office is deprived of some non-essential, less important legal powers, then the office can be said to have retained its identity. There is still a status but consisting in a slightly changed set of normative powers that shape it. Second, if a legal office is deprived of its essential, defining legal powers (e.g., the office of parliament is deprived of the power to issue general legal norms or the office of a judge is deprived of the power to adjudicate cases), but the office still retains certain legal powers or gains new ones (which leaves the officeholder in a position of authority), then such a change of identity happened that one can say that a new legal office has been established. Again, there is a status (albeit a new one), and a new set of normative powers shaping the status. Third, if a legal office is deprived of all its legal powers, then its holders can no longer represent the position of the legal authority, and one can say that the legal office has ceased to exist. Here no powers exist, but also no status (i.e., no legal office). Of course, this does not preclude the office from still existing, as, for example, a political or social office (e.g., the office of the president deprived of all its legal powers). However, if the rules determining the way office-holders are called to the office remain in place, one can conditionally speak of the existence of a so-called empty legal office, that is, 'a legal office' that is awaiting to be assigned the relevant legal powers. Well, strictly speaking, 'an empty legal office' is a *contradictio in adjecto*, for legal offices, by definition, are sets of normative positions and they necessarily include at least one legal power and a minimum liberty to exercise it. However, this seems to be a useful way to describe a situation where there is a rule determining how one becomes the holder of the office in question, the name of the office, and a prevailing understanding that the office should be given the relevant legal powers.

6 Conclusion

This paper analysed the relationship between legal offices and legal powers. I argued that a set of legal positions which constitutes a legal office necessarily includes at least one legal power. This is so since legal offices, by definition, put their holders in a position of legal authority, and legal authority is intrinsically connected to legal powers. One cannot be a legal authority if one does not have legal powers, i.e., powers to affect either the existence or content of a legal norm, or its application. I also argued that legal offices are always constituted by power-conferring norms. While this seems to be obvious in cases of so-called derived legal offices (which are constituted by legal power-conferring norms), I tried to show that even original legal offices (i.e., the first constitution-maker) are norm-based, but that they, unlike derived legal offices, are constituted by social power-conferring norms. This is the case since whoever purports to be the first constitution-maker would not have this institutional status and the power to issue norms on legislation if she were not collectively recognized as such through a social norm of recognition by a relevant community, i.e., a community in respect of which she purports to exercise this power. Furthermore, I argued that legal offices necessarily include at least a minimum liberty to exercise the powers of the office. I claimed that in the absence of such a liberty a purported legal office would fail to count as a member of its artifact kind K since it would be constitutively incapable of performing the characteristic function of members of that kind. Finally, I defended a view that legal offices can never be dissociated from the powers they consist in and rejected the so-called dissociation thesis developed in social ontology literature. On the one hand, examples given to uphold the dissociation thesis do not really show that there can be legal offices without the accompanying legal powers or *vice versa*. On the other hand, there can be no dissociation for the simple reason that offices are, by definition, sets of legal positions which necessarily include legal powers. However, some of the efforts to show the possibility of dissociation have illuminated an important question of the identity of legal offices. While a legal office retains its identity if its non-essential powers are changed, it changes its identity if it is deprived of its essential legal powers (i.e., those conducive to the realization of the office's institutional function), and it ceases to exist (or can, at best, conditionally be described as an 'empty legal office') if it is deprived of all of its legal powers.

References

Almäng J (2016) Legal facts and dependence on representations. J Soc Ontol 2(1):1–15
Atienza M, Manero JR (1998) A theory of legal sentences. Kluwer Academic Publishers, Dordrecht
Bentham J (1970) In: Hart HLA (ed) Of laws in general. University of London, The Athlone Press, London
Bulygin E (2015 (1992)) On norms of competence. In: Bernal C, Huerta C, Mazzarese T, Moreso JJ, Navarro PE, Paulson SL (eds) Essays in legal philosophy. Eugenio Bulygin. OUP, Oxford, pp 272–283
Burazin (2015) Practical concepts of law as an artifact kind. Pravni vjesnik 31(3–4):65–75
Burazin L (2016) Can there be an artifact theory of law? Ratio Juris 29(3):385–401
Burazin L (2018) Legal systems as abstract institutional artifacts. In: Burazin L, Himma KE, Roversi C (eds) Law as an artifact. Oxford UP, New York, pp 112–135
Burazin L (2021) Funciones Jurídicas. Doxa. Cuadernos de Filosofía del Derecho 44:145–157
Crowe J (2014) Law as an artifact kind. Monash Univ Law Rev 40(3):737–757
Essert C (2013) The office of ownership. Univ Toronto Law J 63(3):418–461
Guala F (2016) Understanding institutions. The science and philosophy of living together. Princeton UP, Princeton and Oxford
Hart HLA (1972) Bentham on legal powers. Yale Law J 81(5):799–822
Hindriks F (2020) How social objects (fail to) function. J Soc Philos 51(3):483–499
Horwitz P (2019) The Coxford Lecture. Honour, oaths, and the rule of law. Can J Law Jurisprud XXXII(2):389–411

Horwitz (2020) The two-body problem. JOTWELL (reviewing Renan D, The President's Two Bodies, 120 Columbia L. Rev. 1119 (2020)). https://conlaw.jotwell.com/the-two-body-problem/ Accessed 16 Dec 2020
Koch F (2018) Consent as a normative power. In: Müller A, Schaber P (eds) The Routledge handbook of the ethics of consent. Routledge, London and New York, pp 32–43
Lagerspetz E (1995) The opposite mirrors: an essay on the conventionalist theory of institutions. Springer, Dordrecht
MacCormick N (1999) Powers and power-conferring norms. In: Paulson SL, Litschewski Paulson B (eds) Normativity and norms. Critical perspectives on Kelsenian themes. Oxford UP, New York, pp 493–506
Manero JR (2009) Una tipologia delle norme costituzionali. Ragion pratica 32:277–303
Penner J E (2020) Private law offices. Univ Toronto Law J 70 (Issue supplement 2): 299-314
Raz J (1999 (1972)) Voluntary obligations and normative powers. In: Paulson SL, Litschewski Paulson B (eds) Normativity and norms. Critical perspectives on Kelsenian themes. Oxford UP, New York, pp 451–470
Redondo MC (2016) A legal order's supreme legislative authorities. Revus – J Const Theory Philos Law 29:33–60
Renan D (2020) The President's two bodies. Columbia Law Rev 120(5):1119–1214
Rust J (2017) On the relation between institutional statuses and technical artifacts: a proposed taxonomy of social kinds. Int J Philos Stud 25(5):704–722
Searle JR (1995) The construction of social reality. The Free Press, New York
Searle JR (2010) Making the social world. The structure of human civilization. Oxford UP, New York
Spaak T (2003) Norms that confer competence. Ratio Juris 16(1):89–104
Tuomela R (2002) The philosophy of social practices: a collective acceptance view. Cambridge UP, Cambridge

A Hartian Account of Legal Officials

Jorge Luis Fabra-Zamora

Abstract HLA Hart did not provide a thorough account of legal officials, even though such a notion is one of the central elements of his theory of legal systems. As critics have rightly argued, three related questions remain unanswered: "What is an official?" (the Conceptual Problem); "Who are the officials of a given legal system?" (the Identification Problem); and "How are these officials empowered by the system's secondary rules?" (the Empowerment Problem). These issues have generated suggestions for eliminating legal officials from theoretical inquiries, leading to a larger question: "What role do officials play in legal theory?" (the Explanatory Role Problem). This chapter articulates an account of legal officials that supplements and substantially revises Hart's original formulation in response to these issues. My renewed account reinterprets the central insights of Hart's theory of legal systems as a general theory of practice-based normativity. With this account at hand, responses to each problem are advanced. To address the Conceptual Problem, I argue that officials are agents who make peremptory decisions (enactments and settlements) on behalf of a given community, while legal officials are agents who make such decisions on behalf of political communities. In response to the Identity Problem, I hold that the identification of officials demands the recognition of two kinds of agents: order-constituted officials created by the system's valid norms identified by the rule of recognition and identified through a doctrinal analysis; and order-constitutive officials created by the system's secondary rules and identified through a quasi-sociological inquiry. A detailed clarification of the power-conferring character of social rules is developed in response to the Empowerment Problem. Finally, in response to the Explanatory Role Problem, I clarify the relevance of officials both for jurisprudence and for social philosophy.

I am thankful to Stefan Sciaraffa and Michael Guidice for years of discussion on the central ideas of this chapter, and the editors Torben Spaak and Gonzalo Villa-Rosas for comments that helped me to improve the first draft.

J. L. Fabra-Zamora (✉)
University at Buffalo School of Law, State University of New York, Buffalo, NY, USA
e-mail: jorgefab@buffalo.edu

G. Villa-Rosas, T. Spaak (eds.), *Legal Power and Legal Competence*, Law and Philosophy Library 140, https://doi.org/10.1007/978-3-031-28555-4_11

1 Introduction

Legal officials are one of the central notions of HLA Hart's theory of law.[1] In this account, legal systems are characterized as the union of primary and secondary rules. Primary rules impose duties on the system's subjects. Secondary rules come in three forms: rules that regulate the creation, change, and removal of primary rules (rules of change); rules that concern the application of the system's norms (rules of adjudication); and the standard that identifies the norms that belong to the legal system (the rule of recognition). Officials are agents empowered by the system's secondary rules of change and adjudication to create and apply rules.[2] The introduction of officials who create and apply laws helps to remedy some defects present in "pre-legal communities"—the lack of mechanisms for deliberately adapting the rules and the lack of final and authoritative means of establishing the violation of rules—and thereby their presence is one of the key signals of the emergence of legal systems.

Given these central theoretical roles, it is surprising that Hart did not provide a comprehensive account of legal officials. Several scholars have noted this deficit. For example, Nigel Simmonds complains, "Hart nowhere tells us what an 'official' is and how to identify one."[3] In turn, Keith Culver and Michael Guidice claim: "Hart offered little to explain which rules identify who is to count as a legal official, nor did he take any significant steps towards offering a philosophical explanation of what a legal official is."[4] Similarly, Grant Lamond alleges: "Hart never explains what makes someone an 'official' within a legal system despite the fact the distinction between officials and non-officials is invoked frequently through [*The Concept of Law*]."[5] Finally, Matthew Kramer writes: "Having rightly deplored Austin's inattentiveness to power-conferring laws, Hart damagingly left some significant gaps in his own theory by not fully absorbing the lesson to be drawn from his excoriation of his great predecessor."[6]

This chapter articulates an account of legal officials that supplements and revises Hart's original account. My goal is not to dwell on exegetical disputes or propose the best overall interpretation of Hart's work or legacy. Instead, I will attempt to highlight, further develop, and reformulate some central insights of his account to resolve the main problems that critics have identified and set the stage for further theoretical and doctrinal inquiries.[7] I shall therefore refer to my account as a *Hartian*

---

[1] Hart (2012).

[2] Hart also suggests that the rule of recognition is a power-conferring rule, which has generated exegetical complexities. For simplicity, I will set aside for a different paper the contested power-conferring nature of the rule of recognition and its relationships with official identification.

[3] Simmonds (2008), p. 158.

[4] Culver and Giudice (2008), p. 98.

[5] Lamond (2013), p. 110.

[6] Kramer (2018), p. 47.

[7] The argument relies on an interpretation of Hart's theory that I have developed in Fabra-Zamora (2019, 2023).

account to differentiate it from Hart's own formulations. The argument proceeds as follows. Four problems identified by critics and their theoretical consequences are specified in Sect. 2; these are the Conceptual Problem, the Identification Problem, the Empowerment Problem, and the Explanatory Role Problem. My renewed theory starts in Sect. 3 with a reinterpretation of Hart's account of legal systems as a general account of practice-based normative phenomena. Section 4 offers a novel elucidation of legal officials in response to the Conceptual Problem. The Problems of Official Identification and Empowerment are resolved in Sect. 5 by distinguishing two kinds of officials and providing an account of the power-conferring nature of secondary rules. Section 6 addresses the Explanatory Role Problem by clarifying the relevance of officials for jurisprudence and social philosophy. The final section summarizes my answer to the four problems.

2 The Problems with Hart's Account

Critics have rightly identified three closely related unanswered questions in Hart's account of officials, namely: "What is an official?" (the *Conceptual Problem*); "Who are the officials of a given legal system?" (the *Identification Problem*); and "How are these officials empowered by the system's secondary rules?" (the *Empowerment Problem*). These defects affect the core of Hart's explanation of secondary rules and his understanding of legal systems in different ways. Without a resolution to the Conceptual Problem, officials cannot be decisively distinguished from subjects, and legal systems might not be clearly distinguished from non-legal normative arrangements. Lack of clarity on the Identification Problem affects theorists' ability to describe the system's secondary rules. Finally, lack of guidance on the Empowerment Problem obscures Hart's account of the existence conditions of legal systems. These issues have generated suggestions for eliminating legal officials from theoretical inquiries, leading to a further question: "What role do officials play in legal theory?" (the *Explanatory Role Problem*). This section expands on each of these issues and their theoretical consequences.

2.1 *The Conceptual Problem*

The Conceptual Problem deals with the first part of Simmonds' complaint cited above, namely that "Hart nowhere tells us what an 'official' is."[8] Instead of the "philosophical explanation" requested by Culver and Guidice,[9] Hart provided only some cursory remarks on his account of power-conferring rules—those norms that

[8] Simmonds (2008), p. 158.

[9] Culver and Giudice (2008), p. 98.

provide agents with the ability to change some person's rights, duties or status "by certain specified procedures and subject to certain structures of rights and duties within the coercive framework of the law."[10] Two kinds of powers are distinguished: "Private powers" that confer subjects with "facilities for realizing their wishes," such as the institutions of contracts, wills, and marriages, and "public or official" powers like those created by the secondary rules of change or adjudication.[11] Unfortunately, Hart does not elaborate on this second set of powers but offers examples of officials in domestic law, including the Parliament, courts, police officers, and tax inspectors.[12]

Critics have claimed that Hart's explanation by example is unable to distinguish conclusively between officials and subjects. They note that there exist other agents who exercise powers to create and apply law within domestic legal systems—such as accountants, lawyers, and private security officers—who cannot be readily characterized as officials empowered by the system's secondary rules.[13] For example, Culver and Guidice extensively discuss the case of presidents of Canadian universities, who enjoy substantial statutorily conferred norm-creating and norm-applying powers (such as the power to ban individuals from campus), whose decisions are recognized and supported by state officials.[14] Similarly, subjects also perform significant functions of norm-application when they use powers of citizen arrest or take part in juries, but are not immediately characterized as officials.[15] Hart does not provide enough resources for asserting or denying the "public" character of these powers and the official character of these agents. Meanwhile, other authors have highlighted the critical influence exercised in the legal system by private actors, journalists, academics, lobbyists, critics, charismatic members, and economic, intellectual, or social elites.[16] By contrast, I can add, there are also several state employees in charge of public services (e.g., garbage collection, education, health) whose activities might not be best described as the exercise of normative powers. It is unclear whether the last groups of agents can be appropriately characterized as legal officials in Hart's theory or how such an approach captures and explains their roles in the legal system. As we will see, such conceptual uncertainty is directly connected with the Identification and Explanatory Roles problems.

---

[10] Hart (2012), pp. 27–28.

[11] Ibid., pp. 29–31.

[12] Ibid., pp. 21, 25, 36, 38, 60–61, 122.

[13] The objection is formulated by Culver and Giudice (2010), pp. 8–10; Culver and Giudice (2008), pp. 106–107.

[14] They discuss the examples of university presidents in Culver and Giudice (2010), pp. 47–48. For a different discussion of this example, see Scanlon (1977).

[15] Culver and Giudice (2008), p. 107; Culver and Giudice (2010), p. 117.

[16] Culver and Guidice discuss some of these examples in their inter-institutional theory of law. For example, lobby groups are mentioned in Culver and Giudice (2010), pp. 9, 78. Similarly, Habermas highlights the role of journalists and other actors in the "public sphere." Habermas (1998), pp. 373–379.

The Conceptual Problem has a second consequence. Because the presence of officials is one of the signals of the existence of a legal system, it thereby allows Hart to distinguish between legal systems from non-legal normative arrangements—such as social conventions—that lack specialized agents in change of norm-creation and application. For some critics, the inability to identify the system's legal officials brings unclarity about the distinction between legal and non-legal phenomena. Brian Tamanaha articulates this point as follows:

> Hart uses the presence of secondary rules as the criterion to distinguish "legal" systems from other means of social control—the distinctive nature of law entails institutionalized norm enforcement. (. . .) Writing from a jurisprudential standpoint that takes state law as a starting point, he simply presupposed the status of the legal officials as public. Hart repeatedly refers to "private persons and officials" assuming we know who comprises the latter group. But absent an explicit reference establishing who administers the secondary rules—determining who qualifies as legal officials—Hart's concept of law inexorably leads to the legal pluralist position.[17]

In this passage, "legal pluralism" is the position that recognizes that phenomena other than domestic states (e.g., associations, sports organizations, religious organizations, clubs, educational institutions, transnational norms, etc.) have legal character and interact with state legal orders.[18] Tamanaha's objection underscores that non-state normative arrangements can also exhibit secondary rules and a structure of legal officials. For example, many sports leagues and associations have a complex bureaucracy of norm-applying and -creating agents. The question now is to distinguish between legal and non-legal phenomena, since Hart does not provide an account of officials but merely presupposes state agents. For Tamanaha, without such an account, Hart's theory cannot distinguish between legal systems and non-legal phenomena.

2.2 *The Identification Problem*

The Identification Problem relates to the second part of Simmonds' complaint. Here, the problem is not the concept of officials itself but the related concern of "how to identify one,"[19] namely, the individuation of the particular officials of a given legal system. In Hart's account, to determine whether a specific normative practice is a legal system, theorists need to identify the practice's legal officials, whose attitudes and behavior ultimately constitute the system's secondary rules. At the same time, secondary rules are constituted by the behavior and attitudes of the system's

[17] Tamanaha (2001), pp. 138–139. See also Culver and Giudice (2008), p. 91.

[18] Some writers have endorsed Hart's framework to account for situations of legal pluralism. See e.g., Galanter (1981).

[19] Simmonds (2008), p. 158.

officials.[20] However, disputed cases of officials mentioned in the previous problem complicate such identification. For example, if we cannot determine whether accountants, lawyers, or university presidents are officials empowered by the secondary rules of a given state, the state's secondary rules remain indeterminate. And if theorists cannot identify secondary rules, they cannot decisively determine whether the norms of such a state constitute a legal system or whether the defects of the pre-legal society have been remedied.

Keith Culver and Michael Guidice forcefully make this point concerning putative international legal officials:

> (. . .) without an explanation of what sorts of practices of normative power constitute an office of international legal official, it is not possible to conclude that none or any exist. And without knowledge of whether any international legal officials exist, it is impossible to conclude one way or the other whether an international rule of recognition exists. (. . .) [Hart's argument cannot] capture and distinguish international law and an international legal system from other forms of social order, social norm, and so on.[21]

Although their comment focuses on the rule of recognition in international law, it applies to all other secondary rules of all legal systems. The critical point is that, without identifying the system's particular officials, theorists cannot explain the secondary rules of that system and determine whether the normative practice constitutes a legal system and distinguish it from other legal systems and other non-legal normative practices.

2.3 *The Empowerment Problem*

The idea of social or customary rules is one of the building blocks of Hart's theory. In his view, a social rule is efficacious (i.e., it exists as a social rule) when it is followed by a group where at least some part of the group exhibits a set of pro-attitudes that Hart terms the "internal point of view."[22] Such pro-attitudes are exhibited when agents accept the rules as standards of appropriate behavior, actively seek to conform to the norms, advise and demand conformity from others, acknowledge such criticism and demands as justified, and exercise social pressure or critical reactions against those who do not abide by the shared standards.[23] To use Hart's hackneyed example, we are warranted in concluding that the social rule requiring males to remove their hats when entering the church exists in a group if two conditions are met: (1) that group members generally take off their hats while entering the church, and (2) that part of the community converges in taking the

[20] Many scholars suggest that, for this reason, there is a vicious circularity in Hart's account. I respond to different versions of this objection in a different paper.

[21] Culver and Giudice (2010), p. 33. See also Collins (2015), p. 618.

[22] Hart (2012), pp. 55–60.

[23] Ibid., p. 57.

internal point of view with respect to the normative standard fixed by the pattern of behavior. That is, they take the norm "males should bare the head when entering a church" as a common standard of conduct to which group members are required to conform, and that justifies criticisms and exercises of social pressure against non-compliers.[24]

As evident in the example, Hart's analysis of social rules focuses on duty-imposing norms. However, he also describes the system's secondary rules as social rules that empower officials; that is, they are social power-conferring norms, not duty-imposing ones. Here, an additional deficit of Hart's account arises, the Empowerment Problem, described by Stephen Perry:

> (. . .) [T]here would appear to be an omission in Hart's theory of law, which is his failure to offer an explicit analysis of the character of fundamental power-conferring rules that would correspond to his analysis of the rule of recognition. (. . .) What is apparently required, then, is an account of how customary rules can be power-conferring and not just duty-imposing.[25]

Matthew Kramer also notes this issue:

> . . . what is disconcerting about Hart's otherwise insightful analysis of the internal point of view is that the analysis applies only to duty-imposing norms and not to power-conferring norms. Throughout his discussion of social norms and the internal point of view, Hart was envisaging the categorical requirements established by duty-imposing norms. (. . .) In other words, the social norms contemplated at this juncture by Hart were markedly different from the power-conferring norms which he envisioned when he contended that the role of many of those latter norms is to provide the structures or frameworks of sundry legal arrangements rather than to deter people from engaging in modes of conduct that are perceived as wrongful.[26]

That is, Hart does not explain how secondary rules *qua* social rules empower the system's officials. And without an account of official empowerment, we cannot fully understand what secondary rules are and how they operate.

The Empowerment Problem affects Hart's theory of the existence conditions of the legal system. For Hart,

> There are therefore two minimum conditions necessary and sufficient for the existence of a legal system. On the one hand, those rules of behaviour which are valid according to the system's ultimate criteria of validity must be generally obeyed, and, on the other hand, its rules of recognition specifying the criteria of legal validity and its rules of change and adjudication must be effectively accepted as common public standards of official behaviour by its officials. (. . .) [Officials] must regard these as common standards of official behaviour and appraise critically their own and each other's deviations as lapses.[27]

In this widely discussed passage, Hart holds that officials' acceptance of the system's secondary rules from the internal point of view—and not necessarily the acceptance of subjects—is one of the minimal necessary features for a legal system. In this

[24] Cf. ibid., pp. 81, 91.

[25] Perry (2009), p. 308.

[26] Kramer (2018), p. 47.

[27] Hart (2012), pp. 116–117.

sense, the existence conditions of the legal systems presuppose a theory of social, secondary rules that Hart failed to provide. Therefore, the lack of an account of the social nature of secondary, power-conferring norms obscures Hart's overall explanation of the existence of legal systems.

2.4 *The Explanatory Role Problem*

Finally, these theoretical deficits lead to a more general question about the role that officials should play in jurisprudence that I name the Explanatory Role Problem: If the notion of officials creates so many theoretical problems, do they need to maintain the central role in jurisprudence that Hart attributed to them? Some writers go even further. In their view, the idea of officials is not only rife with problems but also brings with it detrimental assumptions for jurisprudence. For example, it has been argued that Hart makes the existence of law dependent on the recognition of an "elite" of powerful agents, disregarding the views of the system's subjects.[28] For example, Peter Fitzpatrick claims that

> Hart erases the element of the popular. (. . .) The populace is thus excluded and related to a state of Austinian inertness. (. . .) In short, what counts as law becomes exclusively and comprehensively determined by officials and the positivist enterprise is preserved.[29]

By the critics' lights, the result is a "surely patronising and unnecessarily elitist" conception of law[30] which "opens the further possibility of radical alienation" of citizens from their own law.[31]

Because the theoretical problems mentioned above are conjoined with their problematic assumptions, some authors have suggested minimizing the role those legal officials play in legal theory or removing them altogether.[32] Instead of Hart's "official-based" theory, these critics suggest developing alternative conceptions of law in which citizens—or norm users—take the central theoretical role. For example, Gerald Postema has forcefully claimed that theorists need to "turn the pyramid back on its social base," i.e., to develop citizen-centered conceptions of law.[33] Thus, we can capture the influence of citizens and other actors (corporations, lobbyists, etc.) in the legal systems, obscured by Hart's theory. One can argue that this aspect of Hart's theory motivated some of his followers to move away from the categories

---

[28] See Postema (2008), p. 61; La Torre (2013), p. 160; Culver and Giudice (2010), pp. 19–20, 123. See also Ibid., pp. 19–20, 123.

[29] Fitzpatrick (1992), p. 4. See also Ibid., p. 206.

[30] Davies (2010), p. 163.

[31] Postema (2008), p. 51.

[32] Culver and Giudice (2010), pp. 110, 152. See also Taekema (2011), p. 179; d'Aspremont (2011), pp. 203–204; Collins (2015).

[33] Postema (2003), p. 238. See also Culver and Giudice (2010), p. 109; Taekema (2011), pp. 173–174.

of officials and systems. For example, Neil MacCormick developed an influential Hart-inspired theory of law in which institutions, not officials, are the central actors.[34] As one commentator suggests, MacCormick "break[s] rank" with Hart in an effort to promote "a 'norm-user' approach to legal theory, in which, at the end of the day, the internal point of view hinges on the social practices of citizens at large."[35] In sum, the Explanatory Role Problem queries which role, if any, officials should play in legal theory.

3 The Building Blocks

To develop a response to these four problems, this section reinterprets Hart's project as a general theory of practice-based norms and normative complexes. Although Hart's analysis focuses on domestic law, he explicitly claims that some of the "central themes" of his theory of municipal legal systems apply to "any form of social structure" and any situation in which "social rules are observed."[36] Moreover, his examples included games, etiquette rules, social conventions, private associations, and military institutions.[37] This reinterpretation proceeds in six steps. First, I explicate the building blocks of this account, namely, norms, groups, and communities. Then the pivotal idea of normative orders is introduced. Third, a reconsideration of the idea of constitutive rules is presented. Fourth, I develop a distinction between two kinds of normative orders, sets and systems. While these tools can be applied to all sorts of practice-based normative phenomena, fifth, I argue that law is related to those orders that constitute particular arrangements that I term political communities. Finally, a methodological distinction between explanatory and doctrinal inquiries is introduced.

3.1 Practice-Based Norms, Groups, and Communities

Hart's influential theory of law can be understood as a theory of practice-based normativity. Rules or norms (both notions are used indistinctively) refer to any general or particular standard that guides or may be considered to guide the behavior of an individual or group.[38] *Practice-based norms* are those that ultimately depend on the regular behavior of a group, and some group agents sharing attitudes of rule

[34] MacCormick (2007).

[35] Menéndez (2011), p. 217.

[36] Hart (2012), p. vi.

[37] Ibid., Chaps. 3, 5, 7; Hart (1982).

[38] Hart (2012), pp. 82–91. While I use "rule" and "norm" interchangeably, I preserve Hart's familiar expressions of rules of change, adjudication, and recognition.

acceptance that Hart named the internal point of view. Examples of practice-based normative phenomena include or are a feature of social rules, conventions, roles, games, sports, associations, institutions, and nation-states. Practice-based norms contrast with *non-practice-based norms*, namely, those action-guiding standards that exist as propositional entities that a group has not effectively taken up as their actual or potential guides of collective behavior (e.g., Plato's proposal for an ideal state or a bill not yet enacted into law). If norms are no longer practiced, we will not be speaking of extinct normative phenomena (e.g., Roman law); if the norms have never been practiced, the Hartian theories would be referring to proposals for new phenomena.

Any discussion of practice-based norms presupposes a plurality of agents who accept these rules as standards of behavior, act according to them and modify their behavior when they detect deviations and exert social pressure upon those who do not abide by the shared standards. To repeat the example, the rule that forbids men to wear hats in church concerns the conduct and attitudes of a group of churchgoers.[39] Similarly, a token instance of a game relates to the actions of a particular group of players who follow the game's rules. I call *normative groups* those collectives created by practice-based norms, including teams, associations, clubs, boards, committees, military and religious organizations, and states. If a group has permanency and stability in time, I call it a *normative community.* The existence of groups and communities, in my account, is primarily a function of their being guided by the same shared standards. Groups and communities in the normative sense do not require that their members share a common history, moral-political views, values or sentiments, or social, economic, and political interests. In this view, normative practices and groups are co-constitutive notions: a group is a collectivity guided by the same shared norms, and the behavior of this collectivity and the acceptance of the rules by its subjects is what makes these members a "group." Hart's theory—and other contemporary legal theories—thus provide explanations of practice-based norms and their correlative groups.[40]

It should be highlighted that all practice-based normative phenomena are the norms of a particular group that express that group's will, intention, or view of a specific issue. This explanation presupposes an understanding of *group agency*. Unlike mere aggregates and combinations of agents that are unable to act collectively or express a collective will (e.g., a crowd at a mall or the people in the park at 3 p.m.), normative groups and communities are agents capable of having and expressing wills and intentions different from those of their individual members.[41] They do so mainly through creating, modifying, applying, and removing norms. As a result, practice-based duties, rights, powers, reasons, etc., are perspectival: they exist

[39] Ibid., pp. 55–56.

[40] *See* Ibid., pp. 56–57; Raz (1999), p. 52; Finnis (2011), pp. 148–150; Honoré (1987a), pp. 32–52; Raz (2009a), pp. 99–101, 107.

[41] In Sect. 4.1, I suggest that distinction between the sets and systems further develops them the standard theories of collective intentionality.

as a manifestation of the group's will and intentions and insofar as the group practices them.

3.2 *Normative Orders*

A central Hartian methodological prescription is that individual normative components are to be explained in the specific context in which they are meaningful. Hart wrote that "we must never take [legal words, such as duty or right] alone, but to consider the whole sentence in which they play their characteristic role."[42] This insight parallels the *context principle* in philosophy of language that resolves to "never . . . ask for the meaning of a word in isolation, but only in the context of a proposition."[43] In explaining normative phenomena, the context principle translates into the prescription that individual practice-based norms should not be studied individually or in isolation from other rules, but rather in the context of the specific normative in which they are embedded. Raz presented this "major thesis": "a theory of legal systems is a prerequisite of any adequate definition of 'a law.' "[44] This view further echoes a Kelsenian insight: "It is impossible to grasp the nature of law if we limit our attention to the single isolated rule."[45] Less explicitly, Hart suggests that the proper way to analyze legal directives is to be mindful of the "unstated," "background," or "normal context" in which they are meaningful, i.e., an efficacious legal system.[46]

Following this principle, the Hartian theory developed here advances a *contextualist approach* in which individual normative elements should be explained in the context of a relevant complex of norms.[47] This project contrasts with an alternative approach, best illustrated by John Austin, in which the explanation of the idea of "a law" is prior to explaining the complexes of norms.[48] We can call the second approach *compositionalist,* for it mirrors those accounts of language where the meaning of a proposition is primarily the meanings of its constituent elements.[49] Much confusion is derived from the lack of attention to this critical insight.[50] Although here is not the proper place to compare compositionalist and contextualist

[42] Hart (1983a), p. 26.

[43] Frege (1980), p. x.

[44] Raz (1980), p. 2.

[45] Kelsen (1945), p. 3.

[46] Hart (2012), pp. v, 85, 103, 108, 280, 295.

[47] On the centrality of the context principle in jurisprudence, see Toh (2015), pp. 693–695; Waluchow (2011), pp. 363–366.

[48] Austin (1995). For an apt contrast between Austin's and Hart's strategies, see Gardner (2012), pp. 179–180.

[49] See Szabó (2020).

[50] For a discussion, see Toh (2015), pp. 363–366.

approaches, it is critical to note that the compositionalist principle determines the order of explanation of the Hartian theory. This approach does not explain legal phenomena solely by reference to individual normative components, as the compositionalist account does, but starts by identifying the relevant complex of norms and communities that generate it.

There are competing characterizations of the relevant normative complexes in the literature, often using different terminology.[51] To avoid confusion, I introduce the notion of *normative orders*—not present in Hart—to describe one prominent type of normative arrangement characterized by three features: (1) the complex of norms constitutes a certain *domain of behavior* (an activity, collective enterprise, joint action, community, etc.). (2) The complex's norms bear *normatively relevant logical relationships* among them; that is, some norms impose conditions on the application of other norms or impact the operation of other norms. Examples of these "normative relationships," as Raz calls them, include situations when a rule might be applied as a consequence of another rule (e.g., a sanction that follows the breach of a duty); an action in accordance with a rule might result in the creation of a new norm (e.g., the rules created by the exercise of a norm-creating power are related to the rule establishing the power); or one norm might limit the operation of another (e.g., norms that condition or restrict the exercise of a power or right).[52] Finally, (3) that these connections render the group of norms into a *unity* of inter-dependent norms differentiable from other complexes of norms. According to Raz, statements such as "this is a rule of soccer, but it is not a rule of rugby" or "this is a part of English law but there is no such law in the American legal system" "testify to a conception by which certain groups of norms are more than haphazard assemblages of norms."[53] That is, ordinary discourse intuitively relies on a sense of unity to distinguish between different normative practices (e.g., the norms of soccer differ from the norms of rugby) and tokens of the same type of practice (e.g., norms of McMaster University differ from those of the University of Toronto).

The explanation of the features that transform a plurality of norms into normative unity was a central question of legal theory in the twentieth century.[54] While a comprehensive view is not yet developed, I shall rely on standard theories of law to suggest that a complex of norms forms a unity when one or more of the following indicators are present: (i) norms need to be *used jointly* to regulate a domain of action (e.g., norms of a game are typically used together);[55] (ii) they have or constitute *shared points, values, or functions* that do not exist independent of the norms (e.g.,

[51] For example, Raz calls "systems" all complexes of norms, while Hart reserves that label for the more complex arrangements involving officials and secondary rules that Raz termed "institutional systems." Kelsen's term of preference is "order" (*Ordung*), which is also translated as "system."

[52] Raz (1999), Chap. 4.

[53] Ibid., p. 9.

[54] Kelsen, for example, formulated and attempted to resolve this question throughout his career. See Kelsen (1992), p. 55; Kelsen (1967), p. 193; Kelsen (1990), p. 100. For a more recent formulation, see Lindahl (2013), pp. 13–18, 77–81.

[55] See e.g., Raz (1999), pp. 113–115.

winning or losing in the case of a game);[56] (iii) they were created by, or can be traced to, the *same independent norm-creating agent* (e.g., an Austinian sovereign);[57] (iv) they have the *same source of validity* (e.g., the same constitutive document, convention, contract, or agreement);[58] or (v) they empower specific *norm-applying officials* or *institutions* to identify and enforce the order's norms (e.g., referees or judges).[59] In my account, a normative order displays normative relationships among its constituent norms and one or more of these indicators of unity in regulating a domain of action. In sum, a normative order is not a haphazard collection of rules but *a unity of normatively interrelated norms.*[60]

3.3 Order-Constitutive and Order-Constituted Norms

Not all practice-based norms are social rules as described above.[61] For example, enacted norms issued in accordance with power-conferring rules are created by enactment rather than directly by social practice. However, a central insight of Hart's theory is that non-social rules presuppose that a community practices certain social rules.[62] In the example, enacted norms presuppose efficacious social norms that empower certain agents with a norm-creating capacity or create a normative order that contains such a power-conferring norm. In other words, a backdrop of efficacious social norms constitutes—to use an expression from Hart—the "normal, though unstated, background or proper context" in which we can discuss non-social rules.[63]

Having established these parameters, I can recast Hart's familiar yet problematic distinction between primary and secondary rules.[64] He sometimes claims that the division concerns two different types of norms: while primary rules are duty-imposing rules, secondary rules are power-conferring rules.[65] However, elsewhere he suggests that the division concerns different social functions: while primary rules "guide conduct," secondary rules belong to a "different level from primary rules[;] they are about such rules."[66] Critics have rightly noted a contradiction in Hart's

[56] See e.g., Ibid., pp. 117–122.

[57] See e.g., Austin (1995), pp. 30–31, 165–170. See also Hart (2012), p. 53.

[58] See e.g., Kelsen (1982).

[59] See e.g., Hart (2012), pp. 100–110, 122; Raz (1999), pp. 123–140.

[60] For a development of this account, which includes other indicators, see, Fabra-Zamora (2023).

[61] See Sect. 2.3.

[62] Ibid., pp. 88, 103–104, 108. See also Hart (1983a), pp. 33–35.

[63] Hart (2012), p. 85.

[64] Ibid., pp. 81–97.

[65] Ibid., pp. 81, 40–41.

[66] Ibid., p. 94, cf. 97.

view.[67] A rule can impose a duty to apply other rules ("secondary" in the second sense but not in the first), and a rule can confer powers on an agent without directly dealing with other norms ("secondary" in the first sense but not in the second).

To resolve this issue, we should note a critical insight concerning two levels of rules pertaining to any normative order at the core of Hart's confused formulation. I will refer to these levels as *order-constituted* and *order-constitutive norms.*[68] In keeping with the contextualist approach, the constitutive nature of norms should be understood in relationship with their ability to create normative orders. In my account, *order-constitutive norms* are social rules that create and unify a normative order. Meanwhile, *order-constituted norms* are norms and norm-applications that exist only as part of—or which can be made sense of only in the context of—efficacious constitutive social rules. For example, we can distinguish between the regularities of behavior and pro-attitudes of a group that creates a game and empowers that game's umpire (i.e., the game's order-constitutive rules) from the umpire's decisions during the game (i.e., order-constituted rules). These decisions further specify the game's general norms and usually create new individual norms (e.g., "this player committed an infraction and must leave the game") that did not exist before the application. In my explanation, order-constitutive rules are always social rules; order-constituted rules need not be social rules themselves.[69] Although both levels of rules differ in their existence conditions and mode of operation, they are aptly characterized as norms because they guide the behavior of the normative community's members.[70]

Two distinctions with Hart's original formulation need to be acknowledged. First, *pace* Hart's original formulation, there is no reason to restrict order-constitutive norms to power-conferring rules and order-constituted rules to mandatory norms. In

[67] For criticisms of Hart's distinction, see Cohen (1962); Bobbio (1968); MacCormick (1981), pp. 103–106; Tapper (1973); Raz (2009b), pp. 177–179; Gerber (1972); Hacker (1977), pp. 19–21; Ruiz Manero (1990), pp. 100–106; and Bayles (1992), pp. 57–60.

[68] Hart mentions that "rules are *constitutive* of the sovereign" (italics original). Hart (2012), p. 67. The distinction between constitutive and constituted rules was already familiar for Hart. See Rawls (1955), pp. 23–26; Midgley (1958), p. 279; Anscombe (1958), pp. 71–72; Von Wright (1963), pp. 6–7; Von Wright (1971), pp. 150–154; Oakeshott (1975), pp. 56–59; Honoré (1987b), p. 83; and Ross (1987), pp. 53–57.

[69] My account leaves room for constituted social norms, that is, customary norms that lack the capacity to create and unify normative orders. One example is customary norms in state normative systems, which are identified by the criteria of the validity of the Rule of Recognition.

[70] While I do not defend this argument here, I believe that Hartian conception of constitutive rules compares favorably to John Searle's highly influential articulation of the notion. For Searle, rules are not divided between constituted and constituted with regards to their role in the creation of a normative order, but there are two different kinds of norms: "regulative" rules regulate independently existing forms of behavior and constitutive rules define or create new forms of behaviour (X counts as Y in context C). See Searle (1969), pp. 33–36; Searle (1995), p. 28. In my view, Searle develops a compositionalist account of constitutive rules. These defects ultimately generate the problems that other critics have identified, in particular the confusion of regulative and mandatory norms and the neglect of power-conferring rules. See Warnock (1971), pp. 37–38; Raz (1999), pp. 108–109. See also Weissbourd and Mertz (1985), pp. 626–629.

my account, both levels can incorporate all kinds of normative components—i.e., they can establish duties, rights, immunities, etc. Moreover, although Hart describes secondary rules as power-conferring norms, he adds that these powers are "reinforced" by other normative components (duties, rights, etc.) and non-normative elements (e.g., definitions and concepts).[71] Consequently, the constitutive rules of the arrangements that I call below normative systems are best understood as complexes of deontic and non-deontic elements that regulate the central normative activities of a community in which powers play a prominent but not exclusive role. Second, another key difference between my construal and Hart's original formulation should be noted. As formulated here, order-constitutive rules of recognition, change, and adjudication are social rules that exist as standards fixed by community members' behavior and their collective critical acceptance. A system's order-constituted rules—or "primary rules" for Hart—are those identified by the system's rule of recognition. The rules also regulate duties and other normative elements (i.e., conferral of rights, etc.). That is, my explanation allows for order-constituted rules that establish criteria to identify, create, and apply laws, including power-conferring norms, identified by the rule of recognition. Importantly, although order-constitutive rules might be codified or replicated in enacted norms to increase their certainty, such codification does not turn order-constitutive norms into order-constituted ones. As social rules, a community must practice the order-constitutive rules of change, adjudication, and recognition, and their codification would be ineffectual if these rules were not practiced.[72] In this sense, normative systems are ultimately constituted by a complex of "ineliminable" social rules, to borrow Stefan Sciaraffa's apt phrase.[73]

3.4 Sets and Systems

Hart famously introduced the distinction between "pre-legal" communities and societies ruled by "legal systems" through a story in which systems remedy the defects of the pre-legal community. In this view, "pre-legal" or "primitive" communities lack standards for regulating the identification, creation, and application of collective rules, thereby suffering from three "defects": *normative uncertainty* because there are no "common marks" that identify the rules to be obeyed, applied,

[71] Hart (2012), pp. 19, 97, 134.

[72] As Hart puts the point with regard to the Rule of Recognition: "Even if it [sc. 'What the Queen in Parliament enacts is law'] were enacted by statute, this would not reduce it to the level of a statute; for the legal status of such enactment necessarily would depend on the fact that the rule existed antecedent to and independently to the enactment." Ibid., p. 111. For an interesting comment, see Kramer (2018), pp. 92–97. In the Hartian understanding, this point also applies to the constitutive rules of change and adjudication.

[73] Sciaraffa (2011), p. 620. See also Gardner (2012), pp. 68, 102.

and enforced or procedures to settle doubts about membership of norms;[74] the *static character of the rules*, namely, the "lack of mechanisms for deliberately adapting the rules to changing circumstances by eliminating old rules and introducing new ones";[75] and the "*inefficiency of diffuse social pressure* by which the rules are maintained" because the community lacks a "final and authoritative" means of establishing the violation of rules.[76] Societies ruled by "legal systems" include a trio of "secondary" rules of change, adjudication, and recognition that remedy these defects.[77]

In my view, the core of Hart's fable concerns could be reconstructed as concerning three sets of central activities found in normative orders. These are: (1) the identification of the standards that guide the community; (2) the creation, modification, and removal of communal rules; and (3) the monitoring and enforcement of rules, its application to specific cases, and the resolution of communal disputes. Because normative orders are practice-based phenomena constituted and sustained by their participants' continuous engagement with the orders' norms and collective accountability, normative orders that persist in time develop explicit or implicit regulation of their central normative activities. That is, non-transient normative orders develop, through time, membership criteria distinguishing the order's norms from other rules and some standards for creating and applying norms. Consequently, we should understand the fable as concerning the degree of *specificity* and *efficacy* of these regulations rather than (as commonly interpreted) merely relating the existence or absence of regulations in an order's central normative activities.

Two kinds of normative orders thus can be distinguished. *Normative sets* are those orders whose constitutive rules do not provide determinate or efficacious regulations of its central normative activities or empower agents to perform them; this requires community members to identify, create, apply, and enforce the order's norms.[78] These arrangements might (but need not) suffer from Hart's normative "defects" or operational limitations. In contrast, *normative systems* are orders constituted by a trio of social rules—the rules of recognition, change, and adjudication—that determinately and effectively regulate the community's central normative activities and typically empower agents to perform them. The *rule of recognition* specifies determinate *criteria of membership* or *validity*, "some feature or features possession of which by a suggested rule is taken as a conclusive affirmative indication that it is a group's rule to be supported by the social pressure it exerts."[79] That is, the rule of recognition provides authoritative criteria for

[74] Hart (2012), p. 92.

[75] Id. at 92–93.

[76] Hart (2012), pp. 93–94. "Diffuse social pressure" refers to the fact that social pressure in support of norms is exercised by the community as a whole.

[77] Ibid., p. 71.

[78] Hart mentions "Sets" in Ibid., pp. 92, 95, 233–236.

[79] Ibid., p. 94.

identifying the system's norms. The presence of a rule of recognition with criteria of validity thus resolves the problem of normative uncertainty. Meanwhile, *rules of change* regulate the creation, modification, and removal of communal rules,[80] and *rules of adjudication* establish how violations of collective norms should be determined and how communal social pressure should be exerted.[81] These rules, respectively, remedy the static character of the set's rules and the inefficiency of using diffuse social pressure to maintain them. In this reading, the rule of recognition is not a "master rule" that validates all the system's norms, including other secondary rules as suggested by some interpreters.[82] The norms of change and adjudication are not in a subordinate relationship to the system's rule of recognition; rather, they are part of the backdrop of constitutive practice that gives rise to the practice and makes it what it is. In other words, the rules of change and adjudication are constitutive rules of the system that operate in tandem with the rule of recognition in creating a normative system, a type of normative order that exists only when the trio of rules is present.

Hart characterizes the constitutive rules of normative systems as power-conferring rules, because they critically (although not exclusively) endow some agents and institutions with the normative power to create, modify, and apply communal norms. The agents and institutions that perform these normative activities are the *community's officials*. Officials are closely related to offices, a notion mentioned but never defined by Hart.[83] We can now define *offices* as enduring bundles of powers, duties, rights, and other normative components that can be held by different individuals on behalf of the community. The two types of officials are *norm-creators*, who are empowered to issue decisions that alter the system's rules (i.e., enactments), and *norm-appliers*, who are authorized to monitor the compliance of community members, apply rules to particular cases, and issue decisions that resolve communal disputes (i.e., settlements). Norm-appliers can be further divided into *adjudicators*, who resolve disputes and recognize alleged violations of the system's rules (e.g., referees in games or courts in state law), and *enforcers*, who monitor subject compliance with communal rules and settlements and apply social pressure to violators, often at the behest of adjudicators (e.g., domestic executive bureaucrats, police officers, and tax agents).[84] As I expand below, a distinctive

[80] Ibid., p. 95.

[81] Ibid., p. 96.

[82] For example, Dworkin (1978), Chap. 1; Shapiro (2011), p. 80. In the same vein, Keith Culver and Michael Guidice have described the rule of recognition as a "tertiary" rule that validates all rules including secondary rules. Culver and Giudice (2017), p. 63.

[83] Hart discuses the "judicial office," (Hart 2012, pp. 29, 145) and the "office of the legislator" (Ibid., pp. 59, 62, 145.). On the idea of office, see Burazin (2021, 2023).

[84] Hart (2012), pp. 141–142. Hart's analysis focuses on adjudicators because they have a more prominent role in exercising the constitutive function of ascertaining the system's norms. He considers the introduction of adjudicators as a transformation as important as the evolution from a "regime of custom to a mature system of law." Ibid., p. 142. Raz offers a similar argument assigning a central role to "primary institutions," a special form of "norm-applying institutions" whose authoritative decisions are "binding even when [they are] mistaken." Raz (1999), p. 135; Raz

feature of all community officials is their capacity to issue *peremptory decisions*—enactments and settlements—that curtail "deliberation, argument or debate" among community members on normative issues.[85] Consequently, the presence of norm-creating and norm-applying officials who perform normative activities on behalf of the community delivers additional clarity and determinacy to the normative order.

As a result, whereas sets lack precise and effective regulation of their central normative activities, systems feature such guidance and provide their communities with *a concrete idea of their rules, how they are created, applied, and enforced, and by whom.* That is, when constitutive social rules of a normative order regulate a community's fundamental normative activities, they create a *normative system—a distinctive kind of normative arrangement operated by a structure of officials, which provides its community with a concrete account of its normative standards and institutionalized forms of normative discourse and produces distinct doctrinal and politico-moral questions not present in simpler arrangements.* The set/system distinction is a central insight for understanding the social, normative world. For example, theorists can now distinguish between two kinds of sports.[86] Token instances of sports played with one's friends or families, without referees or codified rules, exemplify sets. Professional sports, such as those regulated by the FIFA or the NHL, feature a bureaucracy of administrative agents and referees, and constitute normative systems. Given these features, systems are subjects of theoretical and practical interest and give rise to politico-moral queries that do not apply to less sophisticated arrangements. For instance, as explained in Sect. 6, a plurality of politico-moral questions arises about the authority and legitimacy of the different officials (e.g., the referees and codifiers of norms), their decisions, and the duties of obedience that subjects have toward the order's norms and officials' decisions.

3.5 Law as the Regulation of Political Communities

As noted in Tamanaha's objection (Sect. 2.1), many theorists use the idea of "system" to distinguish between legal and non-legal phenomena. Drawing from Hart's fable, it has been argued the transformation of a set into a "system" through the introduction of secondary rules is the primary mark of legal character. That is, legal practices are those organized as systems, whereas non-systemic practices are not law.[87] Consequently, "primitive law"—i.e., customary practices without

(2009b), pp. 108–109. The enforcement of communal standards, in turn, might be performed by the community at large, by non-specialized officials, or even by officials of other normative orders. For example, state enforcers give efficacy to rules and settlements of private associations, norms from other states as regulated by international private law, and transnational arbitration regimes.

[85] Hart (1982), pp. 253, 136.

[86] This one interpretation of the example Hart introduces in Hart (2012), p. 142.

[87] For examples of this reading, see Tamanaha (2001), pp. 138–139; Roberts (2005), p. 10; Menski (2006), pp. 98–103; and Cotterrell (2012), pp. 506–507.

secondary rules—and international law—which, for Hart, was bereft of secondary rules[88]—were not legal practices.

While not entirely unwarranted (after all, Hart titled a critical chapter "Law as the union of primary and secondary rules"[89]), this reading conflates the concepts of "law" and "legal system." Indeed, Hart wrote: "We shall not indeed claim that wherever the word 'law' is 'properly' used this combination of primary and secondary rules is to be found."[90] More importantly, he also provided different characterizations for each of them. For Hart, "legal system" *qua* union of primary and secondary rules (i) is an "ancillary device"—that is, a theoretically constructed tool—that illuminates the concept of law,[91] and (ii) has a structure in terms of necessary and sufficient conditions for its application.[92] By contrast, "law" is (i) a folk-concept animated by the views of educated citizens that (ii) does not allow for a definitional structure or an account in terms of necessary and sufficient conditions.[93] In Hart's understanding, educated individuals' concept of law comprises not only systemic state law but also primitive law and international law, although they do not constitute systems. Meanwhile, such a concept also excludes associations, universities, and other arrangements that exhibit the hallmarks of normative systems. For this reason, some writers have suggested that Hart's folk-concept of law is structured as a cluster—namely, as a concept characterized by a weighted list of criteria so that no single criterion, or only a few of these criteria, is either necessary or sufficient for membership.[94]

Although Hart did not substantiate this conception of law, his discussion of moral and political obligation offers resources for an alternative and possibly more coherent view on the distinctiveness of legal phenomena.[95] There, Hart suggests that "legal" obligations are created by a sub-type of practice-based norms that impose what he calls "serious" forms of *social pressure*. As mentioned in Sect. 2.3, one of the signals of the existence of a social rule is the exertion of critical reactions against those community members that do not comply with the shared standards. These critical reactions range from "weak" forms of social pressure (i.e., verbal or non-verbal manifestations of disapproval and appeals to feelings of shame, remorse, and guilt) to more "serious" methods, which include physical compulsion or deprivations of the agent's honor, resources, liberty, and even life.[96] These strong forms

[88] Hart (2012) ch. X.

[89] Ibid., p. 79.

[90] Ibid., p. 79. He added: "we have not claimed that the word 'law' must be defined in [terms of a union of primary and secondary rules]." Ibid., p. 205.

[91] Hart (2012), pp. 155, 81.

[92] Ibid., pp. 100, 116, 129.

[93] Ibid., pp. 13–17.

[94] See e.g., Sartorius (1971); Payne (1976); Bayles (1992), pp. 75, 77, 121, 127, 137, 255; Schauer (2012).

[95] See Hart (2012), pp. 86–87. Cf. 179–180. See also Hart (1958).

[96] Cf. Hart (2012), pp. 81, 91.

of social pressure are more commonly used in those orders that regulate morally salient issues, values, and goods of the life of agents like us.[97]

To capture these insights, we can call *normative political communities* or *polities* those groups that effectively impose obligatory or non-optional behavior in morally or politically relevant domains or salient collective goods through the efficacious exercise of "serious" forms of social pressure.[98] For the Hartian, polities merit particular attention for their prominent roles in guiding our collective life. Moreover, given the weighty burdens that polities might impose on their subjects, doctrinal inquiries about the creation and application of their norms and moral-political questions about authority, legitimacy, and justification become especially pressing for participants and theorists. As a result, my renewed Hartian account regards as "law" those practice-based norms and orders that guide the life of political communities. In this account, jurisprudents focus on the legal systems of domestic states because they constitute and regulate some of the most important polities of our time. However, the Hartian would also regard as legal orders the "primitive" law of non-institutionalized communities and international law, which constitute and regulate some political communities, even if—as Hart characterizes them—lack the trio of secondary rules. In contrast, despite the significant level of institutionalization of associations, clubs, sports leagues, and universities, they are not to be considered as legal orders because they do not constitute or regulate political communities as defined here. In sum, while the Hartian conceptual tools provide a general account applicable to several kinds of practice-based normative phenomena, the concept of law captures a sub-type of normative communities, which might be organized as set or systems, that regulate critical moral issues by imposing pressing practical demands on their subjects.

3.6 Explanatory and Doctrinal Inquiries

Finally, a brief comment about this account's theoretical ambitions of practice-based norms is necessary. The Hartian approach focuses on addressing what I call *explanatory inquiries* concerning the existence conditions, central features, individuation, and typology of normative phenomena. Questions like "Is there a social rule or a normative order in place in this situation?", "Does this community have a set or system?", and "Is this practice a legal one?" are examples of explanatory inquiries. Since the existence of practice-based normativity is intricately connected to a certain community, theorists and participants interested in explanatory inquiries about

[97] Ibid., pp. 192–193, cf. 91, 117.

[98] The appeals to political communities are common in contemporary jurisprudence. See Bentham (1988), pp. 40–42; Austin (1995), pp. 178–183; Finnis (2011), p. 147; Honoré (1987a), pp. 33–51; Raz (2009a), pp. 99–101. I develop a richer conception of political community in Fabra-Zamora (2023).

practice-based norms need to refer to the behavior and attitudes of specific groups of agents. However, it is mistaken to say that explanatory inquiries are mere empirical or sociological reports of social facts and beliefs. Very differently, for those who accept Hart's methodological approach, these inquiries demand both the identification of the behavior and beliefs of specific groups and the rational reconstruction of participants' activities and views that animate the practice. We can describe this project as a *quasi-sociological* endeavor to differentiate it from the reports of empirical scholars.[99] It would be no less fitting to refer to this approach as a *socio-hermeneutical* project, for it involves interpreting and reconstructing complexes of human practices.[100]

Importantly, the Hartian account does not attempt to illuminate a different kind of questions that we can call *doctrinal ones* that relate to the determination of the constituted norms that are part of a normative order (or order's content) and the application of these norms to resolve individual cases.[101] Examples of doctrinal investigations include questions such as "Does this order have a rule commanding/forbidding φ?", "Did subject S violate the rules prohibiting φ?", or "Should consequences ψ be applied to the subject for its violation?" For instance, the Hartian account explains the constitutive social rules that create and unify a token instance of a game. That is, roughly, this group at this time and place practices a normative order that constitutes a game where the content of the order-constitutive rules can be roughly described, e.g., "Such behavior constitutes an offside foul," "It is a foul to pick up the ball in your hands," "Goals are scored by kicking the ball into the net," and so on. Moreover, the Hartian account can further explicate whether such an order is a normative set or system, or whether such a practice is a legal one. However, my account does not and need not explore fine-grained doctrinal questions about the details of the order's binding rules or their application to specific cases that players of the game face (e.g., this situation results in an offside offense, penalty kick, red card, etc.). In other words, the theoretical objective of providing an illuminating and fruitful theoretical framework is fully achieved without resolving doctrinal questions about an order's rules. Still, as I argue in Sect. 6, while the results of the Hartian explanation do not have direct implications for doctrinal inquiries, proper quasi-sociological accounts of normative phenomena frame and constrain such further inquiries.

[99] Hart labeled his work an exercise of "descriptive sociology," as it provides a conceptual apparatus to illuminate our empirical inquiries. Hart (2012), p. vi.

[100] Hart referred to his approach as "hermeneutic." Hart (1983b), p. 14. I have added the prefix "socio-" to underscore that the objects under explanation are complexes of behavior and attitudes of social groups, not texts.

[101] I take the label from Ronald Dworkin, who distinguishes between "sociological" and "doctrinal" questions. Dworkin claims, however, that "sociological" questions about the existence of normative systems and the structures of authority that concern us here are not of "much practical nor much philosophical interest." Dworkin (2005), p. 95.

4 Normative and Legal Officials

This section responds to the Conceptual Problem. My central claim is that normative officials are agents who make peremptory enactments and settlements on behalf of a given community, while legal officials are those who make such decisions on behalf of polities. This account allows me to address the critics' concerns, namely to establish a clearer distinction between officials and subjects in disputed cases and distinguish between legal and non-legal phenomena.

4.1 Public Powers Clarified

The Hartian theory developed above provides resources for an improved distinction between public and private powers. From a community's point of view, it is possible to distinguish two kinds of powers: *private powers* are those in which community members express their individual will or intentions through the creation or application of norms; and *public powers* are those in which the agent expresses the communal or collective will or intention on a particular normative issue. Hart's examples drawn from domestic law illustrate this community-based sense of the public-private distinction.[102] The private powers of citizens to form contracts, wills, and marriages regulate how individuals can create norms governing their own affairs and "express their wishes." By contrast, the public power to "legislate" refers not to any act of norm-creation but the enactment of general or individual norms for the domestic community. Likewise, the public power to "adjudicate" is not any act of norm-application but decisions that decisively apply norms on behalf of the state.

Public or collective normative activities are performed differently in sets and systems. Normative sets are communities that have not entrusted specific agents with powers to identify, create, and apply norms, so these activities are applied by a large number of community members. Hence the defects that Hart notes in normative sets. Since any public normative decision involves the participation of numerous community members, it might be difficult to identify the communal norms that regulate certain issues and their content, create new ones, or apply them to specific cases. In contrast, a group governed by a normative system empowers specific agents to perform the central normative activities on behalf of the community, namely, the *normative officials*. The distinctive feature of officials is that they exercise normative powers to issue *authoritative* or *peremptory decisions* about the order's norms.[103] That is, since officials establish the community's rules, how they are applied, and their content, they cut off "deliberation, argument or debate"[104] among community members on normative issues. To borrow from Raz, while subjects might "express

[102] Hart (2012), pp. 29–31.

[103] Ibid., p. 136.

[104] Hart (1982), p. 253.

their opinions" about the order's norms, officials are empowered to "make *authoritative* determinations" about them.[105] Hence, the introduction of officials resolves the problems evident in normative sets.

While it might be possible that all public powers lie in one agent, many persons and institutions often exercise them. Thus, in normative systems, the communal normative labor has been divided between two subsets of members with different normative roles: officials and subjects.[106] Officials are responsible for the community's normative deliberation and decision-making, thereby exercising the communal practical authority and expressing its collective will. In turn, subjects might simply comply with the norms that officials identify, create, and apply.[107] Since officials express the communal will, we can distinguish between "standards of conduct which express the decisions of the community regarding the way people should behave, the entitlements they have, etc., and views about these matters, however sound and however popular, which do not have the imprimatur of the community."[108] Officials will express the group collective might not be the will of the majority of the subjects (e.g., the will of a state on a certain issue, like abortion or euthanasia, it is not necessarily the view of the majority of its subjects).[109] In other words, in those complex situations in which social rules empower officials to decide communal normative issues and subjects have a corresponding duty of compliance, the group of officials exercises practical authority on behalf of the group.

In this account, officials are *agents who exercise normative powers to authoritatively decide normative situations on behalf of a given group*. These might be individual agents (e.g., a judge, or *Rex* of Austin's example) or collective actors (e.g., the Supreme Court or the Parliament). In these characterizations, it should be evident that Hartian officials are not only state actors but any agent in charge of the authoritative identification, creation, and application of norms within a certain normative order. As Roger Cotterrell notes, "nothing in Hart's book seems to indicate that 'officials' for this purpose must be state officials: certainly, the judges of an international tribunal and perhaps the priests of a religious group, the elders of a cultural or ethnic group, the committee of an association, or the directors of a

---

[105] Raz (1999), pp. 134–135; Raz (2009b), pp. 108–109. Authoritative does not mean final. Official decisions can be revised or altered by higher-ranked officials or in the appropriate procedures (i.e., retrial).

[106] For this view, see Hart (2012), p. 117; Green (2012), pp. xxvii–xxx; Raz (1994), pp. 206–207; Raz (2009c), pp. 110–111.

[107] As discussed in Sect. 5.5, Hart suggests that a normative system might be brought to existence through the official acceptance of constitutive rules from the internal point view and their exercise of sufficient social pressure to secure the subject group's general compliance with the norms that they create, identify, and apply.

[108] Raz (2009c), p. 101. Raz's citation refers to what he calls "state" or "political community," but perfectly describes the situation of a community ruled by a normative system.

[109] This is a distinctive insight not well-discussed by standard theories of collective intentionality. Schweikard and Schmid (2021), Sect. 2.3.

corporation could qualify."[110] Officials might exist in every type of normative order, and the "public" nature of their powers is relative to specific practice-based normative orders: umpires and federations are the officials of games, the clergy are officials of religious practices, boards of directors are officials of associations, etc.

We can thus call *normative officials* those agents who issue settlements and enactments on behalf of a group that does not constitute a normative political community. In turn, *legal officials* are those whose powers are part of the normative orders of polities. Such refined understanding does not restrict legal officials to those of the state or domestic polities but allows for international, supranational, and transnational legal officials. For example, we can consider the International Court of Justice or the International Criminal Court as norm-applying officials that apply the norms of international law since they take normative decisions on behalf of the international community.

4.2 Distinguishing Officials and Subjects

The renewed understanding of public power-conferring norms is the critical notion that allows us to distinguish officials from subjects. In the Hartian view, officials exercise peremptory normative powers that exist in some rule-constituted frameworks. We can then distinguish between officials who issue enactments and settlements on behalf of normative communities from other actors they are confused with. Three clarifications are important.

First, we can distinguish officials from a particular type of subjects that I will call *community agents* who work for the group or represent it without exercising powers of norm-creation and norm-application. For instance, a municipal trash collector is a community agent but not an official since he does not exercise normative powers. However, the same agent would be an official as described below[111] if he had powers to fine those who violate the rules about proper garbage disposal. Thus, not all agents who work for or represent a political community are legal officials, only those who exercise normative powers on behalf of the group.

Second, official powers are different from exercises of *de facto* influence in a given community by journalists, academics, lobbyists, critics, charismatic members, and economic, intellectual, or social elites. These *influential subjects,* as we might call them, exercise pressure in the community, particularly in officials' deliberations. Still, they do not qualify as Hartian officials since they do not exercise norm-constituted powers to decide normative situations in the community through their utterances and deeds. Like all other subjects, they can "express their opinions"—which might be communally salient—about the order's norms but are not

[110] Cotterrell (2013), p. 37.

[111] Section 5.2.

empowered to "make *authoritative* determinations."[112] For the Hartian, these actors are sociologically relevant (and thereby central to empirical inquiries) but not central to a legal order's theoretical reconstruction.

Finally, as we will see in our discussion of the Identification Problem, numerous private actors might perform public powers and even be considered officials for certain purposes. However, not all officials are empowered by the secondary or system's order-constitutive rules, so the indeterminacy about an agent's official character does not need to have the dramatic consequences that critics attribute to it.[113]

4.3 *Officials and the Distinctiveness of Law*

Finally, while Tamanaha's objection about the distinctiveness of law affects the standard understanding of Hart's theory, it should be clear that my renewed account directly addresses this concern. In this view, since an official's legal character depends on its origin within a polity, not simply on its relationships to a normative system, I can recognize the existence of officials in legal and non-legal communities. Officials are thus not the mark of legality that Tamanaha suggests but a central tool for understanding social normative phenomena. Finally, since there is no explanatory connection with the modern state or the idea of legal system, this account recognizes as law non-state normative phenomena that create polities, regardless of whether they are organized as sets or systems. In this sense, the polity-based conception captures a foundational distinction between law and non-law while recognizing the possibility of non-state legal phenomena and the fact of legal pluralism that motivates Tamanaha's concern. There might be law without officials and officials without law.

5 The Identification and Empowerment of Officials

This section discusses the Identification and Empowerment problems together, since the responses to these issues are closely related. I start by distinguishing two types of legal officials, order-constitutive and order-constituted. The former are identified using a doctrinal analysis of the system's order-constituted norms; the latter are identified through a quasi-sociological inquiry of the system's constitutive rules. Here we have a partial answer to the Identification Problem; a complete response requires the resolution of the Empowerment Problem. In response to this issue, I develop an account of social rules that explains how constituted officials are

---

[112] Raz (1999), pp. 134–135; Raz (2009b), pp. 108–109.

[113] See Sects. 5.3 and 5.4.

empowered by the system's secondary or order-constitutive rules. After providing the complete answer to the Identification Problem, these elements together answer the consequences of both challenges. On the one hand, I argue that indeterminacy regarding the system's officials does not result in the lack of clarity regarding the system's secondary rules that critics allege. On the other hand, this account clarifies Hart's account of the existence conditions of legal systems.

5.1 Order-Constitutive and Order-Constituted Officials

Based on the distinction between order-constitutive and -constituted norms discussed above, we can distinguish two kinds of officials. *Order-constituted officials* are those created by the system's constituted or "primary" rules, namely, those norms recognized by the system's rule of recognition. In turn, *order-constitutive officials* are created by the constitutive social norms that give rise to the normative system, where "secondary" rules of change and adjudication empower some officials to create and apply norms on behalf of the political community.

To illustrate this distinction, consider a community where *Rex*, the holder of powers of norm-creation and norm-application, confers law-making capacities on a Minister of Economy, who in turn creates a tax agency. Here, *Rex* is the order-constitutive official, for his powers to create and apply laws are generated by the constitutive norms that give rise to and unify the order. That is, *Rex's* powers exist insofar as they are followed and accepted by the community. The Minister and the agency, in turn, are order-constituted officials whose public powers are created and limited by the orders' constituted norms, i.e., norms created under the rule of recognition "Rex's enactments are law." The second set of powers presupposes the efficacy of *Rex's* powers. In other words, there is a set of fundamental power-conferring rules that create and unify a normative order and exist insofar as a particular community practices them. Like all social rules, order-constitutive rules of change and adjudication may be codified or replicated in order-constituted norms. In the example, we could issue a constitution codifying all the system's powers, including *Rex's* order-constitutive ones, which might bring further clarity to the normative system and avoid doctrinal controversies. However, codification of constitutive rules does not transform the order-constitutive powers into order-constituted ones. As social rules, order-constitutive powers of legislation, adjudication, and recognition are operative because a community practices them, and their codification would be a dead letter if the background context of constitutive social rules were not efficacious.

These two types of powers demand different inquiries for their identification. Order-constituted officials created by constituted norms are identified through *doctrinal inquiry* of the system's constituted power-conferring rules. In normative systems, order-constituted officials are identified by finding all public powers established by order-constituted rules valid per the standards established by the system's rule of recognition. That is, it is necessary to consult the relevant constitutional and legislative texts and precedents and other criteria of validity. By contrast, constitutive officials demand an *explanatory quasi-sociological inquiry* into the fundamental social rules that create and unify an order by empowering some agents to identify, create, and apply the laws. Theorists and participants interested in explaining order-constitutive powers cannot limit themselves to the doctrinal study of the system's texts and precedents, but they must refer to the behavior and attitudes of the agents of particular communities. At this moment, the Identification Problem connects with the Empowerment Problem. As Hart did not explain how social rules can confer powers, he failed to explain how order-constitutive officials can be identified. Such an account will be developed in the following subsection.

5.2 Social Power-Conferring Rules

In response to the Empowerment Problem and the Identification Problem concerning order-constitutive officials, I now adumbrate an account of social power-conferring rules. As noted above, there are two requirements for the existence of duty-imposing social rules in Hart's view: (1) *habitual behavior* and (2) *acceptance from the internal point of view*.[114] These two elements also apply to social power-conferring norms. A Hartian social power-conferring rule requires that (1) its members *habitually recognize* the capacity of an individual or collective agent to issue peremptory decisions about the community's normative standards while excluding the community at large and other specific agents from issuing such settlements.[115] This recognition is primarily evidenced by the group's regular compliance with the decision that empowered agent issue. In addition, a social power-conferring norm further requires (2) *collective acceptance from the internal point of view* of the agent's norm-applying capacity by at least some of the group's members. Such an attitude entails acceptance of the decisions that the empowered agent or agents issue or identify as standards of conduct to which group members are required to conform, a disposition to criticize members who fail to recognize such agents' authority to specify such settlements or fail to comply with the specified settlements, and a disposition to apply social pressure against those who fail in these ways. The existence of a power-conferring rule is compatible with some degree of non-compliance with the mandatory norms that officials identify and apply, so long as compliance is monitored, violations are declared, and there are critical reactions against deviators.

A further refinement to the Hartian account needs to be introduced. In most of Hart's examples of duty-imposing social rules, a preponderance of the group members exhibits the internal point of view and exercises critical pressure against

---

[114] See Sect. 2.3.

[115] Cf. Hart (1982), pp. 258–259.

deviators. For example, the majority of community members need to accept the standards about the use of hats in churches for the existence of such a social rule. We can call this situation *articulation by broad support.* However, Hart also describes a second model that we can call *articulation by concentrated pressure.* Social rules of this second kind are established by dint of acceptance from the internal point of view by "a minority of influential and well-organized agents" who compels obedience in the community by exercising social pressure against non-compliers.[116] In this hypothesis, an influential and well-organized minority of churchgoers who accept the standard about the use of hats in churches force other people to comply through the use of social pressure. As we will explain below, this second hypothesis about the emergence of some social power-conferring rules informs Hart's account of the existence conditions of legal systems. Hart accepts that the relevant minority might be constituted only by the system's officials, where such officials mutually accept their respective powers from the internal point of view and exercise social pressure sufficient to secure the larger group's general compliance with the norms that they create, identify, and apply.

The preceding account of social power-conferring rules can be illustrated with Hart's example of the rules about the use of hats in churches. Imagine a community in which priests police compliance with the rule "no hats in the church," where such priests' judgments motivate criticisms and the exercise of social pressure against rule violators. In general, such a community harbors a social power-conferring rule investing its priests with an adjudicative power if the following two conditions are met: (1) community members habitually comply with the priests' judgments with respect to certain rules that the priest identifies as mandatory; and (2) all or some crucial subset of the community members accept the priests' powers from the internal point of view and consequently criticize and exert social pressure against those who do not recognize the priest's power or abide with his settlements. Under the broad support model, the priest's norm-applying power exists by dint of general community acceptance of the priest's power from the internal point of view and its effective enforcement of general compliance with the priest's exercise of this power. In the concentrated pressure model, the priest's power exists by dint of a minority's acceptance of the priest's norm-applying capacity, where the minority is capable of applying social pressure on the group sufficient to motivate general compliance.[117]

Let us further imagine that in this community, the priest issues settlements that decisively establish the violation of mandatory rules, while a group of acolytes exercises the social pressure that gives efficacy to the priest's settlements by verbally censuring deviators. In such a situation, we can characterize the priest as an *adjudicator,* while the acolytes work as communal *enforcers*. The existence conditions of acolytes' norm-enforcing powers have a similar explanation: such power exists if the community habitually recognizes the acolytes' capacity to enforce the priest's settlements, and some members of the community accept such capacity from

[116] Ibid., p. 257.

[117] Hart (2012), pp. 60–61, 114 Cf. 20–21.

the internal point of view. These enforcing powers could also be structured by broad support or concentrated pressure. Of particular interest for present purposes is that under the concentrated pressure model, the priest and acolytes could mutually recognize each other's respective capacities to adjudicate and enforce the communal norms, while the community at large might even be alienated and simply yield to the enforcers' social pressure. In such a case, this practice would be a complex social situation in which a complement of norm-appliers—adjudicators and enforcers—mutually and publicly recognize one another's powers to identify and apply communal norms and secure the compliance of those subject to the norms they identify in accordance with their judgments about the correct application of those norms. Here we have identified a power-conferring rule of adjudication. Similar considerations apply *mutatis mutanda* to the power-conferring rule of recognition.

These considerations show how social rules create powers, which provides a response to Empowerment Problem, the critical gap identified by Perry and Kramer. Two clarifications are relevant. On the one hand, it is essential to note that, even in the second form of articulation, the official character of an agent is not only a function of its capacity to exercise brute social pressure or influence in the community. For someone to be considered an official, the agent's capacity to change or apply norms is created by a power-conferring constitutive social rule. Such a rule is manifested by the relevant officials' practical attitudes and applications of social pressure, and the community's compliance. The key point is that officials normatively empowered in this way are not merely agents who *de facto* exercise social pressure and secure conformity; they are also agents who can create and uphold mutually accepted normative powers through their efficacious exercise of social pressure over a certain community. On the other hand, the Hartian socio-hermeneutical account seeks to identify the critical group of norm-applying officials that constitutes and unifies the practice. What is crucial for the existence of constitutive social power-conferring rules is *sufficient convergence* regarding the critical group of agents obeyed by and large by the community,[118] which is compatible with some disagreement about the precise contours of the community's set of constitutive officials.

5.3 *The Identification of Officials*

With all these elements in place, we can now offer a response to the Identification Problem. In my account, comprehensive identification of normative officials is a two-fold task involving a doctrinal analysis of the power-conferring

[118] Hart claims that, for the existence of the rule of recognition, "what is crucial is that there should be a unified or shared official acceptance of the rule of recognition containing the system's criteria of validity." Hart (2012), p. 115. The Hartian account extends this point to the other secondary rules.

order-constituted rules and a quasi-sociological account of the existence of efficacious order-constitutive social power-conferring rules. For Hart, the "normal context" in which order-constituted rules are used presupposes the efficacy of the order-constitutive rules. Discourse about the officials of extinct or proposed orders proceeds as if the extinct or proposed order were efficacious.[119]

Let us illustrate this account by adumbrating how to identify the officials of a typical state. As mentioned above, a state's order-constituted officials are identified through a doctrinal analysis of all powers created by norms validated by the state's rules of recognition. Thus, the interested agent would need to explore the relevant sources of the legal systems: constitution, legislation, precedents, order-constituted customs, and other criteria established by the rule of recognition. All those executive, legislative, and judicial agents empowered by constituted norms to authoritatively identify, create, and apply laws are the system's order-constituted officials. For example, Hart mentions "a very familiar chain of legal reasoning" in his discussion of the U.K.'s rule of recognition:

> Is this purported by-law of the Oxfordshire County Council valid? Yes: because it was made in exercise of the powers conferred, and in accordance with the procedure specified, by a statutory order made by the Minister of Health. Finally, when the validity of the statute has been queried and assessed by reference to the rule that what the Queen in Parliament enacts is law, we are brought to a stop in [doctrinal] inquiries (. . .)[120]

In this passage, the Oxfordshire County Council and the Minister of Health are order-constituted officials who exercise powers created by the system's order-constituted rules. The Queen in Parliament is one of the order-constituted officials discussed in the next paragraph. The identification of order-constitutive officials, to be sure, might not be an easy task. It might involve complex technical questions about norms of competence, empowerment, and jurisdiction, which are resolved through the interpretative tools provided by the legal system. For instance, treatises of administrative law in domestic legal systems commonly provide intricate reconstructions of the numerous individuals and bodies that exercise public powers on behalf of state political communities and discuss doctrinal controversies that might arise in identifying order-constituted officials.

In turn, following the account of social power-conferring rules developed above, a state's order-constitutive power-conferring rules exist by dint of patterns of treating a critical mass of agents and institutions as empowered to create, police, and apply the system's rules. Order-constitutive norms might be realized by way of acceptance from the internal point of view by either a significant number of community members (broad support) or a cohesive set of agents who can secure communal conformity (concentrated social pressure model). Contemporary states are typically multi-official communities articulated by concentrated pressure. In these cases, the existence of constitutive rules can be verified by locating a critical complement of

---

[119] As Hart puts this point, "One vivid way of teaching Roman Law is to speak *as if* the system were efficacious still." Hart (2012), p. 104 (emphasis in the original).

[120] Hart (2012), p. 107.

norm-creators, adjudicators, and enforcers who mutually and publicly recognize one another's powers to identify and apply communal norms and who can secure compliance among subjects for the standards they identify and the ruling they make. For example, most states have a cohesive set of legislators (e.g., the Queen in Parliament or the Congress), adjudicators (e.g., higher-level courts), and enforcers (e.g., executive officials and police agencies) who create, identify, and apply the state laws. These officials effectively create the system's rules, monitor compliance with the rules they identify and their settlements, exercising social pressure against non-compliers, while the bulk of subjects might or not accept such power-conferring standards from the internal point of view.

This double dimension of official identification is a Hartian account's key contribution. Some critics focus only on order-constituted officials, suggesting that the Identification Problem is resolved with doctrinal analysis of the legal system.[121] This view often reads rules of change and adjudication as constituted rules identified by the system's "master" rule of recognition, failing to recognize the necessary background of constitutive social practice. By contrast, others have focused only on the second dimension. For instance, Brian Tamanaha characterizes legal officials as "whomever, as a matter of social practice, members of the social group (including officials themselves) identify and treat as 'legal' officials."[122] Similarly, Kent Greenawalt suggests that we identify officials by "look[ing] to the population at large to see who are recognized as officials."[123] This strategy fails to acknowledge the possibility of officials created solely by order-constituted rules (that is, without social recognition) or that social power-conferring rules can be articulated through concentrated social pressure (that is, without the broad communal support). In sum, a comprehensive response to the question of "who are the officials" demands *both* doctrinal and quasi-sociological dimensions: the first inquiry is a study of the system's constituted or primary rules, and the second requires a reconstruction of efficacious constitutive rules.

5.4 *Officials and Constitutive Rules*

With these elements, we can begin to address the consequences that critics attribute to these problems, starting with Culver's and Guidice's complaints. In their view, borderline cases of officials and doubts about the Identification Problem are devastating for Hart's theory based on the presupposition that an adequate theory of secondary rules must be able to specify the identity of *all* the system's officials.

[121] See, for instance, Bobbio (1968); Guastini (1999), pp. 307–317.

[122] Tamanaha (2001), p. 142. Jean D'Aspremont endorses this approach to identify the relevant "law-applying authorities" in his theory of international law's "formal ascertainment." d'Aspremont (2011), pp. 203–212.

[123] Greenawalt (2009), p. 4 n. 6.

However, the refined Hartian approach developed here can meet this challenge, for it brings into view a crucial distinction between order-constitutive and order-constitutive officials that has heretofore been overlooked, and not only by those who level the objection. Being official or holding a public power does mean being empowered by the system's constitutive or secondary rules; such norms empower only order-constitutive officials.

For the Hartian quasi-sociological explanation of legal systems only needs to locate the system's order-constitutive officials but needs not generate the fine-grained enumeration of order-constituted officials demanded by critics. As long as the theorist can identify a sufficiently unified set of constitutive officials, the Hartian theorist can individuate particular normative systems and differentiate any such systems from other normative orders. For example, Canada's legal order has a clear set of legislators (e.g., the Parliament), norm-appliers (e.g., the judicial system), and executive authorities (e.g., police and administrative officials) that allows theorists to identify it as a system and separate it from other orders such as the American one and international law. However, this understanding of the system's constitutive rules does not aspire to directly enable or imply a detailed account of all agents who exercise normative power on behalf of the Canadian polity. Rather, the Hartian project seeks to provide a quasi-sociological account of the habitually followed and accepted practices that constitute any legal system. To meet its purposes, it requires no more than a reconstruction of the behavior and shared understandings that animate the constitutive powers in the community.

As an illustration, consider Culver's and Guidice's examples of presidents of Canadian universities. In their view, since under Hart's account it is unclear these agents are officials empowered by the system's secondary rules, this example illustrates the destabilization of Hart's theory of law. However, with the resources developed here, it is evident that this challenge does not need to have the consequences they attribute to it. Instead, these university presidents cannot be deemed order-constitutive officials of the Canadian polity, for they are not part of the compound of agents who identify the standards that guide the community and whose directives are followed by the bulk of citizens. However, it is a matter of doctrinal inquiry to determine whether university presidents exercise powers created by legislated norms to authoritatively decide normative situations on behalf of the state. If the doctrinal examination determines that they exercise such powers, the Hartian could recognize university presidents as order-constituted officials of the Canadian polity. Additionally, the Hartian theory can also approach universities as normative orders of their own, i.e., each university is a unified complex of norms related to but different from the legal system of the Canadian polity. In this second analysis, university presidents are candidate examples of officials who wield powers to issue authoritative decisions on behalf of the university community. Further, these agents might be deemed order-constitutive officials if the quasi-sociological analysis determines that they are part of the critical mass of agents empowered by the efficacious social rules of change and adjudication that constitute and unify the university's normative order. The second perspective illustrates further complexities revealed by the Hartian account. We can see that any application of the Hartian theory departs from the individuation of normative orders, and these normative orders might be organized as normative systems that include their own group of officials. Importantly, nothing precludes the same agent from acting as an official of different communities. For instance, a university's order-constitutive officials might *also* be order-constituted officials empowered by valid norms of state law.

As a result, these considerations show that critics' disputed instances of officials mentioned in Sect. 2.1 do not affect the Hartian account of order-constitutive rules. The examples that critics bring—such as accountants, lawyers, and private security officers—do not involve order-constitutive officials recognized or obeyed by the community at large; but they point to order-constituted officials created by valid rules of the system. Similarly, the Hartian can further acknowledge that citizens might exercise significant "public" powers—citizen arrest or jury participation—without necessarily being empowered by the system's secondary or order-constitutive rules. In fact, not only is it possible to dispute the official nature of a given agent or a particular exercise of normative power without destabilizing the system's secondary rules, but also a great deal of the practice of law in contemporary states entails such doctrinal disputes. For example, courts often discuss issues such as "Is the President allowed to regulate transportation?", "Is education a provincial or federal issue?", "Is this agent acting in his personal or official capacity?", and "Were the police entitled to search this particular house?" States often have standards regulating such issues and allocating individual and collective consequences to the violation of order-constituted power-conferring norms. Crucially, such doctrinal disputes arise within normative systems with efficacious criteria of validity practiced by the critical compound of officials who secure compliance among subjects. In this sense, far from a decisive objection to the Hartian account of legal officials, doctrinal disputes about order-constituted officials are a central feature of normative systems. In sum, the distinction between order-constitutive and order-constituted officials shows that questions of official identification should be distinguished from questions concerning the system's secondary or order-constitutive rules.

5.5 *The Existence Conditions of Legal Systems*

Finally, articulation of social rules through concentrated social pressure informs a response to the consequence of the Empowerment Problem concerning the existence conditions of legal systems—one recurring problem in jurisprudence. By contrast, my account holds that a legal system exists *at least if* its officials accept the trio of constitutive rules and its subjects comply with the peremptory decisions the system's officials specify in accordance with the trio of system-constituting rules.[124] Officials must exhibit the hallmarks of the internal point of view, whereas subjects need not, so long as they generally comply with the settlements that the system's officials

[124] Hart (2012), pp. 116–117.

identify for whatever reason, including habitual conformity, fear of sanction, or a sense of moral duty. Here, Hart accepts that the system's constitutive social rules might be articulated through the concentrated pressure of officials only. To be clear, Hart provides an account of the *minimum conditions* for the existence of a normative system but does not suggest that such a situation is commendable. On the contrary, he deems "deplorably sheeplike" those communities that meet only the minimum requirements while suggesting that subjects in "healthy" communities also display the attitudes typical of the international point of view toward their system's constitutive rules.[125] In other words, Hart's account implicitly suggests that the trio of system-constitutive rules can (but need not) be articulated through concentrated social pressure.

With such a view, he attempts to characterize complex and large-scale normative orders with thousands or millions of participants, such as those constituted by the citizens of a nation-state, the professional soccer players ruled by FIFA, or traders whose transactions are regulated by non-state norms. In these cases, not all community members know—let alone critically accept and display the hallmarks of the internal point of view—the constitutive social rules that give rise to the normative order that governs them and empower their norm-making and norm-applying institutions. The articulation through concentrated social pressure further allows for unhealthy communities where officials might merely coerce subjects. For instance, there might be authoritarian and kleptocratic arrangements where subjects are alienated by the powers of an influential minority of norm-creating and -applying officials who empower themselves by monopolizing serious forms of social pressure. Hart would recognize such cases as legal systems, though corrupt and deplorable ones deserving our condemnation and severe politico-moral criticism.

6 The Explanatory Role of Officials

Finally, this section offers some considerations in response to the Explanatory Role Problem. Critics read Hart as offering an "elitist" conception in which officials are a necessary feature of law that separates and alienates citizens from their own norms. Hence, they call for the minimization of the theoretical role of officials, or their overall removal, to bring citizens or subjects to the central theoretical stage. While such concerns might affect some familiar interpretations of Hart's theory, resources developed by the Hartian account directly reply to the critics' concerns.

As discussed here, officials are not the central feature of all instances of law. Instead, in the Hartian account, officials are agents who authoritatively perform central normative activities in *some* normative orders, including non-legal ones. To repeat the example, consider an informal sport played without officials in which norm-creating and norm-applying activities are advanced by community members

[125] Idem.

directly. In such a case, there might be disputes among the private views of different communal participants about the relevant norms and their application. The defects of sets arise since it might be difficult to reach collective decisions on these issues. By contrast, institutionalized sports typically empower referees as norm-appliers and federations as norm-creators: the federation establishes the norms that regulate collective activities and alters them when necessary, while referees issue settlements that decisively determine the violation of rules and remedy communal tensions. A radical transformation in the community occurs with the introduction of these agents. Now the perspective of the bureaucracy of sports officials—but not necessarily that of the players—is central to resolving doctrinal questions.[126] Moreover, novel politico-questions become appear, including the problems of the *legitimate authority* of those agents who identify, create, and apply the communal norms and the *obedience of subjects* to the norms that officials peremptorily identify and their decisions about them.[127] These questions are specially pressing for theorists and community members in those situations in which officials monopolize strong forms of social pressure. In the Hartian account, the introduction of officials does not connote unconditional benefits or constitute a goal that every set should pursue. Instead, their presence is "purchased at a price."[128] Although systems might remedy possible defects of sets and bring "adaptability to change, certainty, and efficiency," structures of officials are a "luxury" that might generate forms of oppression and alienation unobtainable in societies without officials.[129]

Nothing in the Hartian account suggests that normative complexes with officials are always better forms of social organization than those without them. As Hart indicated, many communities are well-served by sets, particularly groups "closely knit by ties of kinship, common sentiment, and belief, and placed in a stable environment," or when non-centralized social pressure is sufficient to force dissenters to conform.[130] For example, the informal game might be well served by a set, whereas other more complex situations (e.g., a national league) might need normative officials. It should thus be clear that the Hartian account does not make the existence of law dependent on an "elite" of powerful agents, situating these officials as the point of departure of legal theory. By contrast, in keeping with the context principle, this theory begins with the identification of normative orders, some of which regulate political communities. If the normative order lacks officials or their existence is doubted or contested, the community is still ruled by a normative set that likely suffers from the three normative defects. Though, if we can identify a critical mass of agents empowered by social rules to create, identify, and apply collective

[126] Hart (2012), p. 142.

[127] This third problem also covers the issue often called the "political obligation." Dagger (2010). In my terminology, the problem of political obligation exists in those in circumstances where officials monopolize the use of intense forms of social pressure.

[128] Hart (2012), p. 143.

[129] Ibid., p. 204.

[130] Ibid., pp. 91–92.

rules, whose decisions are largely observed by the community and supported by sufficient social pressure, we have identified the system's constitutive rules. By identifying such a trio of rules working in tandem, we have taken the crucial step in identifying a society ruled by a normative system. This does not mean that the subjects are irrelevant to Hart's account of normative system. On the contrary, as for Austin and Kelsen, the Hartian holds that constituted norms needs to be effective for the general population. This condition is stipulated in the first of the two necessary conditions of the existence of a legal system cited above, namely "those rules of behaviour which are valid according to the system's ultimate criteria of validity must be generally obeyed."[131] As John Gardner explains, this type of effectiveness is "relatively easy to come by,"[132] since it is not required that the population at large know, let alone use, the system's constitutive rules, which can be constituted by the concentrated social pressure of officials only. In sum, a great deal of the critics' concerns expressed in the Explanatory Role Problem is misdirected.

Finally, this Hartian understanding of officials applies not only to political communities regulated by law, but to all forms of social normative phenomena. Note that a similar distinction has been developed by social ontologists. For example, Raimo Tuomela has discussed what he calls "operative" members who "not only form goals and views but also have the power to act for the group and to give orders to members."[133] The presence of these members transforms what he calls an "egalitarian" collective, where goals and views are formed by the majority of members, into "structured" or "institutionalized" communities, where there is a division of labor such as the goals and view might be articulated by operative members without the participation of non-operative ones.[134] However, the Hartian account goes further than the account of social ontologists. In addition to a comprehensive account of normative orders and normative powers, this account also clarifies that customary power-conferring rules in large institutional frameworks are commonly, but not necessarily, constituted by dint of being accepted by an influential minority only and the effective social pressure that this influential minority can exert on other members of the community. In this sense, the Hartian theory provides a more perspicuous account of the socially constructed nature of law and normative institutions.

In sum, the Hartian theory need not presuppose an elitist understanding that relies on officials to explain the existence of all legal phenomena as critics suggest. Instead, it provides an account of normative phenomena that elegantly captures pivotal socio-ontological insights and distinctions. Additionally, the refined account compares favorably to familiar socio-ontological theories as it also introduces two types of normative orders and the minimum level of acceptance of subjects and "operative members" while highlighting some doctrinal and politico-moral questions that arise.

---

[131] Hart, 116.

[132] Gardner (2012), p. 284.

[133] Tuomela (2007), p. 3.

[134] Ibid., pp. 127–128.

Therefore, *pace* critics' calls for a "norm-user" approach, it is not necessary to dispense with officials or minimize their role to understand the social foundations of law; on the contrary, their presence or absence helps clarify them.

7 Conclusion

This paper has developed an account of legal officials that addresses the four main concerns advanced by critics. In response to the Conceptual Problem, I argued that officials are agents who make *peremptory decisions* (*enactments* and *settlements*) on behalf of a given community, while *legal officials* are the agents who make such decisions on behalf of political communities. Such an account allows us to clearly distinguish between officials and subjects and resolve disputed cases. In response to the Identification Problem, I held that two kinds of officials with specific types of identification must be distinguished: *order-constituted officials* created by the system's valid norms identified by the rule of recognition and identified through a doctrinal analysis; and *order-constitutive officials* created by the system's secondary or order-constitutive rules and identified through a quasi-sociological inquiry. Thus, inquiries concerning official identity should be separated from questions concerning the identification of secondary rules. Finally, a detailed account of the power-conferring character of social rules was developed in response to the Empowerment Problem. Two different modes of articulation of constitutive social rules were discussed, which further clarified Hart's account of the existence condition of legal systems. Finally, in response to the Explanatory Role Problem, I clarified the relevance of officials for jurisprudence and social philosophy.

References

Anscombe GEM (1958) On brute facts. Analysis 18:69–72
Austin J (1995) The province of jurisprudence determined. Cambridge University Press, Cambridge
Bayles MD (1992) Hart's legal philosophy: an examination. Springer, Dordrecht
Bentham J (1988) A fragment on government. Cambridge University Press, Cambridge
Bobbio N (1968) Ancora Sulle Norme Primarie E Norme Secondarie. Rivista di Filosofia 59:35–53
Burazin L (2021) Funciones jurídicas. Doxa Cuadernos de Filosofía del Derecho 44:145–157. https://doi.org/10.14198/DOXA2021.44.06
Burazin L (2023, Forthcoming) Legal offices and legal powers. In: This Volume. Springer, Cham
Cohen LJ (1962) Critical notice. Mind LXXI:395–412
Collins R (2015) The problematic concept of the international legal official. Transnatl Leg Theory 6:608–634
Cotterrell R (2012) What is transnational law? Law Soc Inq 37:500–524
Cotterrell R (2013) Law, culture and society: legal ideas in the mirror of social theory. Ashgate, Dartmouth
Culver KC, Giudice M (2008) Legal system, legality, and the state: an inter-institutional account. Problema Anuario de Filosofía y Teoría del Derecho 2:85–125

Culver KC, Giudice M (2010) Legality's borders: an essay in general jurisprudence. Oxford University Press, New York
Culver KC, Giudice M (2017) The unsteady state: general jurisprudence for dynamic social phenomena. Cambridge University Press, Cambridge
d'Aspremont J (2011) Formalism and the sources of international law: a theory of the ascertainment of legal rules. Oxford University Press, Oxford
Dagger R (2010) Political obligation. In: Zalta EN (ed) The Stanford encyclopedia of philosophy, Winter 2010
Davies M (2010) The politics of defining law. In: The Hart-Fuller debate in the twenty-first century. Hart Publishing, Oxford, pp 157–167
Dworkin R (1978) Taking rights seriously. Harvard University Press, Cambridge
Dworkin R (2005) Hart and the concepts of law. Harv Law Rev F 119:95–104
Fabra-Zamora (2019) Normative political communities: foundations for a Hartian Theory of State and Non-State Law, Ph.D. Thesis, with McMaster University. https://macsphere.mcmaster.ca/handle/11375/25186
Fabra-Zamora J (2023) Law as normative political communities: foundations for a General Account of State and Non-State Legal Phenomena (manuscript)
Finnis J (2011) Natural law and natural rights, 2nd edn. Oxford University Press, Oxford
Fitzpatrick P (1992) The mythology of modern law. Routledge, London
Frege G (1980) The foundations of arithmetic: a logico-mathematical enquiry into the concept of number, 2nd edn. Northwestern University Press, Evanston
Galanter M (1981) Justice in many rooms: courts, private ordering, and indigenous law. J Leg Plur Unoff Law 13:1–47. https://doi.org/10.1080/07329113.1981.10756257
Gardner J (2012) Law as a leap of faith: essays on law in general. Oxford University Press, Oxford
Gerber D (1972) Levels of rules and Hart's concept of law. Mind 81:102–105
Green L (2012) Introduction. In: The concept of law, 3rd edn. Clarendon Press, Oxford, pp xv–lv
Greenawalt K (2009) The rule of recognition and the US constitution (1987). In: Adler M, Himma KE (eds) The rule of recognition and the U.S. constitution. Oxford University Press, New York, pp 1–45
Guastini R (1999) Distinguiendo: Estudios de Teoría y Metateoría del Derecho. Gedisa, Barcelona
Habermas J (1998) Between facts and norms: contributions to a discourse theory of law and democracy. The MIT Press, Cambridge
Hacker PMS (1977) Hart's philosophy of law. In: Hacker PMS, Raz J (eds) Law, morality, and society: essays in honour of H. L. A. Hart. Clarendon Press, Oxford, pp 1–25
Hart HLA (1958) Legal and moral obligation. In: Melden AI (ed) Essays in moral philosophy. University of Washington Press, Washington, pp 82–107
Hart HLA (1982) Commands and authoritative legal reasons. In: Essays on Bentham: jurisprudence and political theory. Oxford University Press, Oxford, pp 241–268
Hart HLA (1983a) Definition and theory in jurisprudence. In: Essays in jurisprudence and philosophy. Clarendon Press, Oxford, pp 21–48
Hart HLA (1983b) Introduction. In: Essays in jurisprudence and philosophy. Clarendon Press, Oxford, pp 1–18
Hart HLA (2012) The concept of law, 3rd edn. Clarendon Press, Oxford
Honoré T (1987a) Making law bind: essays legal and philosophical. Clarendon Press, Oxford
Honoré T (1987b) Real laws. In: Making law bind: essays legal and philosophical. Clarendon Press, Oxford, pp 69–88
Kelsen H (1945) General theory of law and state. Harvard University Press, Cambridge
Kelsen H (1967) Pure theory of law, Translation from the Second German Edition. University of California Press, Berkeley & Los Angeles
Kelsen H (1982) The concept of the legal order. Am J Juris 27:64–84
Kelsen H (1990) General theory of norms. Clarendon Press, Oxford
Kelsen H (1992) Introduction to the problems of legal theory: a translation of the first edition of the 'Reine Rechtslehre' or pure theory of law. Clarendon Press, Oxford

Kramer MH (2018) H.L.A. Hart. Polity, Cambridge
La Torre M (2013) The hierarchical model and H.L.A. Hart's concept of law. Revus J Const Theory Philos Law 21:141–161
Lamond G (2013) The rule of recognition and the foundations of a legal system. In: Duarte d'Almeida L, Dolcetti A, Edwards J (eds) Reading HLA Hart's 'the concept of law'. Hart Publishing, Oxford, pp 97–122
Lindahl H (2013) Fault lines of globalization: legal order and the politics of A-Legality. Oxford University Press, Oxford
MacCormick N (1981) H.L.A. Hart, 1st edn. Stanford University Press, Stanford
MacCormick N (2007) Institutions of law: an essay in legal theory. Oxford University Press, Oxford
Menéndez AJ (2011) From constitutional pluralism to a pluralistic constitution? Constitutional synthesis as a MacCormickian constitutional theory of European Integration. In: Menéndez AJ, Fossum JE (eds) Law and democracy in Neil MacCormick's legal and political theory. Springer Netherlands, Dordrecht, pp 211–241
Menski W (2006) Comparative law in a global context: the legal systems of Asia and Africa. Cambridge University Press, Cambridge
Midgley GCJ (1958) Linguistic rules. Proc Aristot Soc 59:271–290
Oakeshott M (1975) On human conduct. Oxford University Press, Oxford
Payne M (1976) Hart's concept of a legal system. Wm Mary Law Rev 18:287–319
Perry SR (2009) Where have all the powers gone? Hartian rules of recognition, noncognitivism, and the constitutional and jurisprudential foundations of law. In: Adler M, Himma KE (eds) The rule of recognition and the U.S. constitution. Oxford University Press, New York, pp 295–325
Postema GJ (2003) Law's Melody: time and the normativity of law. Assoc J Leg Soc Theory 7:227–239
Postema GJ (2008) Conformity, custom, and congruence: rethinking the efficacy of law. In: Kramer MH (ed) The legacy of H.L.A. Hart: legal, political, and moral philosophy. Oxford University Press, Oxford
Rawls J (1955) Two concepts of rules. Philos Rev 64:3–32
Raz J (1980) The concept of a legal system, 2nd edn. Clarendon Press, Oxford
Raz J (1994) The problem about the nature of law. In: Ethics in the public domain. Clarendon Press, Oxford, pp 195–209
Raz J (1999) Practical reason and norms, 2nd edn. Oxford University Press, Oxford
Raz J (2009a) Between authority and interpretation: on the theory of law and practical reason. Oxford University Press, Oxford
Raz J (2009b) The authority of law: essays on law and morality, 2nd edn. Oxford University Press, Oxford
Raz J (2009c) On the nature of law. In: Between authority and interpretation: on the theory of law and practical reason. Oxford University Press, Oxford, pp 91–125
Roberts S (2005) After government? On representing law without the state. Mod Law Rev 68:1–24
Ross A (1987) Directives and norms. Humanities Press, New York
Ruiz Manero J (1990) Jurisdicción y normas. Centro de Estudios Constitucionales, Madrid
Sartorius R (1971) Hart's concept of law. In: Summers RS (ed) More essays in legal philosophy: general assessments of legal philosophies. University of California Press, Berkeley & Los Angeles, pp 131–161
Scanlon TM (1977) Due process. Nomos 18:93–125
Schauer F (2012) On the nature of the nature of law. arsp 98:457–467
Schweikard DP, Schmid HB (2021) Collective intentionality. In: Zalta EN (ed) The Stanford encyclopedia of philosophy, Fall 2021. Metaphysics Research Lab, Stanford University, Stanford
Sciaraffa S (2011) The ineliminability of Hartian social rules. Oxford J Leg Stud 31:603–623
Searle JR (1969) Speech acts: an essay in the philosophy of language. Cambridge University Press, Cambridge
Searle JR (1995) Construction of social reality. Simon & Schuster, New York

Shapiro SJ (2011) Legality. Harvard University Press, Cambridge
Simmonds NE (2008) Central issues in jurisprudence: justice, law and rights. Sweet & Maxwell, New York
Szabó ZG (2020) Compositionality. In: Zalta EN (ed) The Stanford encyclopedia of philosophy, Fall 2020. Metaphysics Research Lab, Stanford University, Stanford
Taekema S (2011) Does the concept of law need officials? Problema Anuario de Filosofía y Teoría del Derecho 2:157–182
Tamanaha BZ (2001) A general jurisprudence of law and society. Oxford University Press, Oxford
Tapper CFH (1973) Powers and secondary rules of change. In: Simpson AWB (ed) Oxford essays in jurisprudence. Clarendon Press, Oxford, pp 242–277
Toh K (2015) Four neglected prescriptions of Hartian legal philosophy. Law Philos 34:333–368
Tuomela R (2007) The philosophy of sociality: the shared point of view. Oxford, New York
Von Wright GH (1963) Norm and action: a logical enquiry. Routledge and Kegan Paul, London
Von Wright GH (1971) Explanation and understanding. Cornell University Press, Ithaca
Waluchow WJ (2011) Lessons from Hart. Problema Anuario de Filosofía y Teoría del Derecho 5: 363–383
Warnock GJ (1971) The object of morality. Methuen, London
Weissbourd B, Mertz E (1985) Rule-centrism versus legal creativity. Law Soc Rev 19:623–659

Authority, Reason, and Competence in Issues of Legal Truth

Brian H. Bix

Abstract Legal officials—legislators, heads of administrative agencies, judges, etc.—have the competence to make new law. Sometimes, though, the new law made is via inadvertence or error, and, on such occasions, the content of law as determined through conventional doctrinal analysis may be in tension with recognition of the authorized but mistaken actions of the legal officials. In a sense, this shows an instability in the concept of competence, for the powers to change the law may be, in practice, different from the standards prescribed, and in ways that are not always predictable. This complication for the analysis of legal truth and legal content is exacerbated by the fact that any such errors may or may not be corrected (and the correction may or may not be relatively prompt). Where 'reason' and 'will' get entangled in this way, even simple bivalence may not fully hold: both '**X** is the law' and '**X** is *not* the law' may be correct.

1 Introduction

Legal officials have the competence[1] (the authority, the power) to create new legal norms. Thus, the truth of propositions about what the law is will often be a function of the actions of the community's officials. However, the matter is not as straightforward as it may at first appear: the connections—and the tensions—between legal authority and legal truth are complex. This is due to the fact that legal officials sometimes act outside of their authority (*ultra vires*), and because legal officials, even when acting within their authority, sometimes apply the law incorrectly. Such *ultra vires* or erroneous actions may ultimately be declared invalid by a (higher)

I am grateful for the comments and suggestions of John Mikhail and Torben Spaak.

[1] On (legal) competence, see Spaak (1994, 2009).

B. H. Bix (✉)
University of Minnesota, Minneapolis, MN, USA
e-mail: bix@umn.edu

G. Villa Rosas, T. Spaak (eds.), *Legal Power and Legal Competence*, Law and Philosophy Library 140, https://doi.org/10.1007/978-3-031-28555-4_12

court, but it is also the case that the error might *not* be officially corrected, or at least not be corrected for a very long time. Actions that are *ultra vires* are, narrowly speaking, beyond the competence of the officials or institutions in question, and such actions, in principle should have no legal effect.[2] However, the fact is that sometimes actions that *should* (according to the principles governing the legal system) have no legal effect, in fact *do* have legal effects.[3] This chapter explores the way that improper and erroneous actions by legal officials—subject to correction but not always in fact corrected—are, or should be, understood in terms of legal truth.

This tension within legal systems between authority and correctness is complicated by the role of convention, finality, and acceptance in legal practice. For example, the highest court of a jurisdiction may have the final word regarding a legal issue; thus, there is a sense that the law is whatever the courts say it is. Justice Robert Jackson of the United States Supreme Court famously said: 'We are not final because we are infallible, but we are infallible only because we are final.'[4] On the other hand, it is also the case that a high court sometimes changes its mind (perhaps after a change of personnel) regarding the proper interpretation of an authoritative text, stating that the new interpretation had been the right one all along.[5] What does that say about what the legal truth was during the earlier time, when the highest court took a different view?

The highest court's decision is (in a system like the United States) 'final', in the sense that there is no further appeal available, and judicial decisions are generally not subject to override by any other branch.[6] However, it is also *not* 'final', in the sense

[2] *E.g.*, Spaak (2009), pp. 72–73.

[3] Someone might respond that an official or institution acting outside its competence cannot *really* make new law; at most, other officials may only be acting 'as if' new law was created. Part of the point of this Chapter is to emphasize that such ways of speaking are, at best, unhelpful, if over a very long period of time *all relevant legal actors* view the action as having created new law, it only invites confusion to declare that this is not so.

[4] *Brown v. Allen*, 344 U.S. 443, 540 (Jackson, J., concurring in the result).

[5] The United States Supreme Court has reversed itself on a long list of issues. Among the best known (and most controversial) involved whether children can be required to salute the flag, *West Virginia State Board of Education v Barnette*, 319 US 624 (1943), whether the government can criminalize homosexual sex, *Lawrence v. Texas*, 539 US 558 (2003), whether individuals have a constitutional right to own guns, *District of Columbia v Heller*, 554 US 570 (2008), and whether same-sex couples can be excluded from state marriage laws, *Obergefell v Hodges*, 135 S Ct 2071 (2015).

[6] In the case of a judicial interpretation of a statute, the legislature can pass new legislation affirming the interpretation that had been rejected by the highest court, but that does not change the outcome in the earlier case with which the legislature is disagreeing. (Such a legislative correction or clarification occurred in the United States regarding the question of whether a federal sex discrimination statute covered discrimination based on pregnancy: the 1978 Pregnancy Discrimination Act, 42 U.S.C. §2000e(k), responded to the United States Supreme Court decision in *General Electric v. Gilbert*, 429 U.S. 125 (1976); the Court had said that discrimination on the basis of pregnancy was *not* a form of sex discrimination for the purpose of a federal sex discrimination law, and the 1978 congressional action clarified that it was.)

that, after a passage of time, the same court[7] may reverse itself. And thus, there is no point when matters are entirely 'settled'; the highest court may reverse itself after a few years, or after many decades;[8] there is, as far as we know, no 'point of no return', though, of course, a significant passage of time may increase a court's disinclination to revisit an issue.[9]

The subject of the following discussion is relevant to a number of overlapping rubrics: legal truth, the nature of legal facts,[10] legal objectivity,[11] legal determinacy,[12] the possibility of universal legal error,[13] and legal grounding.[14] (Obviously, there is no space in the current work to get to all these matters in any depth, but there is hope that the present discussion will at least suggest matters to consider for some of them.) The current analysis will also touch on broader debates between legal positivism and natural law theory about the nature of law, and disputes about the proper approach to understanding common law reasoning and legal reasoning in general.

In what follows, the article will consider a series of topics that relate to aspects of the general question: law and truth, doubts about legal truth, will and reason, the problem of legal mistake, the competence (and duty) to change the law, and natural law (universal legal truth), before concluding.

---

[7] Of course, it is usually a different set of judges on the court, but it is still said to be (and is treated as being) 'the same court'.

[8] For example, the well-known United States Supreme Court decision of *Brown v. Board of Education*, 347 U.S. 483 (1954), which held that racial segregation constituted a violation of the Fourteenth Amendment to the United States Constitution, overruled *Plessy v. Ferguson*, 163 U.S. 537 (1896), a decision that had stood for almost 60 years.

[9] Regarding an effort in one case to change the United States Supreme Court's view of a particular provision of the United States Constitution, one Justice wrote: '[T]he original meaning of the Clause is not as clear as [petitioners] suggest and not nearly as clear as it would need to be to dislodge 137 years of precedent.' *McDonald v. City of Chicago*, 561 U.S. 742, 859–60 (2010) (Stevens, J., dissenting).

[10] Theorists do not often write about 'legal facts', and when they do the terms they use may seem jarringly strange to practitioners, and even to some theorists. For example, Rosati writes (2004, p. 286): 'Legal facts are either just facts of some kind about actual or hypothetical human judgments, reactions, or attitudes or they are facts of a different kind.' Of course, that alternative, 'facts of a different kind', is open-ended, but if the first part of the sentence includes the actions and judgments of judges and other legal officials, then it is less clear what content *could* be given to 'facts of a different kind'.

[11] *See, eg,* Greenawalt (1992) and Leiter (2001).

[12] *See, eg,* Solum (1987), Leiter (1995) and Tushnet (1996).

[13] *See, eg,* Kramer (2008) and Bix (2022).

[14] *See, eg,* Rosati (2004) and Chilovi and Pavlakos (2019).

2 Law and Truth

As this chapter focuses on issues relating to 'truth' in law, it is prudent to say a few words about the difficulty or ambiguity of claims of legal truth. One problem is that there are different sorts of propositions, both *within* legal practice and *about* legal practice, which could in principle be described as 'true' or 'false'.

Propositions within and about law can occur at different levels of generality.[15] Some narrow statements regard the content of legal norms: *e.g.*, The speed limit on Highway 494 in Bloomington, Minnesota, is 60 miles per hour. There are what could be described as even more narrow propositions, *applying* legal standards (derived from constitutional provisions, statutes, regulations, contracts, wills, trusts, etc.) to individuals: **A** has the right to protest in front of the *that* government building; **B** has the right under her contract with **C** to be paid four hundred dollars for painting **C**'s apartment; **D** is not allowed to park in *that* parking spot without an official handicapped-person sticker; etc.

In the direction of greater generality and greater abstraction, one can also speak of propositions at the level of legal doctrine, principles of areas of law, or even claims about the nature of law generally. The 'black letter law' one finds in legal treatises is meant to summarize (from statues, regulations, or court decisions) the law on particular issues. Theories of doctrinal areas of law are meant to 'explain' that area of law, to show its essence.[16] Theories of law in general are described in various ways, with comparably diverse objectives (explaining the nature or essence of law or the concept of law, interpreting our legal practices, justifying our existing institutions, naturalistic descriptions of our practices, etc.).[17] Whether propositions at these higher and more abstract levels can be 'truth-apt' is a difficult question. It is like J. L. Austin's observations about the proposition, 'France is hexagonal'.[18] There is a sense in which that is true, but perhaps only 'approximately' or 'more or less' true. Perhaps the same sort of 'more or less true' would apply to claims like 'Contract Law is essentially about promises'.[19] Further discussions of the truth-aptness of more abstract propositions about areas of law or law in general must await another occasion. This chapter will focus on more narrow and less abstract legal propositions.

Relevant to the present discussion, I will also note that in those more general and more abstract categories of propositions, the issues of legal competence—the power of legal officials to make authoritative declarations—generally plays a less central role than it does when speaking about the truth of the kinds of more specific propositions that will be the focus of the present Chapter. This is because the individual actions of particular legal officials are unlikely to alter the law in a

---

[15] See Moore (2003), pp. 24–26.

[16] *See, e.g.*, Moore (2000); see also Bix (2017).

[17] *E.g.*, Dworkin (1985), Raz (2005) and Leiter (2007).

[18] Austin (1975), p. 143.

[19] Fried (2015).

significant enough way to change our view of (*e.g.*) whole doctrinal areas of law or of law in general.

One more general point regarding the truth of legal propositions: It should be noted that, presumptively, truth value claims for law are *relative to* a jurisdiction (legal system) and a time. What is true of twenty-first century British law is often not true of seventeenth century Chinese law, and, even within a single jurisdiction, the law may change from one year to the next, as the legislature passes new statutes, the courts decide new cases, individuals enter new contracts, etc.[20]

3 Doubts About Legal Truth

This chapter will assume, without substantial argument, that there *are* legal truths within and about law. This position has been, on occasion, contested. Focusing on relatively narrow and specific propositions ascribing legal rights and duties to individual parties, some scholars (particularly among the critical legal studies school) have asserted or suggested a position of 'radical legal indeterminacy', that the legal resources are not sufficient to determine that *any* proposition is true or false. Such views have been variously grounded on general semantic indeterminacy (in turn, purportedly based on Jacques Derrida's ideas of deconstruction or Saul Kripke's reading of the later works of Ludwig Wittgenstein) or on competing resources within the law—*e.g.*, conflicting legal principles, or the manipulability of precedent or of canons of statutory interpretation.[21] Arguments about radical legal indeterminacy go far beyond more conventional assertions that there are no right answers in 'hard cases', or that reasonable lawyers and judges could disagree about the legal disputes important enough to be litigated up to an appellate court. It should be noted that there is still a significant practical and theoretical distance between arguing (1) the still-moderate view, that legal resources, on their own, determine a smaller percentage of cases than most lawyers and citizens believe; and (2) the more radical view, that there are rarely, if ever, unique right answers to legal disputes. As truth in and about the law tends to be functions of linguistic meaning and practical reasoning, it would not be easy to construct a broad 'error theory' of legal truth, which managed both to avoid self-contradiction and to be at least mildly persuasive.[22] For that reason, the Chapter will proceed on the assumption that (narrow) legal propositions are generally truth-apt.

[20] Legal truth thus is what philosophers something call "indexical," *see* Braun (2015); *cf.* Green (2009). To save space and avoid some clutter and potential confusion, I will usually *not* include the time when speaking about a legal norm and will also sometimes *not* include the jurisdiction.

[21] For summaries of, and responses to, many of the arguments for radical legal indeterminacy, see, *eg,* Altman (1983), pp. 90–98; Solum (1987); cf Finnis (1985).

[22] *See, eg,* Finnis (1985), cf. Rosati (2004), pp. 287–288.

4 Will and Reason

When one says that it is true (or that it is *not* true) that I have the legal right to park in this parking spot, what is it that makes this proposition true (or false)? Some American legal realist writers famously equated legal truth with predictions of the actions of judges or other legal officials. Oliver Wendell Holmes wrote:

> Take the fundamental question, What constitutes the law? You will find some text writers telling you that it is something different from what is decided by the courts of Massachusetts or England, that it is a system of reason, that it is a deduction from principles of ethics or admitted axioms or what not, which may or may not coincide with the decisions. But if we take the view of our friend the bad man we shall find that he does not care two straws for the axioms or deductions, but that he does want to know what the Massachusetts or English courts are likely to do in fact. I am much of his mind. The prophecies of what the courts will do in fact, and nothing more pretentious, are what I mean by the law.[23]

There is a refreshing worldliness to the equation of law with what judges will decide, with how, more generally, legal officials will distribute punishments and payments,[24] a strong connection being suggested between legal truth and (one kind of) legal competence. From the perspective of average citizens (and not only 'bad people'), and perhaps even lower-level judges and functionaries, this equation of law and official action makes a lot of sense. However, as is well known, the view is significantly less helpful when one looks at the perspective of legal officials, especially higher officials (who are not subject, or at least *less* subject, to reversal by superiors). For them, the law cannot be understood as a prediction of what *other* legal officials will do, and it certainly cannot be a prediction of what *they themselves* will do.

The temptation to tie legal truth closely with (predictions of) what courts decide led H. L. A. Hart to respond with the imaginary game of 'scorer's discretion'. We know the frustrations of watching one's favorite team lose because a referee made the wrong decision about whether a team had scored, causing some to wonder if the scoring rule in this game might be simply: 'a score occurs when the scoring judge says that it has'. Hart would have us think of an imaginary game where that was in fact the only scoring rule.[25] Upon reflection, it is clear that 'scorer's discretion' is very different from the real games we know—and from law. Even bad scoring judges *purport to be applying* (and generally are *attempting to apply*) scoring *rules*.

---

[23] Holmes (1897), pp. 460–461; cf. Llewellyn (1930), pp. 437–438.

[24] Compare Connie Rosati's summary of Brian Leiter's contemporary version of the American legal realist position: 'legal facts are, in some complex way yet to be specified, a function of the actual reactions or practices of most judges.' Rosati (2004), p. 307. An approach of this sort has its own problems, not least the difficulty of explaining legal disagreement. Rosati (2004), pp. 307–308, 312–313.

[25] Hart (2012), p. 142.

Judges[26] (at least those who are not just trying to prevent being reversed on appeal—and, of course, that includes all judges who sit on the highest court in their jurisdiction) will try to discover *what the law is*. However, judges do not always get the answers right (the problem of legal mistake will be explored further in the next section). And this is where many problems of legal truth start. The complexities in discussing the truth within law often derive from legal rules being a product of both 'reason' and 'will'. A statute or constitutional provision may have (objectively speaking, according to the best understanding of the text) one legal meaning, but a court may declare it to mean something different. If one prefers to focus on applications: the correct application of the legal text to a particular dispute may entail that the plaintiff prevails, but the court may apply the text incorrectly, and conclude that the defendant prevails.

The two strains of legal analysis, the reason of doctrine ('legal science') and the will of judicial decision, in such circumstances pull in different directions. The legal doctrinal analysis might indicate one understanding or application of a binding legal text, but the court may give a different interpretation or application. The court's action is binding on the parties, and in many circumstances may bind other officials going forward (unless and until the decision is reversed by a higher court). However, even to speak in terms of the court's having made a mistake (and the possibility of its correction) shows the paradox: because legal officials have the competence (power) to act contrary to the legal standards, with those actions having short-term and long-term legal effects in the world, legal truth can be hard to pin down. As will be discussed below, there are circumstances where both a proposition about the law *and its opposite* can seem to be true.

5 The Competence (and Duty?) to Change the Law

It is uncontroversial that legislators have the competence (the power, the authority) to change the law in their community (by enacting new laws or altering or repealing existing laws), and such changes generally do not raise significant theoretical questions. From a theorist's perspective, matters are more interesting when discussing courts, especially in common law jurisdictions, where they have the authority to alter the law.[27] Here we pick up and elaborate the discussion from the prior Section. Part of the theoretical discussion begins with the question of *when* courts are making new law. For example, in the application of a statute to a set of

[26] Here I assume judges acting in good faith, not ones who are corrupt or for some other reason are making no effort to follow their official duties. I have every reason to believe that in most legal systems almost all judges, almost all the time, are acting in good faith.

[27] There are also matters of theoretical interest connected to administrative agencies, which, in many legal systems, have the authority to make new law through a grant of delegated power.

facts, what is the boundary line between mere 'law application' and 'judicial legislation'?

This is a much-discussed topic, and there is room in the present work only to sample some of the responses. H. L. A. Hart spoke of law having a 'core' of clear application, with a 'penumbra' of uncertain application, where judges would be making new law (through clarifying ambiguities or filling in gaps).[28] Hans Kelsen, by contrast, argued that *every* application of a statute was the creation of a new legal norm.[29] Most commentators see Kelsen's view as extreme and unjustified. Under the standard view, where the application seems straightforward—so-called 'easy cases'—then the court is simply applying existing law, not creating new law.[30] And in many legal systems (again, especially in common law legal systems), it is accepted that judges have the competence (the power), and likely also the duty, to create new law, at least interstitially, and, in some circumstances, to modify existing law. In common law systems, courts can both change the existing law in its application to all parties or create a limited exception for application to a particular case or a small set of cases.

Ronald Dworkin famously offered a view at the other extreme: while there may *appear to be* 'gaps' in the law, in the common law, or in the interpretation and application of statutes or constitutional provisions, there is, he argued, always (or almost always) a right answer regarding what the law requires. This is Dworkin's 'right answer thesis'.[31] He argued that legal systems offered sufficient resources (including legal principles along with legal rules) from which to determine which theories of what the law requires best combine fit with past official actions and moral value. And courts have both a legal and moral obligation to resolve legal disputes based on those right answers. However, the present discussion will assume a more conventional view about courts, rather than Dworkin's right answer thesis.

One set of questions relating to court powers is whether the court has a legal or moral duty to change the law in a particular case. We are familiar with instances of courts being criticized for changing the law, that it was legally or morally wrong to do so. It would make sense that there would also be occasions where a court's decision *not* to change the law, to simply reaffirm and apply the existing law, would

---

[28] Hart (2012), pp. 124–136. There have been challenges and suggested alterations to aspects of Hart's analysis, e.g., Fuller (1958), pp. 646–648, 661–669; Gardner (1988), Schauer (2008), but, in what follows, it will be accepted as roughly right, for purposes of the discussion.

[29] Kelsen (1992), §31(e), p. 70; see also Llewellyn (1933), pp. 72–74, quoted (in translation) in Fuller (1934), p. 445.

[30] In parallel with the conventional view that certain logical or practical entailments of enacted legal rules are also part of law, Dworkin at times argued that *the principles* underlying or justifying the legal rules are also part of the law. He wrote: 'Interpretivism . . . argues that law includes not only the specific rules enacted in accordance with the community's accepted practices but also the principles that provide the best moral justification for those enacted rules. The law then also includes those justifying principles, even though those further rules were never enacted.' Dworkin (2011), p. 402.

[31] *See, e.g.*, Dworkin (1985), pp. 119–145.

be a legal (or moral) error. The theoretical implications of this, and other, legal mistakes is considered further in the next Section.

6 The Problem of Legal Mistake

As discussed earlier, the legal norms of particular legal systems are often the product of both 'reason'—derivation using both logic and other rules of inference—and 'will'—the choices of legal officials and institutions. As already mentioned, the consequence of having legal content being produced by both reason and will is that the two kinds of legal 'product' can conflict. Such conflicts create paradoxes around the idea of legal mistake.

Legal mistake itself is generally a mundane and unproblematic aspect of legal practice. The whole machinery of appeals within court systems (and appeals from the decisions of administrative agencies and executive branch officials to the courts) assumes that legal officials can make mistakes in the declaration and application of the law, and that these mistakes can be, and usually should be, corrected.[32] On the other hand, sometimes mistakes are *not* corrected, and at the time the mistake is made, it is often hard to predict *whether it will be* corrected, and even if one thinks the correction will come, it is often hard to predict how long it will take. (Of course, it is important to keep in mind that reasonable commentators often will disagree about *which* decisions are in fact mistaken.)

Consider one United States Supreme Court decision that nearly everyone agrees to have been mistaken: *Plessy v. Ferguson*,[33] the 1896 decision holding that racial segregation was *not* contrary to the requirement of 'equal protection' established by the 14th Amendment of the United States Constitution (that decision was not corrected for almost 60 years[34]). At the point where the mistaken decision (in this case, *Plessy*) had been made, but before it has been corrected, there is a sense (as Connie Rosati has argued) that the mistaken decision *both is and is not* the law.[35] It *is* the law because a court with the power to bind others has declared it to be the law; it is *not* the law because (by hypothesis) it is contrary to the authoritative standard the court purported to be applying.

This view of two conflicting but true propositions of what the law is, and of perhaps a large-scale divergence between two sets of truths about law, can also be

[32] Obviously, it is possible that we are—collectively and egregiously—wrong about the possibility and nature of legal mistake. Such a radical position would likely have to be grounded in a hard-to-maintain view, along the lines that legal truth equated with the subjective views of individual judges. See, e.g., Rosati (2004), pp. 276–280.

[33] 163 U.S. 537 (1896).

[34] *See Brown v. Board of Education*, 347 U.S. 483 (1954).

[35] Rosati (2004), p. 291. She analyzes this paradox as being caused (in part) by the way that claims about law can have both a descriptive/prognostic function and a critical function. Rosati (2004), pp. 290–291.

found in Dworkin's work. In fact, his approach to law seems to be particularly receptive to the idea that what the law 'really' requires can and does diverge from the actions and decisions of legal officials.[36]

7 Natural Law (Universal Legal Truths)

The principle behind thc Nuremberg Trials of Nazi officials was that there were certain norms that were valid legal rules of all legal systems, even if never supported by any official enactment or pronouncement, and even if official enactments and pronouncements purported to negate those norms entirely or in part. In particular, the argument was that the norm, 'do not commit crimes against humanity' was binding—*legally* binding, not just morally binding—on all people, regardless of what the legal officials of their community had done or said.[37]

Whether it is the case or not that there are certain norms that are parts of (valid in) all legal systems regardless of the actions of legal officials, is, of course, highly controversial. It is a central point of contest between some forms of legal positivism and some forms of natural law theory, and this is not the place to try to resolve that dispute. However, it is worth noting that to the extent that there are such norms, it indicates an interesting aspect to legal truth, and a clear limitation on legal competence.

8 Conclusion

It is a commonplace that legal officials—legislators, heads of administrative agencies, judges, etc.—have the competence to make new law. Sometimes, though, the new law made is via inadvertence or error, and, on such occasions, the content of law as determined through conventional doctrinal analysis may be in tension with recognition of the authorized but mistaken actions of the legal officials. In a sense, this shows an instability in the concept of competence, for the powers to change the law may be, in practice, different from the standards prescribed, and in ways that are not always predictable. This complication for the analysis of legal truth and legal content is exacerbated by the fact that any such errors may or may not be corrected (and the correction may or may not be relatively prompt). Where 'reason' and 'will' get entangled in this way, even simple bivalence may not fully hold: both '**X** is the law' and '**X** is *not* the law' may be correct.

[36] *See* Rosati (2004), pp. 294–295. For a discussion of a 'lost constitution' or a 'constitution in exile', see Barnett (2006, 2013).

[37] *Eg*, Finnis (2020), § 3.

References

Altman A (1983) Critical legal studies: a liberal critique. Princeton UP, Princeton
Austin JL (1975) In: Urmson JO, Sbisà S (eds) How to do things with words, 2nd edn. Harvard UP, Cambridge
Barnett RE (2006) Restoring the lost constitution, not the constitution in exile. Fordham Law Rev 75:669–673
Barnett RE (2013) Restoring the lost constitution: the presumption of liberty, updated ed. Princeton UP, Princeton
Bix BH (2017) The promise and problems of universal, general theories of contract law. Ratio Juris 30:391–402
Bix BH (2022) Objectivity, conventions, and the possibility of universal error. In: McBride M, Kurki VAJ (eds) Jurisprudence without trimmings: the legal, moral, and political philosophy of Matthew Kramer. OUP, Oxford, pp 113–124
Braun D (2015) Indexicals. In: Zalta EN (ed) Stanford encyclopedia of philosophy. https://plato.stanford.edu/entries/indexicals/.
Chilovi S, Pavlakos G (2019) Law-determination as grounding: a common grounding framework for jurisprudence. Leg Theory 25:53–76
Dworkin RM (1985) A matter of principle. Harvard UP, Cambridge
Dworkin RM (2011) Justice for hedgehogs. Harvard UP, Cambridge
Finnis JM (1985) On 'the critical legal studies movement'. Am J Juris 30:21–42
Finnis JM (2020) Natural law theories. In: Zalta EN (ed) Stanford encyclopedia of philosophy. https://plato.stanford.edu/entries/natural-law-theories/
Fried C (2015) Contract as promise, 2nd edn. Oxford UP, Oxford
Fuller L (1934) American legal realism. Univ Penn Law Rev 82:429–462
Fuller L (1958) Positivism and fidelity to law: a reply to Professor Hart. Harv Law Rev 71:630–672
Gardner J (1988) Concerning permissive sources and gaps. OJLS 8:457–461
Green CR (2009) 'This constitution': constitutional indexicals as a basis for textualist semi-originalism. Notre Dame Law Rev 84:1607–1674
Greenawalt K (1992) Law and objectivity. OUP, Oxford
Hart HLA (2012) The concept of law, 3rd edn. OUP, Oxford
Holmes OW (1897) The path of the law. Harv Law Rev 10:457–478
Kelsen H (1992) Introduction to the problems of legal theory (trans: Paulson BL, Paulson SL). OUP, Oxford
Kramer MH (2008) Is law's conventionality consistent with law's objectivity? Res Publica 14:241–252
Leiter B (1995) Legal indeterminacy. Leg Theory 1:481–492
Leiter B (ed) (2001) Objectivity in law and morals. CUP, Cambridge
Leiter B (2007) Naturalizing jurisprudence: essays on American legal realism and naturalism in legal philosophy. OUP, Oxford
Llewellyn KN (1930) A realistic jurisprudence -- the next step. Colum Law Rev 30:431–465
Llewellyn KN (1933) Präjudizienrecht und Rechtsprechung in Amerika, Eine Spruchauswahl mit Besprechung. Weicher, J. Leipzig
Moore MS (2000) Theories of areas of law. San Diego Law Rev 37:731–741
Moore MS (2003) The plain truth about legal truth. Harv J Law Pub Pol'y 26:23–48
Raz J (2005) Can there be a theory of law? In: Golding MP, Edmundson WA (eds) The Blackwell guide to the philosophy of law and legal theory. Blackwell, Oxford, pp 324–342
Rosati C (2004) Some puzzles about the objectivity of law. Law Phil 23:273–323
Schauer F (2008) A critical guide to vehicles in the park. NYU Law Rev 83:1109–1134

Solum LB (1987) On the indeterminacy crisis: critiquing critical dogma. Univ Chic Law Rev 54: 462–503
Spaak T (1994) The concept of legal competence: an essay in conceptual analysis. Dartmouth Pub Co., Brookfield
Spaak T (2009) Explicating the concept of legal competence. In: Hage JC, von der Pfordten D (eds) Concepts in law. Springer, Dordrecht, pp 67–80
Tushnet M (1996) Defending the indeterminacy thesis. QLR 16:339–356

Part V
Theories of Legal Power and Legal Competence

An Analysis of Jeremy Bentham's Quasi-Realistic Model of Legal Competence

Alejandro Daniel Calzetta

Abstract This chapter attempts a reconstruction and analysis of Jeremy Bentham's model of norm creation or legal competence. Bentham's conception of norm creation is dependent on his notion of *power of imperation*, that is the power of the *Sovereign* to create imperatives and other kinds of norms. The exercise of said power is shared by the *Sovereign* and its jurisdictional agents which are called *delegates* and both *Sovereign* and *delegates* fulfil different roles in the creation of norms. The function exercised by the *Sovereign* is called a *de classibus* use of the *power of imperation* and it consist in the creation of norms addressed to a class created by the *Sovereign*. Bentham considers this norm an incomplete one. Is through the *delegate* use of the *power of imperation* that the norm is completed by what Bentham calls a *de singulis determination*. That implies de determination of the concrete individuals that belong to the class created by the *de classibus norm*. The determination done by the *delegate* completes the norm. This, following Giovanni Tarello's reconstruction of the notion of Legal Realism, allows us to considers Bentham's account of norm creation a "quasi" realistic one. Also, some general considerations on Legal Realism are made in order to situate Bentham's theory of legal competence within an appropiate realist framework.

This chapter is part of the results of the project financed by the Fondo Nacional de Desarrollo Científico y Tecnológico, FONDECYT de Iniciación N°11190629, titled "*La formalización de las reglas de creación jurídica*".

A first version of the paper was presented during the Special Workshop on Legal Positivism and Legal Realism during the 29th IVR world congress, at Lucerne, Switzerland. I am extremely grateful for the comments during that presentation, especially those of Juan Pablo Alonso, Francesco Ferraro, Brian Leiter, Julieta Rábanos, Giovanni Battista Ratti, Gabriela Scataglini and Hugo Zuleta. I am also grateful to the members of the Magios Secret Society Reading Group who also discussed this paper: Donald Bello Hutt, Pedro Caminos, Victor Garcia Izaguirre and Sebastián Reyes Molina. I'm also extremely grateful to the editors of the present volume for the invitation to participate in it notwithstanding the fact that I could not participate on the workshop that they chaired at the same congress at Lucerne.

A. D. Calzetta (✉)
Faculty of Law, Department of Legal Sciences, Universidad Alberto Hurtado, Santiago, Chile
e-mail: acalzetta@uahurtado.cl

G. Villa-Rosas, T. Spaak (eds.), *Legal Power and Legal Competence*, Law and Philosophy Library 140, https://doi.org/10.1007/978-3-031-28555-4_13

1 Introduction

The purpose of the present work is rather modest. It aims to offer a reconstruction of the model of legal competence that Jeremy Bentham offers in his manuscript of, for lack of a better term, a "General Theory of Law."[1]

Said manuscript was edited about three times, first in 1945—*The Limits of Jurisprudence Defined*[2]—, then in 1970—*Of Laws in General*[3]—and finally in 2010—*Of the Limits of the Penal Branch of Jurisprudence*[4].

In what follows I will refer exclusively to the 1970 and 2010 editions.[5]

This model of legal competence, or norm creation, is dependent on the concept of "*Sovereign*" that Bentham developed in his manuscript. Therefore, it will be necessary to explain how that concept is defined in the manuscript before discussing the model directly (Sect. 2 of the present work).

Once this has been made, the Benthamite notions of "*power of imperation*" and "*power of contrectation*",[6] as they are presented in both relevant editions of Bentham's manuscript, will be analyzed. Then an analysis of the model of legal competence in Bentham's theory of law will be put forward (Sect. 3).

Once the model has been analyzed, it will be explained in what sense it can be considered as a "*quasi-realistic*" one and what meaning this expression can have. In order to do that it will be necessary to take a not-so-small detour from Bentham's theory in order to explain what I understand "Legal Realism" (and, therefore, "quasi" realism) to mean. In this I will follow Tarello's analysis[7] very closely (Sect. 4).

---

[1] See Chiassoni (2014) for an analysis of Bentham's manuscript (2010 edition) as a "General Theory of Law".

[2] Bentham (1945).

[3] Bentham (1970).

[4] Bentham (2010).

[5] In what follows I will refer to both editions as "Bentham's manuscript" when appropriate, indicating in a note the page reference corresponding to both the 1970 and 2010 editions of the text respectively. This is so because, despite my preference for the text edited by Hart, *neither is really superior to the other* (at least where the account of norm creation is concerned). Both have differences that serve to illustrate Bentham's thinking and, in addition to that, both editions contain a number of appendices different in both quantity and content that are incredibly useful for understanding Bentham's thinking and objectives. By virtue of this, I prefer to use both texts together. I do not think that the publication of the 2010 edition repeals the 1970 edition. As far as bibliography is concerned, it is false that *lex posterior derogat priori*. Also, in the present work, for simplicities' sake, the terms "norm" and "rule" will be used as synonyms.

[6] After this point the terms *power of contrectation* and *power of imperation* and other concept-words of Bentham's theory will be used without inverted commas. Also, every time a term from Bentham's theory appears in italics it is because I am referring to Benthan's conception of said term. If a term does not appear in italics the commonplace conception of the term, and not Bentham's, is the one that I am referring to.

[7] Tarello (1974a).

Finally, I will conclude (Sect. 5) with some considerations about the usefulness of the model under analysis about how it explains satisfactorily the exercise of the legal competence of the bodies entrusted with the creation and application of law.

2 Reconstruction of the Model, Part One: The Notion of a *Sovereign*

As said, Bentham's model of legal competence (and all of his theory of law) is dependent on what he understands by *Sovereign*. By virtue of this, it is convenient to begin by accounting for this central notion in Bentham's thought.

By *Sovereign* Bentham means

> ... any person or assemblage of persons to whose will a whole political community are (no matter on what account) supposed to be in a disposition to pay obedience.: and that in preference to the will of any other person[8]

The way by which the *Sovereign* makes his will known and the means by which it makes the political community submit and willingly render obedience to the *Sovereign* itself is through what today we would call a "*legal norm*", in Bentham's manuscript simply a "*Law*",[9] namely:

> ... an assemblage of signs declarative of volition conceived or adopted by the sovereign in a state, concerning the conduct to be observed in a certain case by a certain person or class of persons, who in the case in question are or are supposed to be subjected to his power: such volition trusting for its accomplishment to the expectation of certain events which it is intended such declaration should upon occasion be a means to bringing to pass, and the prospect of which it is intended should act as a motive upon those whose conduct is in question[10]

When determining which are those powers by which the sovereign subjects the political community Bentham opts for two, the *power of contrectation* and the *power of imperation*.

---

[8]Bentham (2010), p. 18; Bentham (2010), p. 42.

[9]If we are historically and textually strict, this comparison between "*legal norm*" and "*law*" is mistaken, since Bentham does not make the distinction between a normative formulation/source of law ("*law*" in Bentham's usage of the term) and the content of meaning of said formulation/source ("*legal norm*" or "legal rule" in today's theoretical parlance). However, I believe it is pertinent to understand Bentham's "*law*" as today we would understand "*legal norm*" for two simple reasons i) adding to the account the distinction between norm formulations (or legal sources) and norms does not harm the theory under analysis, but rather makes it more sophisticated and more useful; ii) given all that Bentham says about language and his interest in its philosophical analysis (I'm using this term in a Russellian sense), had he known the distinction, Bentham would have adopted it as his own. I thank Francesco Ferraro for this more than pertinent observation. The "solution" or "response" to it consisting on the aforementioned points i) and ii) are my own.

[10]Bentham (1970), p. 1; Bentham (2010), p. 24.

The *power of contrectation* is the power that the *Sovereign* and his *delegates*[11] have in order to make effective, concretize, the threats of pain or sanction and the promises of pleasure or rewards that accompany the orders issued through the use of the *power of imperation*. That is to say, without the *power of contrectation* the mandates issued by the *power of imperation* are a dead letter, they are mere words. In the words of Hobbes, *covenants without the sword are but words*.

Bentham is, however, a bit more complex, given that not only the sword is present in his thinking. The reward is another possibility even if the law, according to our author, almost exclusively appeals to the sword.

The relationship between the two powers is more than important, as well as instrumental. Without *power of contrectation* there would be no way, for better or for worse, to enforce any legal rule. That is why Bentham, always attentive to an empirical analysis of the legal phenomenon, considers that ultimately the entire phenomenon can be reduced only to factual relationships that can be explained by appealing only to the *power of contrectation*.

This power (the same as the *power of imperation*) does not come out of nowhere. It arises, as seen in both definitions, from the disposition of the political community to obey this person or assembly of persons denoted by the word "*Sovereign*". Without this disposition to obedience, which may be based on fear of sanctions, in the belief of the *Sovereign's* right to rule, belief that the *Sovereign* is fair, morally just, merely prudential reasons, etc.,[12] we could not speak of a *Sovereign* in Bentham's sense. This disposition to obedience is, within this scheme, what gives the *Sovereign* these powers to order or command the community (*imperation*) and to force them to comply with said orders or mandates (*contrectation* or, more simply, constraint).

On the other hand, and in general outline, it can be said that the *power of imperation* is the competence of the sovereign to create imperatives, to issue orders backed by threats. Imperatives that, in turn, will be enforced by the *power of contrectation*.

It is the interaction between these two powers that constitutes for Bentham the key to the legal phenomenon. Creating mandates and enforcing them. This is his *key to the science of jurisprudence*. However, the one that is most relevant to us is the *power of imperation*.

Nowadays, with legal theory having already exorcized the idea of sovereign, we would say that the *power of imperation* is the power, on the part of the state, to create *legal norms*. This simple approach to the *power of imperation* is sufficient for the

---

[11] Agents entrusted by the *Sovereign* with "shares" of the *powers of contrectation and imperation*. Said *delegates* could be administrative officials, members of the security forces and police force, judges, etc. In what follows we will mainly use "*delegate*" to refer to judges and their use of shares of the *power of imperation*.

[12] In Bentham's scheme it is not relevant on what the disposition to obedience is based on. His approach is totally empiricist one. The only relevant thing is that the disposition is, in fact, there. What motivates it it's not relevant. A useful scheme of motivation could be that of Ross (2005), pp. 65–92.

time being and one has to keep in mind that this is a terminological question strongly tied to the legal culture and the time in which Bentham wrote. It may be that it has no real importance. But, before specifying or carrying out an analysis of Bentham's model of legal competence, it is necessary to have a more complete knowledge of what Bentham understood by *power of imperation* and what specific functions it fulfilled beyond being the power of the *Sovereign* (in a state) to create imperatives (i.e., prescriptive norms).

In what follows, the aforementioned explanation will be carried out trying to be as clear as possible in the exposition and avoiding, it is hoped, the unattractiveness of Bentham's language.

3 Reconstruction of the Model, Part Two: The *Power of Imperation*

3.1 Definition of the Concept of Power of Imperation

A more precise definition of the *power of imperation* would be the following:

> It is the power to create a legal norm which imposes the duty or obligation of performance or non-performance (prohibition) of an action under the threat of the application of pain or the promise of applying pleasure, based on the performance or non-performance of said conduct.

In Hart's reconstruction of this notion, it is presented crudely and without any subtlety: obligation or duty rests on the carrot or the stick. No more, no less.[13]

This is not without reason. It is coextensive with the general principles of Bentham's philosophy, namely the existence of two guiding principles of human behaviour: the pursuit of pleasure and the avoidance of pain.

These two ideas were extensively developed by Bentham in the first chapters of his *Introduction to the Principles of Morals and Legislation*, a work of which Bentham's manuscript is a direct continuation[14] and where he develops his concepts of *legal norm* ("a law"), *Sovereign*, and normative powers while carrying out the final promise of the *Introduction to the Principles*: to draw the line of demarcation between the penal and civil branches of law.[15]

---

[13] Hart (1982), p. 201.

[14] See Bentham (1996) and both the editorial introductions to Bentham (1970, 2010).

[15] For Bentham, the "penal branch" consists of all legal norms that impose sanctions, including sanctions that today we call "civil" sanctions ("remedies" in the common law tradition). Instead, the "civil branch" consists of all the norms that assign or ascribe rights among subjects, especially property rights. Finally, it is worth clarifying that in Bentham the civil and penal branches are the product of the classifications made by the theorist of the legal material. There would be no truly penal nor civil norms, but these categories are the result of the *Expositor*'s attempt to explain what the law is. For the distinction between the *Censor* and the *Expositor* (and *censorial* and *expository jurisprudence* respectively) see Bentham (1996), pp. 293–300.

Seen in this way, it makes sense that in the very concept of *power of imperation* these two principles represented as corollaries of the imperatives that the *Sovereign* creates to impose duties (in one sense or another) to those who are its subjects.

Legally, the idea of pain translates into the notion of legal sanction or legal punishment and the idea of pleasure in that of legal reward. Despite the fact that the law can apparently use both notions without too many problems, Bentham recognizes that, in general, the law tends to rely more on legal sanctions, that is, the threat of applying some *legal* pain to those who fail to comply with the provisions of a norm.

Now, the *power of imperation*, like the *power of contrectation*, is a normative power[16] that the *Sovereign* possesses due to the political community's disposition to obey the *Sovereign*. It's important to remember that Bentham's *Sovereign* is something purely factual. He does not owe his position as *Sovereign* to any type of normative framework, but rather he is the one who, through the exercise of his powers of norm creation and constraint, creates the normative framework and not the other way around.

The same goes for the concept of *power of imperation*.

Just as the *Sovereign* is defined in factual terms, so does the *power of imperation* that it possesses and the way in which it is exercised. Although Bentham will later try to constrain or legally limit the *Sovereign*'s imperation power through the *Constitutional Code*,[17] it must be remembered that this task belongs to his role as *Censor* and not as *Expositor*. The description that he makes of the *Sovereign* and of powers such as that of imperation are just that, descriptions, not prescriptions, criticisms or recommendations that correspond to the task of the *Censor*.

The *power of imperation*, like the *power of contrectation*, is one of the distinguishing features of the *Sovereign*. It is one of its essential characteristics. It is, in a nutshell, a description of how it creates norms, of how it imposes obligations or prohibitions aided by the application, judicious or not, of the carrot or the stick.

The *Sovereign* is the only titular owner of this power because of the disposition of obedience of the political community. In this sense we can say that it is the supreme holder of this power.

This does not mean that the *Sovereign* is the only one who can exercise it.

In fact, how it is exercised has its own level of sophistication and deserves a certain analysis of its own. If one wants to understand well how Bentham conceived the phenomenon of the creation of norms and what can be apprehended from said conception to nurture a broader conception of the phenomenon of legal competence an analysis of how and by whom the *power of imperation* is exercised should be in order.

---

[16]"Normative" in a descriptive sense, not a justifying one. Both are *normative* powers because both *refer* to norms, be its creation (*imperation*) or application (*contrectation*).

[17]See Bentham (1983).

3.2 *Exercising the* Power of Imperation[18]

Since the *power of imperation* is fundamentally based on the threat of future pain in case of disobedience, the phenomenon of rule-making should, in principle, rest with the *Sovereign* who holds the ownership of said power.

From this it follows that it should be the *Sovereign* who takes the central role when imposing obligations. However, things are not necessarily that simple in Bentham's account.

In fact, Bentham recognizes that the *Sovereign* themselves,[19] despite being the *Sovereign* and holder of all these powers, they cannot do everything by themselves. They require assistance to impose duties. That is, they must share, at least partially, their power to create norms with other agents known as *delegates of the Sovereign* or *delegates* for short.

Bentham maintains that, precisely, to be able to exercise the *power of imperation*, said power must be "broken into shares". That is, it must be divided into portions or shares between the *Sovereign* and its *delegates*, otherwise effective obligations or prohibitions cannot be created.

This works in the following way:

3.2.1 The Central Case: *de classibus imperation*

The essence of this partition into segments is, before going into details such as the *Sovereign* and his *delegates,* what we could call the central case of the exercise of the *power of imperation.*

The central case, as I characterize it, is based on the two ways in which, according to Bentham, the *power of imperation* is exercised.

Bentham calls these two ways of exercising this power *de classibus* and *de singulis.*

The former being the way in which the *Sovereign*/legislator creates norms and the latter the way in which the various *delegates* of the *Sovereign* do.

The *power of imperation de classibus* deals with the creation of imperatives with respect to a class or set.

This is what the *Sovereign* does while acting as a legislator: he creates norms whose addressees is class or set.

Class or set to be clearly designated or created by the *Sovereign* itself.

---

[18] The central notions of this sub-section are from in Bentham (1970), Ch. IX and Bentham (2010), section 11,—both titled "Generality of a Law". Questions related to the *conception* and *adoption* of legal norms are from Bentham (1970), Cap. II and Bentham (2010), section 4.

[19] Normally, here the pronoun "herself" would be used but that would be incorrect. One must remember that Bentham's *Sovereign* does not need to be an individual. It can be an assembly, a group of individuals, etc. So, "themselves" or even "itself" are better pronouns in this case. I thank Julieta Rábanos for this observation.

In this sense, the rules that the *Sovereign* himself creates must be general since they will be applied to an indeterminate number of individuals,[20] who share one or more properties that make them members of the class or set.

Hart, in reconstructing this notion, speaks of natural classes (such as men, pigs, etc.) and artificial classes (such as officials, lawyers, etc.)[21] but in truth this division classes into natural and artificial is as arbitrary as any other type of division or classification that one can conceive (as is clearly exemplified in Borges's *El idioma analítico de John Wilkins*[22]) and all classes are, ultimately, fatally, artificial. Classes or sets are logical-linguistic constructs that cannot be find in nature and are, all of them, mind dependent.

In truth the *Sovereign* would not be limited by these two kinds of classes or sets when it exercises its *power of imperation de classibus*. One is only limited, if this is a limitation, by the number of classifications one is willing to carry out or by the number one can imagine.

Bentham himself makes this clear when he points out the five ways in which, *via de classibus*, subjects and things can be added to the various classes or sets. We will not consider them in depth, because for our purpose it is more than enough to point out the fact of the virtual infinity of possible classes that the *Sovereign* can create or "put" into a statute. We will merely mention that Bentham calls this classifying power of the *Sovereign accensitive power* and that it is subdivided *in personam, in rem, in actum, in locus* or *in tempus*. People, things, acts, locations and time respectively.[23]

Now these general rules that the *Sovereign* creates are, for Bentham, necessarily incomplete ones.

Although they determine what a class should or should not do, these rules would not determine what an individual and concrete member of that class should or should not do. This requires not a general but and individual rule, a "face to face" command so to speak.

If the rules in question are prescriptions, and there is nothing to assume that they are not, a structural problem arises: that of the location of the criteria of membership within the syntactical reconstruction of said prescriptive norms. A brief excursion into the elements of a prescription is, therefore, in order.

3.2.2 The Elements of a Prescription

According to von Wright,[24] who offers the most useful analysis of the logical form of prescriptions such as we can consider it to be the standard account of

---

[20] For this notion of generality see Guastini, Vaquero (trans) (2016), p. 53.

[21] Hart (1982), pp. 203–204.

[22] Borges (2018), p. 338.

[23] From the combination of these five factors, the resulting class types can be infinite. I think this is more than enough for the limits of the present work.

[24] Von Wright (1963).

prescriptions, all prescriptions share three elements which are constitutive of this kind of norms.

These elements, called the norm-kernel by von Wright, are

i) the character of a norm;
ii) the content of a norm;
iii) and the condition of application of norm.[25]

The character of a norm

> depends upon whether the norm is to the effect that something ought to or may or must not be done.[26]

Meaning, the deontic modulation of a norm, whether this norm is an obligation (O), a permission (P), a prohibition (V) or a faculty (F).[27]

The content of a norm is

> that which ought to or may or must not be done. The content of a prescription, in particular, is thus the prescribed (commanded, permitted, prohibited) thing.[28]

And lastly, the condition of application is

> The condition which must be satisfied if there is to be an opportunity for doing the thing which is the content of a given norm.[29]

Meaning that that must happen in order to apply the norm.

Therefore, the (generic) structure of a prescriptive norm (*de classibus*) could be reconstructed like this

$$\mathbf{(x)\ C(x) \supset Op(x)}$$

Basically, for all values of x, if x complies with the condition C, then x has an obligation to perform the action p.[30]

It seems clear, once we distinguish the elements of the norm-kernel of a prescription, that the criteria of membership to a *the classibus* class is included within the condition of application.

Said condition is not only a possible state of affairs that must happen in order to apply the norm but a state of affairs that must be realized by a concrete individual with certain characteristics (i.e., belonging to a certain class). It is therefore the duty

[25] Von Wright (1963), pp. 70–75.

[26] Von Wright (1963), p. 71.

[27] Also known as a bilateral permission, that is a permission to perform an action and to not perform said action. For example, a norm that permits people to do their wills and testaments is better understood as a norm with a character F. It permits to grant the will and permits not to grant it.

[28] Von Wright (1963), p. 71. Underlined in the original.

[29] Von Wright (1963), p. 72.

[30] Bentham's prescriptions are not limited to obligations. A command is not necessarily and obligation, it can also be a prohibition or even a permission, both of which could be *de classibus* formalized as such: $\mathbf{(x)\ C(x) \supset V(x)}$ and $\mathbf{(x)\ C(x) \supset P(x)}$.

of the judge not only to determine if a certain state of affairs occurs but also to determine which concrete individual belong to the class that it is included within the condition of application of the legal norm. That it, to determine which individual (if any) satisfies the intentional criteria stablished by the *Sovereign* in the statute.

This is where the *power of imperation de singulis* and the notion of the *delegate* makes their appearance.

3.2.3 The Delegate's Burden: *de singulis imperation*

In simple terms, the one who exercises the *power of imperation de singulis* is a *delegate* of the *Sovereign*. It holds a share of *power of imperation* granted by the *Sovereign*, which is exercised *de singulis*.

De singulis means that the *delegate* has the power (today we would say that she has the competence) to make the determination of which concrete individuals satisfy the criteria of membership to the class of a norm created by an exercise of *power of imperation de classibus*.

What the *delegate* does is to impose an obligation or a prohibition, with the addition of applying pain in case of non-compliance or pleasure in case of compliance as appropriate to particular individuals. Concrete subjects, not classes.

This always by virtue of a previous *de classibus* norm which imposes an obligation or a prohibition, with the addition of applying pain in case of non-compliance or pleasure in case of compliance, as appropriate, to a class. This class is, normally, composed of a diverse number of members, but the determination of who are the concrete individuals that satisfy the criteria of membership of the class it not done by an imperation *de classibus*, but by an imperation *de singulis*.

In other words, the *de singulis* rule issued by the *delegate* completes ("fills up" says Bentham) the general *de classibus* rule issued by the *Sovereign*.

She makes it effective; she finishes performing the imperative, whatever it may be. From a class, from a set of properties constitutive of an intensional criterion, to a completely determined individual member of said class resulting in a norm like this one

$$\mathbf{C(a)} \supset \mathbf{Op(a)}$$

where "a" represents a concrete individual fully determined by a *de singulis* determination as a member of the class included in C by the *de classibus* legislator.

With this we can see that, for Bentham, norm creation is not something that begins and ends merely with, say, the enactment of a law. This is important, as it sets the general parameters (*in personam, in rem, in actum, in locus or in tempus*) of the imperative. To all X corresponds Y.

But it is in a certain way indeterminate until a delegate of the sovereign determines *de singulis* if individual Z is a member of X. If it is, then Y will correspond to him. But until this determination of the delegate, whose example par excellence is the judge, although it should not necessarily be a judge, happens it is not known for sure if Z corresponds to Y. It can be assumed, it can be believed, but it is not known until this delegate imposes a particular imperative on Z and only on Z.

This exercise of the power of imperation, general and particular, *de classibus* and *de singulis*, is, I believe, the key to understanding how Bentham conceives the creation of norms. The latter is a complex operation where normative power is distributed between an entity called by Bentham "the sovereign", who issues norms affecting various classes, and other sub-entities designated by the main entity determine which specific subjects belong to this or that class and, therefore, what are their legal duties.

It should be clarified that for Bentham the power of dominance goes much further than this I just mentioned. According to it, it serves to explain all creation of norms, whether explicitly dictated by the *Sovereign* (*de classibus*) or by his delegates (*de singulis*), whether they are public agents or not. Even particular rules such as wills or contracts.

Other ways of imperation: conception, adoption, and the limits of delegate imperation

Indeed, as we have seen, the *Sovereign* shares his *power of imperation* with third parties whom we have called his *delegates*. This can be done in two ways; a portion of this power can be conferred to be exercised for the benefit of the *delegate* himself (*power of imperation as beneficiary*) or to be exercised for the benefit of third parties (*power of imperation as fiduciary*).

The classic example of the latter are the judges, who currently benefit a third party[31] when determining *de singulis* what are the obligations that correspond to them for being members of a certain class mentioned in a norm issued *de classibus*. This means that for Bentham the exercise of this power as fiduciary is a constitutional power, that is (in his terminology) a public power and opposed to a private notion of the exercise of said power (that is, as a beneficiary, for the benefit of the person to whom the one who was granted power).

This is because for Bentham every rule, whether public or private, is in a way dictated by the *Sovereign*.[32] Either expressly by the latter when legislating *de classibus* or by their *delegates* when they exercise the portion of the *power of imperation* entrusted to them. It does not matter if this occurs as a holder of this portion as a beneficiary or as a fiduciary. They remain mandates of the *Sovereign* as he pre-adopts them even before they were enacted. This is so for two reasons.

In Bentham the *Sovereign* issues norms in two different ways: by *conception* and by *adoption*. The former does not present too many problems. A norm is created by

[31] Basically, the entire political community within a state of which the *Sovereign* is the recipient of a disposition of obedience by said political community. A *power of imperation as a fiduciary* may also be granted to a *delegate* for the benefit of a single person. For example, a curator, a legal guardian, etc.

[32] This is a theory similar to Kelsen's regarding the unity of legal systems. The main difference is that Bentham's account is one of delegation of competence from the supreme authority in the system to the lowliest one, instead of being an account based on the way the supreme norms in the legal system establish the procedure of creation of the inferior norms of said legal system.

conception when it is the exclusive product of the will, so to speak, of the *Sovereign* and of no one else.[33] On the other hand, *adoption* presents certain complexities since Bentham considers two possible types of adoption: *susception* (or *reception*) and *pre-adoption*.[34]

Reception occurs when the *Sovereign* adopts as his own mandates that have been issued before he has acquired sovereignty. In this case, the current *Sovereign* adopts the norms or mandates created by previous *Sovereigns* and the *delegates* of these previous *Sovereigns*. They adopt them temporarily since they can always repeal them by creating new norms. All of this in order to secure the continuity and unity of the legal order.

Reception is generally tacit. The *Sovereign*, by not expressing a will contrary to the mandates of previous sovereigns and their delegates, adopts those mandates as his own. The reasoning is simple, if somewhat dubious. If you do not express yourself against the mandates of previous *Sovereigns*, it is because you tacitly approve them. This means two things:

i) that the *Sovereign* is aware of everything ordered by his predecessors and their delegates;
ii) that they approve what was commanded, otherwise they would have expressed a contrary will.

This may be too much of a presupposition, but an extensive critique of the concept of normative reception probably exceeds the purpose of this chapter, since the concept of *Reception* is to be intended to deal with the problem of the legal and political continuity of the legal system rather than the problem of legal competence or normative production.[35]

Pre-adoption consists of the *Sovereign*'s adoption of norms issued by his *delegates* that have not yet been issued. In order to *pre-adopt* the norms of the *delegates*, the *Sovereign* makes them, as we have seen, participants in a portion of his *power of imperation*. Meaning that they grant the *delegates* with the legal competence to use said portion of *power of imperation*.

[33] Remember the definition of legal norm or "law" given at the beginning of Sect. 2 of this work.

[34] Bentham (1970), p. 21; Bentham (2010), p. 45.

[35] Some conversations with Julieta Rábanos have opened my eyes to the possibility that perhaps Bentham's reasoning is not at all doubtful. If it is assumed that Bentham is seeing what is actually happening. Then it would be perfectly coherent to impute normative validity to the past mandates of previous sovereigns and their delegates only due to the absence of an expression of contrary will of the sovereign of the moment. This would be the case because the entire Benthamian conception of sovereignty is based in an excessively strong way on the concept of will and its expression through legal norms (laws). The fact of not pronouncing would necessarily imply assent with past wills or mere indifference towards them, a benevolent indifference. This, of course, until the current sovereign changes his mind. In the end Bentham's view is a strange mix of strong empirical observations more commonly associated with some forms of legal realism and the classical legal positivistic doctrine of the will of the legislator. For a critique of this doctrine (and Bentham's use of it) see Olivecrona (1971), chapter 2, pp. 65–78.

Bentham is very clear when he says that the mandates that the *Sovereign* pre-adopts are those issued by the people or classes of people to whom it has conferred participation in the *power of imperation*.[36]

The pre-adopted norms are essentially norms of the *Sovereign* himself because they were dictated by those who participate in the *power of imperation* of which the sole owner is the *Sovereign*.

The other users are only holders of the *power of imperation*, not owners of it. This is so due to the very fact that they have been conferred that portion of power by the *Sovereign*. Without that concession or delegation of (a fraction of the) power, the *delegates* could not issue mandates. Doing so would be a crime (offense) since they would assume a competence that does not belong to them.

However, the fact of participating in the exercise of the *power of imperation* does not allow the *delegates* to issue just any type of norm. The exercise of the power delegated by the *Sovereign* is limited by the other norms dictated by it. With which exceeding the framework delimited by the share granted by the *Sovereign* would be either a crime or an abuse of competence, liable to nullity. This forms a clear material limit to the exercise (competence) of the delegate.[37]

In short, what this notion of *pre-adoption* explains is, basically, the limits of the competence of public and private agents and, necessarily, where their incompetence begins, at least in the material sense.

The function of this delegation is to complete *de singulis* the mandates that the *Sovereign* dictates *de classibus*,[38] which not only results in the mere completeness of the necessarily incomplete general norms that the *Sovereign* conceives. This is also so that individuals can develop their life plans in a more effective way (this is what Bentham calls the power to alienate property and it is a variant of the *power of imperation* in addition to being part of the "civil branch of jurisprudence").

In summary: the norms dictated by the *delegates*, being mandates that are part of a power that in fact belongs to the *Sovereign*, can only be understood as if they were norms issued by the latter. They are in fact mandates of the *Sovereign* that it has pre-adopted before its very issuance by the *delegate* since we are referring about the use of a power that is a constitutive part of sovereignty.

---

[36] Bentham (1970), p. 22; Bentham (2010), p. 46. "As to subordinate power-holders whose mandates the sovereign pre-adopts, these are of course as many and as various as the classes of persons to whom the law gives either powers of *imperation* or contrary powers of *de-imperation*, if such is the name that may be given to the power of undoing what by imperation has been done". Throughout the present work I have only referred to the *power of imperation* for two reasons: i) for expository clarity and ii) because in the passage just cited Bentham questions whether his distinction between *imperation and de-imperation* makes sense. Being the other face of the coin of the *power of imperation*, one could well say that the *power of de-imperation* is superfluous since it consists in replacing one mandate with another. At the end of the day, it is still the same *power of imperation*.

[37] On these material limits and how the operate with the formal limits to the exercise of legal competence see Calzetta (2018).

[38] Bentham (1970), p. 26; Bentham (2010), p. 50.

In this way Bentham accounts for a complex phenomenon that lacked a proper name at the end of the eighteenth century: the concept of legal competence or the theory of competence in law. However, it is not enough to say or imply that Bentham was ahead of his time. Acknowledging his intelligence and his worth is all very well, but what is really important is to take advantage of these ideas to try to develop or improve the problems under study. In this case, normative production and the relation between legislator and judge.

4 A "Quasi" Realistic Model

4.1 Legal Realism and "Quasi" Legal Realism. A Necessary Detour

4.1.1 Some Brief Considerations on the Definition of "Legal Realism"

Attributing a realistic model to Bentham, even if it is a "quasi" realistic one, is difficult for at least two reasons. The first is that it would be a clear anachronism.

Legal Realism is a set of currents of thought that had its first glimpse with the works of Oliver Wendell Holmes, Jr and Axel Hägerström at the end of the nineteenth century and at the beginning of the twentieth respectively and which was mainly carried out during the first half of the twentieth century by what we now call American and Scandinavian Legal Realism respectively.

To say that Bentham was even partially realistic (in the sense of belonging to either of aforementioned versions of Legal Realism) would be a bit rash.

The second reason is that we must be very careful with what we mean by the terms "realism" and "Legal Realism" when we speak about the law.

Nowadays, we can say that there are at least three great realistic currents or movements: the American,[39] the Scandinavian[40] and the Genoese[41] variants of legal realism.

[39] To my mind, American Legal Realism is mainly represented by Arnold, Bingham, Cohen, Cook, Douglas, Green, Llewellyn, Oliphant, Radin and Yntema. Holmes Jr. being more a forefather to American Legal Realism than a realist himself.

[40] To my mind, Scandinavian Legal Realism is mainly represented by i) Hägerström as an initiator to both Swedish (Lundstedt, Olivecrona); ii) and the Danish (Ross) sub-variants. Hägerström firmly belonging to the Swedish sub-variant of Scandinavian Legal Realism as that is the main sub-variant of Scandinavian Legal Realism. The Danish sub-variant of Ross stands alone.

[41] To my mind, Genoese Legal Realism is mainly represented by Tarello, Barberis (even if against his will), Castignone, Chiassoni, Comanducci, Guastini, Pozzolo, Ratti. Kristan, Malagoli and Sardo being the younger members of the Genoese variant. I do not include Redondo as a member of the Genoese variant because she does not consider herself a legal realist. Indeed, she is not. Instead she is one of the finest legal positivist of our age.

For reasons of space, I am not going to analyze them. But at least a general characterization of Legal Realism is in order if one pretends to say something about a (possible?) "quasi" realism.

As with "Legal Positivism",[42] "Legal Realism" is a term which can be quite difficult to define. There are not many attempts to define "Legal Realism" in a general way.

What attempts at definition there is, as I see it, are mostly attempts to arrive a general definition through the attempt at definition of one of the variants of "Legal Realism".[43]

A general attempt at definition is far less common.

Giovanni Tarello, a few years after his attempt at characterization of American Legal Realism, tried his hand at this general definition in his 1967 essay *Realismo Giuridico*.[44]

In what follows I'll shall not depart much from Tarello's account of Legal Realism as I find his approach to be entirely convincing. That notwithstanding, I shall nor refrain on making my own observations about "Legal Realism".

According to Tarello the expression "Legal Realism" can be used to designate the following four main senses:

"Legal Realism" denote

a) Theories regarding the definition of the concept of law;
b) Theories regarding the identification of the field of study of legal experts (*giuristi*);
c) Theories regarding the nature of some legal phenomena or institutions in particular;
d) Theories regarding legal interpretation (which also includes legal adjudication).[45]

---

[42] Regarding the problems of the definition of "Legal Positivism" see Scarpelli (1997), chapters 1 through 5. Scarpelli gives a masterful account of the persistent difficulties of defining "Legal Positivism", both in the Anglo-American as in the Continental tradition of Legal Philosophy.

[43] In regards of American Legal Realism two of the most prominent attempts (the two more interesting in my opinion) are those of Giovanni Tarello and of Brian Leiter (Tarello 1962 and Leiter 2007 respectively). The former being an account of American Legal Realism as through and through empiricist approach to law and the latter as a, albeit a bit anachronistic, naturalized approach in Quine's sense of the term. For a comparison between the two see Chiassoni (2017), pp. 34–41.

[44] Now published as Tarello (1974a), pp. 51–85.

[45] Tarello (1974a), p. 52. Senses "a", "b", "c" and "d" are such named by Tarello. In regard to point "d" Tarello refers to the "so called «legal interpretation»" (*"alla c.d. «interpretazione giuridica»"* in the Italian original). He considers this terminology to be an inexact one and prefers to speak of "the individuation of legal precepts by the judicial and administrative organs" (*individuazione dei precetti giuridici da parte degli organi giudiziari e amministrativi*). For simplicities' sake I'll continue to use "legal interpretation" instead of the more precise, albeit a bit long, formulation of Tarello. One must bear in mind, though, that every time "legal interpretation" appears in the text that term is being used in Tarello's more precise sense. Also, from now on, all translations from Italian to English (with their probable mistakes) are being done by me.

Each one of these senses of the term is in turn constituted by a series of sub-senses. Just in order to be brief I'll enumerate said sub-senses.

Regarding sense ("a"), *definition of the concept of law*, legal realists from several variants put forward or affirm the following sub-senses:

a1) those who give a real definition of law ("Law is such and such") instead of any other kind of definition;
a2) those who use a definition in the sense of a1 because they attribute a specific reality, different from non-legal reality, to the law;
a3) those who use a definition in the sense of a1 because the law exists as a specific reality based on determinate beliefs (denoting a magical thinking or magical reality).[46]

Regarding sense ("b"), *identification of the field of study of legal experts,* legal realists from several variants put forward or affirm the following sub-senses:

b1) those who affirm that the object of legal studies are facts;
b2) those who affirm that the object of legal studies is a specific (legal) reality;
b3) those who affirm that the object of legal studies is the manipulation of natural reality through the use of language and of ritualistic techniques which are considered legal means (magical thinking) of dealing with natural reality;
b4) those who affirm that the object of legal studies is the same as other social sciences since both study the recurrence or certain behaviours;
b5) those who affirm that the object of legal studies is the recurrence or certain behaviours in regard to the resolution of controversies.[47]

Regarding sense ("c"), *the nature of some legal phenomena or institutions in particular*, legal realists from several variants put forward or affirm the following sub-senses:

c1) those who consider that the nature of some legal phenomena coincides with some realities of fact;
c2) those who consider that the nature of some legal institutions (e. g. legal personhood) constitutes a specific legal reality.[48]

Regarding sense ("d"), *legal interpretation*, legal realists from several variants put forward or affirm the following sub-senses:

d1) those who consider that norm individuation is not preordained, and that legal adjudication always involve norm creation (with special consideration to the emergence of new social phenomena);

---

[46] Tarello (1974a), pp. 53–55. According to Tarello Hägerström and Olivecrona affirm a3.

[47] Tarello (1974a), pp. 55–62. According to Tarello Hägerström and Olivecrona affirm b3 and American Legal Realism and Ross affirm b5 and b4 respectively.

[48] Tarello (1974a), pp. 63–65. According to Tarello none of the main variants of Legal Realism affirms c1 or c2.

d2) those who consider that norm individuation is not preordained, and that legal adjudication must always refer to global legal experience;
d3) those who consider that norm individuation is not preordained and that in the process legal adjudication considerations of magical qualifications intervene;
d4) those who consider that concrete solutions of legal problems need an empirical approach because they are factual and with, at best, a possible connection, not a necessary one, with preexisting legal norms;
d5) those who affirm that legal interpretation is a practical, not a theoretical problem, in which its relevant characteristic is not the recurrence of problems of interpretation itself, but the solution reached by the law-applying organs at large ("*Law is what the judges do*").[49]

It is quite obvious that not all legal realist affirms the aforementioned fifteen senses that "Legal Realism" has but all legal realist affirms at least two of said senses.

For instance, according to Tarello, American Legal Realism can be defined as the variant of Legal Realism that affirms both b5 and d5. Interpretation being a practical problem for them and the field of study of legal experts is oriented to the resolution of controversies. Obviously, an American Legal Realist can affirm any other of the fifteen senses but these two are the core of that variant of Legal Realism. If one considers herself and American Legal Realist one must affirm b5 and d5.

Scandinavian Legal Realism is more complicated in Tarello's view. The Swedish sub-variant is divided between Lundstedt (b3 and d3) and Hägerström and Olivecrona (a3 and b3). The core of the Swedish sub-variant seems to be the affirmation of b3 as Tarello defines it as sharing a3, b3, and d3.

The Danish sub-variant, that is, Alf Ross, is an altogether different case since it affirms neither a3, b3 nor d3, but b4 and d4. It is considered a variant of Scandinavian Legal Realism because Ross originally found inspiration on Hägerström works but he later developed a completely original variant of legal realism of his own.[50]

Notwithstanding the case of Ross and his place in Scandinavian Legal Realism, it seems that, according to Tarello, one is a realist if one shares one of the pairs of senses that he considers to be the *more appropriate senses* (*usi opportuni*). Those pairs being *b5 and d5*, *b4 and d4*, *b3 and d3* (a3 being optional).[51]

[49] Tarello (1974a), pp. 65–74. According to Tarello American Legal Realist affirm d5 and Lundstedt, from the Swedish sub-variant affirms d3. Hägerström and Olivecrona does not seem to affirm any of the d senses.

[50] I'm of course referring to the theory expounded in Ross (2005). If this is correct then grouping Ross with the Scandinavian Legal Realists is something done just for geographical and biographical reasons, not for theoretical ones. Even Tarello recognizes this, as he points out that Ross' cultural formation and substantive thinking makes it dubious to group him with the other Scandinavians (see Tarello 1974a, p. 79). Maybe it's time to start to consider Ross as a more autonomous kind of legal realist, one not bound by geography and/or schools, tributary in a way to Hägerström but independent of him and his school.

[51] Tarello (1974a), p. 74 ss. For an analysis of Tarello's claims, see Hierro (1981), pp. 66–69. I believe that the "a3, b3, d3" grouping could be problematic. For that see footnote 53.

This, at least to me, seems to signify (at least in Tarello's appropriate senses of the expression) that one is a legal realist if one shares or affirms at least two of the main senses regarding the "*identification of the field of study of legal experts*" (b) and of "*legal interpretation*" (d), other senses (a, c) being optional and not part of the core of appropriate meaning.[52]

Of these two senses, b and d, I believe that d is the more important one of the core of Legal Realism.

Legal Realism, at the end of the day, deals mainly with what judges do, meaning legal interpretation and adjudication.

In order to do that some ideas about what legal interpretation is are necessary. From that can (and often does) follows an interest on what legal experts do, as they are those who furnish judges with competing argumentative strategies and conceptions of legal institutions for them to apply while interpreting legal sources and adjudicating cases. That is what constitutes the kernel of Legal Realism in my view and that is the logical priority between what I consider to be Tarello's two main senses of the expression "Legal Realism".

Basically, sense d leads to sense b, then one could be considered a legal realist in the appropriate sense of the expression and then senses a and/or c *may* follow, since neither of those senses seem necessary in order to be a realist.[53]

---

[52]What about the Genoese variant? What are its "appropriate" core senses? That is difficult to say since Tarello does not apply his analysis to himself. To many, even to some of the Genoese themselves, the School of Genoa (if there is such a thing, not all of the Genoese agree) seems to be defined by a shared method of legal analysis than by shared theses or affirmed senses. It's my opinion that the senses that different members of the school share, if they share any, are the result of a shared methodological approach and some shared concepts developed by Tarello such as those of "legal culture" and the distinction between "legal provisions" (*disposizioni giuridiche*) and "legal norms" (*norme giuridiche*) which points to some specific senses and sub-senses of "Legal Realism". Even so, if one were asked which one of the pairs of Tarello's opportune senses are affirmed by the Genoa School one would answer that none of them are affirmed by that school. I would argue that the Genoa School can identify with the following main senses: b3 because of how in legal matters brute facts are understood through an institutional lens and d2 if one equates the expression "global legal experience" with the notion of "legal culture" developed by Tarello. Senses a3 and c2 (this one understood as complementary to b3) being optional for some members of the school. This does not mean that "b3, d2" is an inappropriate sense of "Legal Realism", it just one that Tarello did not include due to lack of self-analysis. "b3, d2" point out to a variant of realism deeply concerned with the relation of legal interpretation and with the manipulation of fact by the legal experts. That hardly seems inappropriate. Of course, this only works if one reads d2 in the way I'm reading it. This is, clearly, just my opinion and the Genoese will probably reject it outright. On the notion of "legal culture", central to the Genoese School, Tarello defines it in several works where he distinguish between internal and external senses of "legal culture". For Tarello"s uses of the notion of "legal culture" see the following works: Tarello (1972), (1974b), pp. 475–521 and (1976). For that of "legal provision"/"legal norm" see Tarello (1980), chapter 3. For a brief but excellent reconstruction of said notions, see Guastini and Rebuffa (2002).

[53]What does this mean for Hägerström and Olivecrona since, according to Tarello, they do not affirm any of the d senses? Are they legal realists or not? Answering that question goes beyond the scope of the present work but it is an interesting conundrum. As we have seen, within the Swedish sub-variant of Scandinavian Legal Realism, only Lundstedt affirms one the d senses (d3). It could

4.1.2 On "Quasi" Realism

But, what happened if one shares some of the main senses but not all of them?

It depends. I believe if one shares one (or part of) of the b senses one could not be considered a realist. If one shares one (or part of) of the b senses one has a non-orthodox view of legal experts, but nothing more. In this case one is clearly not a realist but also one is not necessary an anti-realist.

Things change dramatically, I believe, if one shares some (or part of) the d senses. D senses are the cornerstone of Legal Realism. Sharing one of these senses is a sure way of becoming, with time, either a legal realist or a kind of very unorthodox legal positivist. That is because d senses present a quite different view on legal interpretation that those generally defended by legal positivists of all traditions of Legal Positivism.[54]

This theoretical situation, a realistic approach to legal interpretation within a (commonly understood) non-realistic general theory of law, will be called a "quasi" realistic approach or "quasi" realism.

I use the word "quasi" because a theory such described accepts what I consider to be the central element of the kernel or Legal Realism (a variant of one of the d senses) without necessarily being a realistic theory of law since it neither has a realistic conception of the field of study of legal experts (b) nor attempts a realistic definition of law (a) and does not (necessarily) have an opinion on the nature of legal phenomena and/or institutions (c).

Said theory could still be considered a legal positivistic theory. That depends on the concrete theory under discussion, but it is at least a partially realistic one.[55]

---

be said that the Swedish sub variant is a realist one since it combines the interest of Lundstedt on legal interpretation with those on legal epistemology of Hägerström and Olivecrona. That is what Tarello does when he considers "a3, b3, d3" to be one of the appropriate senses of Legal Realism but this to me seems to be forcing a grouping in order to respect an already made classification a School. As we have seen, all legal realist variants (even the Genoese on my account) share at least one of the b and d senses. In Tarello's analysis of the Scandinavians this also the case but only because he is forcing a grouping of one believer of d3 with two non-believers of said sense only because they share a belief on b3. This to me seems forced, since all the members of the other variants believe in one of the d senses. On these sense-centric approach, I believe there is no clear theoretical reasons for grouping Lundstedt with Hägerström and Olivecrona. They are Scandinavian Legal Realists only in a historical sense but not in a theoretical one. Notwithstanding that, the question remains open for me and could be problematic for the account of Legal Realism that I'm using.

[54] For those traditional and orthodox legal positivistic views on legal interpretation see Bobbio (1965), Bulygin (2007), Carrió (2006), Hart (2012). According to Chiassoni (2016) Kelsen is a particular case in this regard.

[55] Kelsen's general theory of law could also be read as a "quasi" realistic one if one follows Chiassoni's view on Kelsen's theory of legal interpretation as a realistic one (while the rest of Kelsen's theoretical apparatus remains a classical legal positivistic one). See Chiassoni (2016), chapter 6.

This is the case of Bentham's theorization of the *power of imperation*, which can be read as a both a theory of norm production (legal competence) and a theory of legal interpretation at the same time.

4.2 Bentham's Account of Imperation *as "Quasi" Realism*

Although the three main variants of Legal Realism have quite a few differences between them, there is something in which they all clearly coincide: an affirmation of one of the d senses. According to the d senses, law is not determined by the legislative function,[56] but it is determined, case by case, by the jurisdictional function. In other words, the law, in the sense of the content of legal norms, depends on ultimate instance on the judges, not on the legislators.

If we stick to the description of Bentham's model as discussed in Sects. 2 and 3, we will see that this is partially true in the case of Bentham. It is not that the law is completely indeterminate at the legislative level, but that it is partially indeterminate in a particular way.

In Bentham's reconstruction of norm creation and interpretation,[57] sources created by the legislative bodies which enact (in Bentham's parlance) *de classibus norms*, that is, legal formulations that once interpreted by the *delegate*[58] constitute incomplete norms which only mention or constitute classes or sets.[59]

[56]That is, legal sources (mainly those produced by a legislator of any kind since I'm nor referring to legal customs in this work) are indeterminate in some fashion. For different kinds of legal indetermination that can affect legal sources, see Tarello (1980), chapter 3, Guastini (2011), Part I, chapter 3, Chiassoni (2019), pp. 227–228.

[57]I'm referring to what can be called Bentham's theory of legal interpretation, meaning what Bentham considers, in his model, what judges (*delegates* of the political *Sovereign*) actually do while manipulating the legal (*de classibus*) enactments of the *Sovereign*. I'm not referring to what Bentham considers the judges should or must do in a particular case and neither to what Bentham considers a "good" interpretation of the law to be. That is what is called an interpretative ideology, a prescriptive discourse addressed mainly to judges and other interpreters of the law. Instead, a theory of legal interpretation is a descriptive enterprise or discourse about what judges and other interpreters of the law actually do. Said descriptive discourse is similar to those of Tarello (1980), Guastini (2011) and Chiassoni (2019). For an analysis of Bentham's interpretative ideology see Ferraro (2011).

[58]From now on Bentham's *de classibus norms* shall be referred as "*de classibus norm formulations*".

[59]I'm being deliberately ambiguous in this case and using "mention" for so-called "natural classes" and "constitute" for so-called "artificial classes". I am not going to settle or solve the problem here but suffice it to say that, as I said before in this paper, I do not believe that natural classes exist. Classes are the product of the human intellect. They are logic-linguistic constructions which groups things together by virtue of (at minimum) a single common property to create what we call a class or set. Every class is due to the arbitrary selection of that common property, designated as such by the classifier. Classes are not found in nature; they are created *ex nihilo* by virtue of the voluntaristic design of their creator. Outside of that there is nothing more to say about the misnamed "nature" of classes.

These norms are partially indeterminate because, although they mention a class (for example: the class or set of testamentary heirs) they do not make use of it. That is, they do not determine the concrete individuals that are members of the class or use the class to attribute to a specific subject i) membership in it and ii) a specific legal position that follows for belonging and being a member to said class or set.

The *de classibus norm formulation* are minimally limited to mentioning the intensional criteria that an individual must satisfy in order to belong to the class or set, but they do not carry out the work of individuating the concrete members of the class or set defined by said intensional criteria. Said work is carried out by the *delegate* by interpreting said *de classibus norm formulation*. Said interpretation does not only include determining the meaning and reach of the intensional criteria set by the *Sovereign* but also includes the *de singulis determination of at least one individual member of said class or set.*

In a certain sense, in this model at least, what many may call "application" of the law or of legal norms is nothing more than determining (almost concretizing them in Guastini's sense[60]) them to the point of creating an individual norm that has a specific human being (or specific human beings) as its subject or addressee.

The application of the law can be understood as just the complex operation of legislating *de singulis*, which would be nothing more than to concretize a general proposition filling its empirical gaps, following Bentham's metaphor, among which is the membership of a class mentioned by the norm.

It could also be argued that the model is partially or quasi realistic due to the fact that it is not a mere historical curiosity. Realism seeks to describe legal reality as it is, particularly that of legal interpretation as we have seen in the precedent section. Hence its name. If we take that for granted, we should also consider this model partially realistic, however anachronistic it may be to use this term to refer to Bentham, in the way already described. This is so, because, despite the anachronism of the term, Bentham's model describes the task and role of judges in current legal systems quite well.

That is because Bentham's descriptive account of norm creation and legal interpretation is a theoretical model, is not an historical reconstruction. It is a system of concepts furnished to advance our understanding on how norms are created. And, in Bentham's view, norm creation is a very complex enterprise that need both the legislator and the judge.[61]

If one sticks to what a judge does when passing sentence in the twenty-first century, it can be seen that the task that the judge undertakes is not so different from what Bentham theoretically reconstructed during the late eighteenth and early nineteenth centuries. The judge takes the sources created by the legislator (*de classibus norm formulations*), from which he extracts a partially determined norm that refers to classes of individuals, but not to any concrete individual, and then, analysing the facts of the case, determines whether they satisfy the intensional class

---

[60] See Guastini (2011), Part II, chapter 3.

[61] See Sect. 3 of the present work.

criteria mentioned in the *de classibus norm formulation*, "filling it up" and arriving at an individual legal norm that applies the class criterion to a specific individual and ascribe to her a specific legal position.

In this sense, the Benthamian model fits completely into current legal systems and the way legal interpretation and adjudication is carried out. It would only be necessary to make minimal adjustments, for example, to the notion of *Sovereign* (which could be replaced or adjusted by a concept of a legal system "holder" and a source of the *powers of imperation*) and to the notion of *power of imperation* itself.

All of the above can be seen in the following reconstruction of a *de singulis* use of the *power of imperation*. Something we may call the *Benthamite judicial syllogism*.[62]

In Bentham's model interpretation and adjudication proceeds as such:

1) $(x)\ C(x) \supset Op(x)$	**Assumption. De classibus norm**[63]
2) $C(a)$	**Assumption. De Singulis determination**
3) $C(a) \supset Op(a)$	**1, Elimination of the universal quantifier**
4) $Op(a)$	**2, 3, Elimination of the conditional**

The *power of imperation* is conjunctly the legal competence of both the *Sovereign* and their *delegates* to produce legal norms. However, this is too limited, especially if we consider that for Bentham the normative production extends beyond mere orders backed by threats.

The *power of imperation* should be replaced by a differente notion, that of a power of regulation or norm creation that implies the creation of norms, whether these are imperative or not, and i) that is attributed to the *Sovereign* or to the legal system and ii) that it can be divided into fractions among the different law creating/applying organs of said legal system.

These changes are nothing more than theoretical updating an approach in some of it's terminology that, in general terms, still works today and still manages to describe the functioning of current legal systems without much problems.

[62] Where

i) "x" is a free variable, a subject yet to be determined;

ii) "a" is an already determined subject;

iii) "C" is a condition of application in von Wrights sense (see Sect. 2 of this article), meaning, a circumstance or set of circumstances that have to actually happen in order for the norm to be applied. In this reconstruction the membership criteria to the class has been subsumed into the condition of application as already defined;

v) "⊃" is the notion of implication for the conditional;

vii) "Op(x)" is a normative solution in terms of Alchourrón and Buligyn (2012), chapters 1 and 3, meaning, an action, represented by the letter "p", to be carried out by a subject x as ordered by a legal norm. "O" in this context means, of course, the notion of duty or obligation.

I am specially indebted to Torben Spaak for some comments and criticisms on the original formulation of the syllogism and to Giovanni Battista Ratti for his invaluable help in improving on the formalization of it.

[63] This being the result of the *delegate*'s interpretation of the *de classibus norm formulation*.

The usefulness of said modifications can be seen if the model is applied to a non-mandatory rule, one that could not be considered an imperative.[64]

For example, a rule that establishes the subjective right to testify.

Let's take, for example, the case of the holographic will"[65] in the current Civil and Commercial Code of the Argentine Republic.

> Article 2477. Requirements
>
> The holographic will must be entirely written with the characters of the language in which it is granted, dated and signed by the testator's own hand.
>
> The lack of any of these formalities invalidates the act, except if it contains statements or material elements that allow the date to be established in a certain way.
>
> The signature must be located after the provisions, and the date can be placed before or after the signature.
>
> The error of the testator on fixing the date does not affect the validity of the act, but the will is not valid if the testator voluntarily set a false date in order to violate a public order rule.
>
> The additions written by any strange hand invalidate the testament only if they have been made by order or with the consent of the testator.[66]

A superficial reading would say that this article only expresses one concept, that of a holographic will, and nothing else. It does not express or determine any class. That is mistaken. A good reading, which goes in depth and does not remain floating on the

---

[64] That is, a norm that neither imposes and obligation nor a prohibition. For instance, a permissive norm or a facultative norm.

[65] The term in Spanish is "testamento ológrafo" which apparently is translated into English as "holographic will". As native Spanish speaker this came as quite a surprise to me. In Spanish "ológrafo" and "holográfico" ("holographic") are not synonyms and "holográfico" does not refer in any sense to documents such as will and testaments, just to holograms. It must be said that holograms are beyond the scope of this work.

[66] Artículo 2477. Requisitos

> El testamento ológrafo debe ser íntegramente escrito con los caracteres propios del idioma en que es otorgado, fechado y firmado por la mano misma del testador.
>
> La falta de alguna de estas formalidades invalida el acto, excepto que contenga enunciaciones o elementos materiales que permitan establecer la fecha de una manera cierta.
>
> La firma debe estar después de las disposiciones, y la fecha puede ponerse antes de la firma o después de ella.
>
> El error del testador sobre la fecha no perjudica la validez del acto, pero el testamento no es válido si aquél le puso voluntariamente una fecha falsa para violar una disposición de orden público.
>
> Los agregados escritos por mano extraña invalidan el testamento, sólo si han sido hechos por orden o con consentimiento del testador.

The way in which the article is drafted is less than ideal, but that is a problem of the whole Civil and Commercial Code that is currently in force in Argentina. I have translated it to English to the best of my abilities.

merely grammatical surface of the text, would see that a class is also built into this arrangement.

This class is the class or set of holographic testators, and it is made up of every individual subject who, at the time of writing a document that purports to be a will and testament creates, an instance of the concept of holographic that is mentioned in the (interpreted) rule expressed by the article.

The class in question is not used but is merely mentioned when speaking of writing a document that satisfies the concept of a will created by this legal provision. Its mention is indirect; it only occurs within the framework of the creation of the concept of holographic will. This is carried out by mentioning the properties that constitute the will in question and how they are related (or grouped) to each other. This is done through the enumeration of said properties that make the concept susceptible to be instantiated.[67]

Those properties have to be grouped, in fact, by someone in particular and in a concrete (factual) case, otherwise nothing happens and there is no will. That someone is an individual who is a member of the holographic testator class. The mention of the class is indirect since it is logically presupposed in the concept of holographic will that is established in the legal provision. In other words, there are no wills without testators.

So far this is a mere *de classibus* regulation. A class is indirectly created (*in personam*) that has the possibility of implementing an instantiation of a particular concept.

From a Benthamite point of view, this falls short of constructing a subjective right to grant wills for two reasons.

The first reason is that the exercise of *power of imperation de classibus* is limited to classes, not concrete individuals for which, to the extent that it is allowed, the legislative formulation only establishes the rights that the class possesses (and that after it is interpreted by a *delegate*).

This *de classibus norm* is still undetermined in terms of actual membership of the class it creates. We do not know who the specific members of the class are (or if there are any). The legislative function gives us the intensional criteria that must be satisfied to belong to the class, but it does not include a list of members of said class. In this sense the classes, and the norm, are *partially indeterminate*.

This indetermination is, I believe, a different one from those that have been recently analyzed by Chiassoni.[68] Those kinds of indetermination occur at the level of what Guastini calls "interpretation *in abstracto*",[69] that is when the delegate interprets the *de classibus norm formulation* to arrive at the *de classibus norm*.

---

[67] Said properties are mentioned in the first paragraph of the article: "*entirely written with the characters of the language in which it is granted, dated and signed by the testator's own hand*". In Argentinian law a Holographic will is equal (the same as) the conjunction of all of those properties.

[68] Chiassoni mentions five different kinds of legal indetermination: adjudicative, textual, normative, methodological and ideological. See Chiassoni (2019), pp. 227–228.

[69] Guastini (2011), Part 1, chapter 2.

The indetermination that I'm referring to could be called, for lack of a better name, "logical indetermination" or "logical indeterminacy". It occurs while moving from the first step of the *Benthamite legal syllogism* to the second one. This indetermination consists on the lack of determinacy of the actual values of the variable or variables expressed in the *de classibus norm formulation* which constitute the intensional criteria constitutive of the class or set to which the *de classibus norm* is addressed. Said values finally being equal to a concrete individual and to the concrete instantiation of the properties mentioned in the criteria. This logical indeterminacy is resolved by the judge (*delegate*) through a *de singulis* determination as seen in Sect. 3.

In order to close or resolve the logical indeterminacy, the judge/*delegate* must refer to both, the *de classibus norm formulation* and the facts of the case under analysis. In order to do this, Chiassoni's five kinds of legal indeterminacy[70] must be resolved or closed during the interpretation *in abstracto* of the *de classibus norm formulation*. One of these kinds of indeterminacy, the methodological indeterminacy, could anticipate some or all the problems of the logical indeterminacy in what Chiassoni calls "systemic indeterminacy",[71] being the result of a norm (*de classibus norm formulation*) which contains an open and un-ordered class or set.[72]

The second reason is that, for Bentham, both rights and duties and any legal position whatsoever, depend on specific authoritative decisions. They cannot be wholly general. What exists, prior to a concrete authoritative decision, is at the most an expectation of belonging to a class or set X mentioned by a norm Y.

Following this line of thought, until a judge exercises what we may call the power of regulation *de singulis*, an individual, at most, can count on the expectation of belonging to the class of testators by virtue of the fact that said person considers that he created a valid instance of the concept of holographic testament as defined by article 2477 of the Civil and Commercial Code of Argentina.

She has no certainty of belonging to the class, just a mere expectation. In the absence of an authoritative decision made by a delegate of the *Sovereign*/legal system, said expectation ends up being just that, an expectation. Her membership to the class, and the rights that come with it, remain undetermined.

The construction of the subjective right to grant wills is only completed when an individual, equipped with a fraction of *power of imperation* (or power of regulation in the updated terminology), completes or "fills up" the legal norm by individuating a specific and concrete individual as a member of the class by a *de singulis* determination or exercise of aforementioned power. When corroborated as such by the judge/*delegate*, the individual *now* happens to have the properties of a member of the class mentioned by the legal norm.

---

[70] Or those presented in a particular and concrete legal interpretation. Could be any number between one to five.

[71] Chiassoni (2019), p. 228.

[72] This could mean that if, as I believe, logical indeterminacy is unavoidable, then methodological indeterminacy is also unavoidable.

In the case in question, if a subject is individuated and certified as a member of the class of holographic testators, then he becomes the holder of a subjective right to grant holographic wills by means of that specific instrument.

This is, effectively, the way the courts operate. When passing judgment, they corroborate or reject expectations of different individuals and retroactively recognize or ignore the (possible) adscription to an individual of a certain legal position. In our example, the subjective right to grant holographic wills, or formally, "Subject X has the faculty[73] of granting holographic wills according to article 2477 of the Code".

5 Conclusions

i) the Benthamite approach to norm creation and legal interpretation is presented as "quasi" realistic one, given the central role that judges play in this model in determining the content of legal norms, which can be read as affirming, at least partially, one of the d senses of Tarello's reconstruction of the meaning of Legal Realism.
ii) It also offers a faithful reconstruction the practice of the courts while dealing with the interpretation of legal sources.
iii) It does so by the following reconstruction:
iv) legislators produce norm formulations that, once interpreted are still indeterminate in a logical sense.
v) From this follows that norm creation is not limited to *de classibus* rulemaking exercises and that norm creation involves the collaboration of the judiciary.
vi) While collaborating with the legislative organs, the judges are not limited merely to performing exercises of abstract interpretation (determining or assigning meanings to legal formulations), but they also legislate via *de singulis* determinations, completing the rule by designating an individual as a member of a class in the way seen in what we called the *Benthamite judicial syllogism.*
vii) This also reveals that the process of exercising legal competence is much more complex than assumed, since it is not limited to the mere phenomenon of the legislative function.
viii) It is a continuum that goes from legislation to adjudication, which leads to the determination of the legal positions of specific individuals, a legal position they hold only because they belong to a certain class created by the legislator and whose membership is determined by the judge.
ix) Norm creation is a collaborative work in which the legislator aims to create and determine legally relevant classes for legally relevant cases, plus the legal positions that would correspond to the members of said classes just for the fact of being members of them.

[73] See footnote 27.

x) The judge, on the other hand, has the unenviable job of completing said classes by creating individual norms, expressed in judicial rulings, which determine that a specific subject belongs to a specific class and, for that fact alone, possesses a specific legal position.

These conclusions are, of course, provisional. Bentham's model needs to be adjusted along the lines indicated in the preceding section. This does not mean that it is incorrect in general lines and that it does not manages to describe quite clearly the way in which legal competence is exercised, and the way that this exercise takes until it reaches an individual with clearly determined rights and duties.

The model also seems to show, to the extent that this may matter to someone despite the undersigned, that individuals, that is, us, guide their conduct not based on law, but on expectations we have in relation to what we beleive the content of certain legal documents to be.

In some sense, prior to any jurisdictional decision, we move as in a house of mirrors, believing we see things that maybe are not in fact there. Only very rarely do we succeed, almost miraculously, in discerning reality and correctly identifying the law by ourselves.

I am referring, of course, to those cases in which we successfully anticipate the judge's decision.

References

Alchourrón C, Buligyn E (2012) Sistemas Normativos. Introducción a la Metodología de las Ciencias Jurídicas, 2nd edn. Astrea, Buenos Aires (First Edition in English: Alchourrón C, Buligyn E (1971) Normative systems, library of exact philosophy. n°5. Springer Verlag, Wein & New York)

Bentham J (1945) In: Everett CW (ed) The limits of jurisprudence defined. Columbia University Press, New York

Bentham J (1970) In: Hart HLA (ed) Of laws in general. The Athlone Press, London

Bentham J (1983) In: Rosen F, Burns JH (eds) Constitutional Code, vol I. Clarendon Press, Oxford

Bentham J (1996) In: Burns JH, Hart HLA (eds) An introduction to the principles of morals and legislation. Clarendon Press, Oxford

Bentham J (2010) In: Schofield P (ed) Of the limits of the penal branch of jurisprudence. Clarendon Press, Oxford

Bobbio N (1965) Giusnaturalismo e positivismo giuridico. Edizioni di Comunità, Milano

Borges JL (2018) El idioma analítico de John Wilkins. In: Inquisiciones/Otras Inquisiciones. Sudamericana, Buenos Aires, pp 333–339

Bulygin E (2007) Il positivismo giuridico. Giuffrè Editore, Milano

Calzetta AD (2018) Competencia y constitutividad. Las normas de competencia en la obra de Riccardo Guastini. In: Chissoni P, Commanducci P, Ratti GB (eds) L'arte della distinzione: scritti per Riccardo Guastini, vol I. Marcial Pons, Madrid, pp 275–294

Carrió C (2006) Notas sobre Derecho y Lenguaje, 5th edn. Lexis Nexis. Abeledo-Perrot, Buenos Aires

Chiassoni P (2014) Bentham on legal order. In: Tusseau G (ed) The legal philosophy and influence of Jeremy Bentham. Essays on 'On the Limits of the Penal Branch of Jurisprudence'. Routledge, London, pp 47–70

Chiassoni P (2016) Da Bentham a Kelsen. Sei capitoli per una storia della filosofia analitica del diritto. Giappichelli, Milano

Chiassoni P (2017) El realismo americano según un abogado de provincia. In: Tarello G (ed) El realismo jurídico americano (trans: Troncoso M). Palestra, Lima

Chiassoni P (2019) Interpretation without truth. A realistic enquiry. Springer, Cham

Ferraro F (2011) Il giudice utilitarista. Flessibilità e tutela delle aspettative nel pensiero giuridico di Jeremy Bentham. Edizioni ETS, Pisa

Guastini R (2011) Interpretare e argomentare. Giuffrè Editore, Milano

Guastini R, Rebuffa G (2002) Introducción. In: Tarello G, Pérez M, Luis J (eds) Cultura Jurídica y Política del Derecho. Editorial Comares S.L., Granada, pp 1–36

Guastini R, Vaquero NV (trans) (2016) La Sintaxis del Derecho. Marcial Pons, Madrid

Hart HLA (1982) Legal powers. In: Essays on Bentham, jurisprudence and political theory. OUP, Oxford, pp 194–219

Hart HLA (2012 (1961)) The concept of law, 3rd edn. Clarendon Press, OUP, Oxford

Hierro L (1981) El realismo jurídico escandinavo. Una teoría empirista del derecho, 1st edn. Fernando Torres-Editor, S.A, Valencia

Leiter B (2007) Naturalizing jurisprudence: essays on American legal realism and naturalism in legal philosophy. OUP, Oxford

Olivecrona K (1971) Law as fact, 2nd edn. Steven & Sons, London

Ross A (2005) Sobre el Derecho y la Justicia. Eudeba, Buenos Aires

Scarpelli U (1997) Cos'è il positivismo giuridico. Edizioni Scientifiche Italiane, Napoli

Tarello G (1962) Il realismo giuridico americano. Giuffrè Editore, Milano

Tarello G (1972) Teorie e idiologie nel diritto sindacale. L'esperienza italiana dopo la Costituzione. Edizione di Comunità, Milano

Tarello G (1974a) Realismo Giuridico. In: Tarello G (ed) Diritto, enunciati, usi. Studi di teoria e metateoria del diritto. Il Mulino, Bologna, pp 51–85

Tarello G (1974b) Atteggiamenti culturali sulla funzione del giurista-interprete. In: Tarello G (ed) Diritto, enunciati, usi. Studi di teoria e metateoria del diritto. Il Mulino, Bologna, pp 475–521

Tarello G (1976) Storia della cultura giuridica moderna. I. Assolutismo e codificazione del diritto. Il Mulino, Bologna

Tarello G (1980) L'interpretazione della legge. Giuffrè Editore, Milano

von Wright GH (1963) Norm and action. A logical inquiry. Routledge & Kegan Paul, London

Merkl's Stufenbaulehre in the History of the Theory of Legal Power

Gonzalo Villa-Rosas

Abstract This chapter explores the contributions of the *Stufenbau* theory advanced by Adolf Julius Merkl in his writings *Die Lehre von der Rechtskraft* (1923) and *Prolegomena einer Theorie des rechtlichen Stufenbaues* (1931) to the development of power qua power conferred by the law. The main thesis of this paper argues that Merkl's theory of *Stufenbau* is based on the rejection of any pre-legal foundation of power not only with respect to the ultimate basis of the legal system, but also with respect to the power to enter into voluntary legal obligations. The *Stufenbau* theory corresponds to an analytical achievement that grounds the formal separation thesis of law and morals by reacting not only against the remnants of historical positivism that still echoed in its time but also against *Gesetzpositivismus*, that is, the doctrine that held that the law is created by the legislator and the law is restricted to what the legislator commands.

1 Introduction

The normative account of legal power[1] provides an explanation of legal power through the study of the rules that confer and regulate it. The importance of this account lies in the fact that, through an understanding of these rules, it is possible to explain the fundamental characteristics of any legal system, such as its formal

[1] Although Merkl uses the term 'competence' (see e.g., Merkl 1931, p. 281) on the basis of a long series of writings (e.g., Alexy 2008, p. 43; Spaak 1994, pp. 1–4; Bulygin 1991, pp. 201–202; Lindahl 1977, p. 194), for the purposes of this chapter, I will assume that this term is synonymous with the term 'legal power'.

G. Villa-Rosas (✉)
Centre for Research in Philosophy and Law, Externado University, Bogotá, Colombia

Department of Legal and Constitutional History, Faculty of Law, University of Vienna, Vienna, Austria
e-mail: gonzalo.villa@uexternado.edu.co; gonzalov93@univie.ac.at

G. Villa-Rosas, T. Spaak (eds.), *Legal Power and Legal Competence*, Law and Philosophy Library 140, https://doi.org/10.1007/978-3-031-28555-4_14

structure and its changes as a result of normative creation.[2] The notion of legal power qua power conferred by the law makes the normative account of legal power possible. Although legal power qua power conferred is an ancient technique, the theoretical construct of legal power qua power conferred by the law is relatively recent.

This chapter explores the contributions of the *Stufenbau* theory[3]—advanced by Adolf Julius Merkl in his writings *Die Lehre von der Rechtskraft* (1923) and *Prolegomena einer Theorie des rechtlichen Stufenbaues* (1931)[4]—to the theoretical development of power qua power conferred by the law. The main thesis of this chapter argues that Merkl's theory of the hierarchical structure of the legal system provides a general scope to the normative account of legal power as it provides a legal foundation of power regarding the ultimate basis of the legal system and its intermediate and lower structures, as well as with respect to the power to enter into voluntary legal obligations.[5] The *Stufenbau* theory corresponds to an analytical achievement that formally grounds the separation thesis of law and morals by reacting, on the one hand, against the remnants of the Pandectist movement that still echoed in its time, and on the other, against nineteenth-century statutory positivism (*Gesetzespositivismus*)—that is, the doctrine that held that 'all the law is created by the legislator of the state and exhausted in her orders'.[6]

Merkl's *Stufenbau* theory rejects any formal pre-legal foundation of power. The structure of this chapter follows not only this certainty but also the methodological constraint, according to which the full recognition of the contributions of Merkl's *Stufenbaulehre* to the theory of legal power requires a comparative historical

[2]Kelsen (2017 (1960)), § 133, p. 140. As stated by Paulson, '[a] creative dimension [in law] is undeniable, for there is an unavoidable element of discretion involved in the issuance of the lower-level norm. In other words, the determination of lower-level norm by higher-level norm is never complete.' (Paulson 2013). In fact, the relationship between legal power and normative creation was emphasised by Kelsen when analysing the difference between the dynamic and static concept of law. (See Kelsen 1945, pp. 122–123.)

[3]The contributions of the *Wiener rechtstheoretische Schule* to the theory of legal power also include the contributions of Alfred Verdross, who developed a theory of hierarchical normative structure (*Stufenbaulehre*) with which he intended to establish a monism based on the primacy of international law. See Verdross (1923).

[4]Although Merkl offered the most systematic exposition of his *Stufenbaulehre* in these two writings—*Die Lehre von der Rechtskraft* (1923) and *Prolegomena einer Theorie des rechtlichen Stufenbaues* (1931)—Merkl had already presented substantial elements of his theory in *Das Recht im Licht seiner Anwendung* (1916, 1917, 1919. These remarks focus on the reading of the version published in Merkl (1993–2009), vol. 1, pt. 1, 85–146, esp. pp. 96–116).

[5]As stated by MacCormick, '[v]oluntary obligations are of course those which arise from contracts and promises, obediential include, e.g., those whose incidence is determined by the law of delict.' (MacCormick and Raz 1972, p. 59). As we shall see, voluntary obligations have been associated with the concept of act-in-the-law (*Rechtsgeschäft*) in the continental European tradition since the advent of the Pandectist movement. (See Guzmán Brito 2004.)

[6]Wieacker (2016 (1967)), p. 458. See Merkl (1931), p. 254. On statutory positivism in the Imperial Germany see Schröder (2005), pp. 571–586. On the difference between scientific positivism and statutory positivism, see Wieacker (2016 (1967)), pp. 458–467.

analysis.[7] In fact, I resolve these caveats by dividing the chapter into two parts. In the first part, I revisit the relevant theories upon pre-legal foundations of legal power; I devote the second part to Merkl's theory of construction of levels (*Stufenbaulehre*).[8]

2 The Pre-legally Founded Legal Power

The roots of the technique of legal power qua conferred power in European legal history go back to the *Liber Extra* promulgated by Pope Gregory IX in the thirteenth century.[9] This exclusive compilation for all of canon law developed not only an almost-stable vocabulary on validity[10] but also power-conferring institutions on the representatives of the church.[11] Nonetheless, the theoretical construct of legal power qua power conferred by the law is relatively recent. This theoretical construct and its general explanatory scope concerning any legal system endorsed the rejection of pre-legal foundations of power, not only with respect to its ultimate basis but also regarding the foundation of the power to enter into voluntary legal obligations.

---

[7]This methodological constraint has been inpired by Paulson's insights advanced in *Zur stufenbaulehre Merkls in ihrer Bedeutung für die allgemeine Rechtslehre* (Paulson 1990).

[8]Paulson (2021).

[9]Two main reasons can be advanced against the view that the Roman jurists carved out a notion of power as power conferred by the law. On the one hand, the pragmatic character of Roman jurists hampered the development of general concepts that would serve as a basis for the use of a stable language referring to legal validity—in the sense of membership of a legal system. Moreover, on the other hand, the impact of the Roman political history on the public law (see Köpcke 2019, pp. 39–41) and the formalism within the field of voluntary obligations (Zimmermann 1992 (1990), pp. 32, 508–509) prevented Roman jurists from adding conferring-power as a uniform category to the functions of law. Roman jurists restricted the functions of law to command, prohibit, permit and punish as noted by Modestinus (D. 1, 3, 7) and, as Thon argued, the Romans maintained a constant linguistic rupture which can be appreciated through the use of terms such as '*potestas*', '*facultas*', '*licentia*' and the more general name '*ius*' (see Thon 1878, p. 341). The same reasons may be held against that view which maintains that the conception of legal power as conferred power was already found in Gratian's *Decretum.* It is true that an express recognition of a power conferring-function of law is also absent in *Liber Extra* (*Quinque Libri Decretalium*) promulgated by Pope Gregory IX, and that, according to this source, the ultimate foundation of power is still pre-legal (according to L. I, Tit. II, Cap. III: '*Potestas legem condendi et mutandi est penes vicarium Christi.*'). Nevertheless, as stated in the text, it has been recognised on the one hand that this source presents, perhaps for the first time, an almost steady language regarding legal validity (Köpcke 2019, pp. 68–72) and, on the other hand, that this source expressly deals with power-conferring institutions on the representatives of the church brought together in its Liber I. (See https://www.hs-augsburg.de/~harsch/Chronologia/Lspost13/GregoriusIX/gre_0000.html#3.)

[10]See Köpcke (2019), pp. 68–72.

[11]See Liber I, Tituli I to XLIII. *Liber Extra* (*Quinque Libri Decretalium*) promulgated by Pope Gregory IX. https://www.hs-augsburg.de/~harsch/Chronologia/Lspost13/GregoriusIX/gre_0000.html#3.

As stated by Köpcke, for centuries legal thought operated without an ultimate legal basis for legal power.[12] This method of operation was reflected in theoretical strands not only from natural law but also from classical English legal positivism. On one side, regarding natural law, we find pre-legal ultimate foundations of legal power both in theories defending a divine justification of power[13] and in non-theological natural law theories of the modern age.[14] Analysing these latter non-theological theories, Klippel distinguished two characteristic currents.[15] Firstly, throughout the seventeenth century, the natural law as political theory shaped the foundations of enlightened absolutism. Indeed, a common doctrine of seventeenth-century natural law theories maintained that whereas the power of the sovereign was based on the state of nature, her subjects leave this state through the social contract.[16] This contract fulfilled the function of an ideal ethical order that legitimised the power of the sovereign, who was then understood as a political entity superior to the legal order—*supra leges civiles*—and, therefore, as a political entity unbound by the law—*legibus solutus*.[17] Secondly, from the mid-eighteenth century onwards, various currents of natural law strongly gravitated towards the absolute validity of freedom and human rights.[18] These theories offered not only a normative theoretical framework prior to the sovereign's power established by nature or by reason but also a source of restrictions to her legal power in the form of individual subjective rights.[19] Within the latter current, Kant posited *a priori* principles as pre-legal foundations of legal power,[20] transforming a theory of natural law 'from a normative theory of action into a normative theory of legislation'.[21] On the other side, for the authors of classical English legal positivism,[22] the ultimate pre-legal foundation of legal power rests on the sovereign, whose existence is at the heart of the command theory. Indeed, Bentham and Austin's theories share a common core[23] according to which being subject to the law is tantamount to paying habitual obedience to the

[12] Köpcke (2019), 8, pp. 115–145.

[13] On the importance of theories of divine right in the development of the theory of sovereignty see i.a. Burgess (1992).

[14] See Klippel (1976, 1987). The analysis presented above is largely based on Brockmöller (1997), pp. 35–42.

[15] The analysis presented by Klippel should be assumed to be illustrative, as it is restricted to the modern Germanic world of the seventeenth, eighteenth and nineteenth centuries. See Klippel (1987), p. 267; Klippel (1976).

[16] Klippel (1987), p. 272. On this development of natural law see Klippel (1976), pp. 92–112.

[17] Klippel (1987), p. 272; Klippel (1976), pp. 92–112.

[18] Klippel (1976), pp. 113–134.

[19] Klippel (1987), pp. 273–277; Klippel (1976), pp. 113–134.

[20] Kant MdS RL (1999 (1785)), AB 44.

[21] Dreier (1979), p. 27 Note 77.

[22] See i.a. Freeman (2008 (1959)), pp. 247–269.

[23] On the conceptual relationships between Bentham's and Austin's theories and the concept of positivism see Schauer (2013).

sanction-backed commands of a sovereign.[24] This means that despite differences in their positions on sovereignty,[25] Bentham and Austin posit the sovereign as a necessary condition for legal power. Whoever holds the pre-legal position of sovereignty[26] cannot lack competence[27] and, consequently, her mandate 'may be cruel; it may be impolitic'[28] but 'it cannot be void and invalid'.[29]

Moreover, only recently has the power for voluntarily entering into an obligation been grasped as power legally conferred.[30] As Köpcke argued, for centuries this power was also attributed a pre-legal foundation.[31] The fact that Roman jurists were not overly concerned with bringing the law into a neat systematic order[32] and that the enforceability of contractual obligations was restricted to certain types of *iuris vincula* according to the manner with which they were concluded[33] prevented Roman jurists from finding a uniform basis for their voluntary obligations. As stated by Zimmermann, according to the Roman Law a *nudum pactum*—that is, an agreement that did not fit into one of the categories *verbis*, *re*, *litteris* or into one of the *numerus clausus* of consensual contracts[34]—was not actionable.[35] This Roman practice was summarised by Ulpianus in the *regula iuris* '*nuda pactio obligationem non parit, sed parit exceptionem*'.[36] However, the influence of

---

[24] Hart (2011 (1967)), p. 226; Moreso (1989), p. 352.

[25] On the differences between the indivisible and illimitable Austin's sovereign and Bentham's notion of sovereign see i.a. Hart (2011 (1967)), pp. 222–227; Turégano Mansilla (2001), pp. 313–346; Raz (1970), pp. 7–9.

[26] Authors such as Manning (Manning 1963 (1933), p. 180) and Cotterrell (Cotterrell 1989, p. 67) defended a formal interpretation of Austin's conception of the sovereign - Stone raised some criticisms against consistency of Austin's position (see Stone 1964, pp. 73–88). According to the formal interpretation of Austin's sovereign, Austin posits an entity determinable according to its general non-legal normative characteristics that do not depend on any particular person and that, as a presupposition of legal power, allows for the identification of a normative system as the ultimate source of its validity (On Austin's sovereign as a source of validity see Turégano Mansilla 2001, pp. 340–345; Garzón Valdes 1981; Moreso 1989).

[27] Hart (2011 (1967)), p. 226.

[28] Bentham (1970 (1780)), p. 16.

[29] Hart (2011 (1967)), p. 226.

[30] Indeed, this has also been a topic of contemporary debates. An example of this can be found in Raz's defense of the necessary nature of the exercise of normative powers for the conclusion of promises as sources of voluntary obligations as opposed to MacCormick's position, for whom legal enforceability was a sufficient condition to explain the obligations derived from promises. See MacCormick and Raz (1972).

[31] Köpcke (2019), p. 140.

[32] Zimmermann (1992 (1990)), p. 24.

[33] Zimmermann (1992 (1990)), p. 32.

[34] According to Roman sources, only if the *consensus* between the parties could be classified as *emptio venditio*, *locatio conductio*, *mandatum* or *societas* was it enforceable (see Zimmermann 1992 (1990), p. 508).

[35] Zimmermann (1992 (1990)), p. 508.

[36] D. 2, 14, 7, 4; Ulp. D. 19, 5, 15; Paul. Sent. II, XIV.1.

commercial practice, as well as the contribution of canon and natural law, led to the acceptance of the rule of consensualism. According to this rule, all pacts are binding, regardless of whether they are clothed or naked.[37] Nevertheless, canon law found the basis for this rule not in the positive law but rather in the Christian mandates[38]—although the applicability of some of those mandates in the *foro civile* remained in dispute over the centuries.[39] Likewise, Suarez argued that the source of the validity of acts was a '*potestas moralis*'.[40] Similarly, Grotius[41] and Pufendorf[42] maintained that *fides* as ground of justice requires that promises must be kept regardless of the manner in which they have been made. This pre-legal foundation of the power to enter into legally binding voluntary obligations, which leaves to the law the function of restricting and shaping the power to prevent its abusive use,[43] corresponds to the strand that inspired the first wave of codification with the great legislative works of France, Austria and Prussia.[44]

Although a reaction against this first wave of codification set the stage for German nineteenth-century positivism,[45] this positivism did not completely renounce the legitimation of law by natural law foundations.[46] This can be seen in the efforts made

---

[37] Zimmermann (1992 (1990)), p. 576.

[38] Zimmermann (1992 (1990)), p. 542.

[39] Zimmermann (1992 (1990)), p. 543.

[40] Suarez (2010 (1612)): V, XXXI, 11: '. . .*cum potestas sit primum fundamentum valoris actus*'; II, XII, 4: '*[T]ollitur principium substantiale (ut sic dicam) valoris actus, quod est potestas moralis, id est, quae habeat adiunctam sufficiemtem voluntatem; sine potestate autem et voluntate non est actus validus'; V, XXVI, 25: 'voluntas humana ex iure naturae habet hanc potestatem contrahendi, donandi et alia similia faciendi.*'

[41] Grotius (2005 (1625–1630)), Lib. II, Ch. XI, §I-XXII. For a Latin version see https://www.digitale-sammlungen.de/de/view/bsb10040700?page=6. On Grotius' contribution to the instrumentality of the civil law category of the *pactum* see Calasso (1959), pp. 336–342.

[42] Pufendorf (1998 (1684)), Lib. III, Cap. IV, § 2: '*Pacta servanda Sunt. Si quae autem inter homines ineuntur pacta, ilia sancte observanda esse, sociabilis natura hominis requirit. [. . .] Igitur religiosissimum juris naturalis praeceptum, & quod universae humanae vitae decus, modum, atque rationem temperat, habetur: Ut quilibet fidem datam servet, seu promissa atque pacta expleat.*'

[43] Köpcke (2019), p. 141.

[44] A paradigmatic position of this first European codification movement with respect to the Roman law of obligations is expressed by Pothier in the following terms: '*Les principes du droit romain sur les différentes espèces de pactes, et sur la distinction des contrats et des simples pactes, n'étant pas fondés sur le droit naturel, et éiant très-éloignés de sa simplicité, ne sont pas admis dans notre droit.*' (Pothier 1761, § I, p. 6).

[45] See e.g. Brockmöller (1997), pp. 83–111.

[46] This comment comes from Kelsen (1934), p. 39: '*Der Positivismus des 19. Jahrhunderts verzichtet zwar nicht völlig auf eine Legitimierung des Rechts durch einen überpositiven Wert; aber er tut dies nur indirekt, gleichsam unter der Oberfläche seiner Begriffe*'. In the same line, Bockmöller considered that with only some exceptions—e.g. Bierling and Bergbohm—none of the jurists considered as leaders of the emergence of the legal discipline 'represents a positivistic concept of law in the sense of the separation thesis; also none of them assumes that law can be obtained purely system-immanently, without extra-legal evaluations, or that all law is state-generated statutory law and is exhausted in the commands of the legislator. An essential idea for

by authors of the Pandectist movement to free themselves from[47]—or at least attenuate their commitment to[48]—a pre-legal foundation of the power to enter into legally binding voluntary obligations rooted in the 'province of the independent mastery of the individual will'.[49] The Pandectists searched for a definition of power which not only could serve as a general explanatory basis for all acts-in-the-law (*Rechtsgeschäfte*) but also whose use would, first, only be legitimate in relation to legal sources and, second, would be reflected in a uniform terminology.[50] Windscheid reminds us that an attempt at such a definition was proposed by Brinz.[51] In fact, Brinz emphasises the distinctive feature of legal power (*rechtliches Können*), highlighting its differences with legal permission (*rechtliches Dürfen*) and physical power (*physisches Können*). According to Brinz, although it is true that where there is legal power with respect to acts-in-the-law, there is usually also legal permission to enter into them, 'sometimes the former exists where the latter is missing'.[52] Moreover, whereas a legal permission may occur both with respect to ordinary acts and with respect to acts-in-the-law, legal power occurs only with respect to the latter; that is, 'in the broad sense of the term, only with respect to those acts imposed or adopted by law for the achievement of its invisible legal effects'.[53] Second, although neither legal permission nor legal power can be used without physical power, physical power differs from both. For, whereas ordinary acts can occur only if one has physical power and even in the absence of permission, acts-in-the-law without legal power are null and void.[54]

---

the jurisprudence of the 19th century is that law is supposed to realize justice and, due to its historical process of development, also increasingly incorporates material contents that finally guarantee justice.' Brockmöller (1997), p. 275.

[47] In searching for the objectification of the concept of act-in-the-law (*Rechtsgeschäft*), Bierling understood by act-in-the-law (*Rechtsgeschäft*) 'a form of law formation, more precisely: a fixation of legal rules on the basis of any already existing subordinate legal rule.' For Bierling, an act-in-the-law (*Rechtsgeschäft*) involves 'the creation or dissolution or, at least, the alteration of a legal relationship.' These changes of a legal relationship amount to 'the establishment of a legal rule'. Bierling maintained that this direct link between acts-in-the-law (*Rechtsgeschäft*) and the creation of norms was 'completely absent in the old concept of act-in-the-law (*Rechtsgeschäft*)' (Bierling 1898, p. 118). Nevertheless, as Merkl stated, in the quest for objectification, Bierling turned the theory of acts-in-the-law (*Rechtsgeschäft*) into a theory of the legal sources (Merkl 1923, p. 195).

[48] According to Windscheid, '*[i]n der neueren Zeit aber tauchen Stimmen auf, die bereits nicht mehrvereinzelte genannt werden dürfen, welche der Erklärung als solche, unabhängig davon ob sie die Trägerin eines wirklich vorhandenen Willen ist, in grösserem oder geringerem Masse Wirkung beizulegen geneigt sind.*' Windscheid (1878), §1, pp. 3–4; Thon (1878), §12, p. 358.

[49] Savigny (1867 (1840)), p. 271. Windscheid (1862), § 69, pp. 145–148.

[50] Thon speaks of the varied terminology used in his time and refers in particular to the following expressions '*rechtlicher Macht*', '*rechtliches Können*' and '*Befugnis*.' See Thon (1878), §7, p. 341.

[51] Brinz (1873), §65, pp. 211–212.

[52] Brinz (1873), §65, pp. 211–212.

[53] Brinz (1873), §65, pp. 211–212.

[54] Brinz (1873), §65, pp. 211–212.

However, Brinz's contributions to the quest for a consistent terminology to refer to legal power could not overcome the restrictions imposed by the Pandectist tradition. On the one hand, the search for this terminology was restricted to the reflection on acts-in-the-law (*Rechtsgeschäfte*). On the other hand, the Pandectist movement failed to bring about a radical break with the pre-legal foundation of the power to enter into voluntary obligations. In contrast, the blossoming of a new interest in another area of legal scholarship provided us with the conceptual repertoire necessary to posit an ultimate legal foundation for legal power.

3 The Legally Founded Legal Power: Merkl's Theory of *Stufenbau*

Various political changes in the nineteenth century seeded the blossoming of public and state law studies in continental European legal scholarship. For example, in Central European legal systems, the strengthening of the rule of law—which entailed both the guarantee of recognition of fundamental rights in German Imperial and Austrian constitutional law and the establishment of administrative courts in the most important *Länder* in the second half of the nineteenth century—led to a upsurge of interest in state and administrative law studies at universities and in the legal scholarship.[55] Indeed, this legal scholarship mirrored the quest for predictable state activity that characterises the rule of law. As Stolleis argued, 'by interpreting state activity as a development of the law and leaving to politics the goals this development pursues, jurisprudence abandoned the old terrain of political science, but conquered the terrain of the universality of categories such as equal rights, predictability and surveillance over the actions of the state—above all the category of "administrative act" (*Verwaltungsakt*)—and the recognition of its own work as a science'.[56] In understanding studies of the state as a descriptive explanatory science,[57] and state activity as a development of law, the German scholarship underpinned the overcoming of the state sovereignty concept as a necessary theoretical construct for the foundation of the law. Consequently, Jellinek—perhaps the most prominent leading figure of nineteenth-century Austrian studies of the state—understood state power as 'governing power arising from itself',[58] and law as a set of rules that 'have as a necessary characteristic their validity'.[59]

[55] Stolleis (2002), p. 43.

[56] Stolleis (2002), p. 43.

[57] Jellinek (1929 (1914)), p. 9.

[58] Jellinek (1929 (1914)), pp. 489–490.

[59] Jellinek (1929 (1914)), p. 333.

As a result of these developments, the concern for the validity of law and its sources was not far from the debates of *fin de siècle*.[60] This is shown by the contributions of Bülow,[61] Haenel,[62] Bierling[63] and the Free Law School (*Freirechtsschule*),[64] on which Merkl based his theory of the hierarchical structure of the legal system. With this theory, Merkl intended to respond to the traditional line of thought on legal sources that dominated at the time and which, by excessively privileging the law enacted by parliament, denied the multiplicity of sources, reducing them essentially to just two: statutory and customary law.[65] Merkl included in the general category of legal phenomena the various sources of law. By investigating the logical relationships between these phenomena, Merkl postulated the legal foundations of power not only regarding the ultimate basis of the legal system but also with regarding the power to enter into voluntary legal obligations. Merkl thus articulated a normative theory of legal power that is based on power qua power conferred by the law.

According to Merkl's theory, there are non-legal orders—such as morals and customs—which can demand compliance with their norms yet cannot be enforceable.[66] In contrast to these non-legal orders, the constant increase of contents, as well as their relentless refinement and specialisation, characterise the law.[67] These characteristics show that the law supposes not only procedures but also a plurality of bodies involved in its creation.[68] These bodies comprise the States. Thus, the more complex the structure of the State, the more diverse the norms used for the creation of law.[69] In this sense, according to Merkl, although the state is not identical to the law, it is completely conditioned by it.[70] Merkl argues that the object of his analysis is the material created by the bodies that comprise the State.[71] To determine the criteria for ordering this material, Merkl introduces, on the one hand, the notion of legal phenomena (*Rechtserscheinungen*), in which he groups together both legal norms (*Rechtsnormen*) or statements (*Rechtssätze*) and factual acts of execution (*faktische Vollzugsakte*),[72] and, on the other hand, the notion of legal form

[60] A description of the atmosphere of fundamental debates at the end of the century can be found at Stolleis (2002), pp. 51–52.

[61] Merkl (1923), pp. 182–190.

[62] Merkl (1923), pp. 190–194.

[63] Merkl (1923), pp. 194–197.

[64] Merkl (1923), pp. 197–198.

[65] Merkl (1931), p. 254.

[66] Merkl (1931), p. 253.

[67] Merkl (1931), p. 253.

[68] Merkl (1931), p. 253.

[69] Merkl (1931), p. 253.

[70] Merkl (1931), p. 253.

[71] Merkl (1931), p. 255.

[72] Merkl (1923), p. 218. As Borowski argued, 'Merkl does not distinguish between a legal norm and a legal statement. On the contrary, he follows the widespread linguistic usage according to which a

(*Rechtsform*) to refer to classes of legal phenomena determined according to formal criteria—in particular the class of legal norms.[73] To determine the logical relationships between the various legal forms and their components, Merkl proposes the application of the structural analysis of historically determined legal material.[74] The resulting arrangement of the legal forms and their components found in this material corresponds to a construction of levels.[75] This construction evidences an archetypal relationship between conditioning and conditioned norms and acts.[76] In this archetypal relationship, the conditioning norms prescribe the form and content with which the norms we call conditioned are created.[77] Thus, the latter cannot come into existence in any form other than that prescribed by the former.[78] Conditioning norms thus not only possess temporal but also logical priority, insofar as a certain conditioned norm is not only always created after a conditioning norm but only from it, in such a manner that the conditioned norm cannot be thought of without considering the conditioning norm from which it derives its validity.[79] Thus, the conditioning norm appears superior to the conditioned norm. The series of conditioning and conditioned norms build the series of levels, which, taken together, comprise a staggered construction composed of higher and lower ranks.[80]

According to Merkl, the finding that law regulates its own creation is based on the fact that 'the legal order consists of two components with different contents: on the one hand, the norms of conduct (*Verhaltensnormen*) and, on the other hand, the norms regulating the establishment, formation and, ultimately, creation of these

legal norm or a legal statement represents a hypothetical judgment about the state's willingness to impose a consequence to an act against the law' (Borowski 2005, p. 132).

[73] On the clarification of the definition of *Rechtsformen* in accordance with Merkl's use of the term see Borowski (2005), p. 144.

[74] Merkl (1931), p. 255.

[75] Merkl uses different metaphors to refer to the resulting arrangement of the legal forms and their components 'such as that of a chain, a family tree or a stream of water, a technical production process, etc.. . . .' Nevertheless, he considers that 'that of a sequence of levels, a construction of levels, is probably the most unadorned, but the most striking and meaningful' picture to refer to the phenomenon (Merkl 1931, p. 283).

[76] Merkl (1931), p. 273.

[77] Merkl lays the foundations of a theory of discretion. For Merkl, the competent subject is bound to the higher-level norms. Nevertheless, what is not already decided by these norms is left to the decision of the competent subject. In this way, what is not already decided by these norms amounts to the competent subject's margin of discretion. This margin makes the subjective aspect possible when the competent subject applies the higher-level norms. Through this aspect 'extra-legal motivations can penetrate' to the legal decision (Merkl 1927, p. 152). However, from the perspective of the competent subject of a lower level, once the application of the norms by her superior has been completed, both the subjective and the objective component of the application of the norms appear united in the superior's decision, which thus constitutes the objective framework of the new normative application (Merkl 1927, p. 219).

[78] Merkl (1931), p. 275.

[79] Merkl (1931), p. 275.

[80] Merkl (1931), p. 276.

norms of conduct'.[81] Consequently, in the absence of the latter rules, the legal order would only be conceivable as a static order.[82] Nevertheless, it is not possible to question the statement that law is created from legally relevant actions carried out by bodies that serve as instruments of law creation that are provided by the legal order itself.[83] The legally relevant actions through which law is created must as a condition have been carried out by bodies created by delegating legal norms—the so-called competence norms.[84] Thus, Merkl continues, 'just as a human being is only legitimized as a body and in particular as a producer of law by such a competence norm that delegates the production of law to him, so a certain human action only turns out to be a legal product, in particular a legal norm, through following all the norms of law production decided in the conditioning legal sphere'.[85]

From this fundamental description, Merkl argues that every legal system contains at least two typical legal forms, without which it is not conceivable.[86] These are the original norm (*Ursprungsnorm*) and the factual act of execution (*faktische Vollzugsakt*).[87] The original norm or constitution in the legal-logical sense is the ultimate norm that regulates the creation of law insofar as it grants the organs the competence to create law.[88] That is, the original norm qua pure conditioning norm is the ultimate basis of legal power. Merkl contrasts this necessary form at the upper end of any legal system with a necessary form at the lower end corresponding to the factual act of execution; that is, the purely conditioned act that constitutes the level of pure application of law.[89] This ideal scheme differs from the structural analysis of the Parliamentary Rule of Law. Regarding the latter, Merkl concludes that the necessary legal forms predicable of every legal system must be supplemented by the necessary legal forms predicable only of this type of state. In other words, Merkl argues that in addition to the pure conditioning original norm and the pure conditioned factual act of execution, the Parliamentary Rule of Law is composed of both conditioning and conditioned intermediate forms. In the Parliamentary Rule of Law according to Merkl, 'the constitution is presented as the rule of generation of law enacted by the parliament (*Gesetzgebung*), the constitution and the law enacted by the parliament as rules of generation of administrative regulations (*Verordnungen*), and formal and material justice laws as rules of generation of administrative acts (*Verwaltungsakte*) and judicial decisions as well as acts-in-the-law (*Rechtsgeschäfte*)'.[90] In this manner, Merkl includes acts-in-the-law

[81] Merkl (1931), p. 281.
[82] Merkl (1931), p. 281; Merkl (1923), p. 217.
[83] Merkl (1931), p. 281.
[84] Merkl (1931), p. 281.
[85] Merkl (1931), p. 281.
[86] Merkl (1923), p. 213.
[87] Merkl (1923), p. 218.
[88] Merkl (1923), pp. 209–210.
[89] Merkl (1923), pp. 213, 217.
[90] Merkl (1931), pp. 280–281.

(*Rechtsgeschäfte*) as conditioned legal forms that do not differ from 'the judicial decision and the administrative act, by their logical structure, but only by their technique of creation'.[91] Therefore, if acts-in-the-law (*Rechtsgeschäfte*) are parts of law, then they must be created from relevant legal actions. As every relevant legal action that creates law must be carried out by a body created by competence norms, there must be rules conferring competence on individuals. These rules constitute the legal basis for entering into legal voluntary obligations.

4 Conclusion

As Kohler observed, the hierarchical structure of the legal system is the most important achievement of the Vienna School of Legal Theory.[92] Its importance lies in the fact that it provides a general scope to a normative explanation of legal power. The normative account of legal power clarifies the fundamental characteristics of any legal system, such as its formal structure and its changes as a result of normative creation. As I have shown, the normative account of legal power is premised on the theoretical construct of legal power qua power conferred by the law. Merkl's theory of the hierarchical structure of the legal system provides a general scope for the normative account of legal power as it offers a legal foundation of power not only with respect to the ultimate basis of the legal system, its intermediate and lower structures, but also with respect to the power to enter into voluntary legal obligations. The capital importance for the history of the theory of legal power of Merkl's *Stufenbaulehre* was recognised by Kelsen when he integrated this theory as an essential component of the Pure Theory of Law.[93] As Paulson argued, this integration had vast implications that led Kelsen to reformulate his general theory of norms in terms of empowerment, beginning in the 1930s, and his own concept of law.[94]

Nevertheless, the profound impact this integration had on continental jurisprudence meant that an important difference between Merkl's and Kelsen's insights was, perhaps, lost to obscurity. As Merkl did not renounce the attribution to natural law of 'the mission' to be the 'extra-legal regulative principle of positive law',[95] a sound interpretation of his work should highlight that his theory of the hierarchical structure of the legal system is founded on a formal rather than a content-based separation between law and morality. Indeed, in his famous treatise *Das doppelte Rechtsantlitz. Eine Betrachtung aus der Erkenntnistheorie des Rechts* (1918), he

[91] Merkl (1931), p. 261.

[92] Koller (2005), p. 106.

[93] It was not for nothing that Kelsen considered Merkl to be the 'co-founder' (*Mitbegründer*) of the Pure Theory of Law (see Kelsen 1959/1960, p. 313).

[94] Paulson (2019); Paulson (2000), esp. pp. 146–150; Paulson (2013).

[95] Merkl (1914), p. 578.

held that '[n]o legal system, however constructed, is without a kind of root of natural law. Moreover, every positive legal proposition has at some point passed through the stage of normative natural law; the accusation of "natural law" is out of place where the foundation stones of the legal edifice are to be laid. [These stones] cannot be made of the material of positive law, no matter how much a purely positivist legal edifice is built on their foundation'.[96] Here I have inquired about the importance of the *Stufenbaulehre* for the history of the theory of legal power. Nonetheless, an inquiry into the significance of the *Stufenbaulehre* for Merkl's own work must be left for the future.

References

Alexy R (2008) Alf Ross' Begriff der Kompetenz. In: Hoyer A, Hattenhauer H, Meyer-Pritzl R, Schubert W (eds) Gedächtnisschrift für Jörn Eckert: 15. Mai 1954 bis 21. März 2006. Nomos, Baden-Baden, pp 43–64

Bentham J (1970 (1780)) In: Hart HLA (ed) Of laws in general. The Athlone Press, London

Bierling E (1898) Juristische Prinzipienlehre. Mohr, Freiburg

Borowski M (2005) Die Lehre vom Stufenbau des Rechts nach Adolf Julius Merkl. In: Paulson SL, Stolleis M (eds) Hans Kelsen – Staatslehrer und Rechtstheoretiker des 20. Jahrhunderts. Mohr Siebeck, Tübingen, pp 122–159

Brinz A v (1873) Lehrbuch der Pandekten, vol 1, 2nd edn. [u.a.], Erlangen

Brockmöller A (1997) Die Entstehung der Rechtstheorie im 19. Jahrhundert in Deutschland (Studien zur Rechtsphilosophie und Rechtstheorie 14). Nomos, Baden-Baden

Bulygin E (1991) On norms of competence. Law Philos 10:201–216

Burgess G (1992) The Divine Right of Kings reconsidered. English Hist Rev CVII (CCCCXXV, 1, Oct):837–861

Calasso F (1959) Il negozio giuridico, Lezioni di storia del diritto italiano. Giuffrè, Milan

Cotterrell R (1989) The politics of jurisprudence. A critical introduction to legal philosophy. Butterworths, London

Dreier R (1979) Zur Einheit der praktischen Philosophie Kants. Perspektiven der Philosophie: Neues Jahrbuch 5:5–37

Freeman (2008 (1959)) Introduction to jurisprudence. Thomson Reuters (Legal) Limited, London

Garzón Valdes (1981) Acerca de las limitaciones legales al soberano legal. Sistema: Revista de ciencias sociales 43/44:43–56

Grotius H (2005 (1625–1630)) The rights of war and peace. Book II, Ch. IX, § II to IV. Liberty Fund, Indianapolis. https://www.digitale-sammlungen.de/de/view/bsb10040700?page=6. Accessed 5 June 2022

Guzmán Brito A (2004) Para la historia de la formación de la teoría general del acto o negocio jurídico y del contrato, IV: Los orígenes históricos de la noción general de acto o negocio jurídico. Revista de Estudios Histórico-Jurídicos [Sección Historia del Derecho Europeo] XXVI:187–254

Hart HLA (2011 (1967)) Sovereignty and legally limited government. In: Hart HLA (ed) Essays on Bentham. Studies in jurisprudence and political theory. Oxford University Press, Clarendon, pp 220–268

[96] Merkl (1918), p. 29; Merkl (1923), p. 210.

Jellinek G (1929 (1914)) Allgemeine Staatslehre. Dritte Auflage unter Verwertung des handschriftlichen Nachlasses durchgesehen und ergänzt von Dr. Walter Jellinek. Verlag von Julius Springer, Berlin

Kant I (1999 (1785)) Grundlegung zur Metaphysik der Sitten. Felix Meiner Verlag, Hamburg

Kelsen H (1934) Reine Rechtslehre. Einleitung in die rechtswissenschaftliche Problematik. Deuticke, Wien

Kelsen H (1945) General theory of law and state. Harvard University Press, Cambridge

Kelsen H (1959/1960) Adolf Merkl zu seinem siebzigsten Geburtstag am 23. März 1960. Österreichische Zeitschrift für öffentliches Recht 10:313–315

Kelsen H (2017 (1960)) Reine Rechtslehre. Mit einem Anhang: Das Problem der Gerechtigkeit. Studienausgabe der 2. Auflage 1960 unter Berücksichtigung von Kelsens Änderungen anlässlich der Übersetzung ins Italienische 1966 herausgegeben und eingeleitet von Matthias Jestaedt. Mohr Siebeck Verlag, Wien

Klippel D (1976) Politische Freiheit und Freiheitsrechte im deutschen Naturrecht des 18. Jahhunderts. Schöningh, Paderborn

Klippel D (1987) Naturrecht als politische Theorie zur politischen Bedeutung des deutschen Naturrechts im 18. Und 19. Jahrhundert. In: Bödecker HE, Herrmann U (eds) Aufklärung als Politisierung – Politisierung der Aufklärung. Felix Meiner Verlag, Hamburg

Koller P (2005) Zur Theorie des rechtlichen Stufenbaues. In: Paulson SL, Stolleis M (eds) Hans Kelsen. Staatsrechtslehrer und Rechtstheoretiker des 20. Jahrhunderts. Mohr Siebeck, Tübingen, pp 106–121

Köpcke M (2019) A short history of legal validity and invalidity. Foundations of private and public law. Intersentia Ltd, Cambridge

Lindahl H (1977) Position and change: a study in law and logic. Springer Science, Dordrecht

MacCormick N, Raz J (1972) Voluntary obligations and normative powers. Proc Aristot Soc, Suppl Vol 46:59–102

Manning CAW (1963 (1933)) Austin today; or 'the province of jurisprudence' re-examined. In: Jennings WI (ed) Modern theories of law. Wildy & Sons Limited, London, pp 180–226

Merkl A (1914) Buchbesprechung von: Erich Jung, Das Problem des natürlichen Rechts. Zeitschrift für öffentliches Recht, I. Jg., 570–578. Reimp. In: Mayer-Maly D, Schambeck H, Grussmann W-D (eds) Adolf Julius Merkl. Gesammelte Schriften, vol 1 Grundlagen des Rechts, Pt. 1. Duncker & Humblot, Berlin, pp 3–18

Merkl A (1918) Das doppelte Rechtsantlitz. Eine Betrachtung aus der Erkenntnistheorie des Rechts. Wien: Sonderabdruck aus den Juristischen Blättern. Selbstverlag des Verfassers. Reimp. In: Mayer-Maly D, Schambeck H, Grussmann W-D (eds) Adolf Julius Merkl. Gesammelte Schriften, vol 1 Grundlagen des Rechts, Pt. 1. Duncker & Humblot, Berlin, pp 227–252

Merkl A (1923) Die Lehre von der Rechtskraft. Entwickelt aus dem Rechtsbegriff. Wiener Staatswissenschaftliche Studien. Franz Deuticke, Leipzig

Merkl A (1927) Allgemeines Verwaltungsrecht. Springer, Vienna

Merkl AJ (1931) Prolegomena einer Theorie des rechtlichen Stufenbaues. In: Verdross A (ed) Gesellschaft, Staat und Recht. Untersuchungen zur Reinen Rechtslehre, Festschrift Hans Kelsen zum 50. Geburtstag gewidmet. Springer, Vienna, pp 252–294. Reimp. In: Mayer-Maly D, Schambeck H, Grussmann W-D (eds) Adolf Julius Merkl. Gesammelte Schriften, vol 1 Grundlagen des Rechts, Pt. 1. Duncker & Humblot, Berlin, pp 437–492

Merkl AJ (1993–2009 (1916, 1917, 1919)) Das Recht im Licht seiner Anwendung. In: Mayer-Maly D, Schambeck H, Grussmann W-D (eds) Adolf Julius Merkl. Gesammelte Schriften, vol 1 Grundlagen des Rechts, Pt. 1. Duncker & Humblot, Berlin, pp 85–146

Moreso J (1989) Cinco diferencias entre Bentham y Austin. Anuario de Filosofía del derecho VI:351–375

Paulson SL (1990) Zur stufenbaulehre Merkls in ihrer Bedeutung für die allgemeine Rechtslehre. In: Walter R (ed) Adolf J. Merkl. Werk und Wirksamkeit. Ergebnis eines

Internationalen Symposions in Wien (22.-23. März 1990). Manzsche Verlags- und Universitätsbuchhandlung, Vienna, pp 93–105
Paulson SL (2000) The weak reading of authority in Hans Kelsen's pure theory of law. Law Philos 19:131–171
Paulson SL (2013) How Merkl's Stufenbaulehre informs Kelsen's concept of law. Revus. J Const Law Philos Law 21:29–45. https://doi.org/10.4000/revus.2727. Accessed 9 Mai 2022
Paulson SL (2019) Empowerment: Hans Kelsen e la teoria radicale delle norme giuridiche. Analisi e diritto 1:21–66
Paulson SL (2021) The Stufenbau Yields Legal Powers. Aspects of Hans Kelsen's Norm Theory (Manuscript). https://youtu.be/pwcF8nnZ-BU. Accessed 29 June 2022
Pope Gregory IX. Liber Extra (Quinque Libri Decretalium). https://www.hs-augsburg.de/~harsch/Chronologia/Lspost13/GregoriusIX/gre_0000.html#3. Accessed 5 June 2022
Pothier RJ (1761) Traite des Obligations. Tome Premier. Orleans: Chez Rouzeau-Montaut, Imprimeur du Roi, de la Ville, & de l'Université. https://books.google.de/books?id=MY1EAAAAcAAJ&pg=PA5&hl=de&source=gbs_toc_r&cad=4#v=onepage&q&f=false. Accessed 9 May 2022
Pufendorf S (1998 (1684)) De jure naturæ et gentium. Erster Teil: Text (Liber primus – Liber quartus). Akademie Verlag, Berlin
Raz J (1970) The concept of a legal system. Clarendon Press, Oxford
Savigny FC (1867 (1840)) System of the modern Roman law, vol I. J Higginbotham Publisher, Madras. https://babel.hathitrust.org/cgi/pt?id=wu.89097651095&view=1up&seq=7&skin=2021. Accessed 9 Mai 2022
Schauer F (2013) Positivism before Hart. In: Freeman M, Mindus P (eds) The legacy of John Austin's jurisprudence. Springer, Dordrecht, pp 271–290
Schröder J (2005) Gab es im deutschen Kaiserreich einen Gesetzespositivismus? In: Baumann W, von Dickhuth-Harrach H-J, Marotzke W (eds) Gesetz, Recht, Rechtsgeschichte. Festschrift für Gerhard Otte zum 70. Geburtstag. Sellier. European Law Publishers, Munich, pp 571–586
Spaak T (1994) The concept of legal competence. An essay in conceptual analysis. Dartmouth Publishing Company Limited, Aldershot
Stolleis M (2002) Geschichte des öffentlichen Rechts in Deutschland. Vol. 3, Staatsrechtwissenschaft und Verwaltungsrechtswissenschaft in Republik und Diktatur. Weimarer Republik und Nationalsozialismus. C. H. Beck, Munich
Stone J (1964) Legal system and lawyer's reasonings. Maitland Publications Pty Ltd, Sydney
Suarez F (2010 (1612)) Tractatus de legisbus ac Deo legislatore. Liber V: De varietate legum humanarum et preasertim de odiosis. Centro Superior de Investigaciones Científicas, Madrid
Thon (1878) C. A. Thon, Rechtsnorm und Subjektives Recht. Hermann Böhlau, Weimar
Turégano Mansilla (2001) Derecho y moral en John Austin. Centro de estudios políticos y constitucionales, Madrid
Verdross A (1923) Die Einheit des rechtlichen Weltbildes auf Grundlage der Völkerrechtsverfassung. J.C.B. Mohr, Tübingen
Wieacker F (2016 (1967)) Privatrechtsgeschichte der Neuzeit. Unter besonderer Berücksichtigung der deutschen Entwicklung, 3rd edn. Vandenhoeck & Ruprecht, Göttingen
Windscheid B (1862) Lehrbuch des Pandektenrechts. 1. Band. Buddeus, Düsseldorf
Windscheid B (1878) Wille und Willenserklärung: Eine Studie. Druck von Alexander Edelmann, Leipzig
Zimmermann R (1992 (1990)) The law of obligations Roman foundations of the civilian tradition. Juta & Co, Ltd., Cape Town

Empowerment and the Act of Will in Hans Kelsen's General Theory of Norms

Monika Zalewska

Abstract The aim of this paper is to examine the concept of empowerment in Hans Kelsen's General Theory of Norms and to enquire whether it is capable of maintaining coherence of the conception of the hierarchical structure of law considering the rejection of the logic of the norms of the norms by Kelsen. It will be argued that the empowerment understood by Kelsen as an act of commanding and defined as "conferring on an individual the power to posit and apply norms" occurs in the vertical and horizontal aspect of law. Empowerment covers multiply functions, among others takes over the function ascribed to hierarchical structure of law, allowing to understand the act of granting a competence to lower organ. Moreover, the horizontal aspect allows to combine empowerment with imputation understood in terms of supervenience. Empowerment is bound with imputation in a way that it belongs to the states of affairs understood as a consequence. Since an individual without empowerment cannot create law, empowerment is one of the criteria of understanding as law and turning subjective meaning of the norm into objective one.

1 Introduction

Traditional legal theory perceives the legal system as a set of rules imposing obligations. This perspective was abandoned by Kelsen in *General Theory of Norms* (GTN), the ultimate revision of his theory. In the final phase of his work, Kelsen favours empowering norms.[1] Empowerment occurs in both the vertical and

This project was funded by Polish National Centre of Science. Project number: 2021/41/B/HS5/01174.

[1] I would like to thank Carsten Heidemann for the feedback and discussion which helped me to clarify some crucial points in this chapter. Paulson (1988), p. 58.

M. Zalewska (✉)
Department of Theory and Philosophy of Law, University of Łódź, Lodz, Poland
e-mail: mzalewska@wpia.uni.lodz.pl

G. Villa-Rosas, T. Spaak (eds.), *Legal Power and Legal Competence*, Law and Philosophy Library 140, https://doi.org/10.1007/978-3-031-28555-4_15

horizontal aspects of law. In the vertical aspect, it is bound up with the hierarchical structure of law (*Stufenbau*), which Kelsen understands in formal terms. Namely, the higher organ empowers another organ to issue a certain norm. At the top of the *Stufenbau* is the constitution, which draws its validity from the basic norm; this interpretation, however, causes complications stemming from the fact that Kelsen reformulated his theory in its final phase. This reformulation includes the definition of the norm as the meaning of the act of will emphasising an empirical aspect of the will of the lawmaker.[2] Consequently, Kelsen denied the possibility that logic could be applied to norms. These changes highlighted the need to reformulate further elements of Kelsen's theory, including the hierarchical structure of law and empowerment. While the former lost its significance, the latter turned out to be one of the main categories of the new structure.[3] Hence, the significance of the problem concerning the hierarchical structure of law lies in the new definition of the norm as the meaning of an act of will and consequently as the rejection of the logic of norms. Namely, Kelsen claimed that the laws of logic do not apply to norms, since norms are understood in terms of will. The will is not an intellectual act, ruled by logic: on the contrary, it can be irrational.[4] In such framework, the hierarchical structure of law, understood as competence being granted by a higher organ to a lower one to issue a certain norm, might not have much sense, due to the possibility of irrational acts of will. If what counts is the act of will which does not fall under the rules of inference, then in the worst-case scenario, the will, which lies behind a decision maker might disregard the content of higher norms, including the constitution. In such case, the hierarchy of norms might collapse and the empowerment of the higher organ might become inefficacious.

Contrary to the vertical aspect, the horizontal one is bound up with the application of law; the act of empowerment is commanded,[5] hence empowerment implies a command to the addressee of the norm. As such, empowerment is bound up with imputation in the sense that it belongs to the state of affairs understood as legal consequence. The question is how to understand the nature of imputation in *GTN*, since in the revision, it lost its Neokantian function of a relative *a priori* category. In the following paragraphs, I will address the aforementioned problems.

The aim of the first part will be to examine the idea of empowerment in the vertical aspect of the 'General Theory of Norms' framework and highlight the problems with *Stufenbau* in GTN mentioned above. This part will examine the potential consequences of the norms' logic rejection combined with the norm understood as the meaning of the act of will. The second part will address a binding of the higher organ empowerment with the lower organ will, and is going to investigate the potential solution to be used to save the coherence of the conception of the hierarchical structure of law. I will discuss the possibility of coherence

[2] Kelsen (1979), p. 2.

[3] Paulson (1988), pp. 58–59.

[4] Kelsen (1979), pp. 170–174.

[5] See Paulson (1988), pp. 68–69.

restoration due to distinction between legal norms and the statements about the legal norms. The third part of the paper will examine the horizontal aspect of empowerment and its relations with imputation; it will pay particular attention to the character of the relationship connecting empowerment to imputation, which lost its function as a relative *a priori* category in GTN. This part will argue that imputation is in fact a supervenience relationship tying the condition to its consequence, empowerment.

2 The Problem with Empowerment in Vertical Aspect

2.1 The Concept of Empowerment

Empowerment is understood as "conferring on an individual the power to posit and apply norms". As Stanley Paulson notes, Kelsen perceives empowerment as a fundamental type of norm.[6] Especially in Kelsen's late works the empowerment took prominent position, however this construction had already been present since the 1930s.[7] Carsten Heidemann notes that the competence from which the concept of empowerment stems can be understood in three ways depending on the phase in which Kelsen was writing:[8] (1) In his Neokantian phase, competence is a "transcendental scheme", the result of cognition and the use of the category of Ought or imputation; (2) In the Realist phase, competence plays a normative function, being understood as the major premise in the syllogism of legal validity;[9] as such, it states the legal conditions for the existence of the norms; (3) In *General Theory of Norms*, Kelsen describes competence (empowerment) as a "conditional command", as an act of commanding defined as "conferring on an individual the power to posit and apply norms".[10] Empowerment in GTN is one of the modalities which are understood by Kelsen as Ought. As Stanley Paulson notes, Kelsen introduces empowerment in order to eliminate the concept of legal obligation as an independent concept. As a result, empowerment is the main modality, while obligation has the status of a derivative notion.[11] Such understood empowerment exists in the hierarchical structure as well as in the context of the coercive act. Kelsen distinguishes three types of empowerment. He understands it in its narrowest sense as the "capacity of creating legal norms", a broader definition supplemented with the condition to impose a coercive act as legal, and an even broader one that includes the conditions leading to

---

[6]Paulson (1988), pp. 58–72.

[7]Paulson (2020).

[8]Heidemann (2000), pp. 263–264.

[9]The major premise is that the norm including a command should be objectively valid; minor premise is the fact of commanding; conclusion is the statement of the validity of the norm, that one ought to behave in commanded way (RR2, 205).

[10]Kelsen (1979), p. 102.

[11]Paulson (2020), p. 54.

imposing a coercive act.[12] For the purposes of this paper, I will restrict my analysis to the first and second meaning, referring to the activity of legal organs. In the next paragraph, I will discuss the problems with empowerment emerging in the former, vertical aspect.

2.2 *Act of Will and* Stufenbau

Kelsen's best-known book, Pure Theory of Law, presents a Neokantian account of law, where a normative chain of norms constructs the hierarchical structure of law. This formulation lies in Kelsen's conviction, stemming from Neokantian principles, that the method of cognition constitutes the object of cognition. The lawmaker only produces legal raw material, which is subsequently cognized as legal norms.[13] However, beginning in his realist phase, Kelsen perceives norms as cognition-independent entities granting the lawmaker a more central position in his theory. From now on, the "chain of validity" consists of competence norms and the organ empowered to issue the next norm. In *General Theory of Norms*, through acceptance of the definition of the norm as the meaning of the act of will, and rejecting the logic of norms, Kelsen goes even further.

The definition of the norm as a meaning of an of act of empirical will, the key principle in GTN, has several implications which serve to distinguish GTN from the more renowned "Pure Theory of Law"; even though, at first glance, the changes may seem to be minor. Two important consequences result from this fact: firstly, the connection between the norm and the fact uses a definition in which the empirical will is contained in the definition of the norm. Secondly, the new version rejects the logic of norms. Since the will is by no means an intellectual act of thinking but rather a violative act, rules of logic, specifically the rule of contradiction and the rules of inference, cannot apply to the relations between norms.[14] The act of will opposed to the act of thought, which is subject to logic, hence the norms cannot be defined as contradictory, or not, to one another because this logical category becomes irrelevant in such case. The same applies to the rules of inference. The rejection of the logic of norms affects the hierarchical structure of law, and raises the question of empowerment function.

The rules of inference provided the tool that guaranteed an empowered organ would issue a norm in accordance with the content of the empowering norm. Since such rules are gone, due to the highlighted function of the act of will (which meaning is the norm), such link between the higher organ empowerment and the empowered norm seems to be absent. What remains in law-making process is the act of will of the lawmaker, which might or might not conform with empowerment stemming

[12] Kelsen (1967), p. 146; Heidemann (2000), p. 273.

[13] Heidemann (2000), pp. 271–273.

[14] Kelsen (1979), pp. 170–174, 211–225.

from the higher norm. Hence, the question arises, what causes the lower norm to be in accordance with the empowerment, if the logical inference is ruled out? The rule of contradiction aided the Pure Theory of Law framework in this aspect. The rule of contradiction guaranteed that the legal order was meaningful (*sinnvoll*) and was the assumption stemming from the basic norm. In GTN highlighting one's empirical will as the aspect of the norm implies a loss of the legal system's rationality, embodied in the rule of non-contradiction.[15] This state of affairs raises a question regarding the limits of the lawmaker's will. Namely, since the lawmaker's empirical will is the essential feature of the norm, can one assume that the lawmaker can create norms which are not agreeable with higher norms? In such a framework, what could possibly prevent the lawmaker from creating a chaotic and contradictory set of norms instead of a coherent legal system?

This issue reveals the underlying problem of the originating source of the power. The power might come from the legal system in the framework of the *Stufenbau*, or from the will of the lawmaker. Initially, regarding the "No imperative without imperator" rule, which Kelsen accepted in "general Theory of Norms"[16] it seems that the power is in the hands of the lawmaker, not the legal system. However, this brings consequences unwanted by Kelsen. Namely, if the lawmaker decides whether, which, and how to apply the norm, the clarity, between what law is and what law is not, vanishes. Especially, if the lawmaker's will departs from what is written in law. Perhaps the lawmaker's statement is not actually observed by the people, because they counter-claim his/her statement, deeming it to be in violation of the law.

To illustrate this problem let us examine a hypothetical example. It is a simplified version of the real case study of Poland in years 2015–2020. In 2020 due to covid19 pandemic the government prohibited gatherings by issuing an ordinance instead of a parliamentary act, as the constitution prescribed. At the same time, the Constitutional Court, where some of the judges were unlawfully appointed (against the rules of the constitution) in 2015, banned abortion. Consequently, women went out on the streets to protest and argued the legality of such gatherings, on the basis of the constitutional protection of the right to gather. This right can only be limited through introduction of a state of emergency. Meanwhile, the government, being under the pressure of the protesters, did not publish the ruling of the Constitutional Court, meaning that the case is suspended. As a result, the medical staff doubts whether the abortion is still allowed. Even if the ruling was published, the doubts would still exist, due to unlawfully selected members of the Constitutional Court. There is also a doubt, whether women should be punished for their gatherings. Hence, the question is not only: "who holds the power?", but also, whether the issuer and addressee of the norms agree about that with the government. If not, then probably the court will issue decisions in each particular case. For Kelsen, due to the *res judicata* rule, such a

---

[15] Kelsen (1945), pp. 407–410.

[16] Compelling and interesting analysis of such concept of the norm and the rule "no imperative without imperator" was presented by: Jabloner (1988), pp. 1–22.

ruling is valid even if it goes against a higher norm.[17] As it can be seen in this example, the law lost some of its power. The outcome concerning abortion and the legality of the gatherings is resolved in the courts, which will decide in each particular case whether what matters is the constitution or the will of the lawmaker. In this way, the certainty of law vanishes, and the situation caused by the unlawful actions during the law-making process makes the legal system irrelevant. What counts is the judge's decision influenced by his particular views, and in case he is in opposition to the government directives, his decision depends on the factual power government has or does not have over him. This seems to be an essential departure from Kelsen's main doctrine. Kelsen's "innocent" reformulation of the definition of the norm and the rejection of the norm's logic brought significant consequences. Instead of slight change, the definition of law moves from the normative area of norms into the power relations in the sphere of Ought. Hence, it is not theoretical shift but rather significant change in the understanding of the concept of law with practical implications. Depending on how the inquiry where the legal power lies is addressed, be it in legal norms, or be it a will of lawmaker, the practical consequences affect the matter whether the formal rule of law exist; and the formal rule of law functions only in the legal systems with respected hierarchy. As it was demonstrated in the example above, the understating of law reduced to the will of the lawmaker, impairs the formal rule of law. Such reduction is possible, when the connection between the empowerment and the will of the empowered organ is perceived as not necessary. To put it in other words, when the will of the lawmaker is superior toward the legal hierarchy. The rules of inference and the rule of contradiction between norms created necessary link in legal hierarchy and the departure from these rules is the departure from some ideal type of what law is. In GTN, when such rules are gone, the will of the lawmaker seems to be unlimited. If the legal power lies in the will of the lawmaker, then his actions are legitimized. This consequence seems to be contrary to Kelsen's intentions.

In order to prevent such unwanted interpretation of Kelsen's doctrine, the proper interpretation of Kelsen's definition of the act of will in the context of *Stufenbau* is essential. Either what matters is only the will of the lawmaker, or there are some links between the higher and lower norms preventing randomness of the act of will. These two interpretations of where the power lies would affect the rulings of the judges. In case when the power lies in law, judge's rulings are rather predictable. If the legal power lies outside the law, at the hands of the decision makers, there are no rules enabling predictions as to how judges will rule. In such case, the law would rather remind random set of rules determined by the factual power-struggles of the legal organs on different levels of the hierarchy. This would mean that Kelsen's theory is leaning towards the Is sphere in a way which could decompose Kelsen's sophisticated idea of law embedded in normativity. In the following paragraphs, I will demonstrate how Kelsen could avoid this trap and how to interpret his General

[17] Kelsen (1979), p. 248.

Theory of Norms in a manner in which the *Stufenbau* still has some significance, and providing predictability to judges' rulings.

3 Empowerment, *Stufenbau* and Statements About the Norms

Empowerment is one criterion of understanding the law and turning the subjective meaning of the norm into an objective one (equivalent of a valid norm), since an individual without empowerment cannot create law. However, as it was demonstrated above, this mechanism can be impaired, if the act of will of the lawmaker is what it counts and the logic does not apply to a norm. In the light of what is presented above, the main question is, if a norm is the meaning of an act of will, and if the will can sometimes be irrational, how can empowerment be of any relevance to norms? The next step considers a possibility to maintain the concept of a coherent legal system based on empowerment and grounded in GTN, as opposed to a chaotic set of norms.

As it was stated before, according to Kelsen, the legal system has a specific hierarchy, which he names "*Stufenbau*", based on the chain of empowerments: a higher organ empowers a lower organ to issue the certain norm with certain content. When issuing a norm, the legal organ simultaneously empowers another organ to issue another norm, with this empowerment entailing the framing of the content of the norm. This construction assumes that empowerment requires the new legal norm to be in accordance with the content of the empowering norm. Such hierarchy can be regarded as a hierarchy of conditions or a hierarchy of derogation. While the hierarchy of conditions regulates the law-making process, the derogation hierarchy concerns the elimination of the legal norms from the system in case of their conflict in accordance with *lex superior derogat legi inferiori rule*.[18] In the context of legal power, more problematic is the hierarchy of conditions. As Paulson notes, the conditional character of the hierarchy means that the higher norm is the necessary condition for the validity of the lower norm. In theory, if the conditions are not satisfied, the issuance of the lower norm fails.[19] However, as was noted before, in the framework of *GTN*, this is not obvious due to the definition of the norm and the rejection of the logic of norms. Furthermore, it is important to consider the possibility that such a norm might not be in accordance with constitution, despite being in accordance with the empowering norm. Based on the analysis done in the former paragraph, what follows is that the answer depends on the perception of the hierarchical structure of law. Focussing only on this particular form of empowerment, it is possible to imagine a situation where the legal norm is in accordance with quite a narrow empowering norm, however, at the same time, this norm impairs

[18] Borowski (2014).

[19] Paulson (2020), p. 66.

some much broader constitutional provisions. This results in unwanted consequences, such as unpredictability of judicial decisions and dependence of law on factual power. The assumption behind Kelsen's understanding of law is the entire legal system, not just that of individual norms lacking the context created by other norms. In such an all-encompassing case, it is necessary to consider the entire chain of empowerments starting from the Constitution, rather than examining only the final empowerment, and each legal norm should be in accordance with all of them. In this context, the most interesting empowerment is the one stemming from the Constitution; and it must be asked whether such empowerment includes the assumption that the norms issued on its behalf must conform to all the provisions of the Constitution. In the case of the latter, the concept of empowerment is indeed able to bring coherence to the hierarchical structure of law.

In such a framework, the query remains, however, how such a mechanism could possibly work, since Kelsen eliminated the rules of inference and contradiction from the normative sphere. So far, it was demonstrated that empowerment related to the constitution brings coherence to *Stufenbau*. What remains is to reveal the binding relation between the empowerment and the act of will of the lawmaker, which would subordinate, at least to some extent, the will of the lawmaker to the empowerment stemming from higher norms limiting its randomness.[20] Hence, the second issue worth discussing is the nature of the logical relationship between the act of will and empowerment.

Kelsen partially solved this dilemma pointing out that although the rules of inference and the rule of contradiction do not apply to legal norms, they apply to the statements about the norm, which are the statements of legal science.[21] Hence, in the legal science framework (but not on the level of norms) the rules of inference and contradiction still exercise the function of unifying legal order and binding the acts of will with the higher norms, preventing the randomness in the process of legal creation. However, these statements are of use not during the law-making process, which is volatile in nature. They serve intellectual ex post analysis of the legal application which has already occurred. Hence, such approach does not solve the problem of link between empowerment and the empowered act of will during the process of legal creation; it brings the criteria to distinguish the lawful from unlawful action. The application of rule of logic to statements about the legal norms makes evaluation of the law-making process possible stating that a certain norm as a product of the act of will was created against the empowerment; either through direct empowerment to create the norm, or the empowerment stemming from the constitution. Such vision of law presupposes that law-making process of the lower

[20] It is worth to highlight that this quest is carried out on the grounds of Kelsen's GTN. In reality, much more is dependent on a willingness of authorities to obey the constitution. What makes a difference is whether the acts of will violating constitution are considered as law or unlawful acts. The aim of interpretation of GTN is to avoid deriving the consequences possibly leading to the conclusion that each willful act of the authority, regardless if it is in accordance with constitution or not, is law.

[21] Kelsen (1979), p. 227.

norm can violate the higher norms in the hierarchy. Hence, the evaluation on the level of legal propositions is unable to prevent unlawful law creation. However, the evaluation provides powerful tools, for instance to judges, to assert what the law is and what is not. As a result, the statements about the norms and possibility to apply the logic to them have ability to sustain the power in the framework of a law.

It seems that such vision of law is quite accurate. In practice, the lawmaker can violate the legal order by issuing the norms which are contradictory to the higher norms. However, such norms are still evaluated as unlawful, providing powerful tool to judges, and especially the constitutional court, to reinstate the legal order in their decisions following the constitutional norms.

4 Empowerment in Horizontal Relations

By horizontal relations, I mean the process resulting in the application of a coercive act. As Paulson notes, since 1930s Kelsen perceived a sanction norm as fitted with empowerment which results in the application of a coercive act.[22] The coercive act in turn is the last level of the chain of *Stufenbau*, starting with the constriction and ending on coercion. As Kelsen notes: "The coercive act alone is consequence without itself being condition".[23] Thus, it is worth to distinguish this category of empowerment, which results in the application of a coercive act. The most important element, one setting the entire process in motion, is imputation, understood as the link between condition and consequence; it is analogical to causality, but of a normative character. Comparing to Neokantian phase, in GTN Kelsen simplifies this category. Not only it is no longer a relative category *a priori*, but also Kelsen uses a more general definition designed for both legal and moral norms. In such a framework, Kelsen understands imputation as produced by legal norm and existing in the statement about the norm, hence, the legal science statement, which Kelsen accounts to ought-sentences. In the most classic version, the condition and the consequence are described in the ought sentence, of the sanction norm, hence, they belong to the normative sphere.[24] With such a description the following problem appears: since imputation does not have the function of cognizing norms, what exactly is its nature? The statement that imputation is analogical to causality seems vague. Kelsen's claims that imputation has the same logical nature as the causality formulated in Is-sentences do not help either. In such a framework, imputation does not seem to add much to Kelsen's theory. In the doctrine, the best-known attempt is to assign pragmatic function to imputation. This way its construction, known from the Neokantian phase, would be sustained. The relative category a priori would be substituted by linguistic paradigm. With such approach

[22] Paulson (2020), p. 67.

[23] Kelsen (1967), pp. 145–146.

[24] Kelsen (1979), pp. 24–25.

still it is unclear what kind of mechanism lies behind the "logical link" which has pragmatic function.

There might be alternative approach. Within this interpretation imputation can be perceived as supervenience. Supervenience is the relationship defined as "there cannot be A-difference without B-difference", with the most widespread version concerning properties on two levels, of which (B) is the more basic. One of the most well-known examples concerns two paintings, an original and a perfect, identical forgery. Obviously, there are features which make them different: one of them is a forgery and the two works were painted by different persons. It is argued, however, if the two paintings are the same on the molecular level, then they must be the same in terms of such physical features as colour, contrast and light impact, and more controversially, they should have the same aesthetic value. This dependence of higher-level properties, in this case aesthetics, on lower level properties, physical features, is an example of a relationship of supervenience: how the painting looks supervene on its molecular properties.[25] It is enough to affirm that two paintings on molecular level are identical to the extent that they are the same for human's eye.

Since supervenience is defined as "There cannot be A- difference without B-difference", it is necessary to define the elements that are bound by imputation, i.e. the condition and the consequence, and determine which should be understood as A and which as B. Since supervenience is the link between two levels of properties and the level (B) is more basic, the level (A) is more complex, this brings the difficulty to traditionally understood concept of imputation. Traditionally, in Kelsen's Pure Theory, the condition and the consequence are at the same, normative level. In order for supervenience to work, the condition should be on the level of facts and the consequence on the level of norms. Such interpretation would mean the extension of Kelsen's study and such extension must be justified. On one hand, there is no doubt that the fact of breaking the law initiates normative consequences. Hence, we can assume that even if not mentioned by Kelsen, such type of imputation can be derived from his theory. Furthermore, such understood imputation can potentially bring some added value to the comprehension of the legal phenomena providing more understanding to the relations between the norm and the fact. In GTN, such weakening of the separation between Is and Ought already exist, for instance, when the norm is defined as the meaning of the empirically understood act of will.

In such framework, the facts of breaking the norm which are limited to behaviour and circumstances is understood as the condition, and since it is more basic, it is understood as B, with A being the consequence; the precise nature of the consequence remains initially unclear. In GTN, Kelsen suggests the act of coercion, but he does so in the context of both moral and legal norms. In case of legal norms, and considering the context of other elements, such as importance of empowerment in GTN, or the relationship between primary and secondary norms,[26] it would make

[25] McLaughlin and Bennett (2018).

[26] Kelsen (1979), p. 143.

more sense to regard empowerment to impose the sanction as the consequence. In such case, two rules regarding supervenience would apply:

1. If the conditions are the same, the empowerments to impose the sanction are the same.
2. If the empowerments to impose the sanction are different, the conditions are different.

These two rules seem to correctly reflect the way lawyers think. Identical circumstances should imply identical consequences, while different consequences should result from different circumstances.

The alternative rules which cannot apply as supervenience:

(1) If the facts surrounding breaking of the norm are different, the consequences are also different, and
(2) if the consequences are the same, the facts surrounding the breakage of the norm are also the same,

do not apply to understanding of law. It is entirely possible that two different crimes, for instance manslaughter and bank robbery, may be punished by the same sanction.

At this stage, the main question would concern the specific nature of the empowerment. It cannot be the empowerment in general norm, but rather the empowerment concerning an individual decision of the court to impose a specific sanction issued to the executive organs. Such supervenience reveals implicit conviction about the law where in the ideal conditions, if two cases were alike on the matter of circumstances and behaviour, then the consequences should be alike. This formula resembles equality rule that comparable cases should be treated alike. One might have doubts whether such equality rule is not against Kelsen's intention to eliminate all the values from the form of law. It does not seem to be the case. In the framework of the positivistic conception of law Herbert Hart derived the principle of equality from the general character of the legal norms,[27] hence, the imputation understood as supervenience just confirms the existence of such principle in the positivistic paradigm.

5 Summary

In this paper, I have analysed the problem of empowerment in the context of vertical and horizontal relations in *GTN*. Empowerment encompasses multiple functions, including those ascribed to the hierarchical structure of law, and allows competence to be granted to a lower organ. This interpretation maintains the coherence of Kelsen's vision of legal system. Even though Kelsen denied logic of norms and especially rules of inference, and contradiction, the concept of *Stufenbau* can be

[27] Hart (1958), pp. 623–624.

defended. Due to empowerment and specification of the connection of particular chain links on the level of legal science, it can be asked ex post when the act of will of the lawmaker is not random. In the legal system the act of will is subject to the rules, which ensure continuance of the system. Such an ideal type of the legal system can serve as a guideline to distinguish a normal case from anomaly, when the will of the lawmaker departs from the rules of *Stufenbau*.

In the horizontal aspect, empowerment can be understood as a consequence in the imputation relationship. In addition, peripheral imputation can also be understood as a form of supervenience. Imputation understood in terms of supervenience departs from the classical understanding of imputation which linked two normative elements. However, since in *GTN* Kelsen deconstructed the concept of imputation, depriving it of its primary function and making it more ambiguous, this gives us a reason to look for an alternative interpretation of this concept, provided that the new interpretation brings some added value. The concept of imputation as supervenience explains relations between norms and facts, as well as includes the category of equality from Kelsen's Pure Theory. Such interpretation proposed departs from standard Kelsen's findings; however, it does not contradict Kelsen's theory. Elements already existing within the theory constructed this explanation, and any new elements, such as supervenience, are merely accounting for any gaps. In this case, the gap can be defined as a question regarding the nature of imputation, and what kind of link it is. This interpretation, which serves as a departure from the classical understanding of Pure Theory of Law, has the added value of providing a coherent solution to the problem of empowerment.

References

Borowski M (2014) Concretized norm and sanction qua fact in the Vienna School's Stufenbaulehre. Ratio Juris 27(1):79–93. https://doi.org/10.1111/raju.12036

Hart HLA (1958) Positivism and the separation of law and morals. Harv Law Rev 71(4):593–629. https://doi.org/10.2307/1338225

Heidemann C (2000) The creation of normative facts. Law Philos 19:263–281

Jabloner C (1988) Kein Imperativ Ohne Imperator. Anmerkungen Zu Einer Theorie Kelsens. Schriftenreihe des Hans Kelsen Instituts 12:1–22

Kelsen H (1945) General theory of law and state. Harvard University Press, Cambridge

Kelsen H (1967) Pure theory of law. The Lawbook Exchange, Ltd., New Jersey

Kelsen H (1979) General theory of norms. Clarendon Press, Oxford

McLaughlin B, Bennett K (2018) Supervenience. In: Zalta EN (ed) The Stanford encyclopedia of philosophy (Spring 2018). Metaphysics Research Lab, Stanford University, Stanford CA. https://plato.stanford.edu/archives/spr2018/entries/supervenience/

Paulson SL (1988) An empowerment theory of legal norms. Ratio Juris 1(1):58–72

Paulson SL (2020) Hans Kelsen as outlier: the defence of a radical norm theory. In: Bertea S (ed) Contemporary perspectives on legal obligation. Routledge, London & New York, pp 54–67. https://doi.org/10.4324/9780429293412-4

Printed in the USA
CPSIA information can be obtained
at www.ICGtesting.com
LVHW011408110823
754736LV00004BA/122

9 783031 285547